NAJICA BLITZ TACTICS 2

TAKUYA TASHIRO

CREATOR: STUDIO FANTASIA • AFW/NAJICA Project

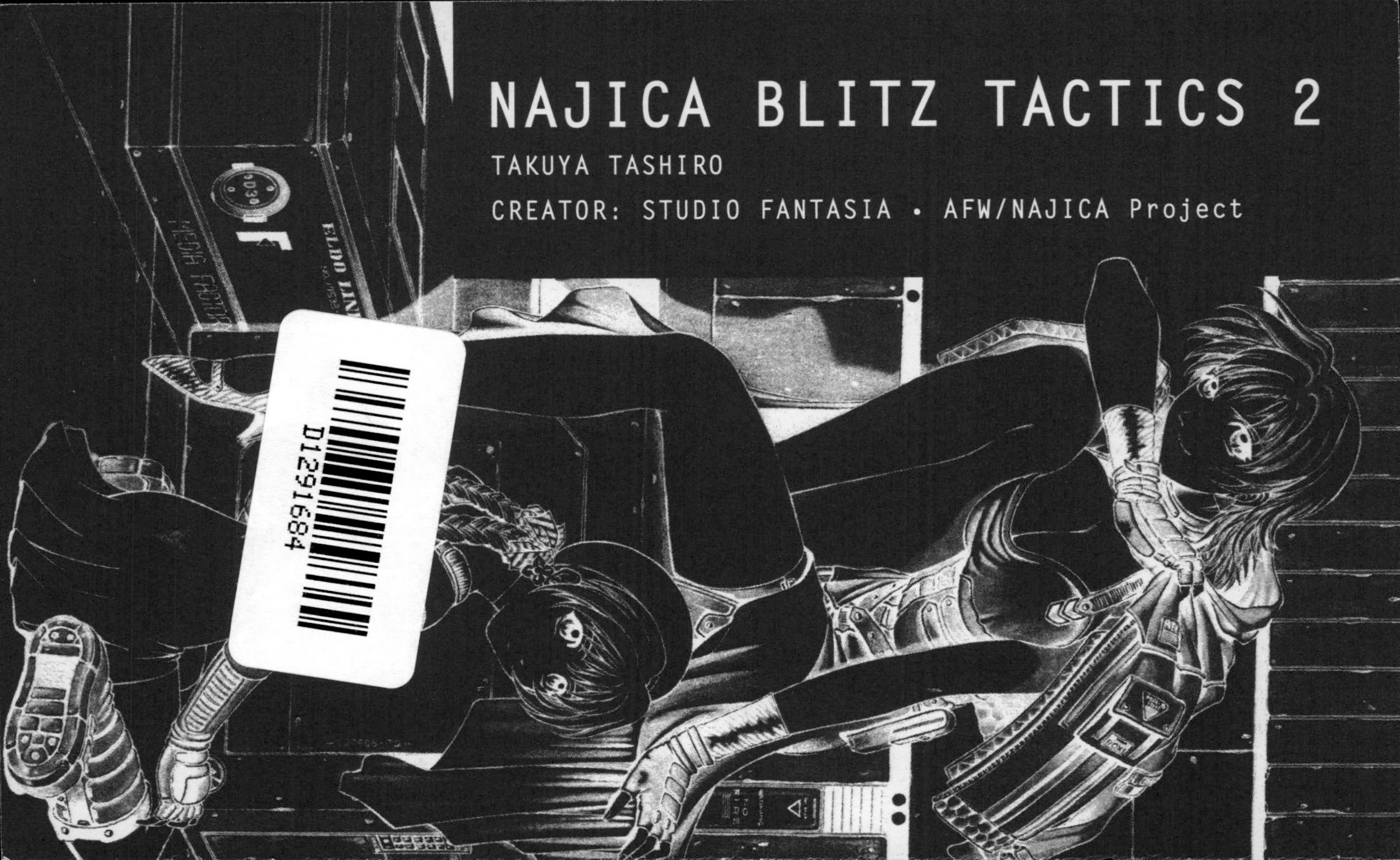

C O N T E N T S

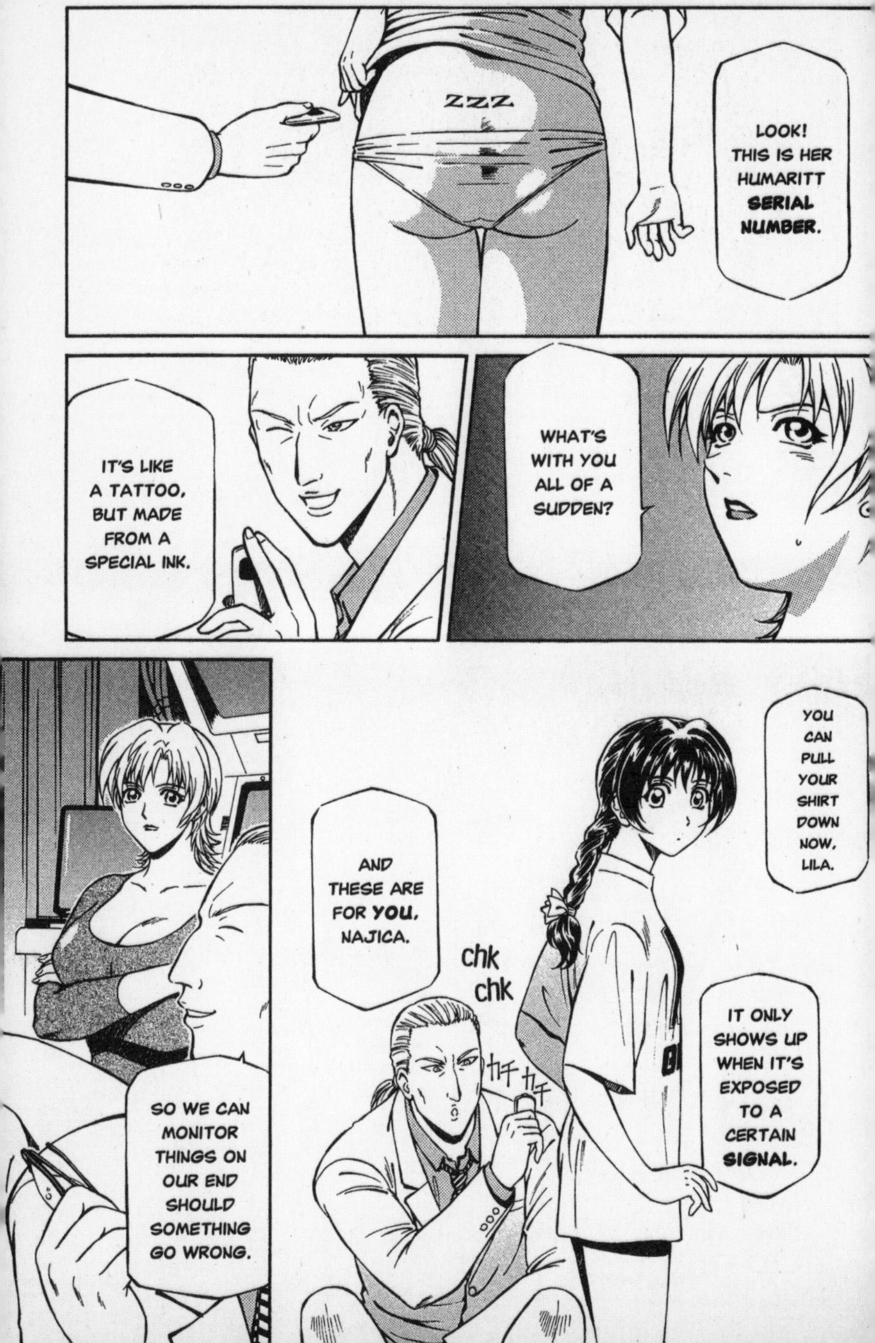
ZZZ
LOOK! THIS IS HER HUMARITT SERIAL NUMBER.
WHAT'S WITH YOU ALL OF A SUDDEN?
IT'S LIKE A TATTOO, BUT MADE FROM A SPECIAL INK.
YOU CAN PULL YOUR SHIRT DOWN NOW, LILA.
IT ONLY SHOWS UP WHEN IT'S EXPOSED TO A CERTAIN SIGNAL.
AND THESE ARE FOR YOU, NAJICA.
chk chk
カチ カチ
SO WE CAN MONITOR THINGS ON OUR END SHOULD SOMETHING GO WRONG.

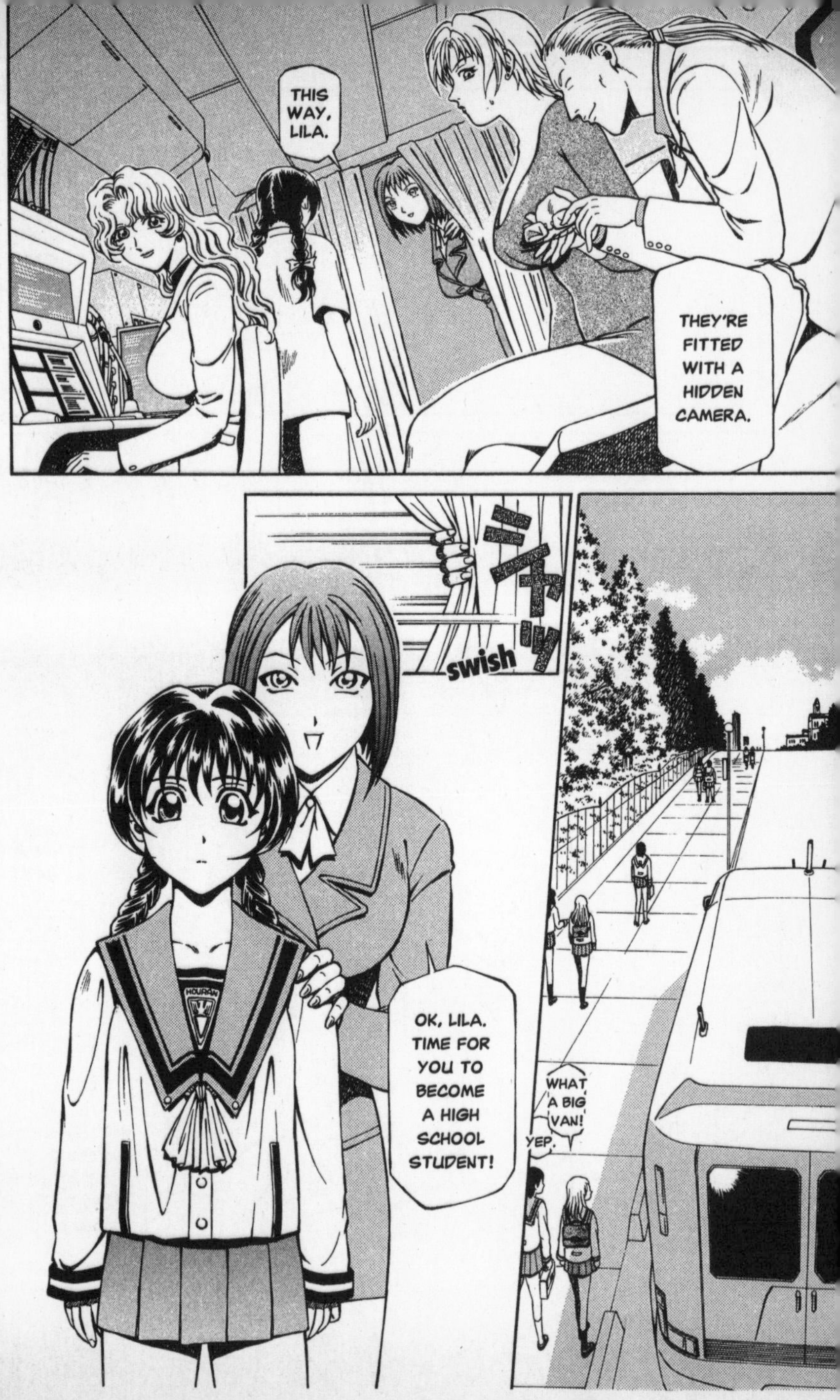

THEY'RE FITTED WITH A HIDDEN CAMERA.
THIS WAY, LILA.
WHAT A BIG VAN!
YEP.
シャッ
swish
OK, LILA. TIME FOR YOU TO BECOME A HIGH SCHOOL STUDENT!

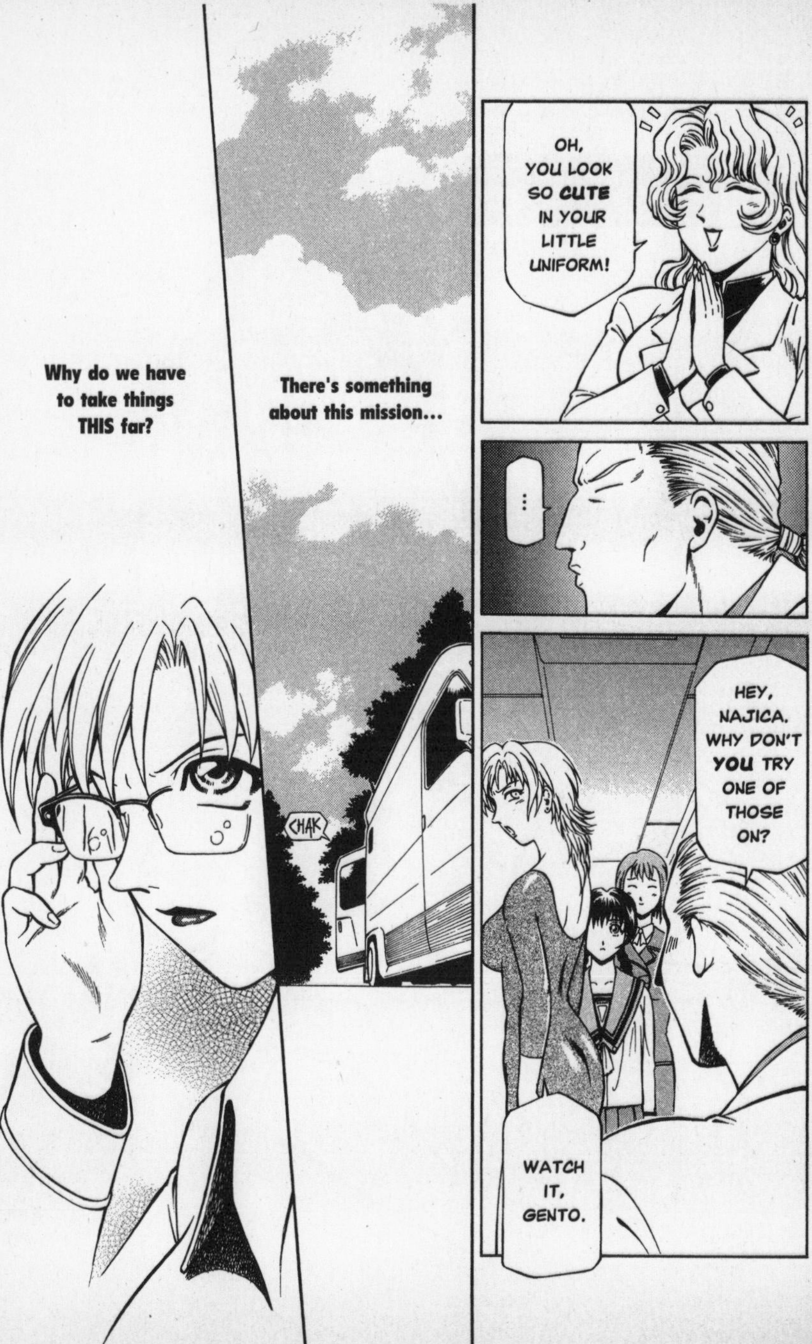
OH, YOU LOOK SO CUTE IN YOUR LITTLE UNIFORM!
...
HEY, NAJICA. WHY DON'T YOU TRY ONE OF THOSE ON?
WATCH IT, GENTO.
There's something about this mission...
CHAK
Why do we have to take things THIS far?

Operation.7
INFILTRATE THE ALL GIRLS' HIGH SCHOOL

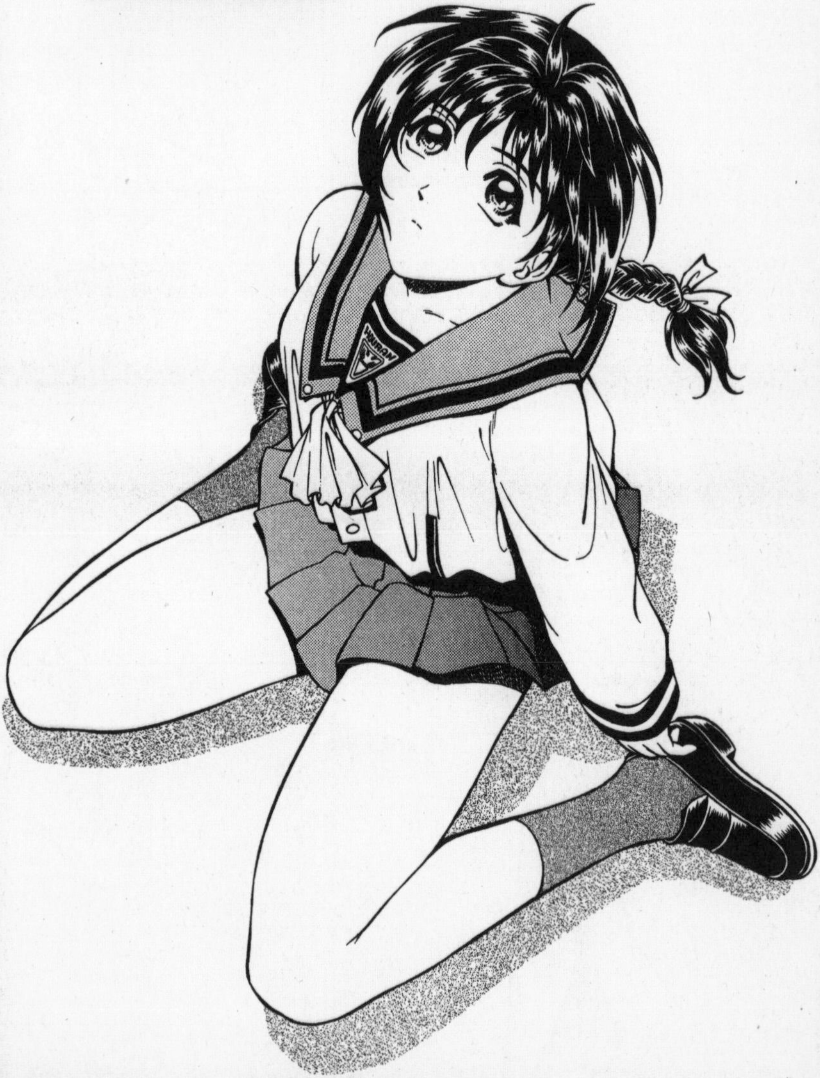

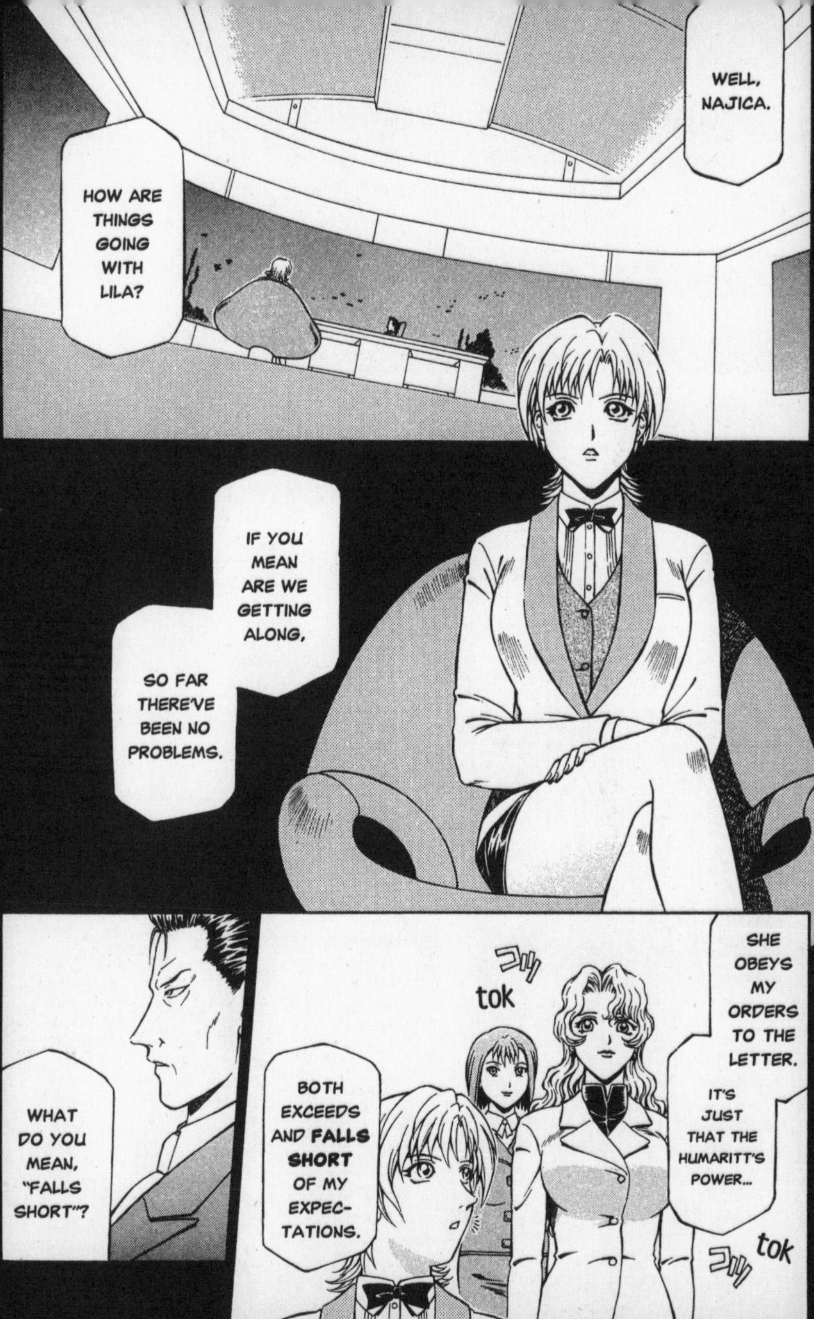
WELL, NAJICA.
HOW ARE THINGS GOING WITH LILA?
IF YOU MEAN ARE WE GETTING ALONG,
SO FAR THERE'VE BEEN NO PROBLEMS.
SHE OBEYS MY ORDERS TO THE LETTER.
コツ tok
IT'S JUST THAT THE HUMARITT'S POWER...
BOTH EXCEEDS AND **FALLS SHORT** OF MY EXPECTATIONS.
コツ tok
WHAT DO YOU MEAN, "FALLS SHORT"?

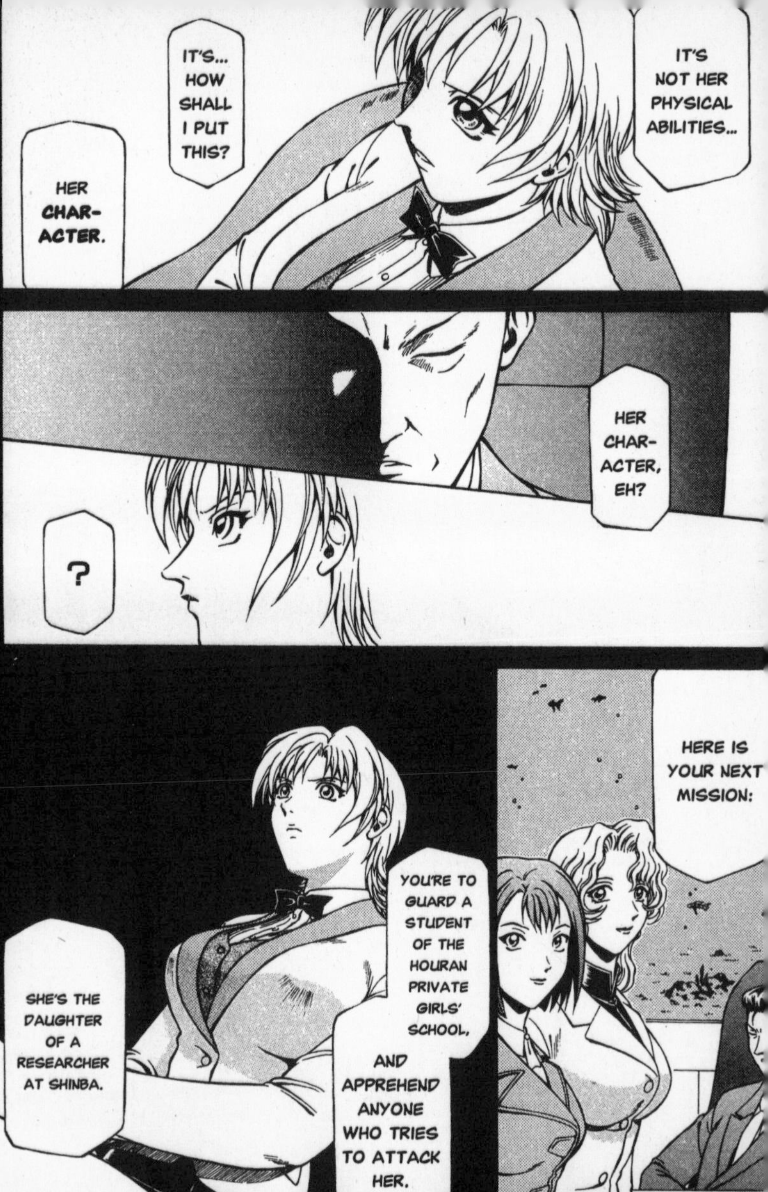
IT'S NOT HER PHYSICAL ABILITIES...
IT'S... HOW SHALL I PUT THIS?
HER CHARACTER.
HER CHARACTER, EH?
?
HERE IS YOUR NEXT MISSION:
YOU'RE TO GUARD A STUDENT OF THE HOURAN PRIVATE GIRLS' SCHOOL,
AND APPREHEND ANYONE WHO TRIES TO ATTACK HER.
SHE'S THE DAUGHTER OF A RESEARCHER AT SHINBA.

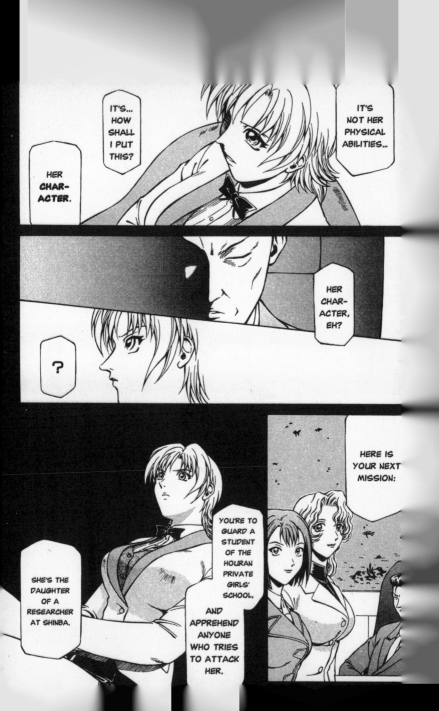

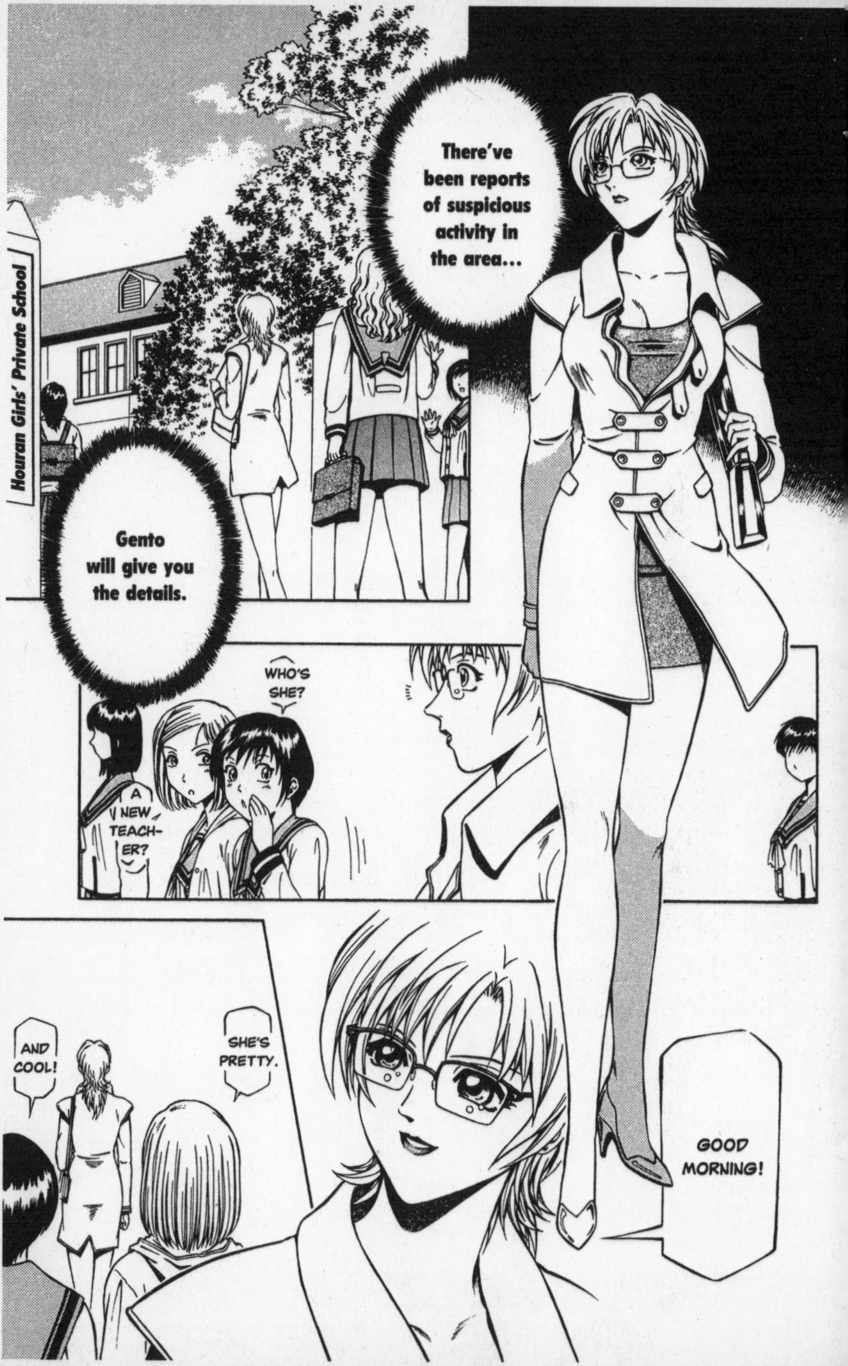

There've been reports of suspicious activity in the area...
Houran Girls' Private School
Gento will give you the details.
WHO'S SHE?
A NEW TEACHER?
GOOD MORNING!
SHE'S PRETTY.
AND COOL!

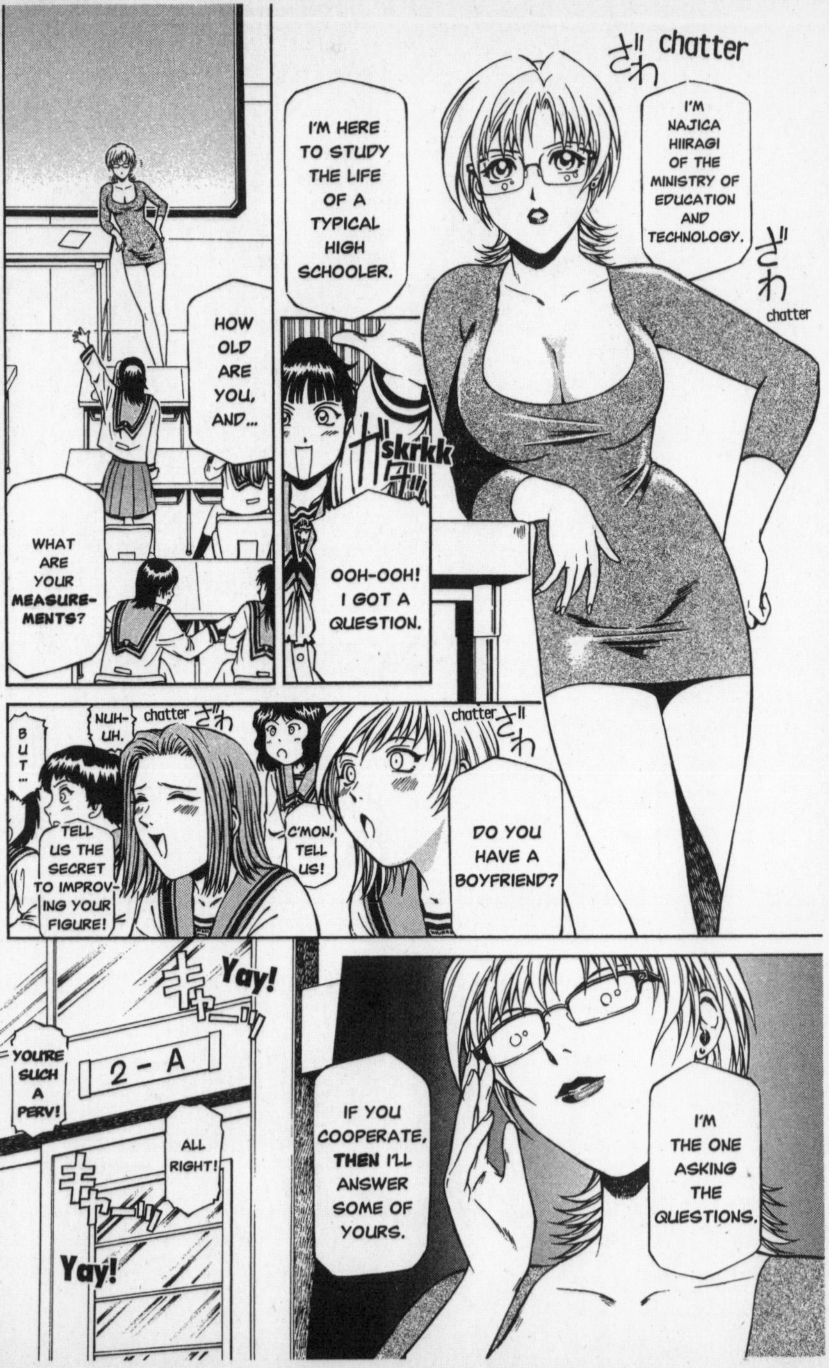
ざわ chatter
I'M NAJICA HIIRAGI OF THE MINISTRY OF EDUCATION AND TECHNOLOGY.
ざわ chatter
I'M HERE TO STUDY THE LIFE OF A TYPICAL HIGH SCHOOLER.
OOH-OOH! I GOT A QUESTION.
skrkk
HOW OLD ARE YOU, AND...
WHAT ARE YOUR MEASUREMENTS?
DO YOU HAVE A BOYFRIEND?
chatter ざわ
C'MON, TELL US!
chatter ざわ
NUH-UH.
TELL US THE SECRET TO IMPROVING YOUR FIGURE!
BUT...
I'M THE ONE ASKING THE QUESTIONS.
IF YOU COOPERATE, THEN I'LL ANSWER SOME OF YOURS.
Yay!
YOU'RE SUCH A PERV!
2 - A
ALL RIGHT!
Yay!

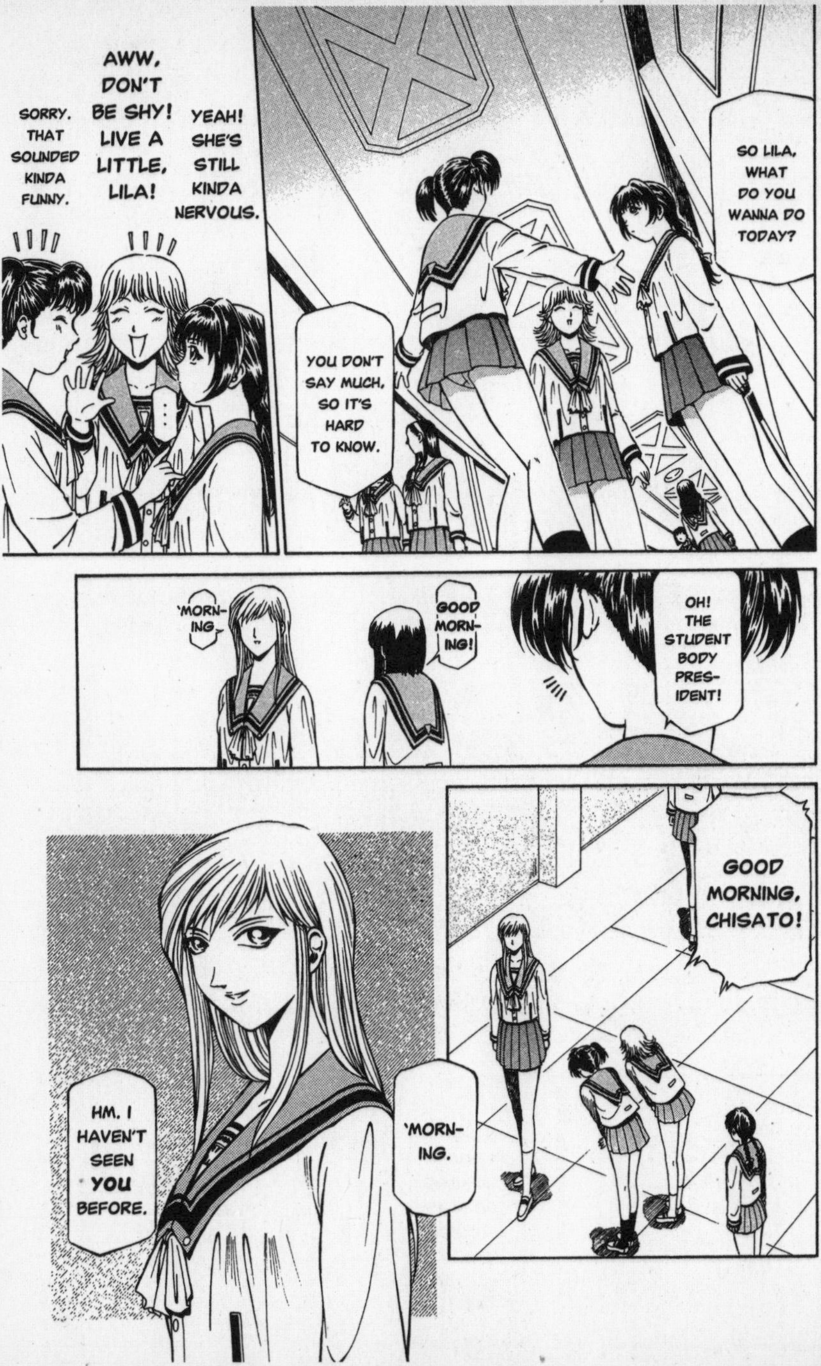
SO LILA, WHAT DO YOU WANNA DO TODAY?
YOU DON'T SAY MUCH, SO IT'S HARD TO KNOW.
YEAH! SHE'S STILL KINDA NERVOUS.
AWW, DON'T BE SHY! LIVE A LITTLE, LILA!
SORRY. THAT SOUNDED KINDA FUNNY.
OH! THE STUDENT BODY PRES-IDENT!
GOOD MORN-ING!
'MORN-ING.
GOOD MORNING, CHISATO!
'MORN-ING.
HM. I HAVEN'T SEEN YOU BEFORE.

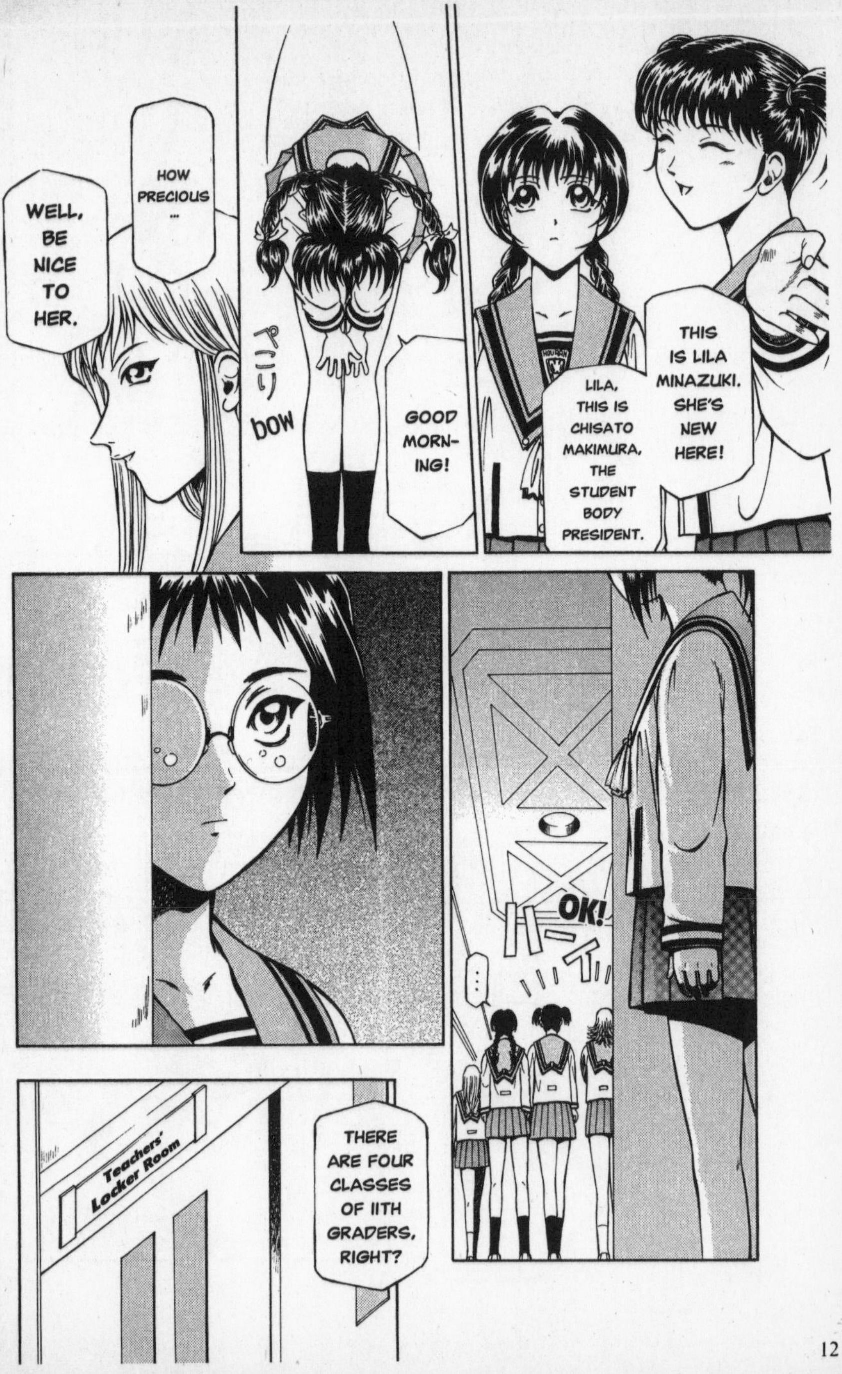
THIS IS LILA MINAZUKI. SHE'S NEW HERE!
LILA, THIS IS CHISATO MAKIMURA, THE STUDENT BODY PRESIDENT.
ぺこり
bow
GOOD MORNING!
HOW PRECIOUS ...
WELL, BE NICE TO HER.
ハーイ
OK!
...
Teachers' Locker Room
THERE ARE FOUR CLASSES OF 11TH GRADERS, RIGHT?

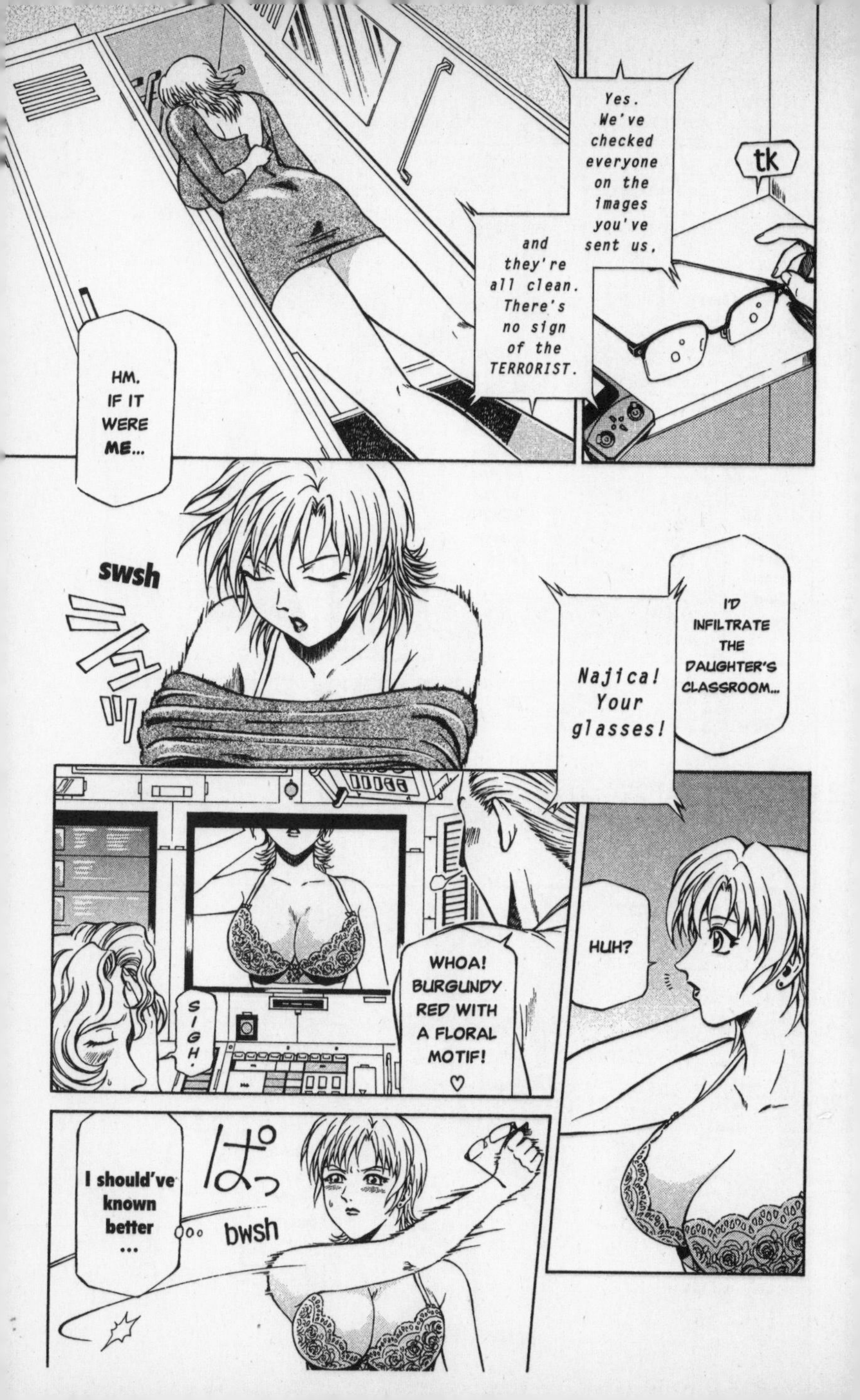
tk
Yes. We've checked everyone on the images you've sent us,
and they're all clean. There's no sign of the TERRORIST.
HM. IF IT WERE ME...
I'D INFILTRATE THE DAUGHTER'S CLASSROOM...
swsh
シュッ
HUH?
Najica! Your glasses!
WHOA! BURGUNDY RED WITH A FLORAL MOTIF! ♡
SIGH.
ぱっ
bwsh
I should've known better...

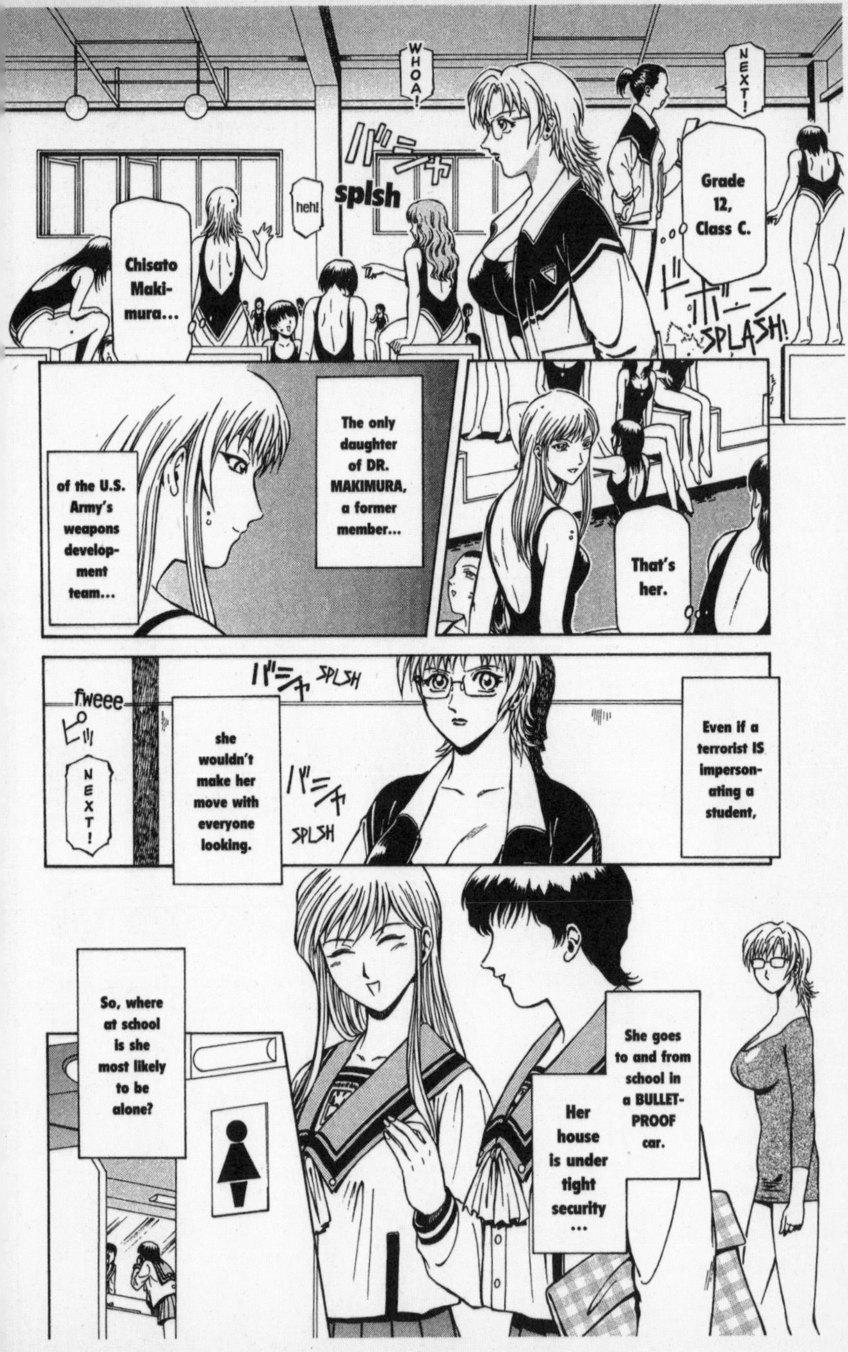
NEXT!
Grade 12, Class C.
ドボーン
SPLASH!
WHOA!
バシャ
splsh
heh!
Chisato Maki-mura...
That's her.
The only daughter of DR. MAKIMURA, a former member...
of the U.S. Army's weapons development team...
Even if a terrorist IS impersonating a student,
バシャ
SPLSH
バシャ
SPLSH
she wouldn't make her move with everyone looking.
fweee
ピッ
NEXT!
She goes to and from school in a BULLET-PROOF car.
Her house is under tight security...
So, where at school is she most likely to be alone?

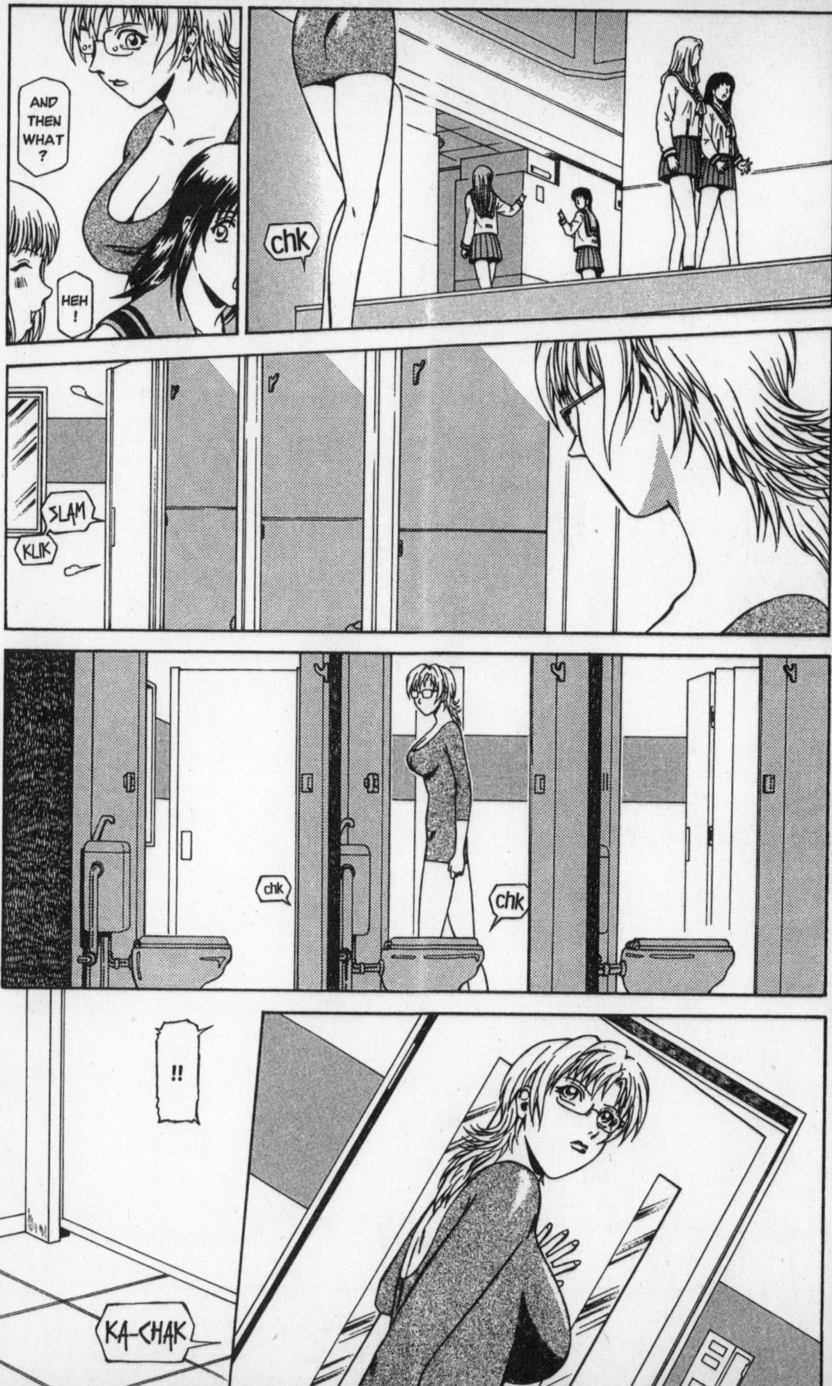
chk
AND THEN WHAT ?
HEH !
SLAM
KLIK
chk
chk
!!
KA-CHAK

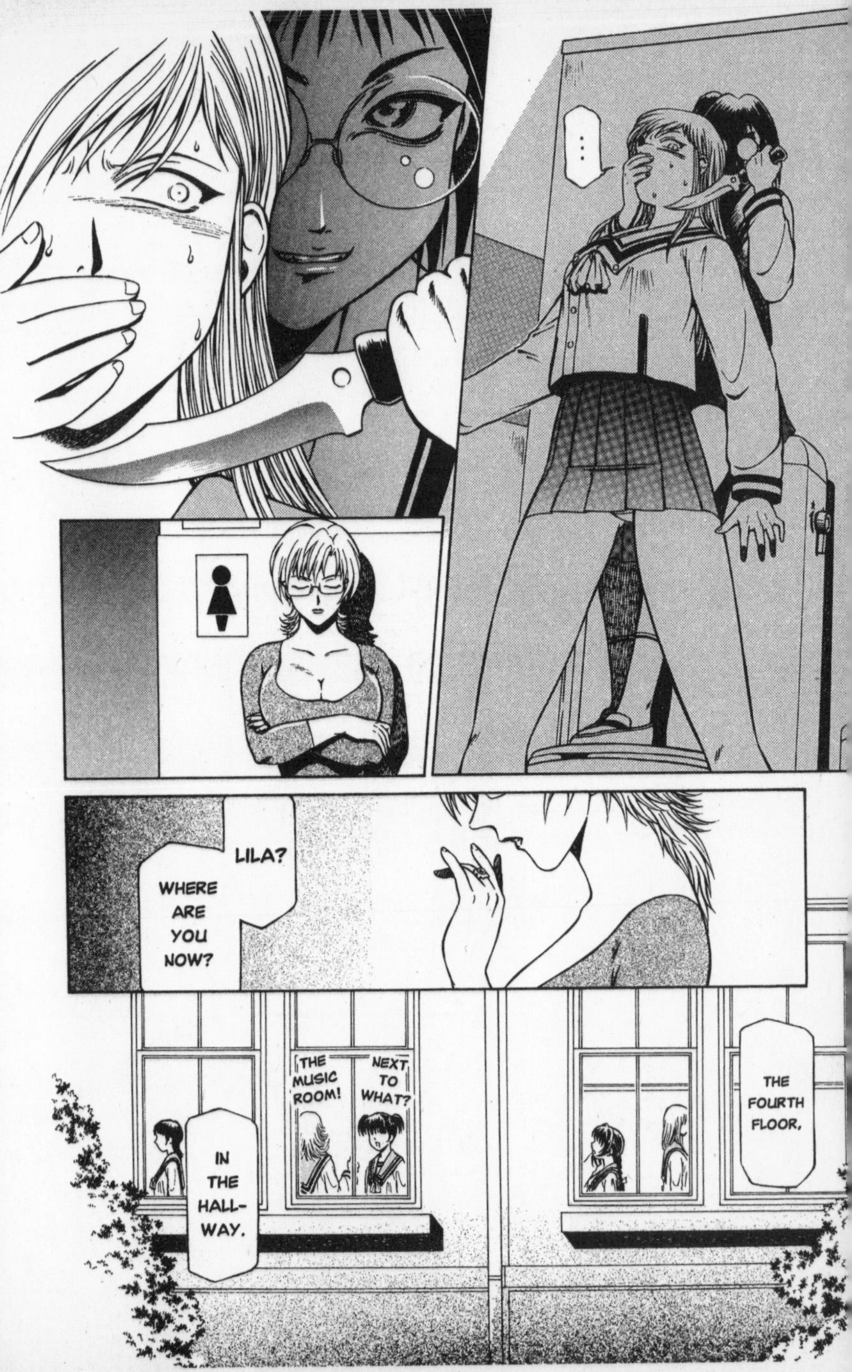
...
LILA? WHERE ARE YOU NOW?
THE FOURTH FLOOR,
NEXT TO WHAT?
THE MUSIC ROOM!
IN THE HALL-WAY.

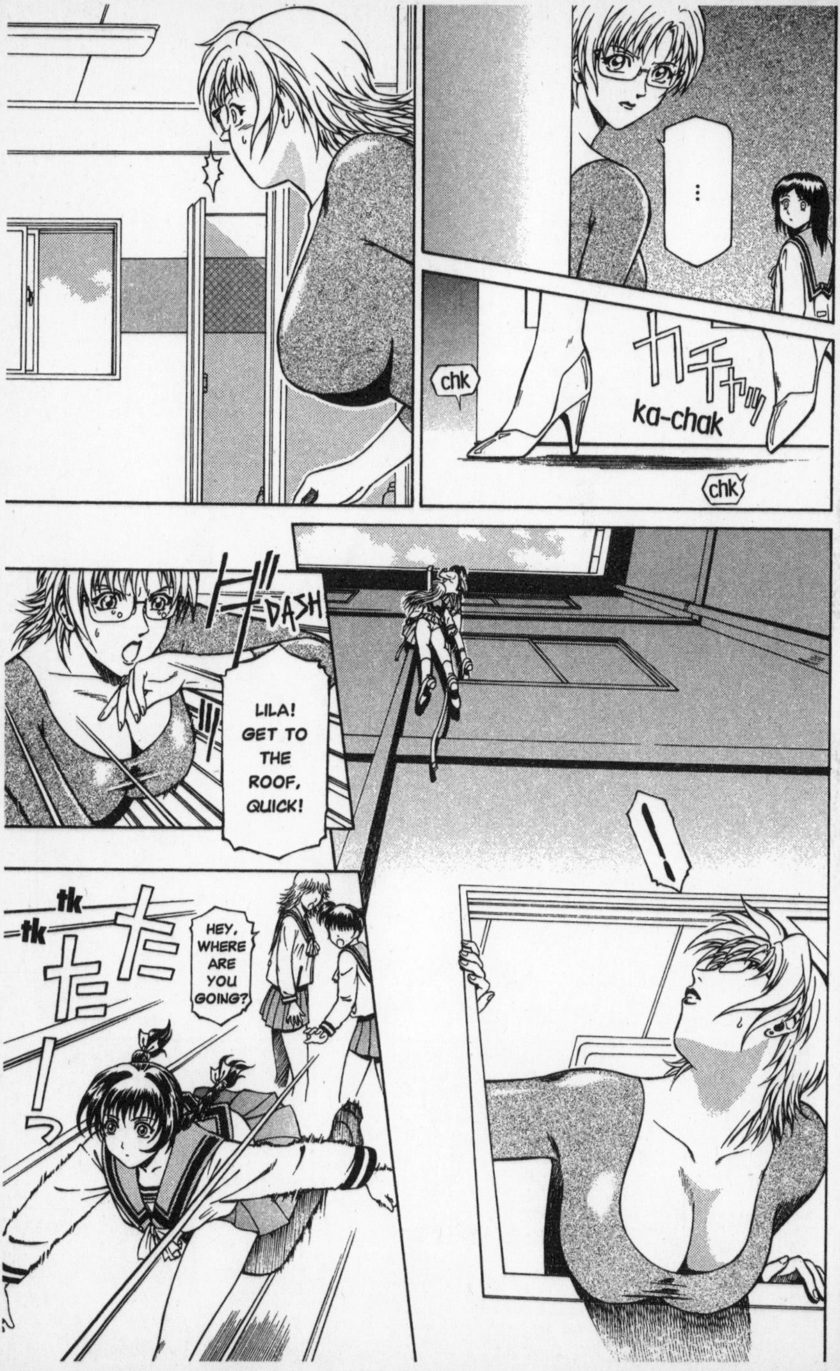
…
カチャッ
ka-chak
chk
chk
!
DASH
LILA! GET TO THE ROOF, QUICK!
HEY, WHERE ARE YOU GOING?
たたたーっ
tk
tk

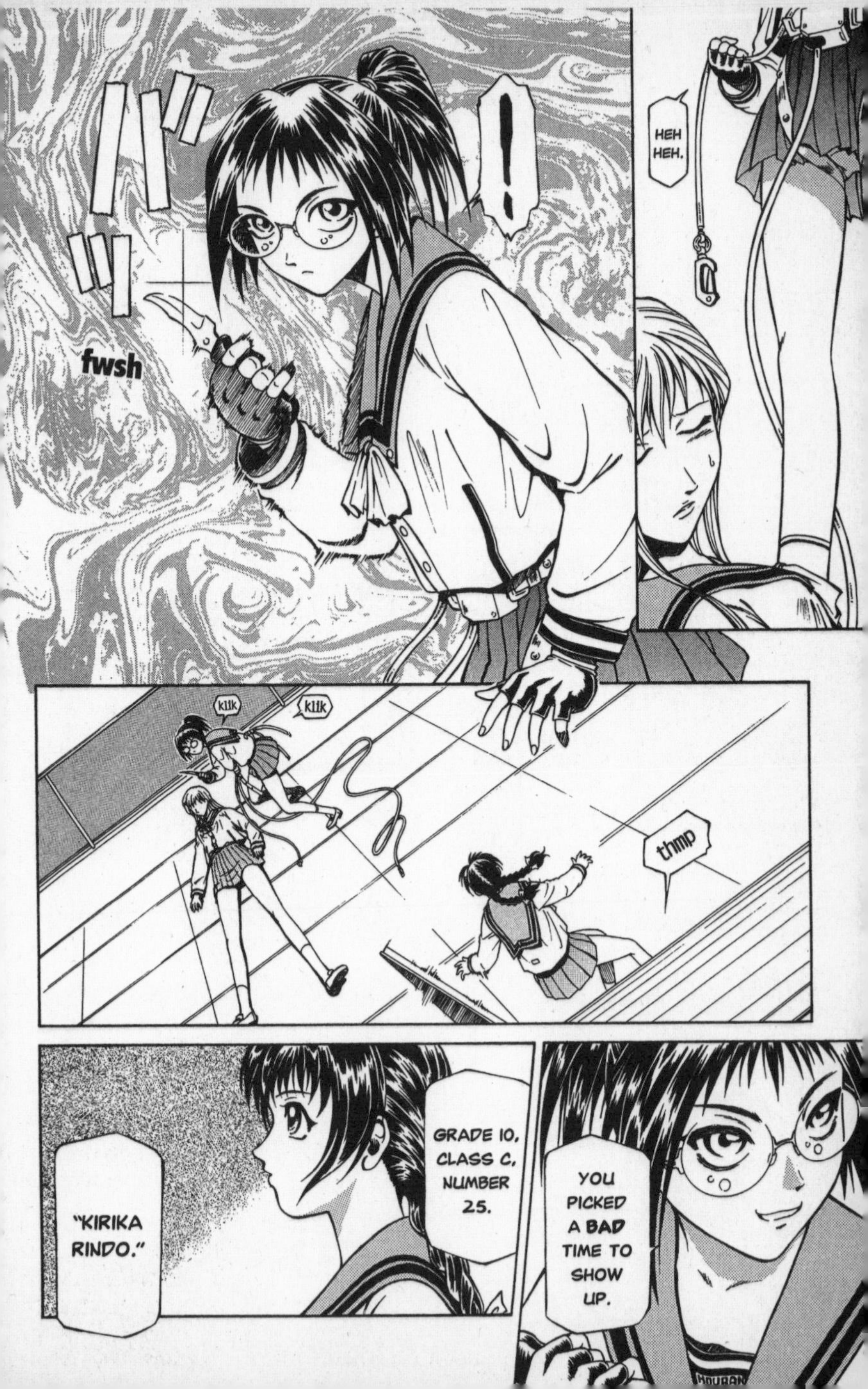
HEH HEH.
!
fwsh
klik
klik
thmp
YOU PICKED A BAD TIME TO SHOW UP.
GRADE 10, CLASS C, NUMBER 25.
"KIRIKA RINDO."

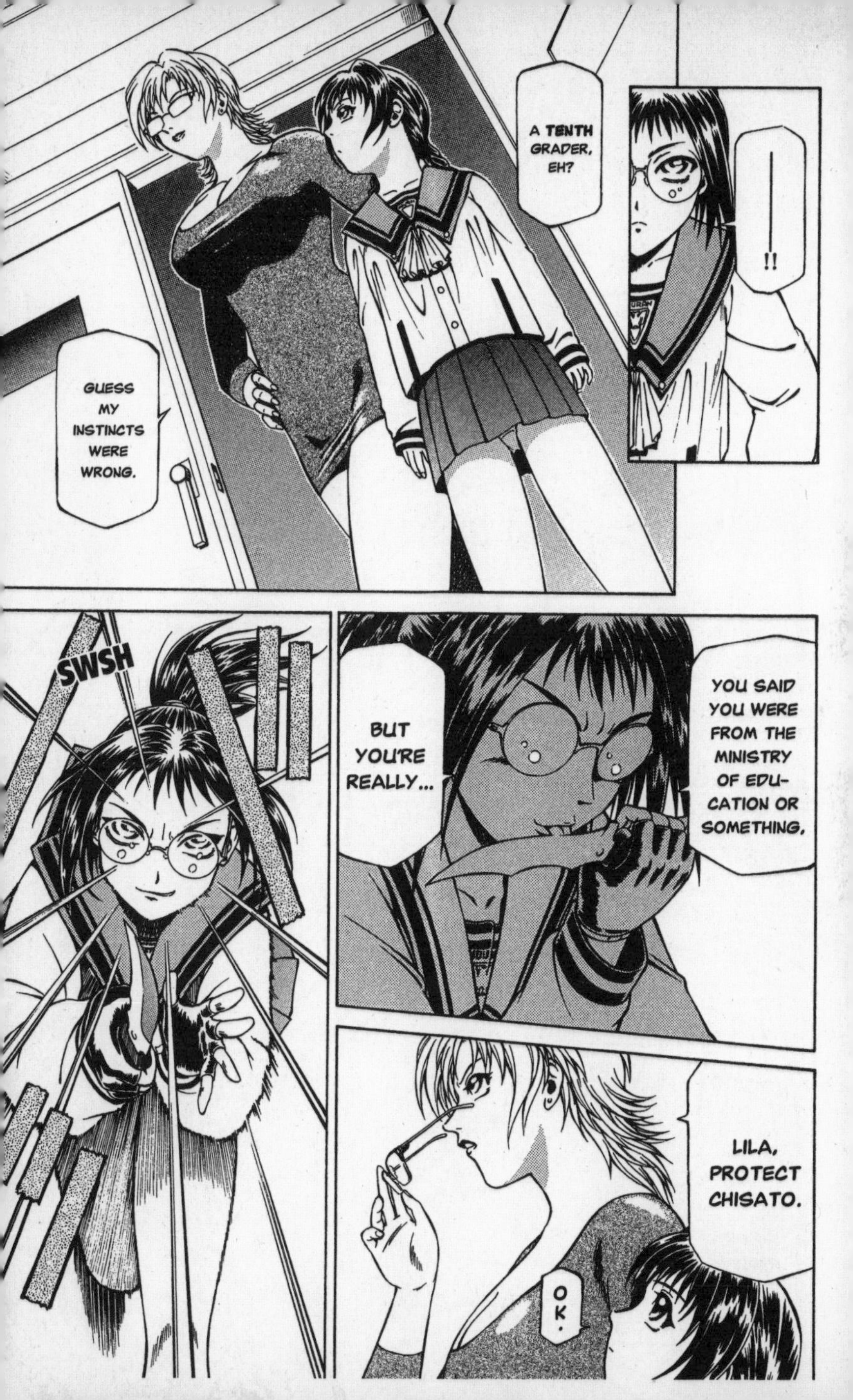
!!
A TENTH GRADER, EH?
GUESS MY INSTINCTS WERE WRONG.
YOU SAID YOU WERE FROM THE MINISTRY OF EDU-CATION OR SOMETHING,
BUT YOU'RE REALLY...
LILA, PROTECT CHISATO.
OK.
SWSH

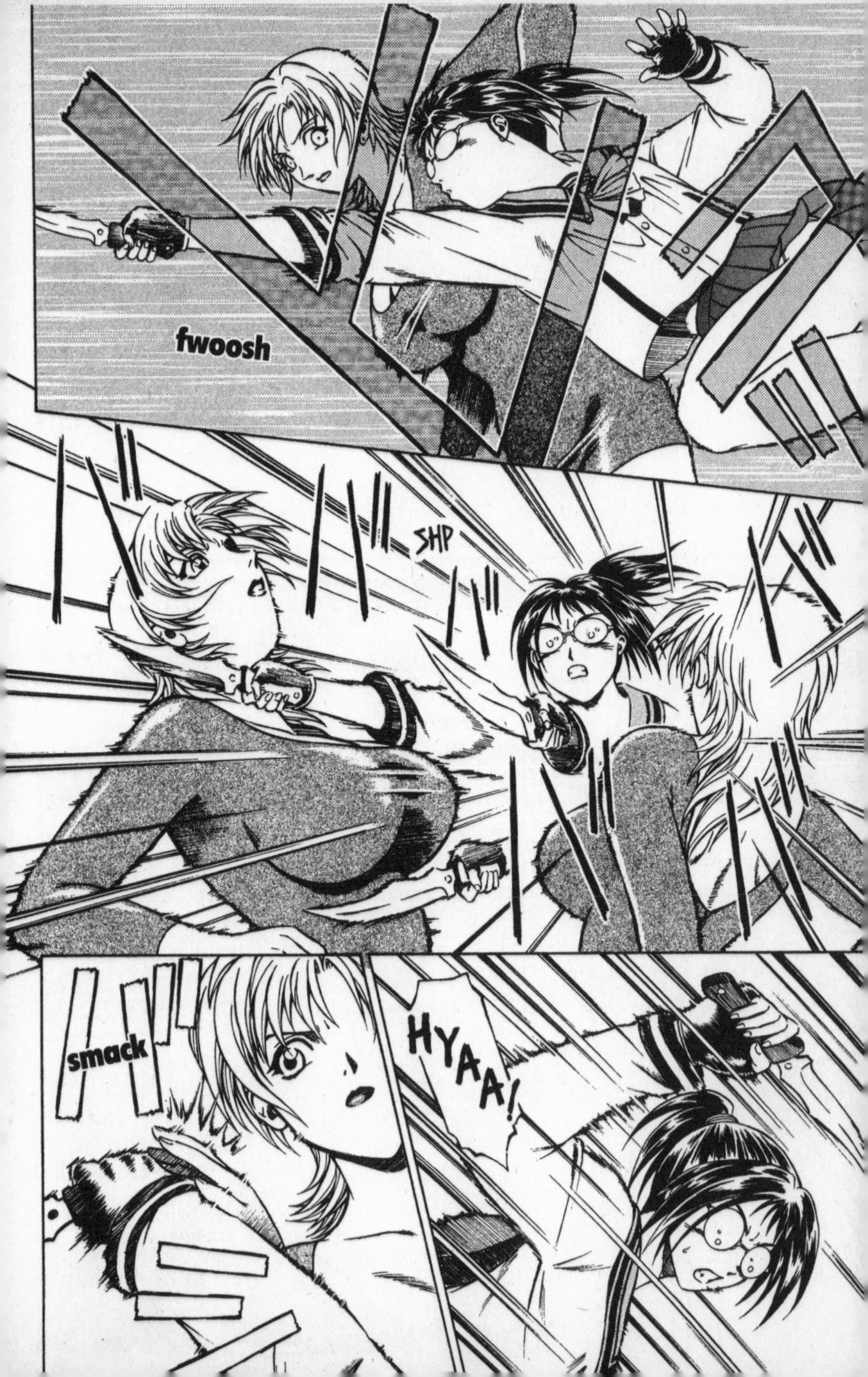
fwoosh
SHP
HYAAA!
smack

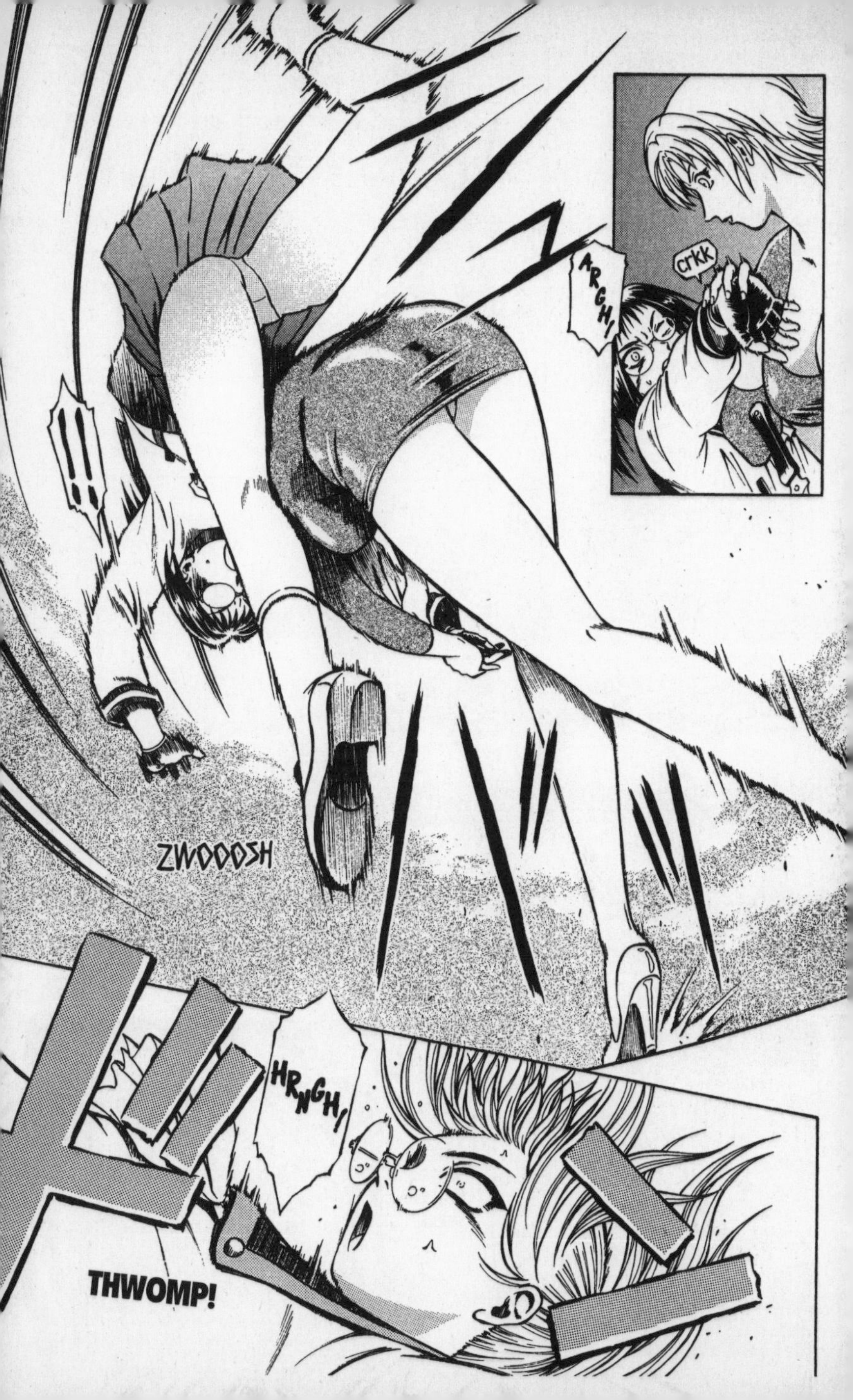
crkk
ARGH!
!!
ZWOOOSH
HRNGH!
THWOMP!

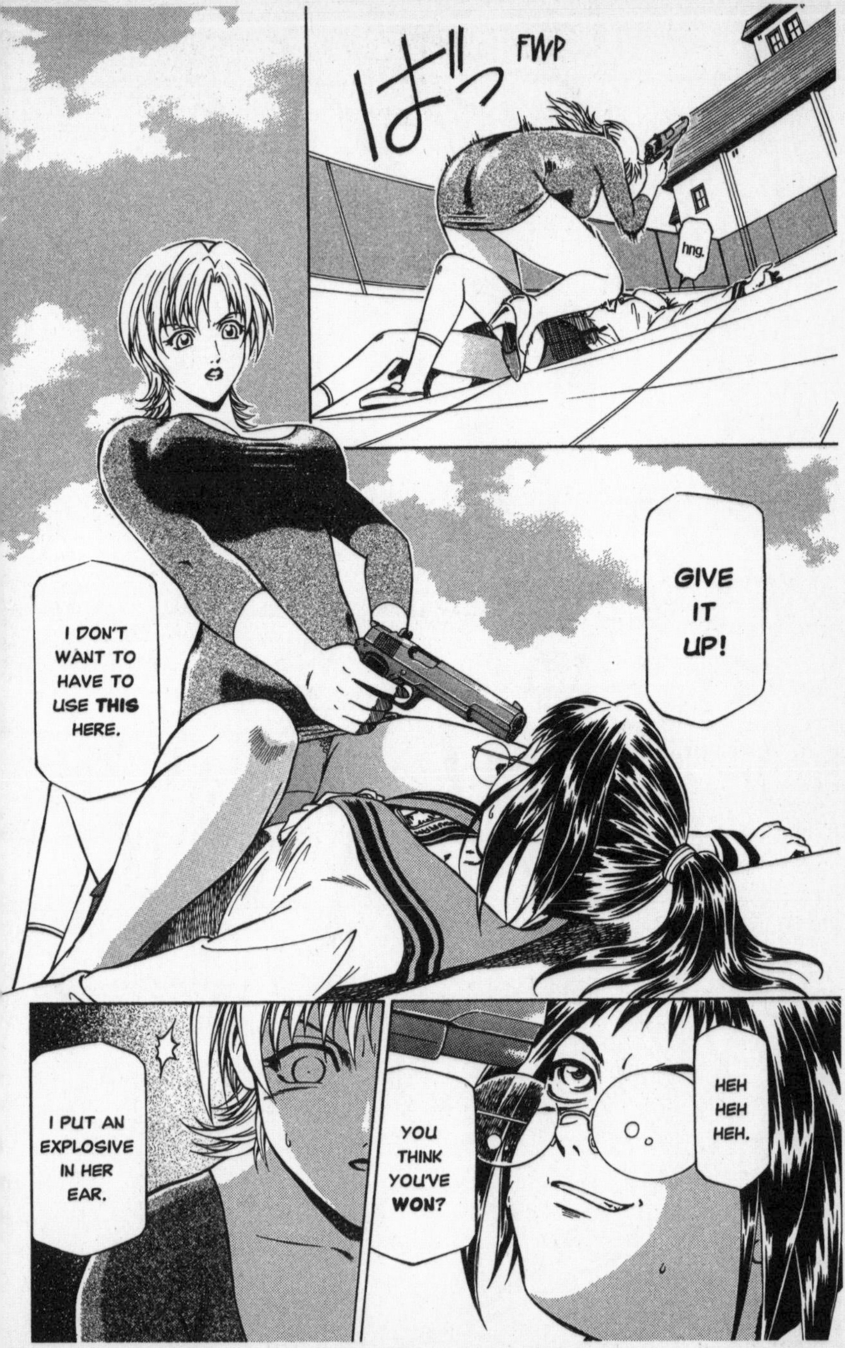
ばっ
FWP
hng.
GIVE IT UP!
I DON'T WANT TO HAVE TO USE THIS HERE.
HEH HEH HEH.
YOU THINK YOU'VE WON?
I PUT AN EXPLOSIVE IN HER EAR.

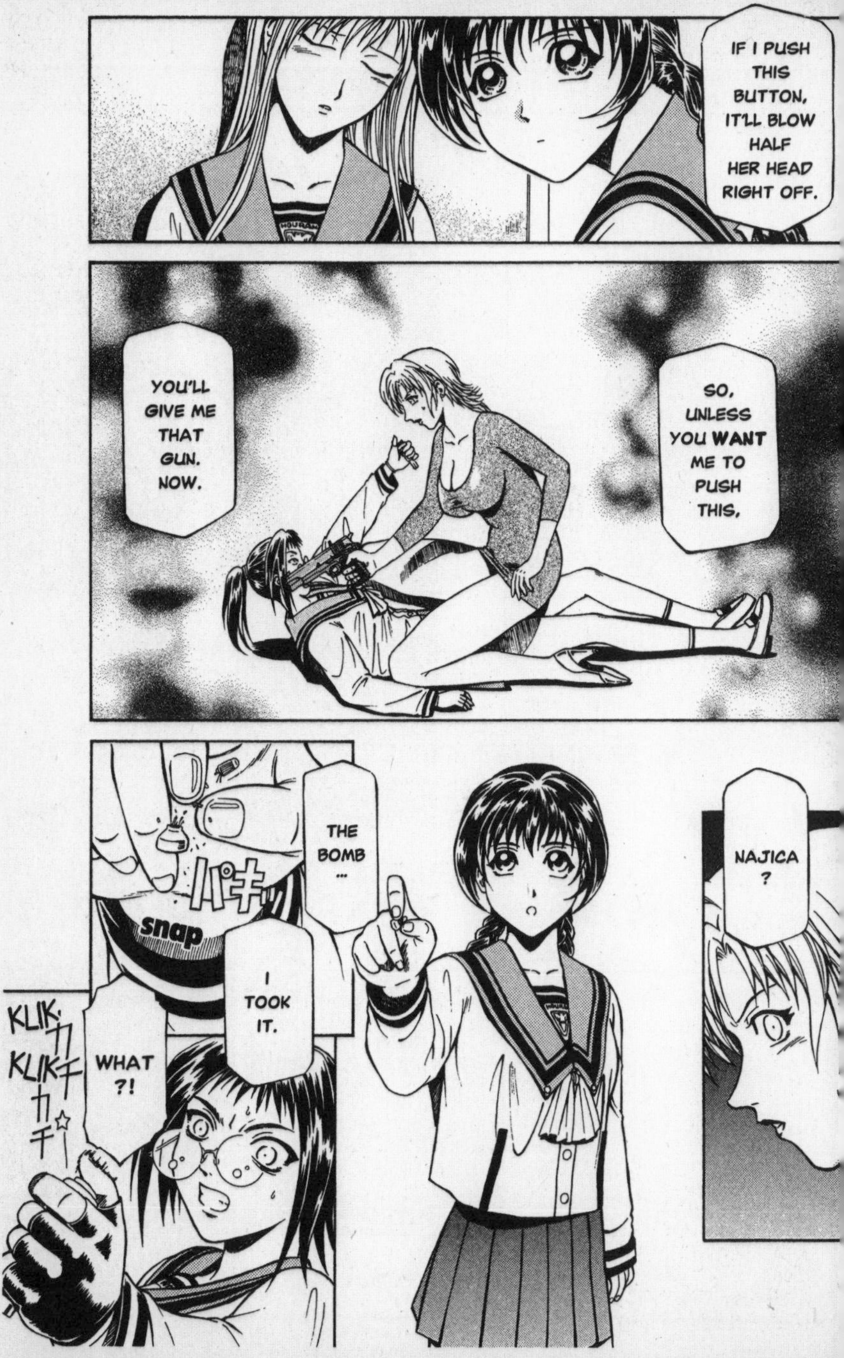
IF I PUSH THIS BUTTON, IT'LL BLOW HALF HER HEAD RIGHT OFF.
SO, UNLESS YOU **WANT** ME TO PUSH THIS,
YOU'LL GIVE ME THAT GUN. NOW.
NAJICA ?
THE BOMB ...
パキッ
snap
I TOOK IT.
KLIK KLIK
カチ カチ☆
WHAT ?!

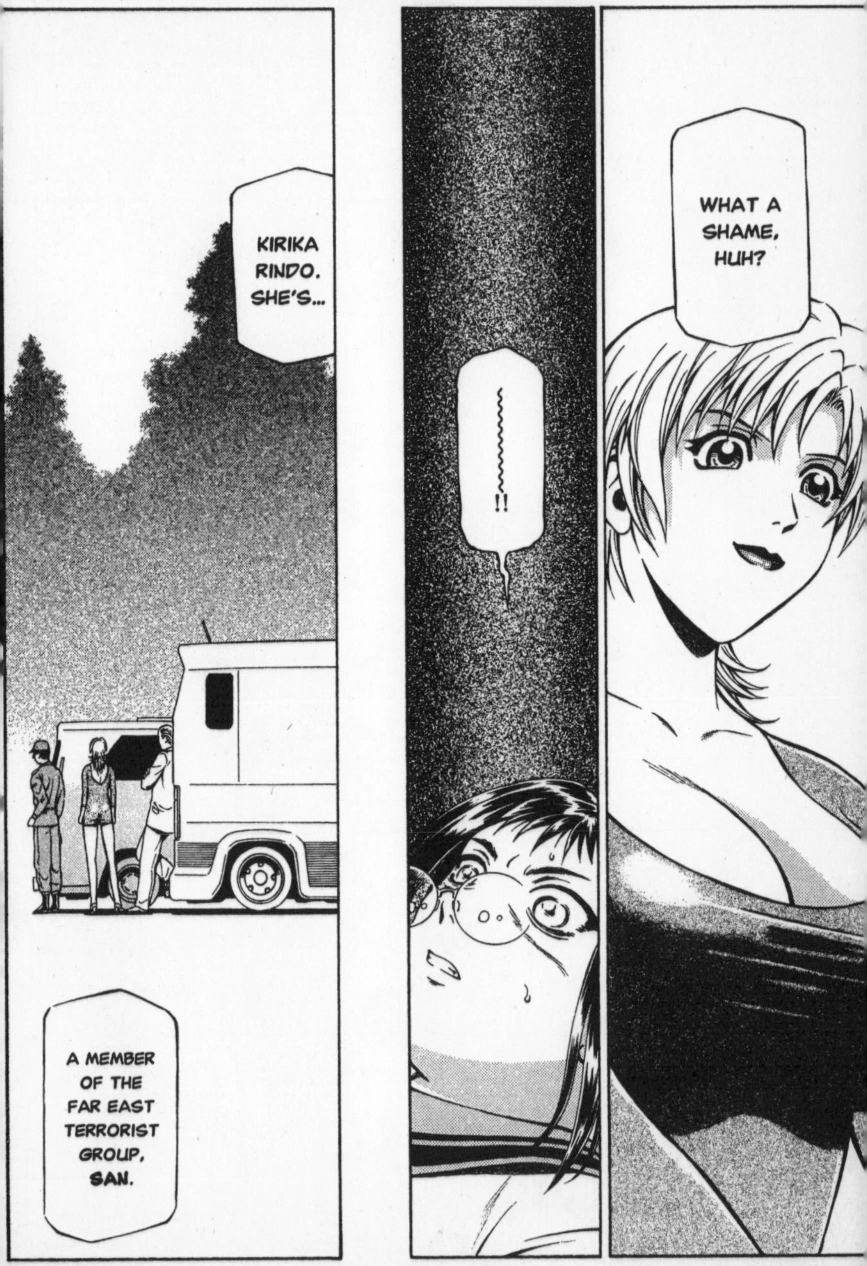
WHAT A SHAME, HUH?
~~~~!!
KIRIKA RINDO. SHE'S...
A MEMBER OF THE FAR EAST TERRORIST GROUP, SAN.
~~~~

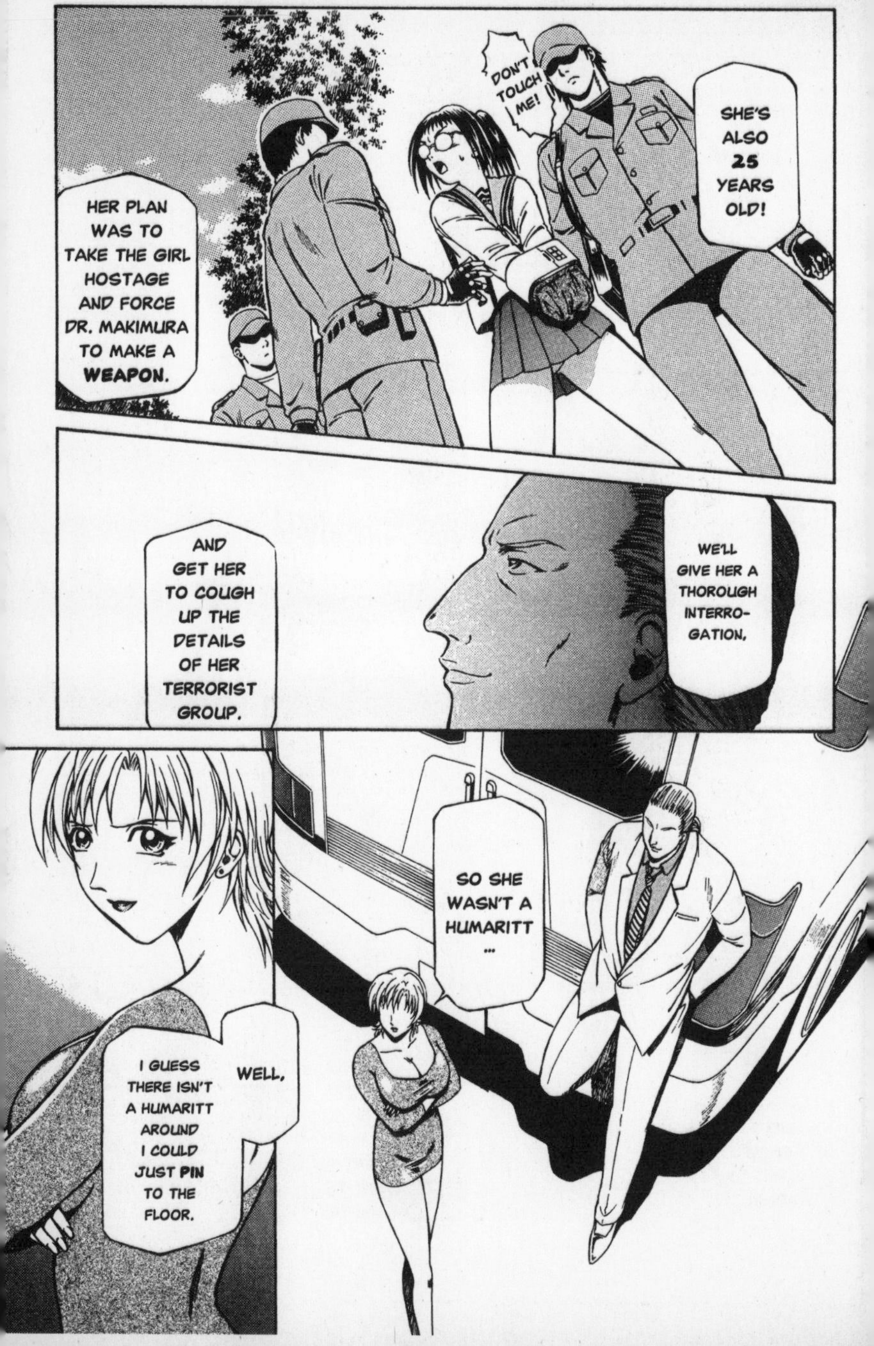
SHE'S ALSO 25 YEARS OLD!
DON'T TOUCH ME!
HER PLAN WAS TO TAKE THE GIRL HOSTAGE AND FORCE DR. MAKIMURA TO MAKE A WEAPON.
WE'LL GIVE HER A THOROUGH INTERRO-GATION.
AND GET HER TO COUGH UP THE DETAILS OF HER TERRORIST GROUP.
SO SHE WASN'T A HUMARITT ...
WELL,
I GUESS THERE ISN'T A HUMARITT AROUND I COULD JUST PIN TO THE FLOOR.

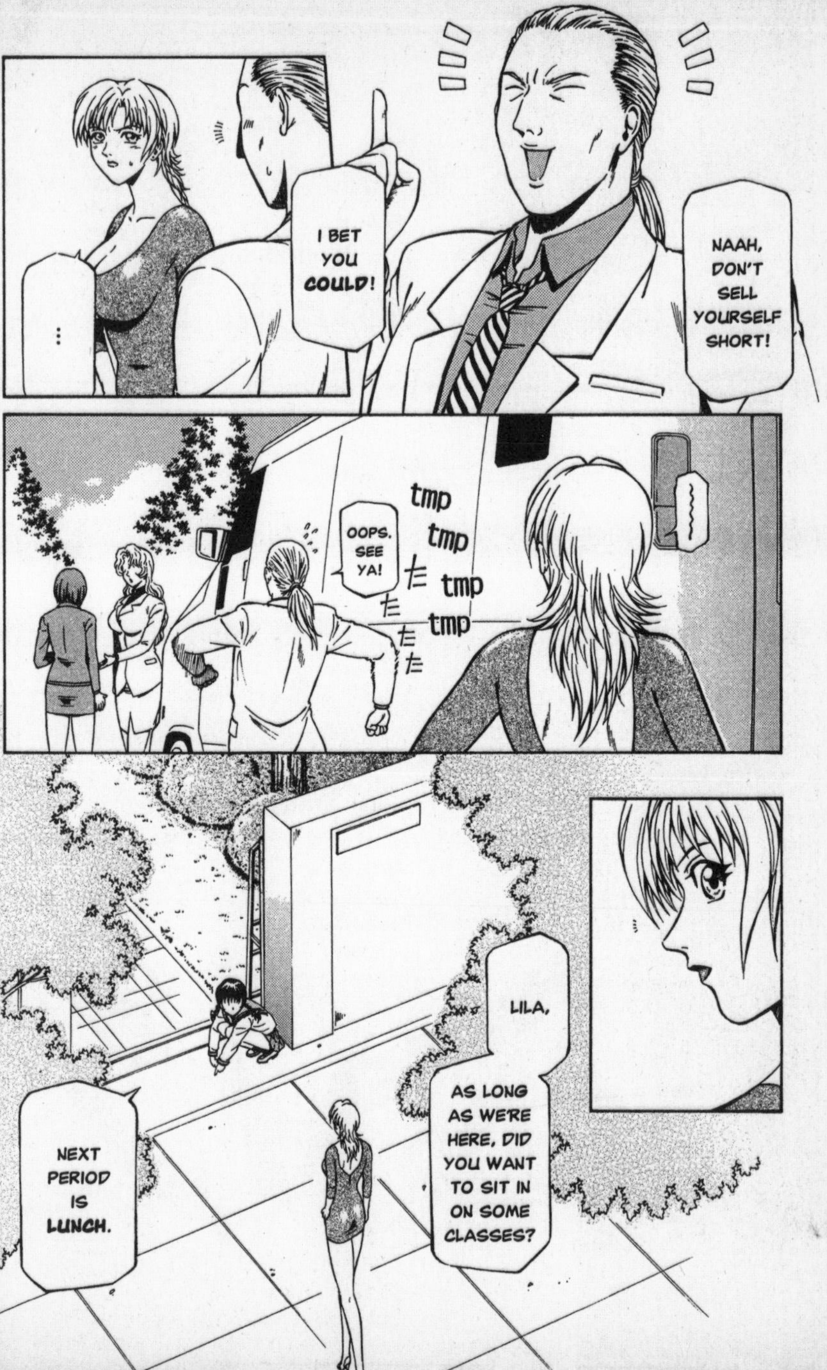
NAAH, DON'T SELL YOURSELF SHORT!
I BET YOU **COULD**!
...
tmp
tmp
tmp
tmp
OOPS. SEE YA!
た
た
た
た
LILA,
AS LONG AS WE'RE HERE, DID YOU WANT TO SIT IN ON SOME CLASSES?
NEXT PERIOD IS **LUNCH**.

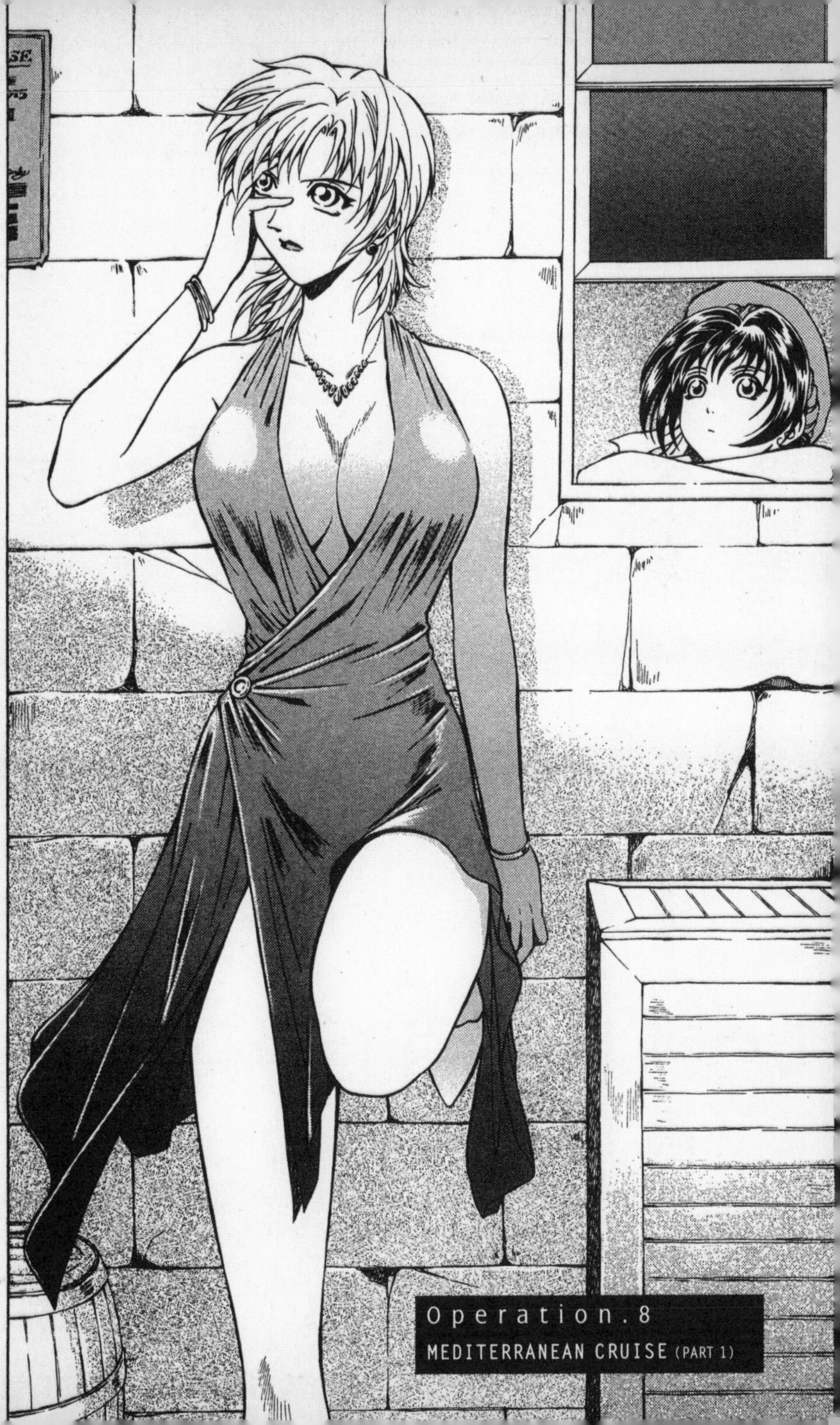
Operation.8
MEDITERRANEAN CRUISE (PART 1)

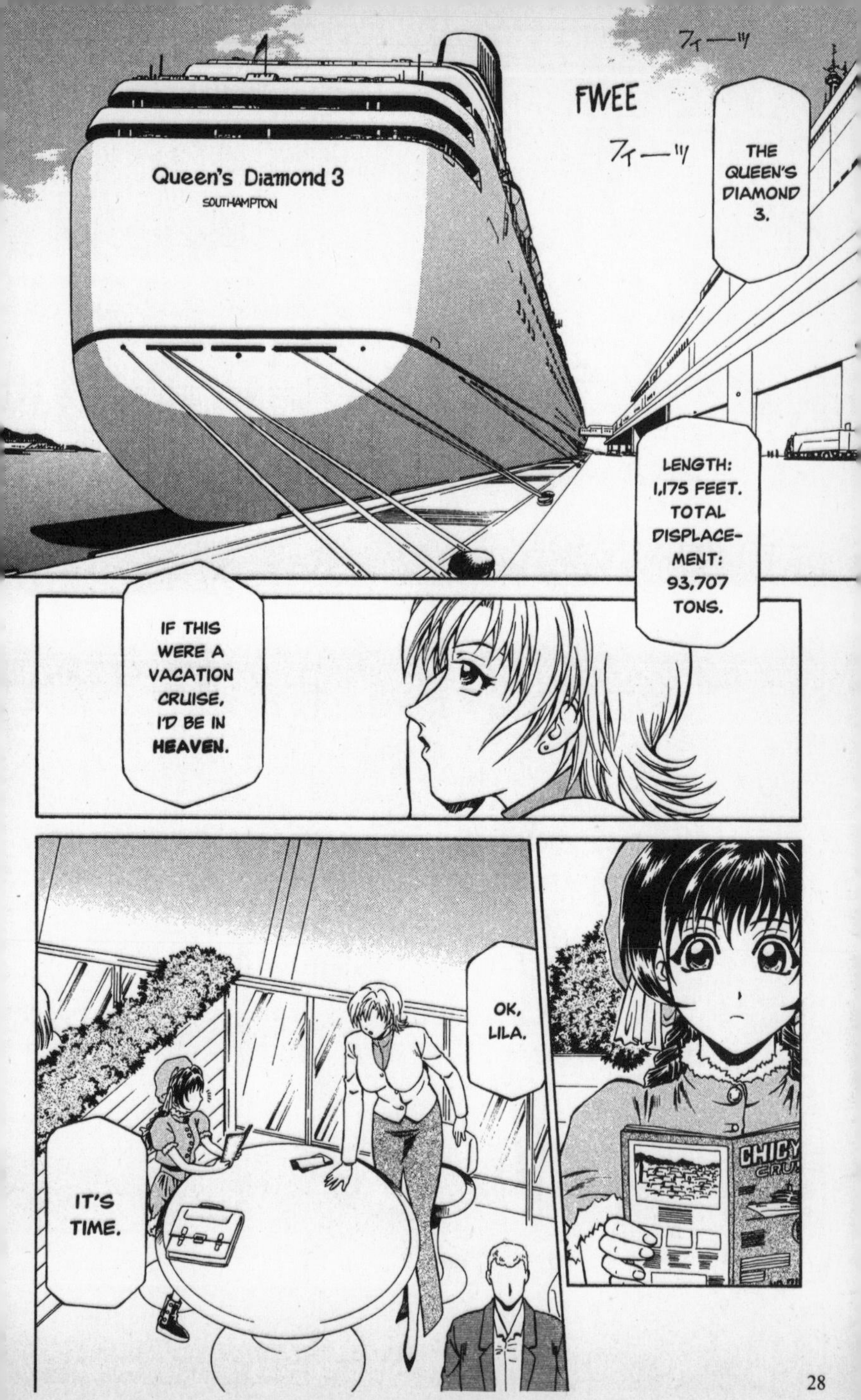

フィーッ
FWEE
フィーッ
Queen's Diamond 3
SOUTHAMPTON
THE QUEEN'S DIAMOND 3.
LENGTH: 1,175 FEET. TOTAL DISPLACEMENT: 93,707 TONS.
IF THIS WERE A VACATION CRUISE, I'D BE IN HEAVEN.
OK, LILA.
IT'S TIME.

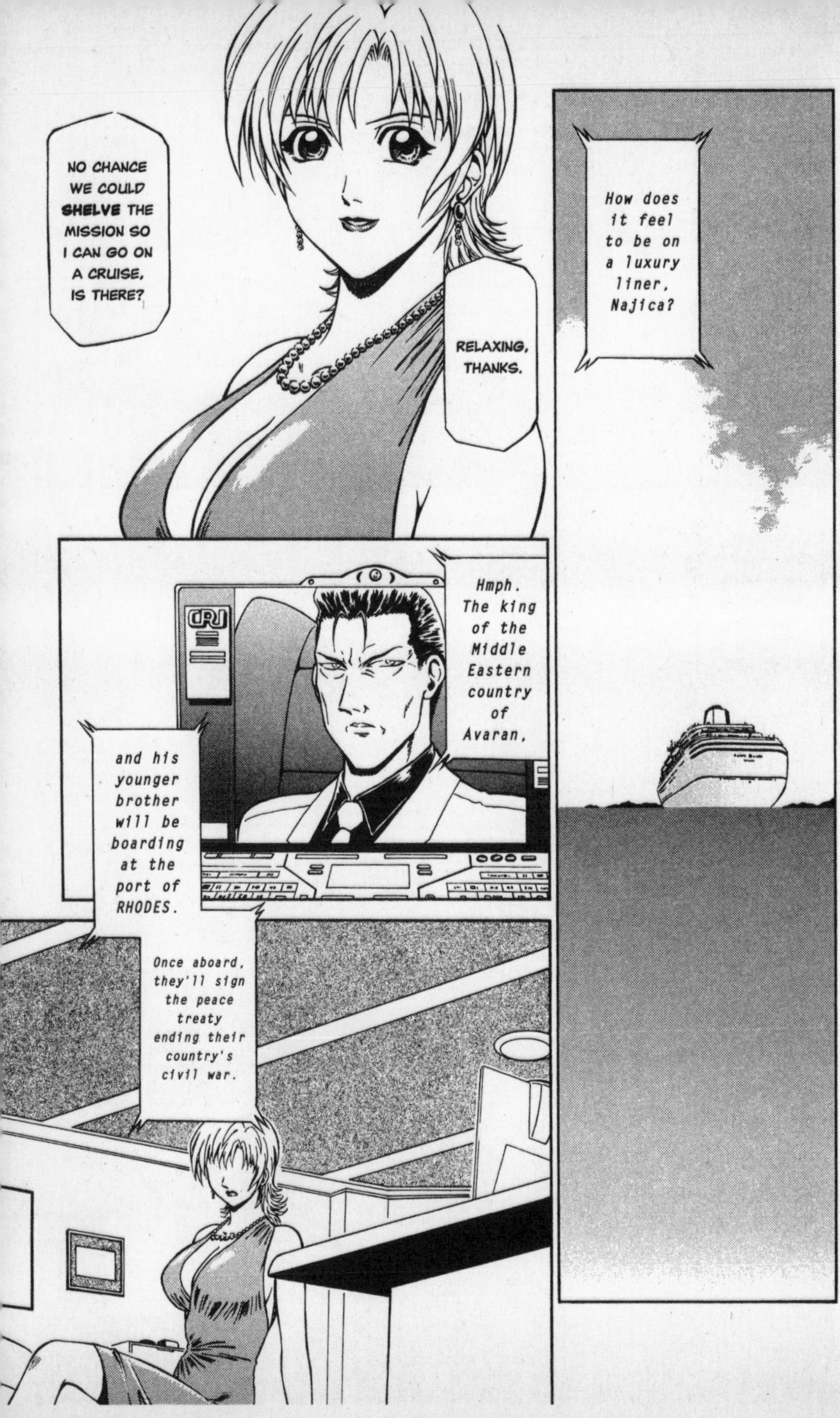
How does it feel to be on a luxury liner, Najica?
RELAXING, THANKS.
NO CHANCE WE COULD **SHELVE** THE MISSION SO I CAN GO ON A CRUISE, IS THERE?
Hmph. The king of the Middle Eastern country of Avaran,
and his younger brother will be boarding at the port of RHODES.
Once aboard, they'll sign the peace treaty ending their country's civil war.

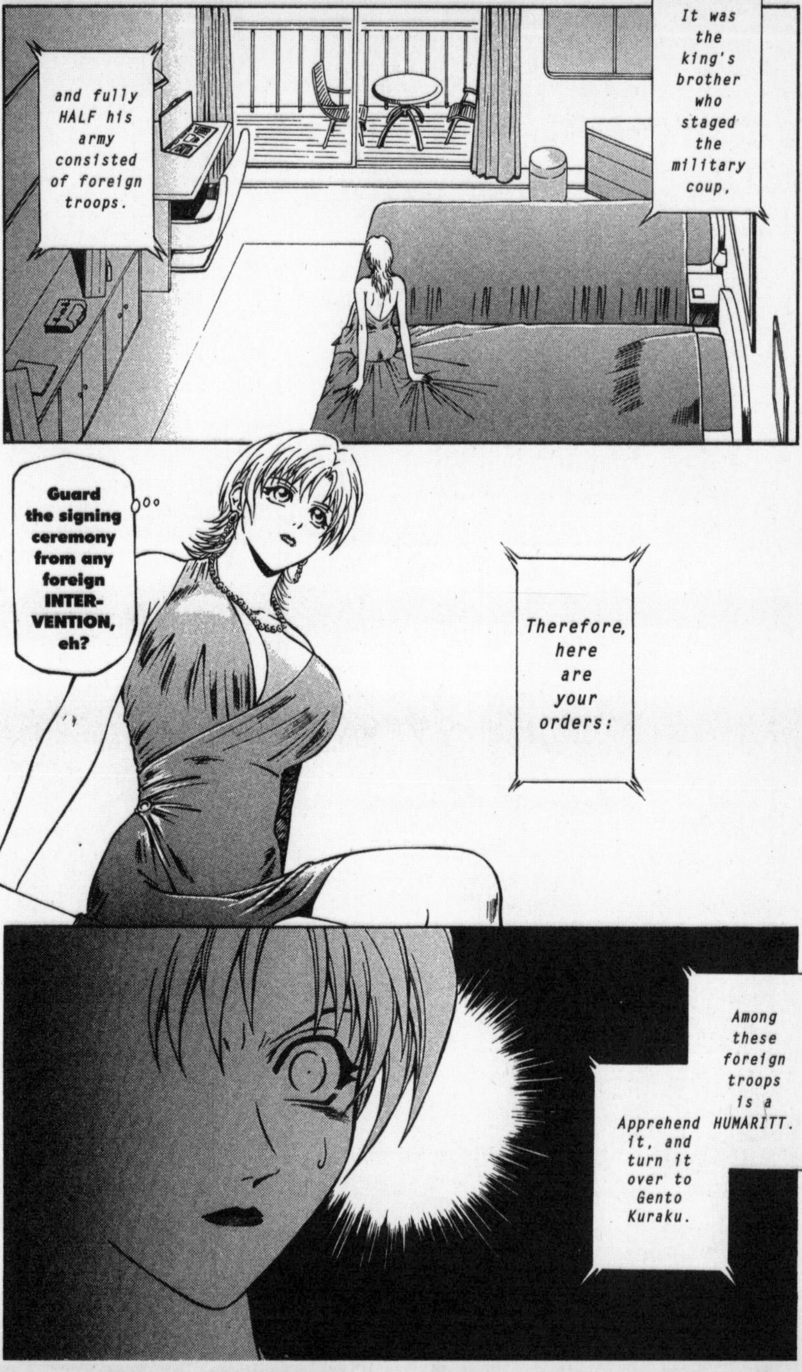

It was the king's brother who staged the military coup,
and fully HALF his army consisted of foreign troops.
Guard the signing ceremony from any foreign INTER-VENTION, eh?
Therefore, here are your orders:
Among these foreign troops is a HUMARITT.
Apprehend it, and turn it over to Gento Kuraku.

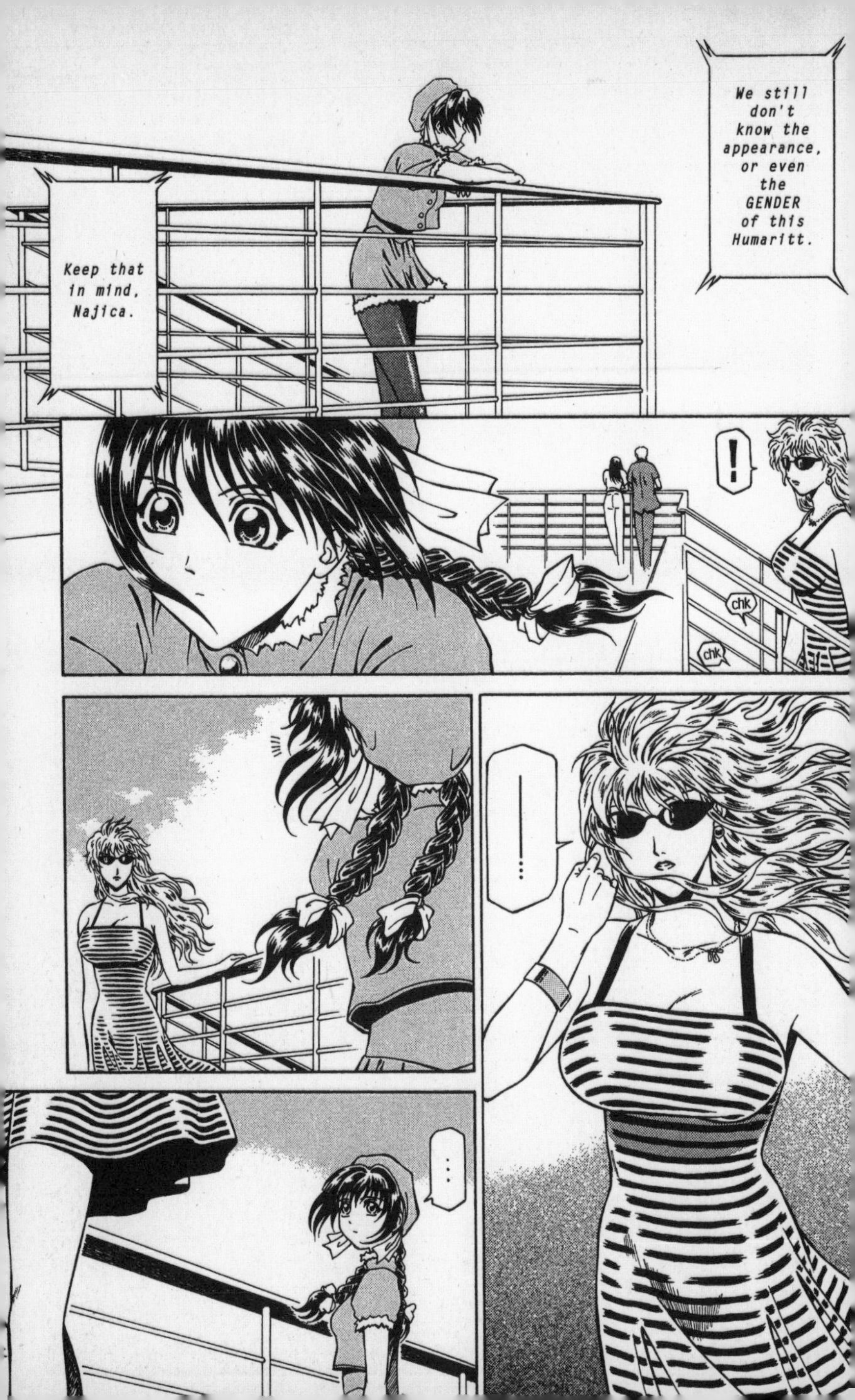
We still don't know the appearance, or even the GENDER of this Humaritt.
Keep that in mind, Najica.
!
chk
chk
......
...

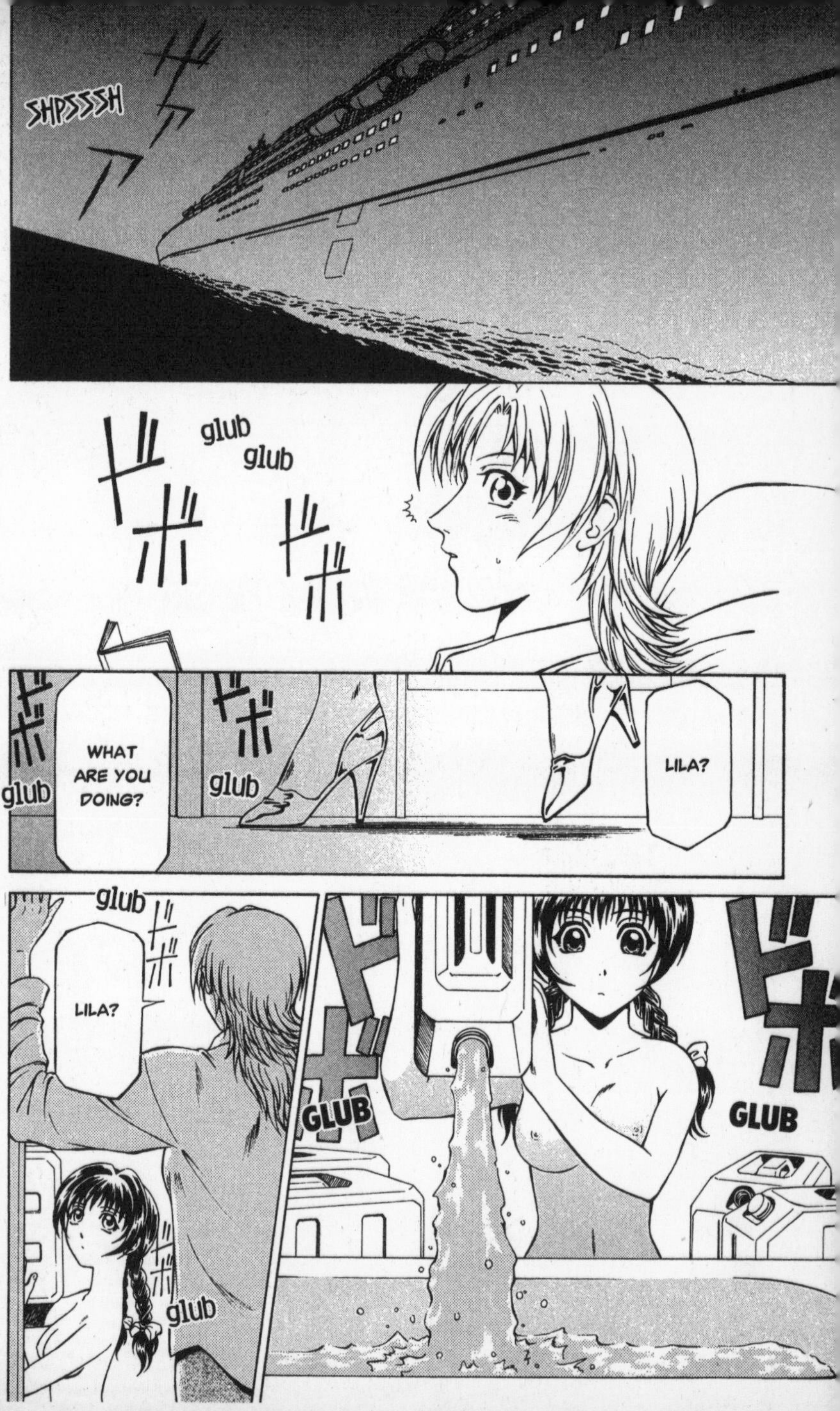
SHPSSSH
glub
glub
LILA?
glub
glub
WHAT ARE YOU DOING?
GLUB
GLUB
glub
LILA?
glub

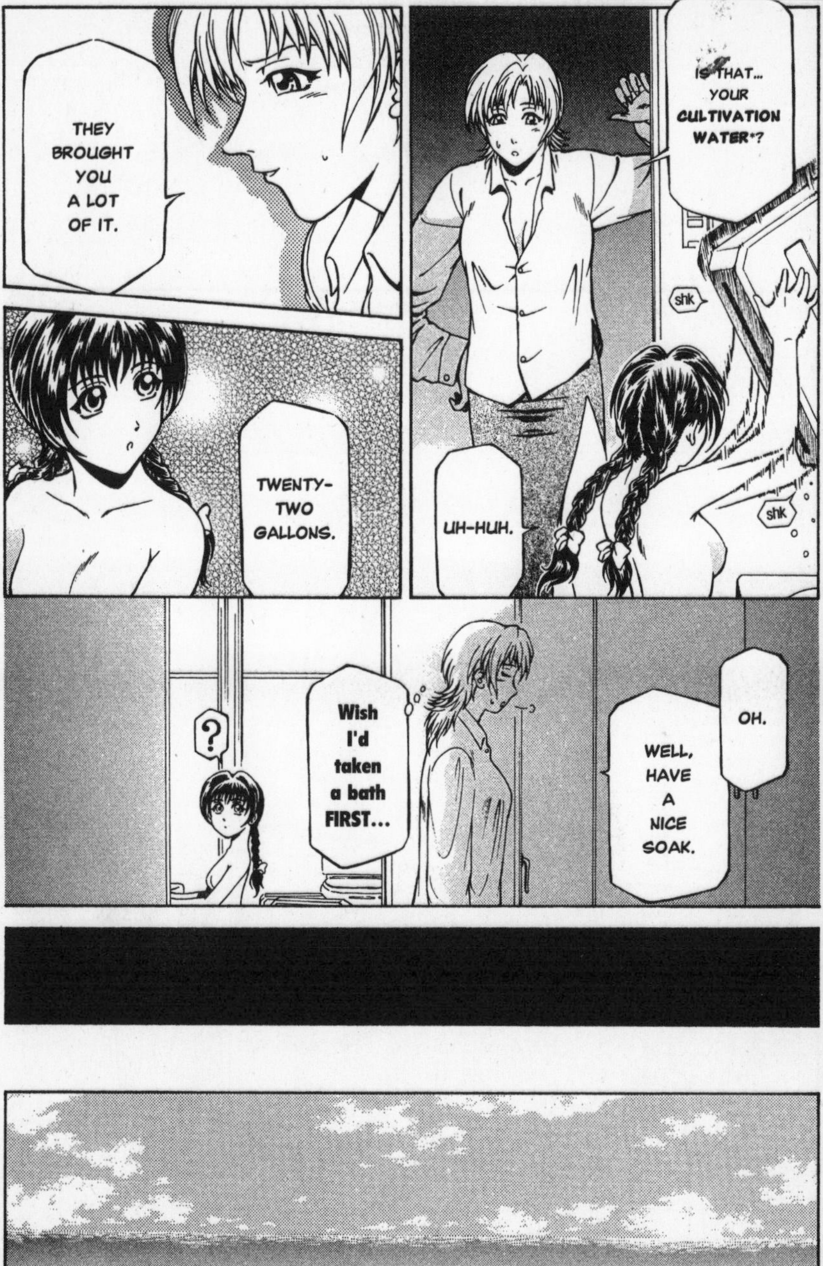
IS THAT... YOUR CULTIVATION WATER*?
shk
shk
UH-HUH.
THEY BROUGHT YOU A LOT OF IT.
TWENTY-TWO GALLONS.
OH.
WELL, HAVE A NICE SOAK.
Wish I'd taken a bath FIRST...
?

*A SPECIAL FLUID THAT LILA BATHES IN.

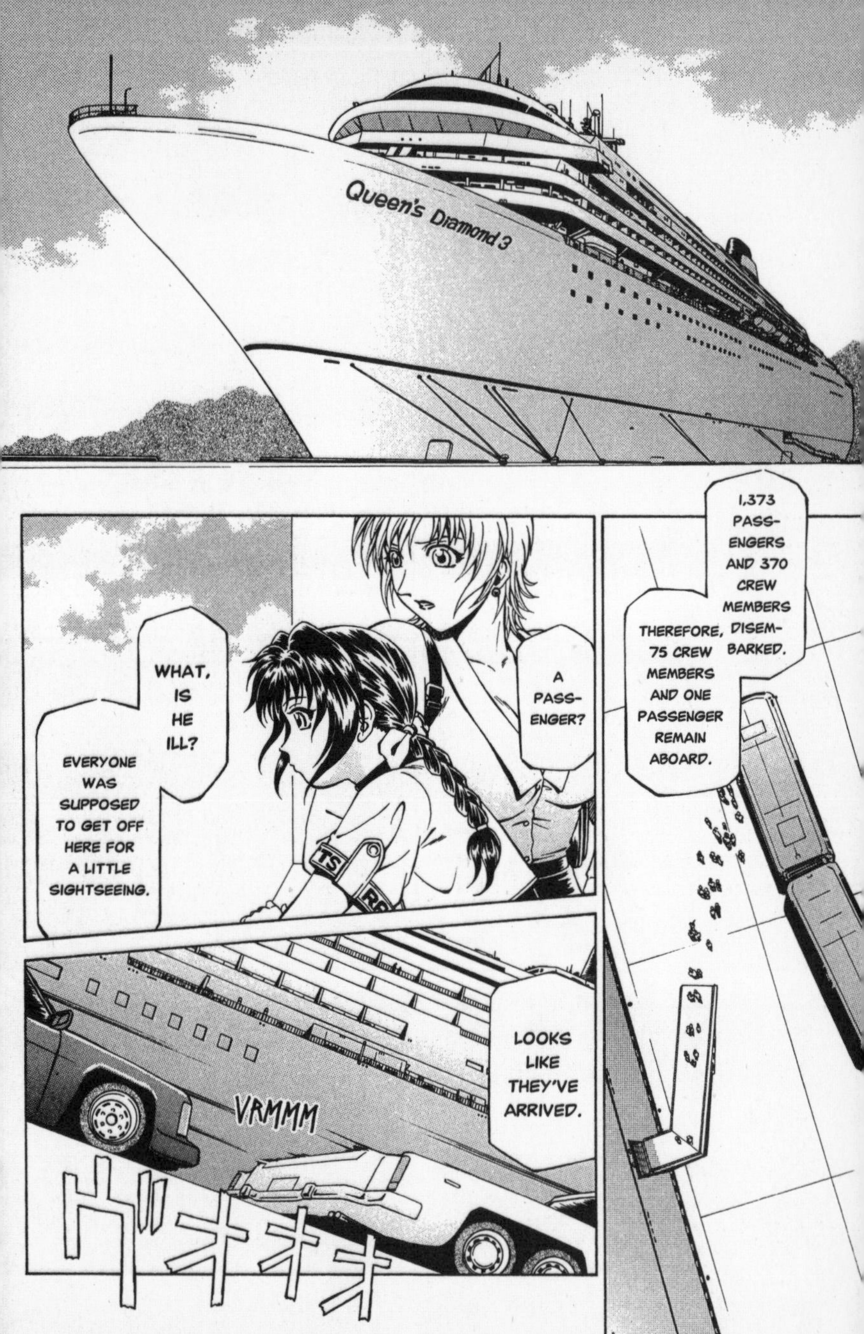
Queen's Diamond 3
1,373 PASSENGERS AND 370 CREW MEMBERS DISEMBARKED.
THEREFORE, 75 CREW MEMBERS AND ONE PASSENGER REMAIN ABOARD.
A PASSENGER?
WHAT, IS HE ILL?
EVERYONE WAS SUPPOSED TO GET OFF HERE FOR A LITTLE SIGHTSEEING.
LOOKS LIKE THEY'VE ARRIVED.
VRMMM
ヴオオオ

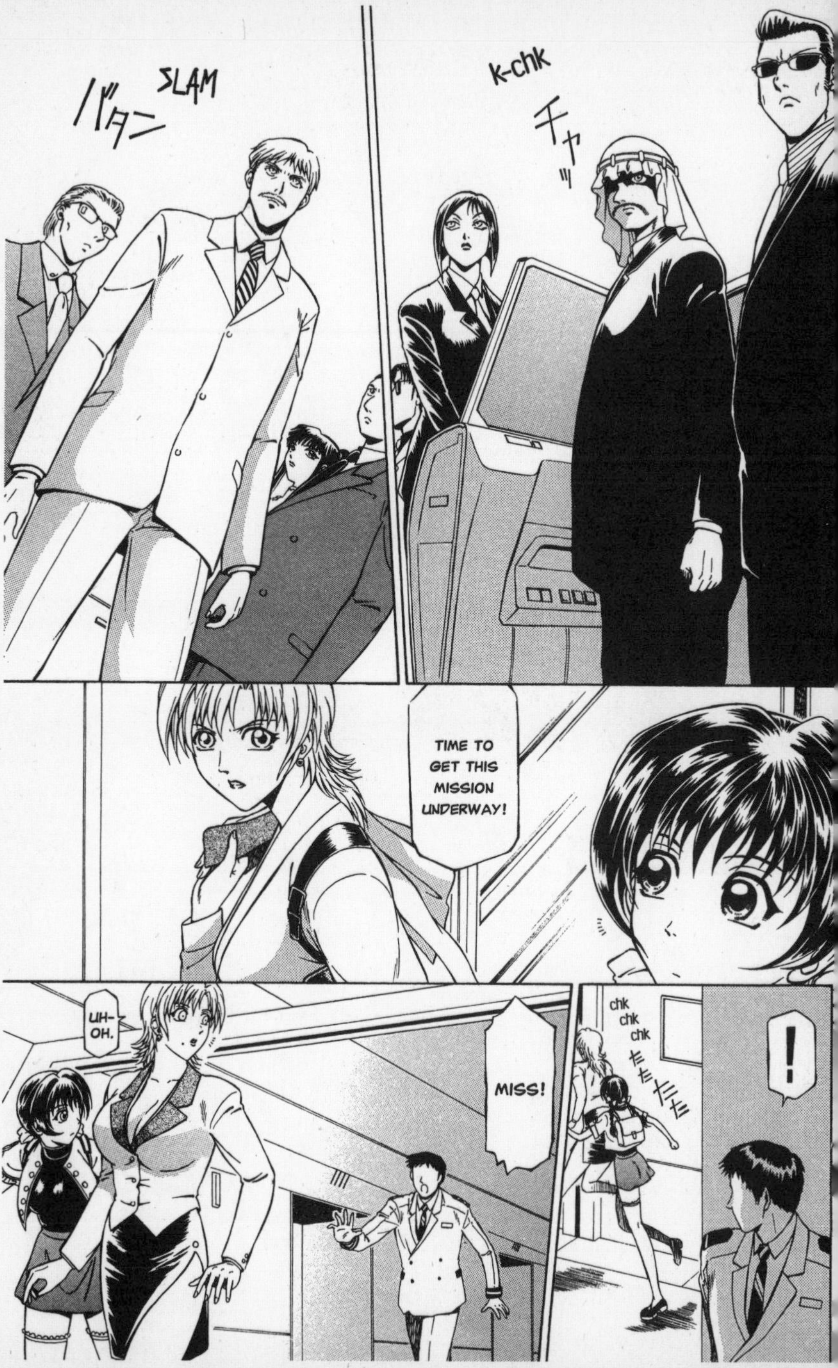
k-chk
チャッ
SLAM
バタン
TIME TO GET THIS MISSION UNDERWAY!
!
chk chk chk
たたたたた
MISS!
UH-OH.

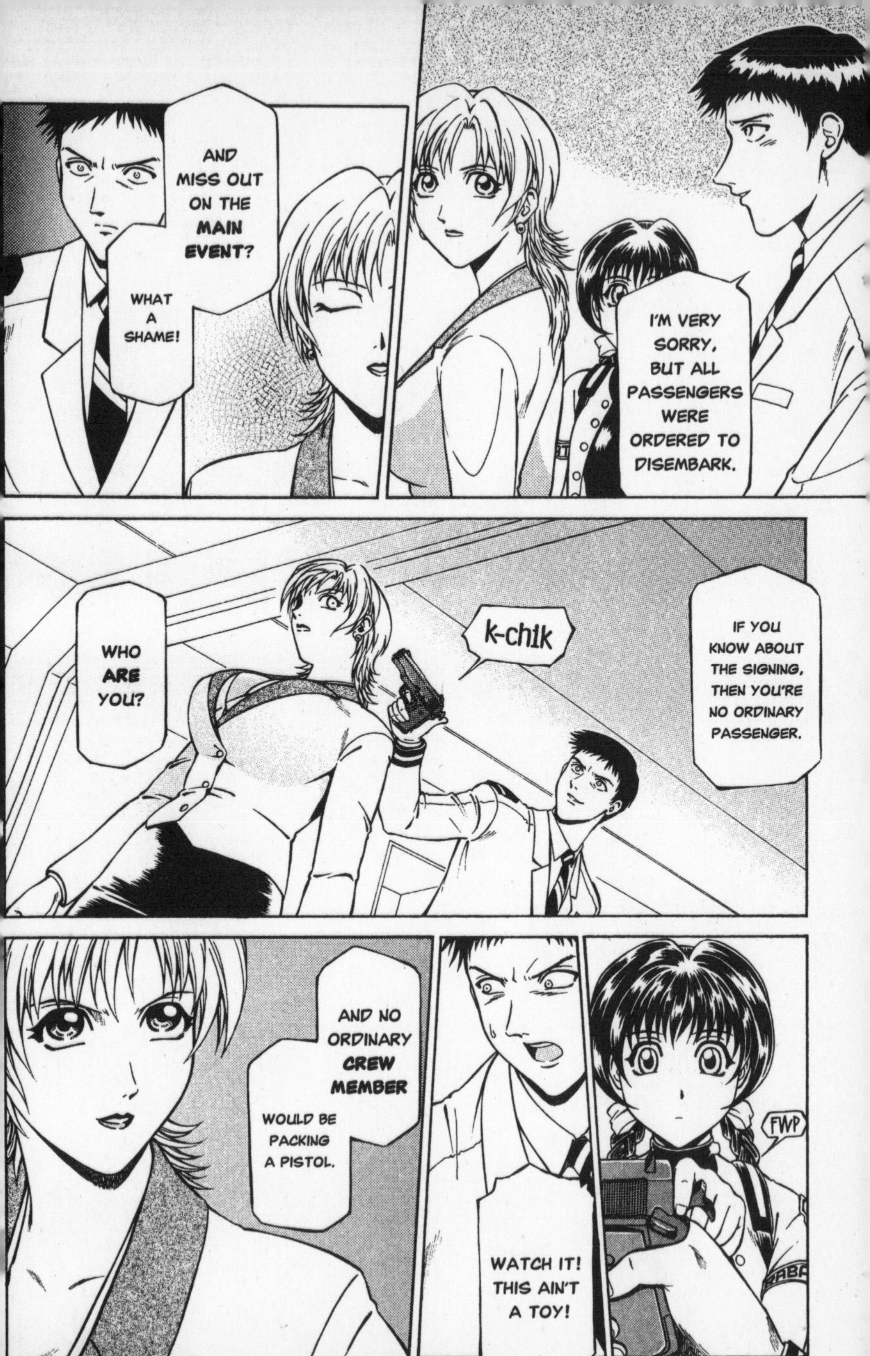
I'M VERY SORRY, BUT ALL PASSENGERS WERE ORDERED TO DISEMBARK.
AND MISS OUT ON THE MAIN EVENT?
WHAT A SHAME!
IF YOU KNOW ABOUT THE SIGNING, THEN YOU'RE NO ORDINARY PASSENGER.
k-chik
WHO ARE YOU?
FWP
WATCH IT! THIS AIN'T A TOY!
AND NO ORDINARY CREW MEMBER
WOULD BE PACKING A PISTOL.

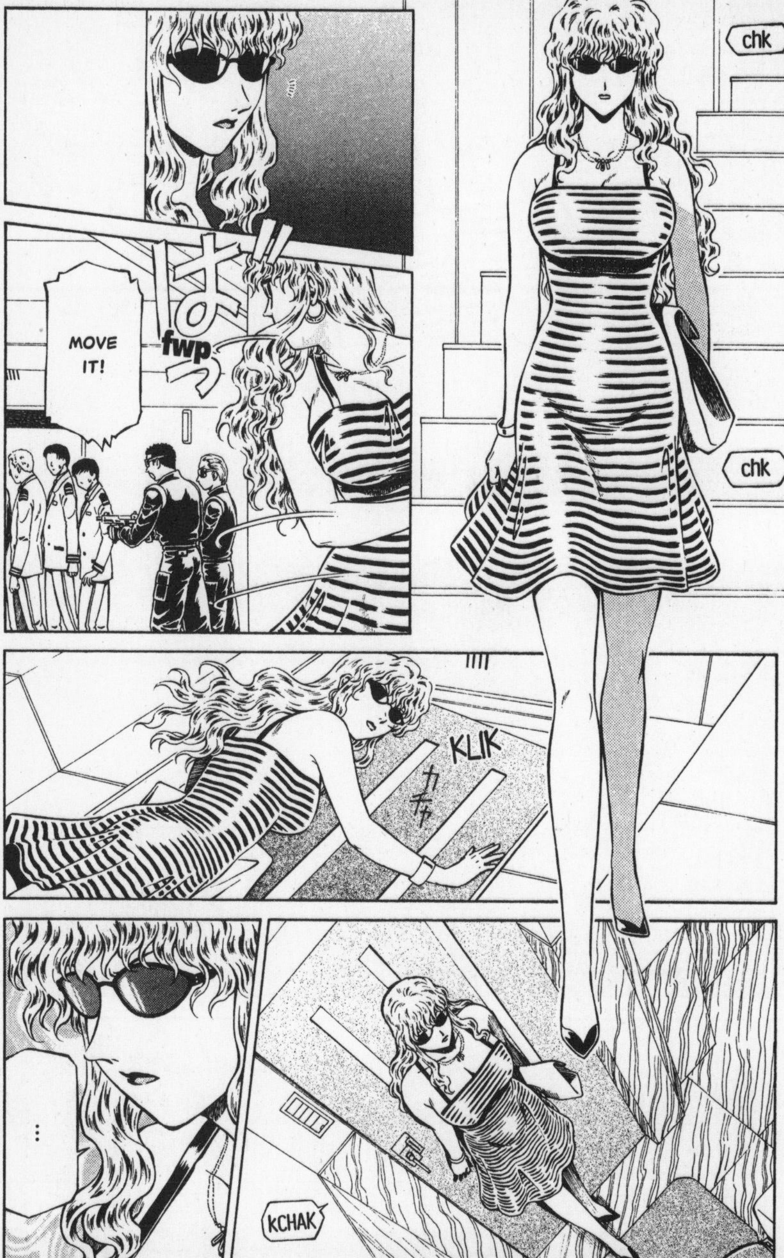
chk
chk
はっ!!
fwp
MOVE IT!
KLIK
カチャ
kCHAK
...

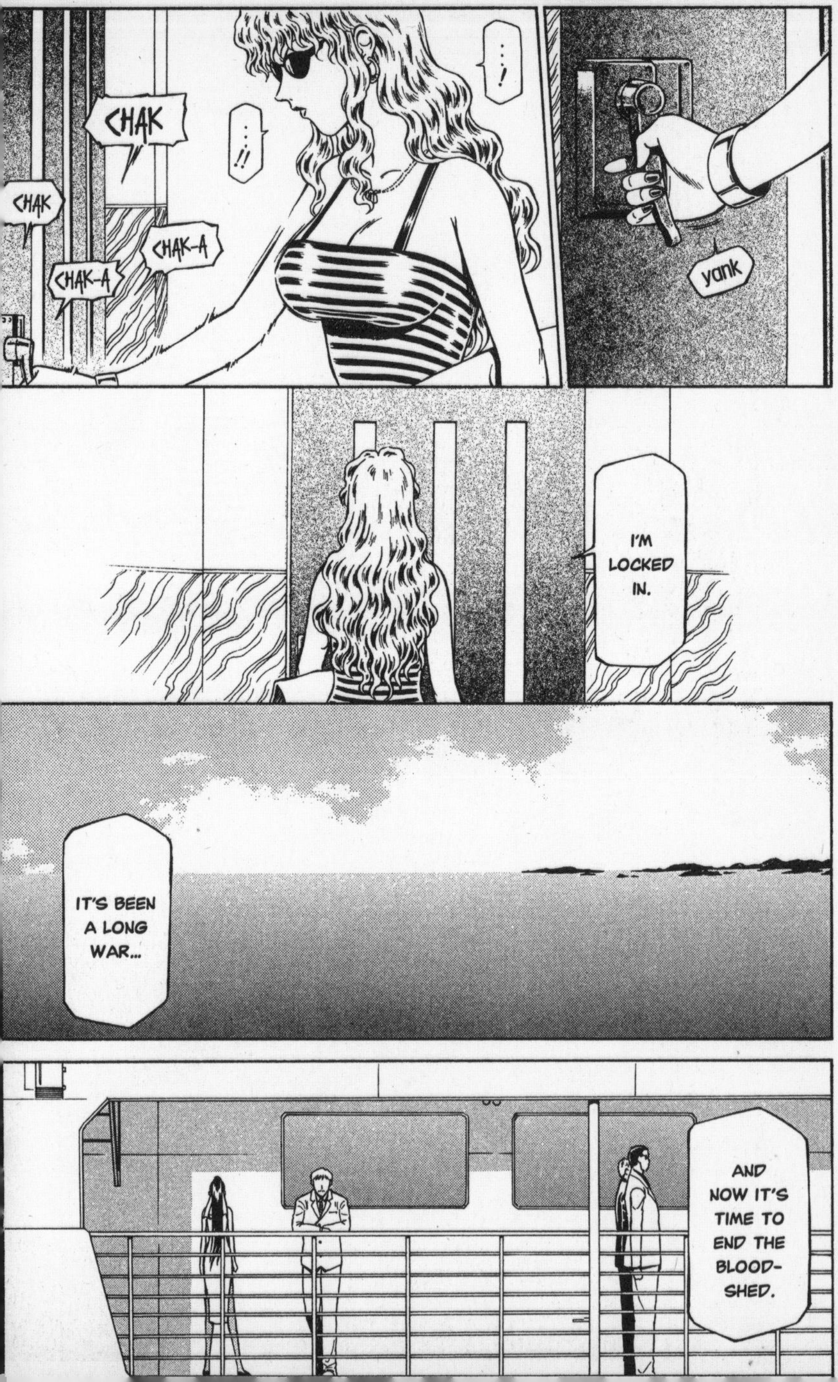
yank
...!
...!!
CHAK
CHAK-A
CHAK
CHAK-A
I'M LOCKED IN.
IT'S BEEN A LONG WAR...
AND NOW IT'S TIME TO END THE BLOOD-SHED.

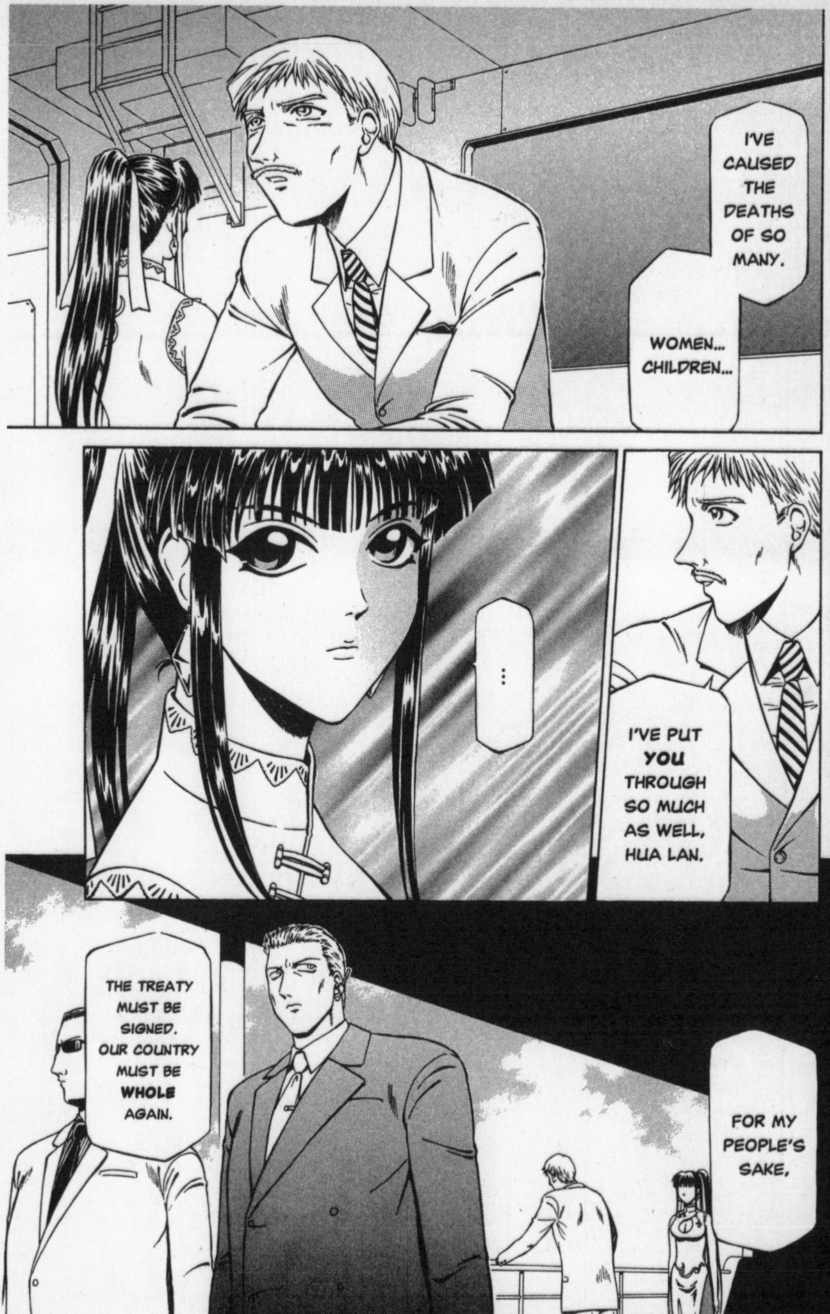
I'VE CAUSED THE DEATHS OF SO MANY.
WOMEN... CHILDREN...
I'VE PUT **YOU** THROUGH SO MUCH AS WELL, HUA LAN.
...
FOR MY PEOPLE'S SAKE,
THE TREATY MUST BE SIGNED. OUR COUNTRY MUST BE **WHOLE** AGAIN.

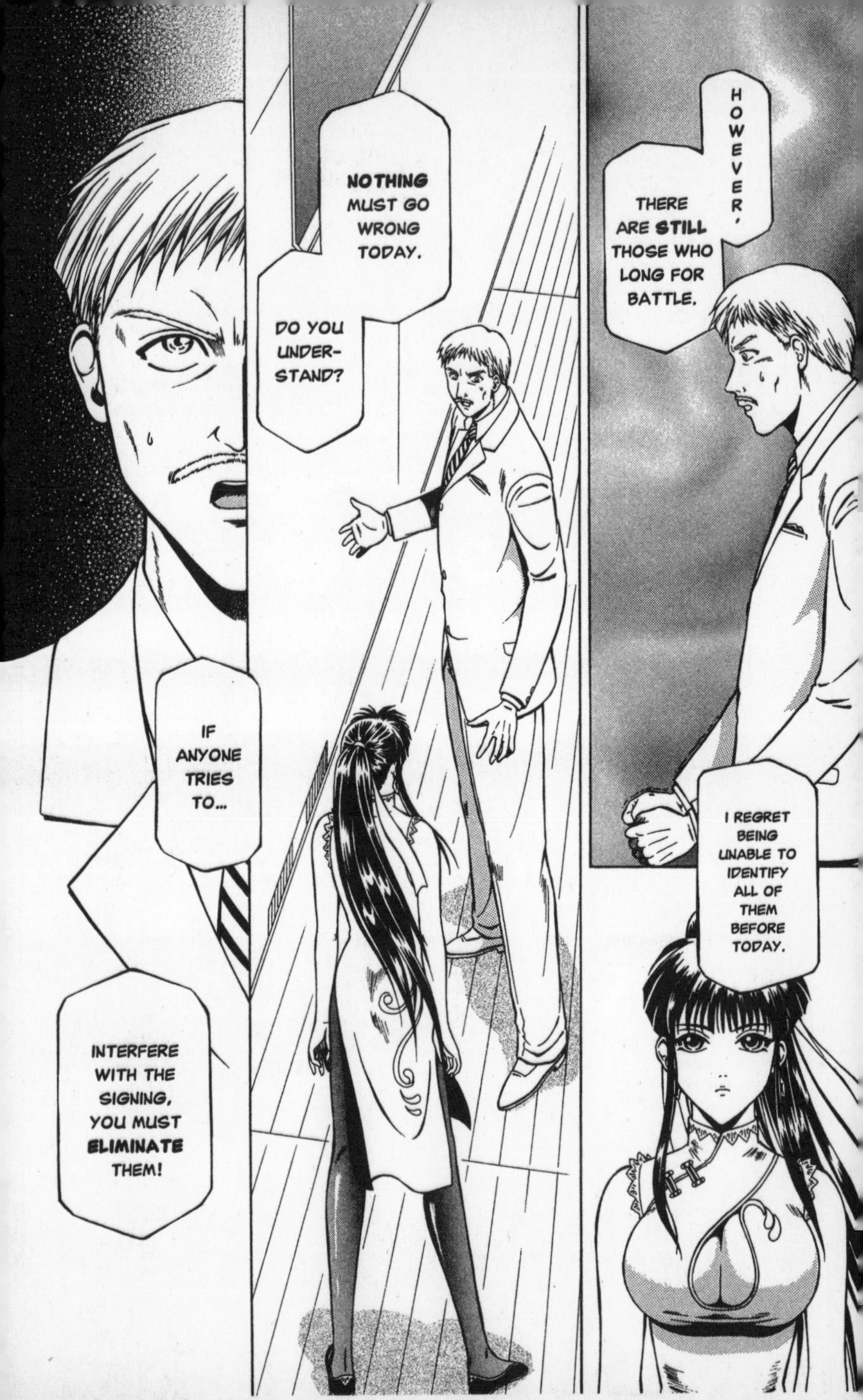
HOWEVER,
THERE ARE STILL THOSE WHO LONG FOR BATTLE.
I REGRET BEING UNABLE TO IDENTIFY ALL OF THEM BEFORE TODAY.
NOTHING MUST GO WRONG TODAY.
DO YOU UNDERSTAND?
IF ANYONE TRIES TO...
INTERFERE WITH THE SIGNING, YOU MUST ELIMINATE THEM!

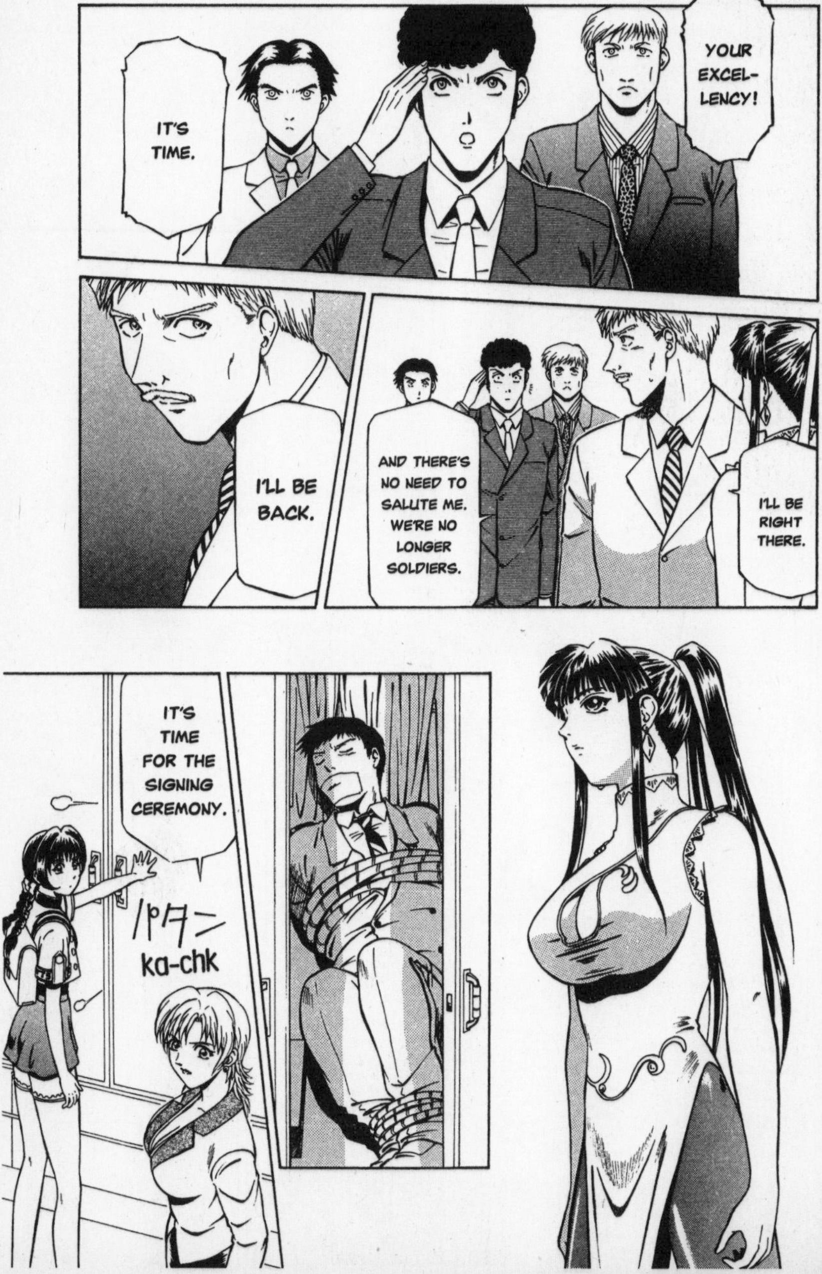
YOUR EXCEL-LENCY!
IT'S TIME.
I'LL BE RIGHT THERE.
AND THERE'S NO NEED TO SALUTE ME. WE'RE NO LONGER SOLDIERS.
I'LL BE BACK.
IT'S TIME FOR THE SIGNING CEREMONY.
パタン
ka-chk

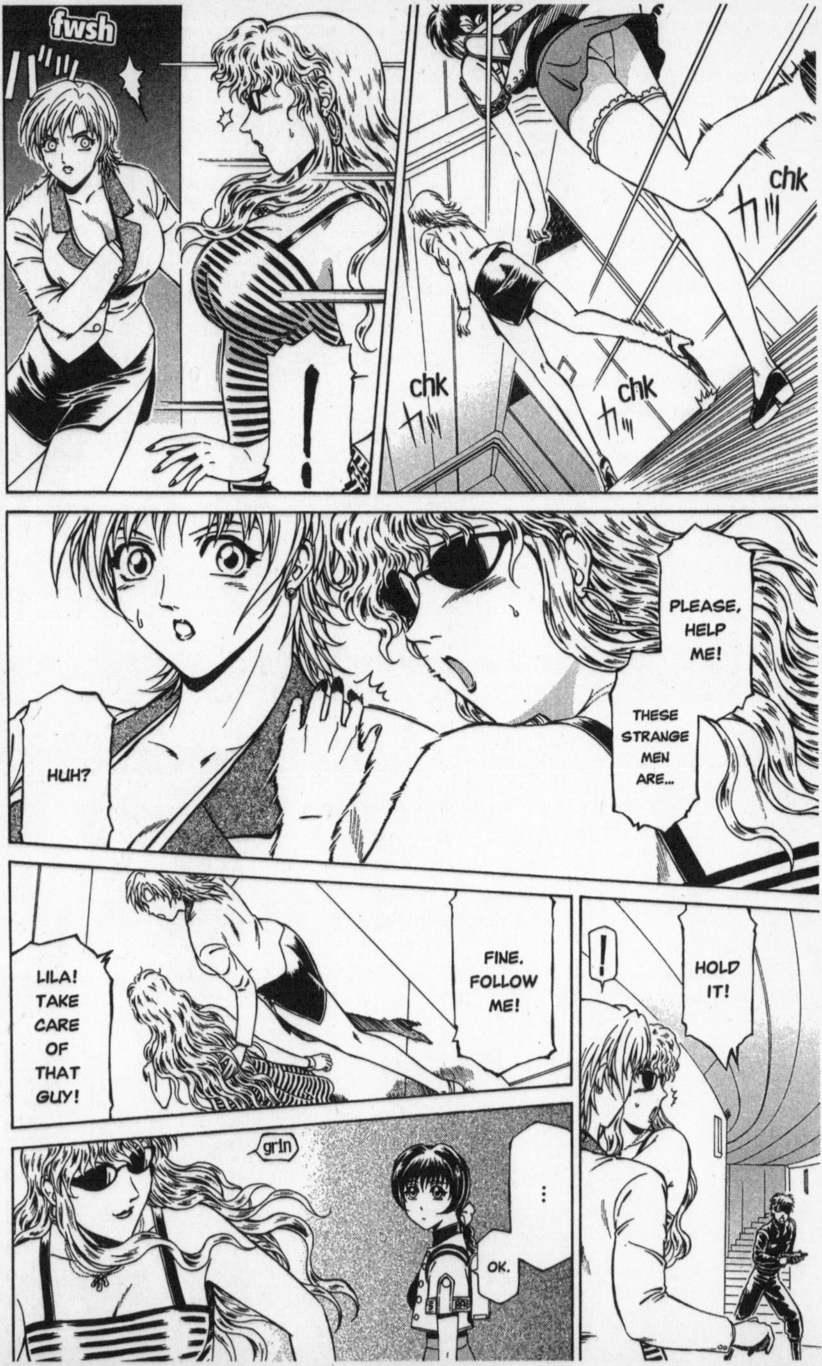
chk
chk
chk
fwsh
!
PLEASE, HELP ME!
THESE STRANGE MEN ARE...
HUH?
HOLD IT!
!
FINE. FOLLOW ME!
LILA! TAKE CARE OF THAT GUY!
...
OK.
grin

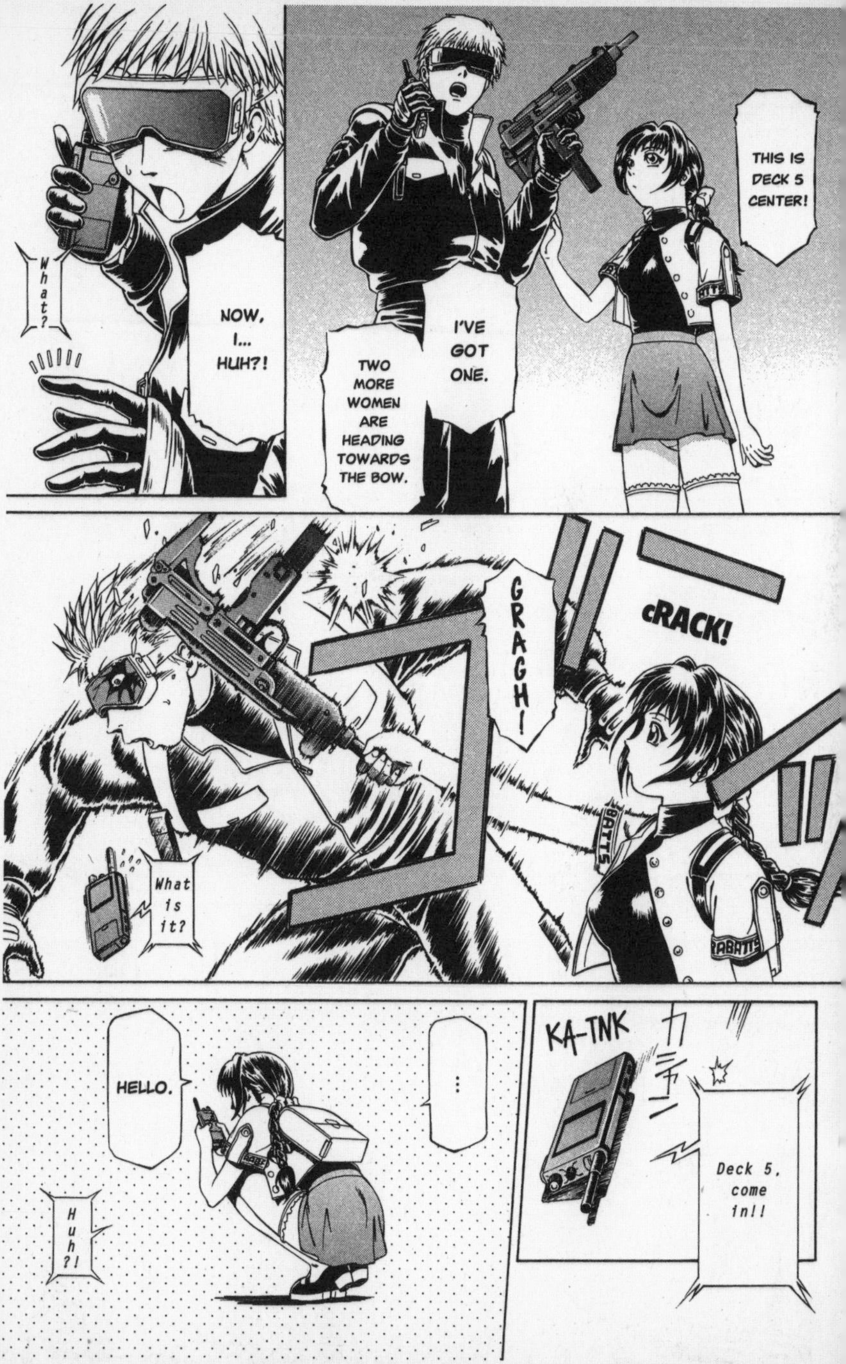
THIS IS DECK 5 CENTER!
I'VE GOT ONE.
TWO MORE WOMEN ARE HEADING TOWARDS THE BOW.
NOW, I... HUH?!
What?
cRACK!
GRAGH!
What is it?
KA-TNK
Deck 5, come in!!
...
HELLO.
Huh?!

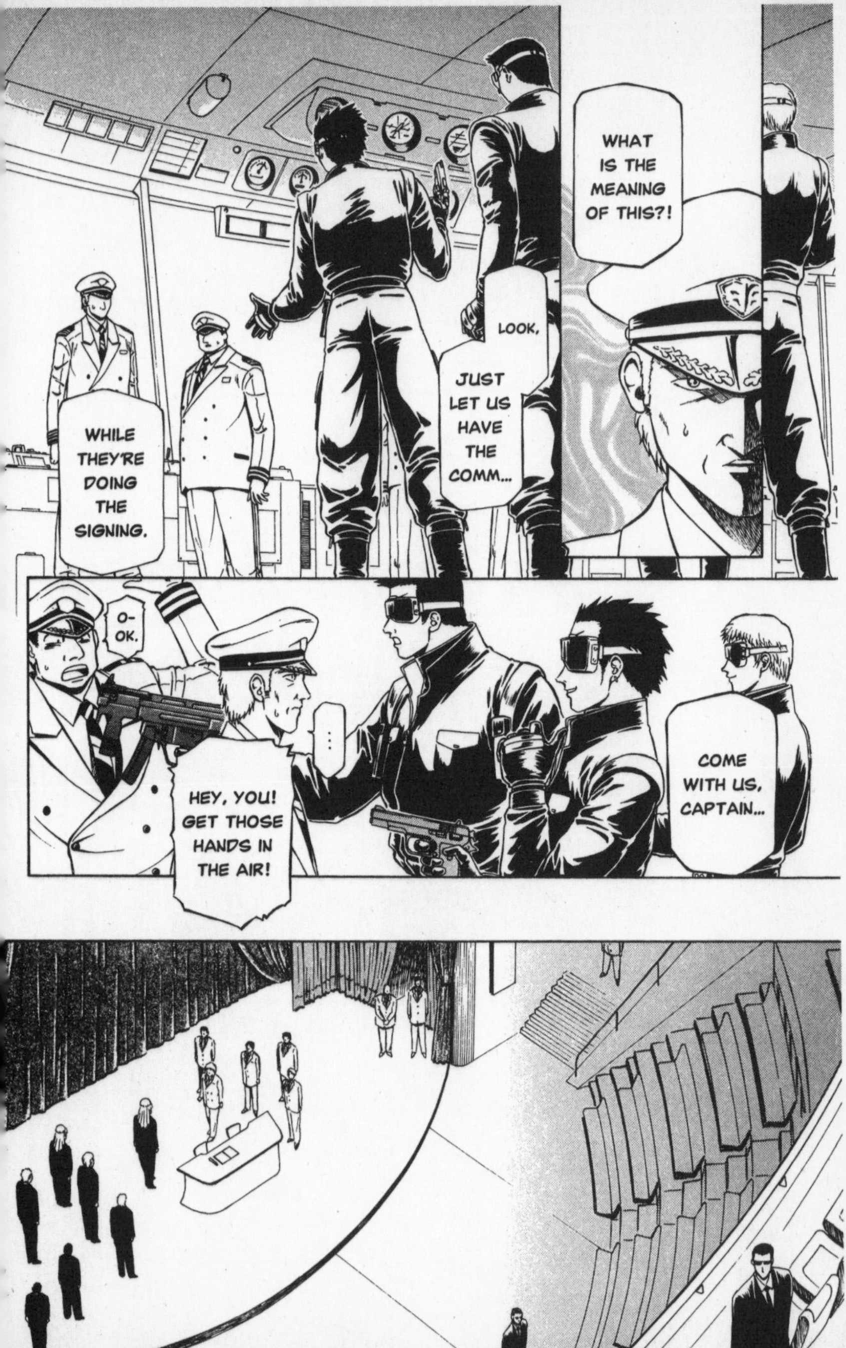
WHAT IS THE MEANING OF THIS?!
LOOK,
JUST LET US HAVE THE COMM...
WHILE THEY'RE DOING THE SIGNING.
COME WITH US, CAPTAIN...
...
HEY, YOU! GET THOSE HANDS IN THE AIR!
O-OK.

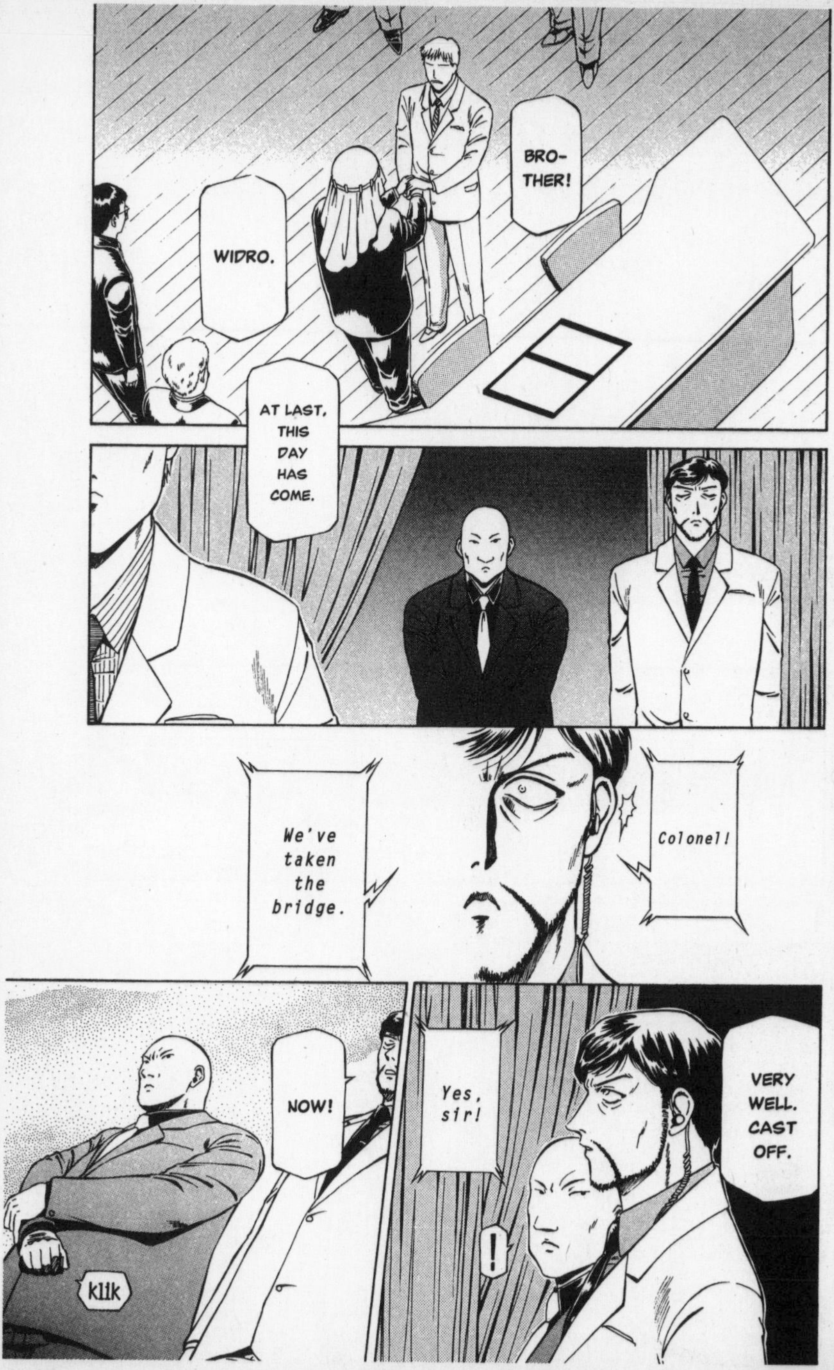
BROTHER!
WIDRO.
AT LAST, THIS DAY HAS COME.
Colonel!
We've taken the bridge.
VERY WELL. CAST OFF.
!
Yes, sir!
NOW!
klik

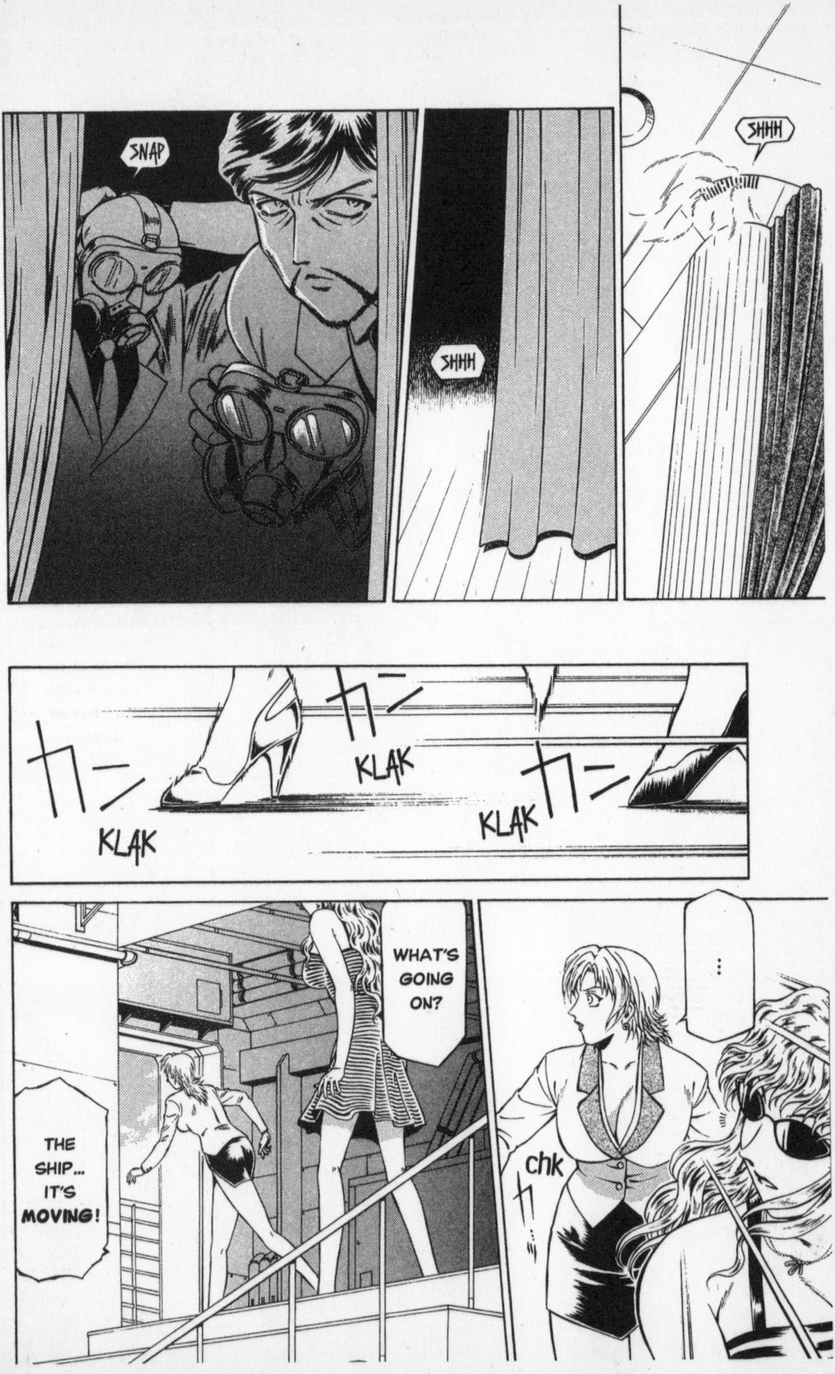
SHHH
SHHH
SNAP
カー
KLAK
カー
KLAK
カー
KLAK
...
chk
カ...
WHAT'S GOING ON?
THE SHIP... IT'S MOVING!

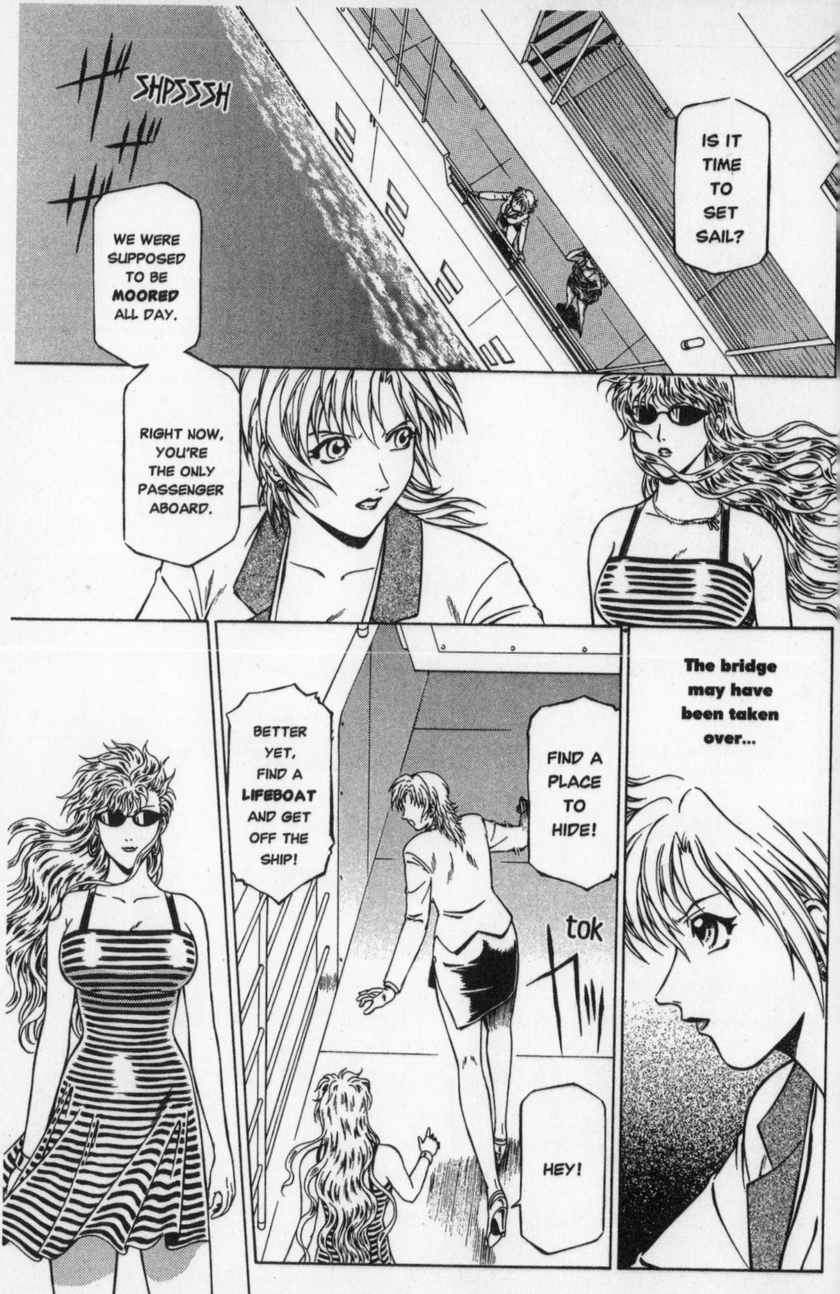
IS IT TIME TO SET SAIL?
SHPSSSH
WE WERE SUPPOSED TO BE MOORED ALL DAY.
RIGHT NOW, YOU'RE THE ONLY PASSENGER ABOARD.
The bridge may have been taken over...
FIND A PLACE TO HIDE!
BETTER YET, FIND A LIFEBOAT AND GET OFF THE SHIP!
tok
HEY!

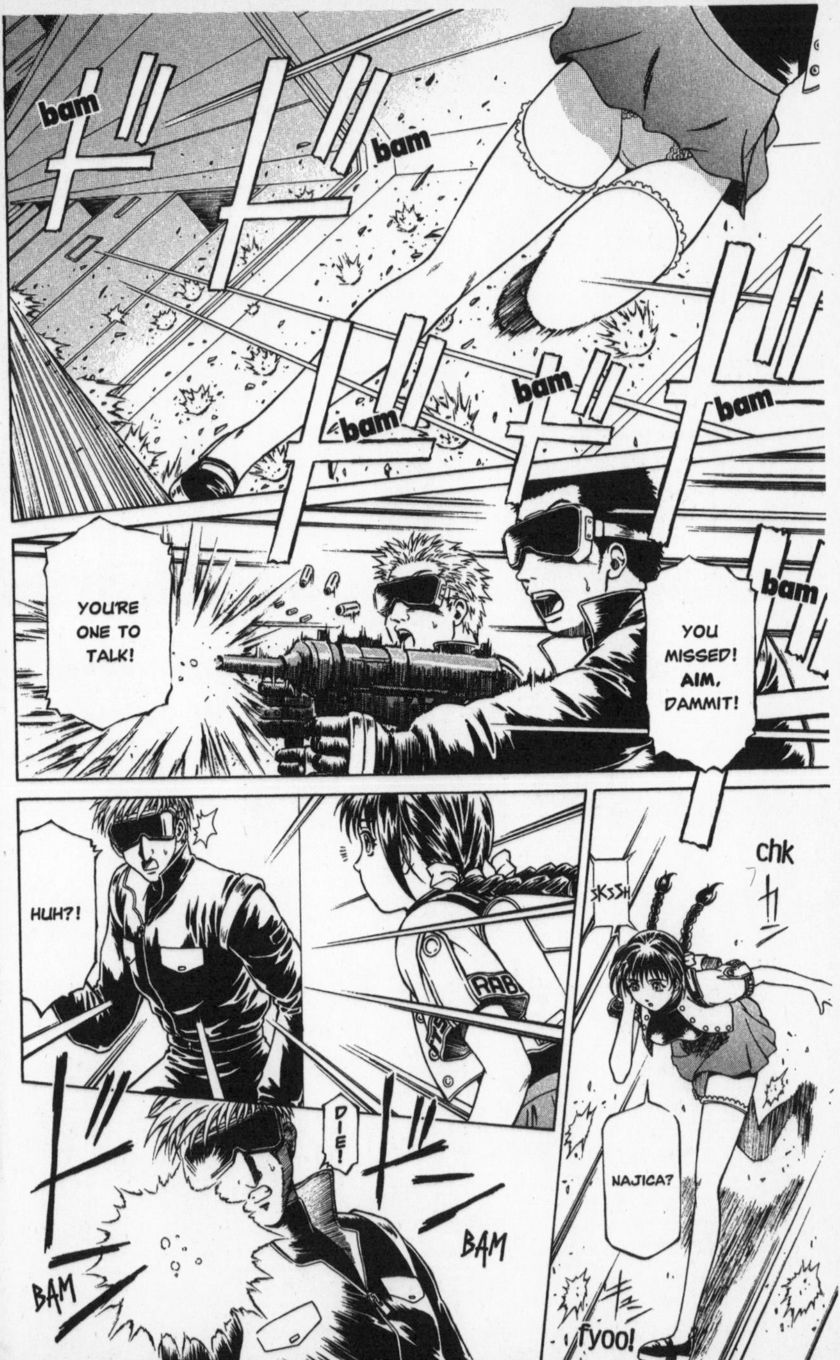
bam
bam
bam
bam
bam
bam
bam
YOU MISSED! AIM, DAMMIT!
YOU'RE ONE TO TALK!
chk
SKSSH
NAJICA?
fyoo!
HUH?!
DIE!
BAM
BAM

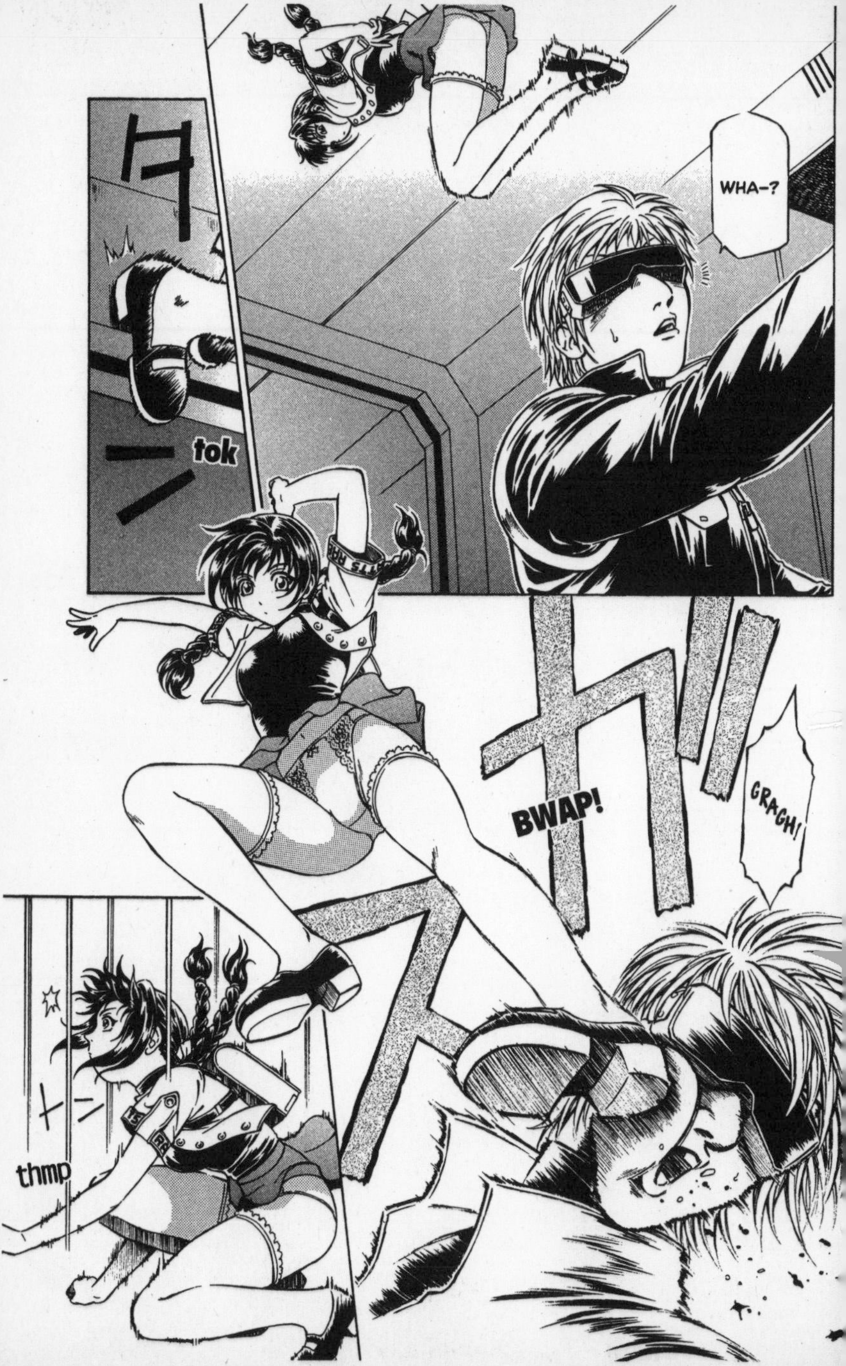
WHA-?
tok
GRAGH!
BWAP!
thmp

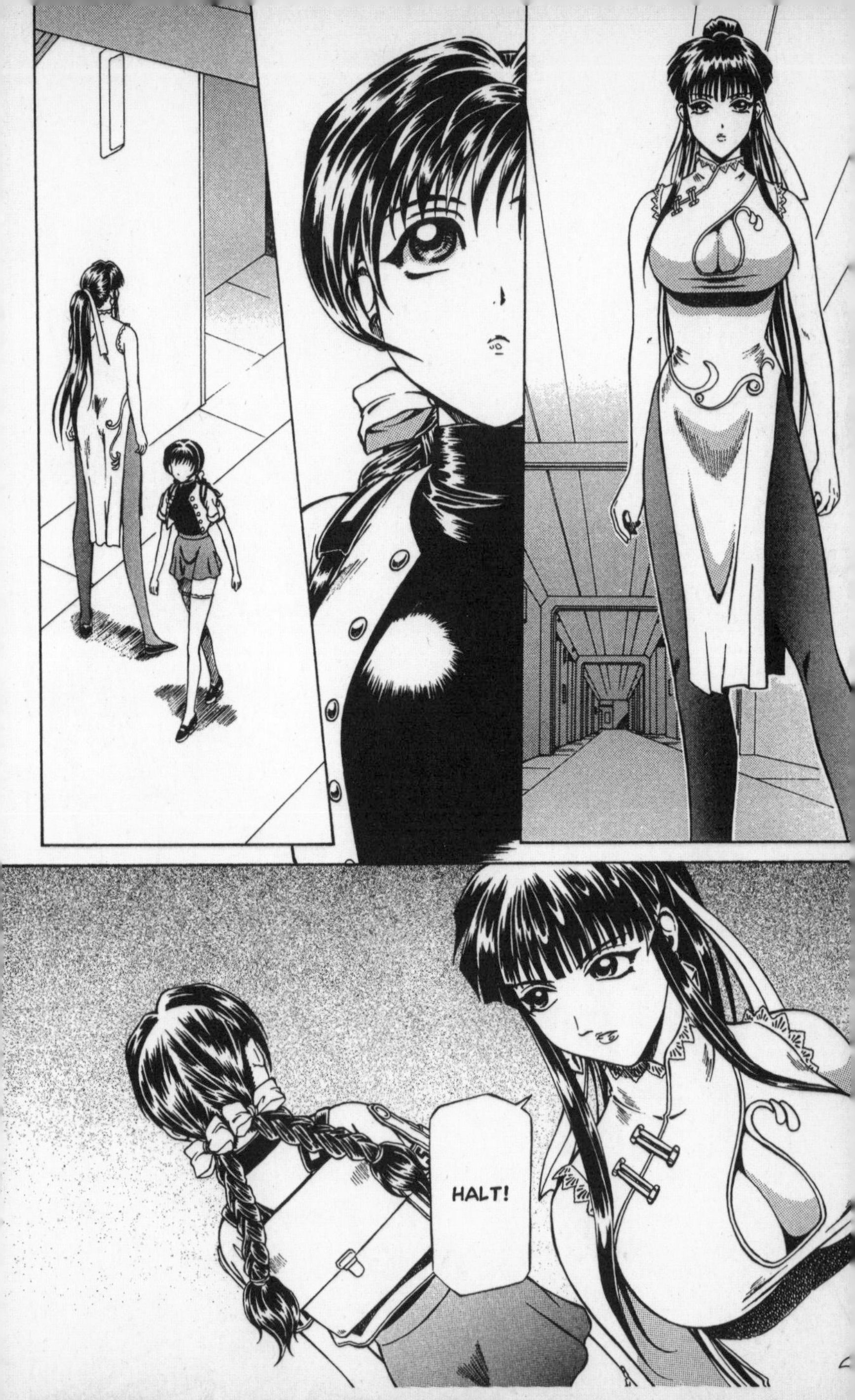
HALT!

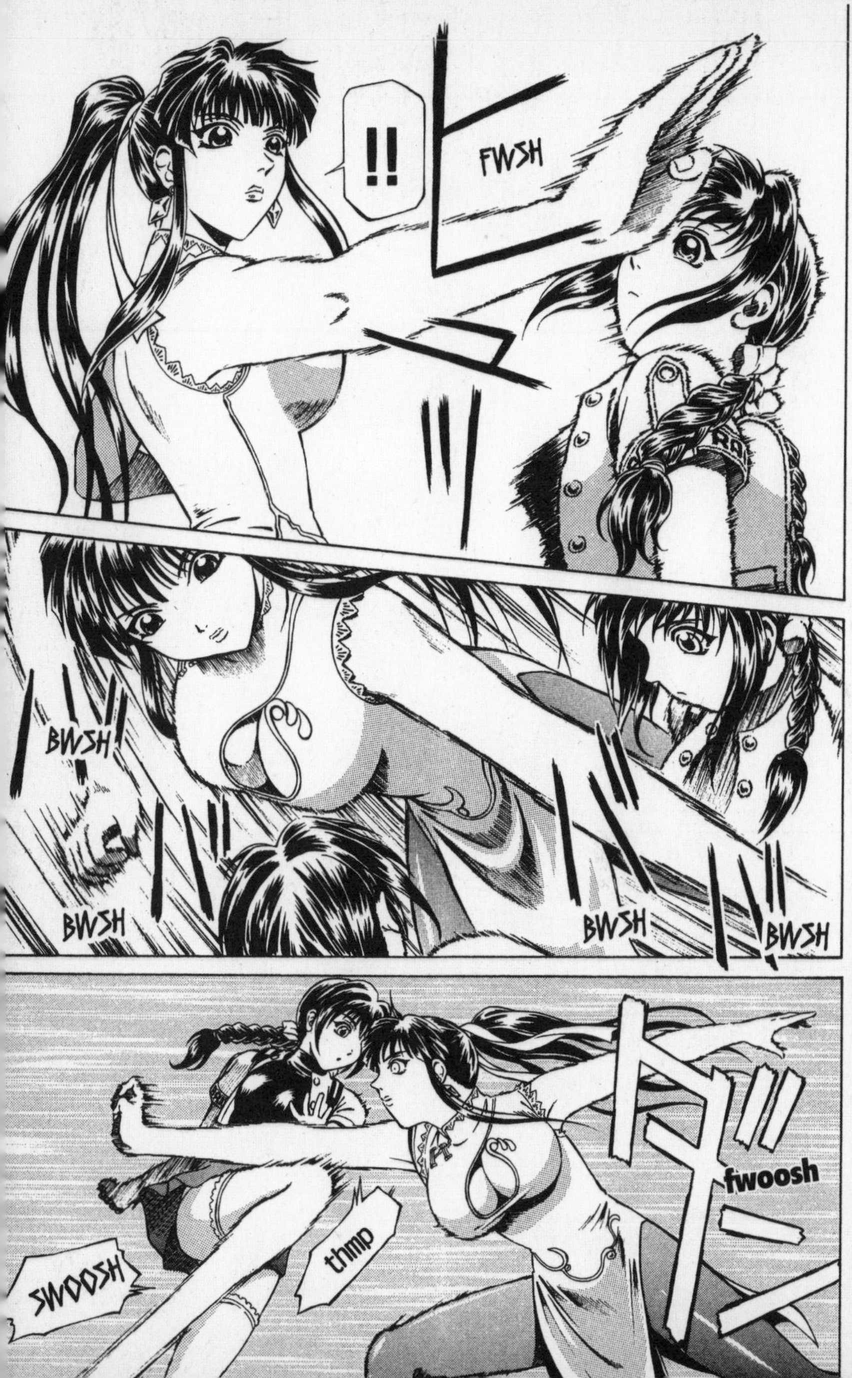
FWSH
!!
BWSH
BWSH
BWSH
BWSH
fwoosh
thmp
SWOOSH

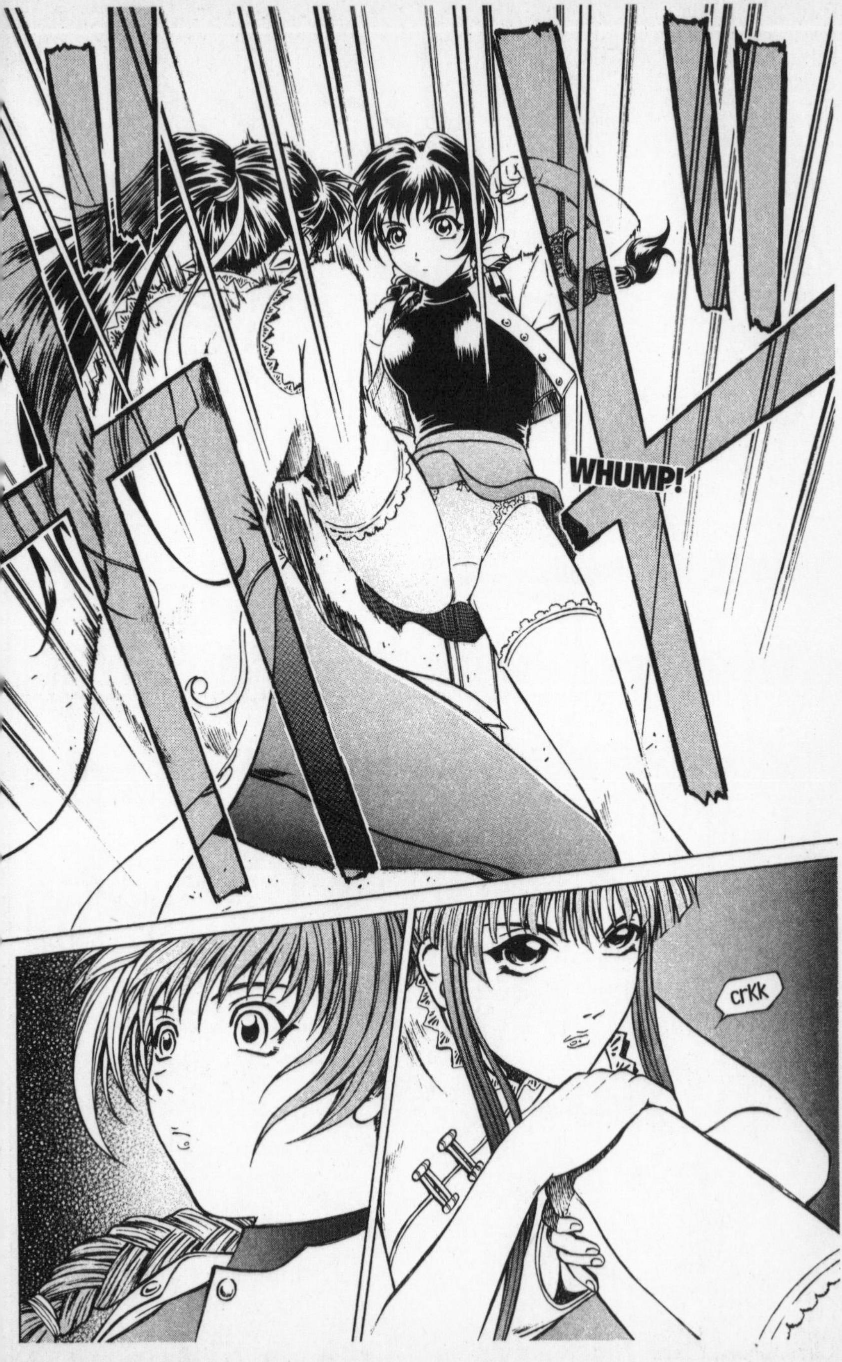
WHUMP!
crKk

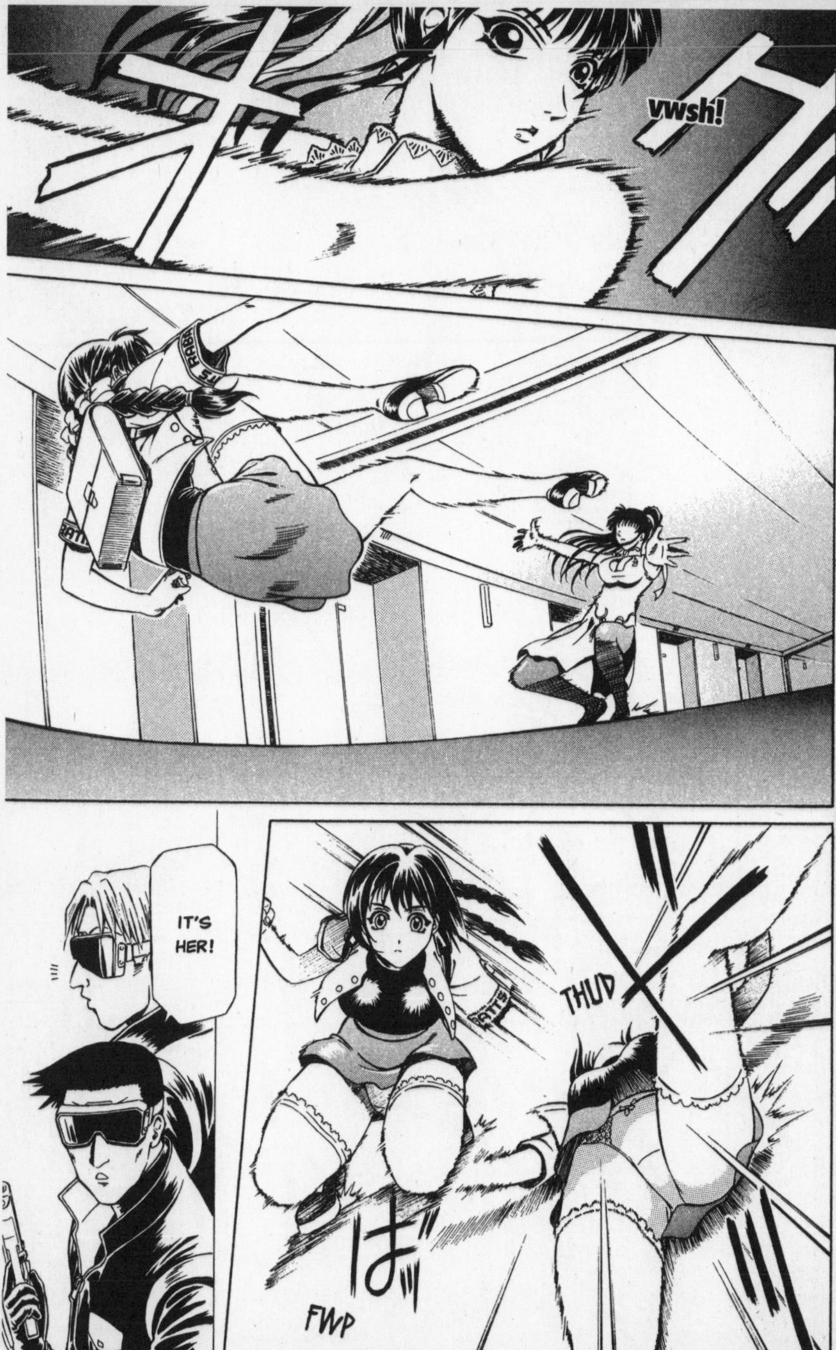
vwsh!
THUD
FWP
IT'S HER!

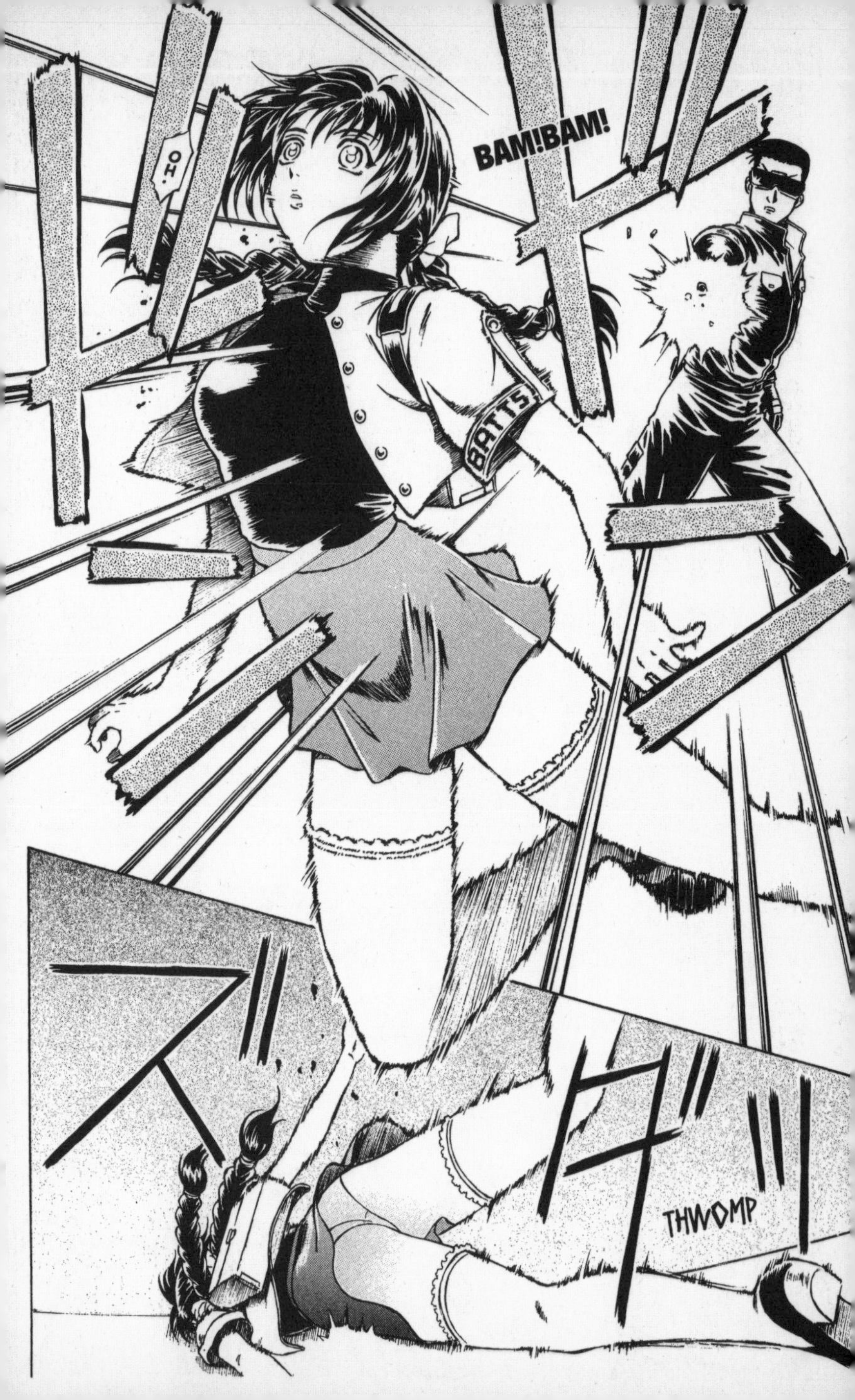
BAM!BAM!
OH.
BATTS
THWOMP

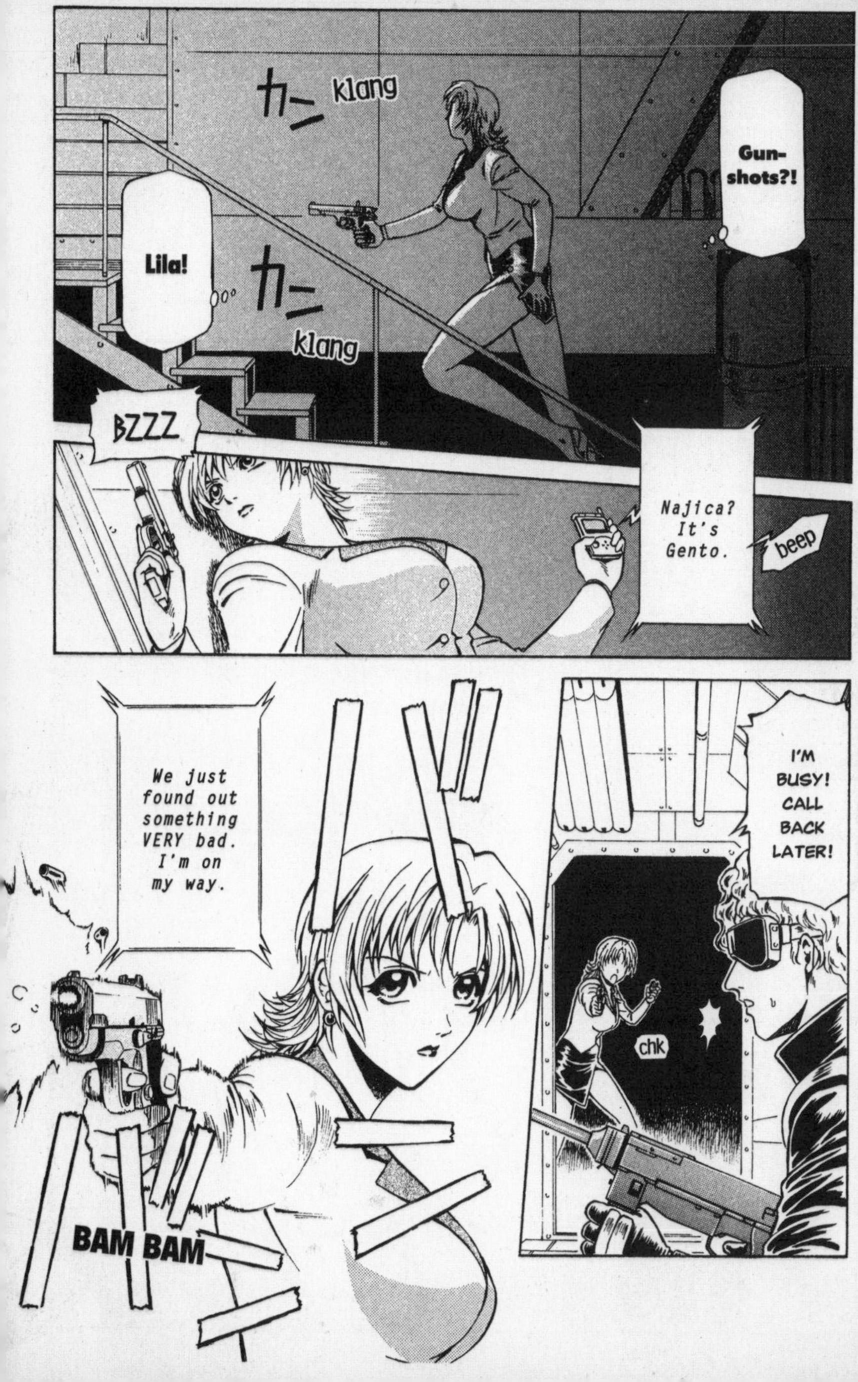
Gun-shots?!
カン
klang
Lila!
カン
klang
beep
Najica? It's Gento.
BZZZ
I'M BUSY! CALL BACK LATER!
chk
We just found out something VERY bad. I'm on my way.
BAM BAM

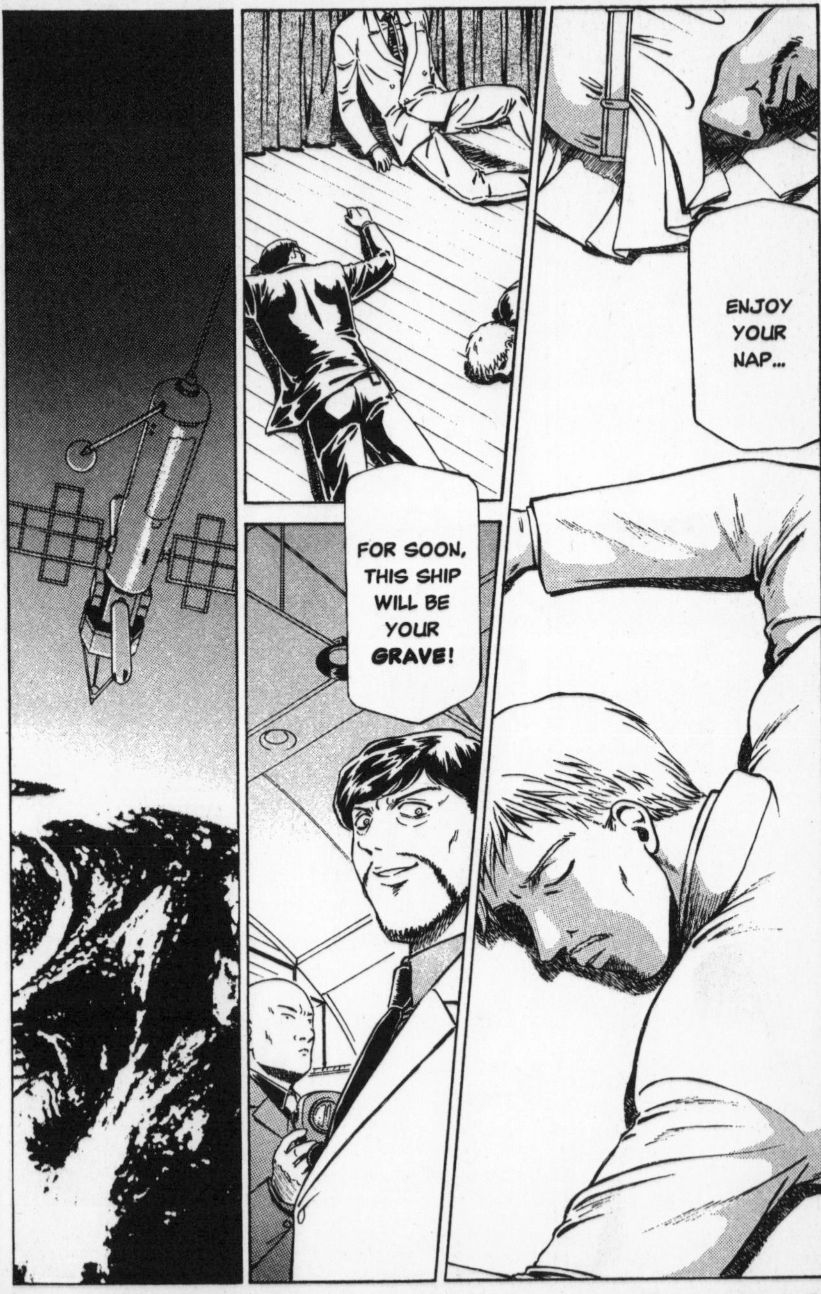
ENJOY YOUR NAP...
FOR SOON, THIS SHIP WILL BE YOUR GRAVE!

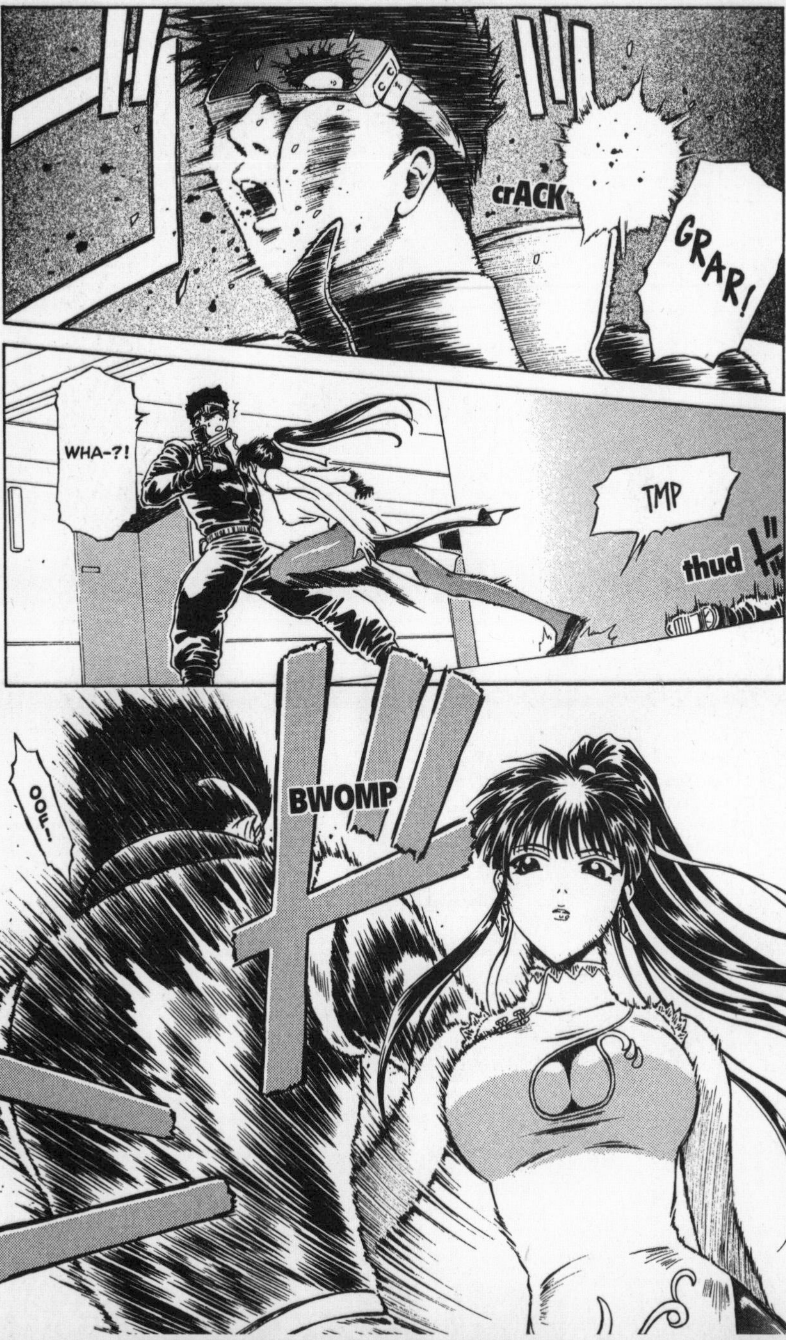

GRAR!
crACK
TMP
thud
WHA-?!
BWOMP
OOF!

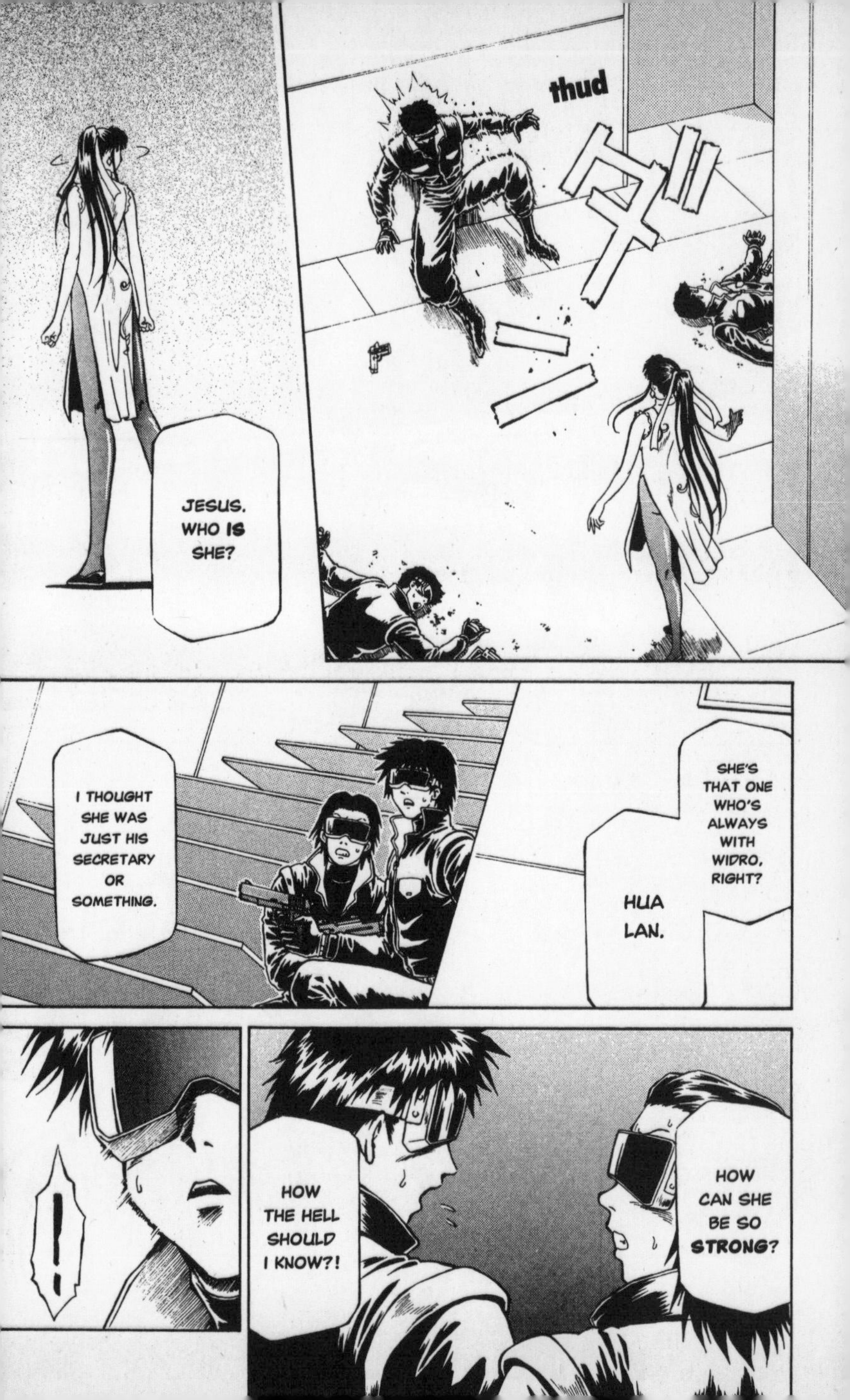
thud
ダ
JESUS. WHO IS SHE?
SHE'S THAT ONE WHO'S ALWAYS WITH WIDRO, RIGHT?
HUA LAN.
I THOUGHT SHE WAS JUST HIS SECRETARY OR SOMETHING.
HOW CAN SHE BE SO STRONG?
HOW THE HELL SHOULD I KNOW?!
!

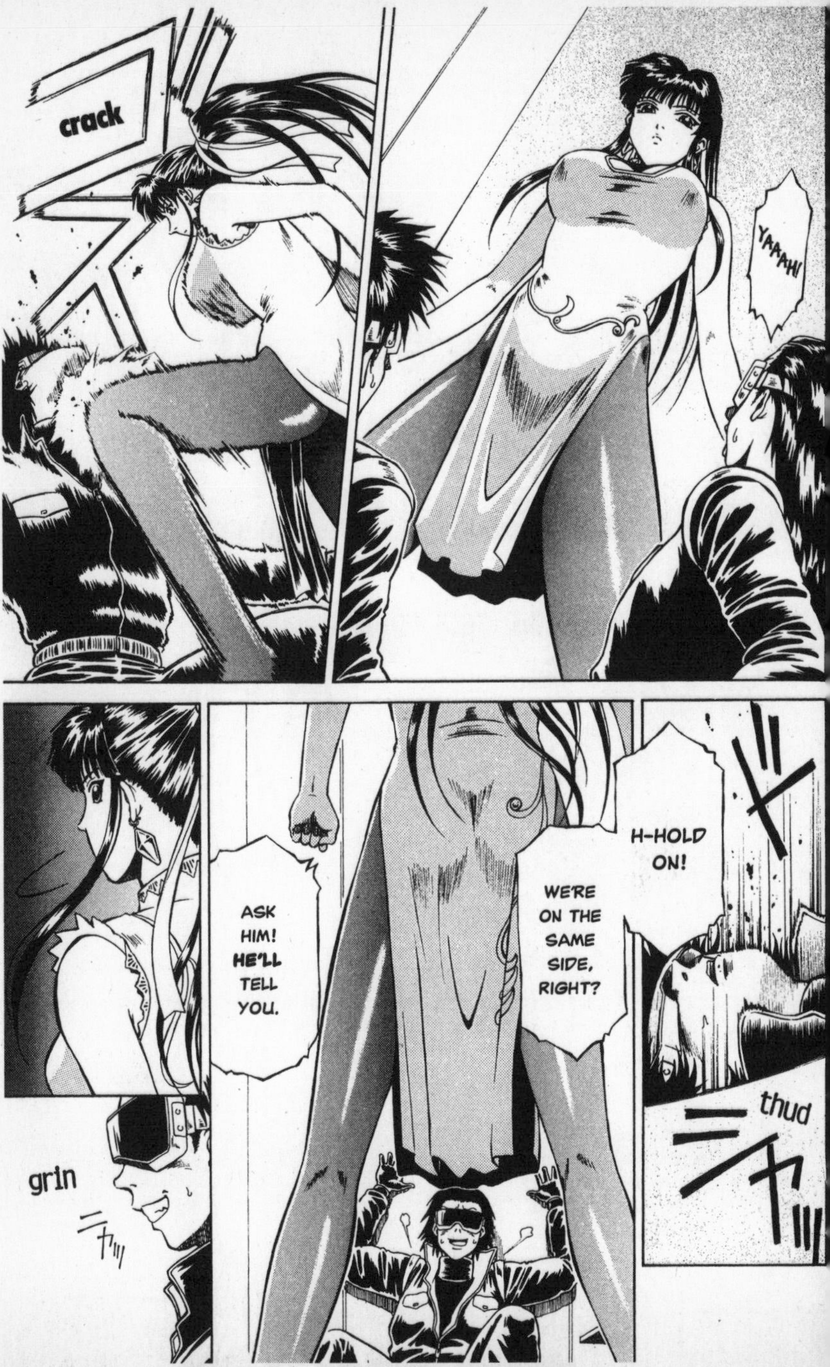
YAAAH!
crack
H-HOLD ON!
thud
WE'RE ON THE SAME SIDE, RIGHT?
ASK HIM! HE'LL TELL YOU.
grin

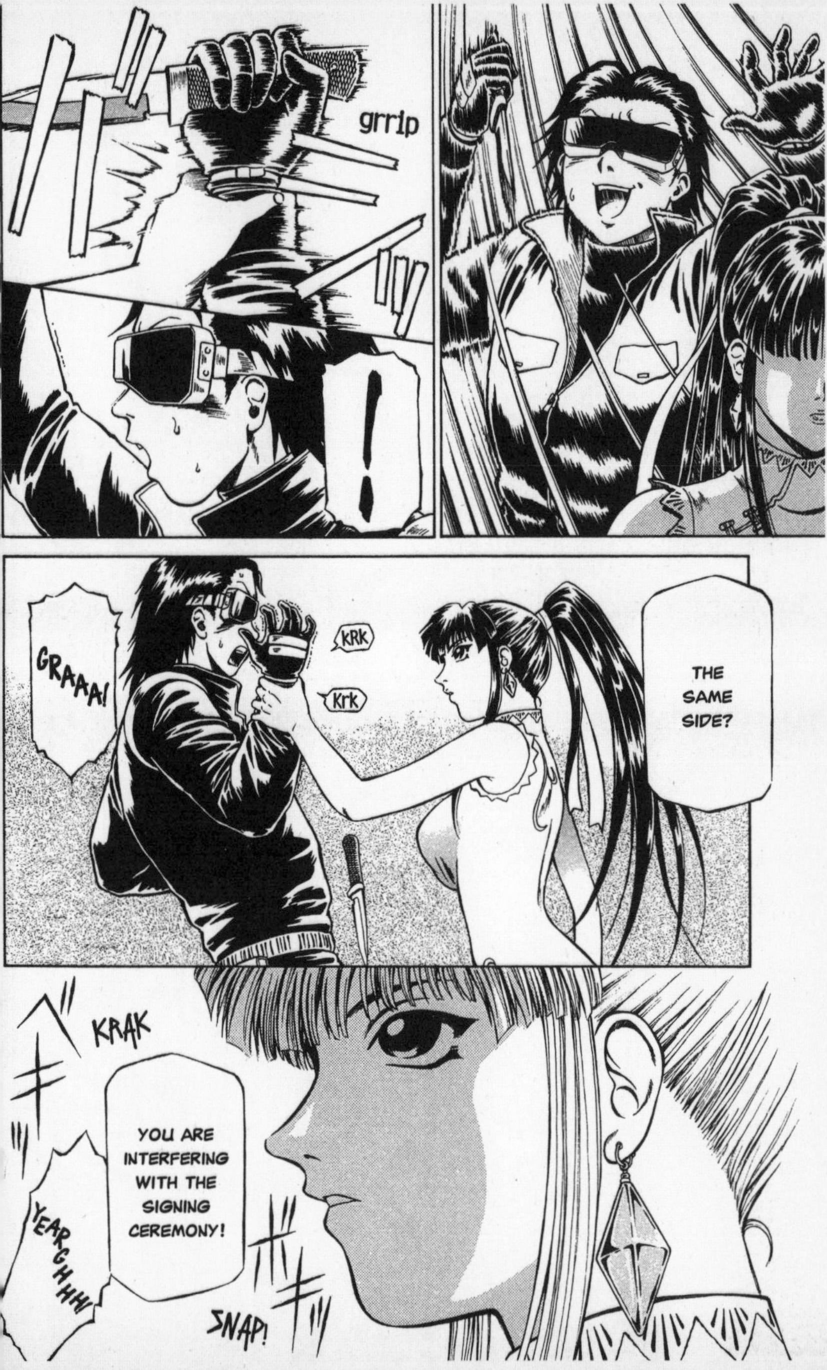
grrip
!
THE SAME SIDE?
KRK
Krk
GRAAA!
KRAK
YOU ARE INTERFERING WITH THE SIGNING CEREMONY!
YEARGHHH!
SNAP!

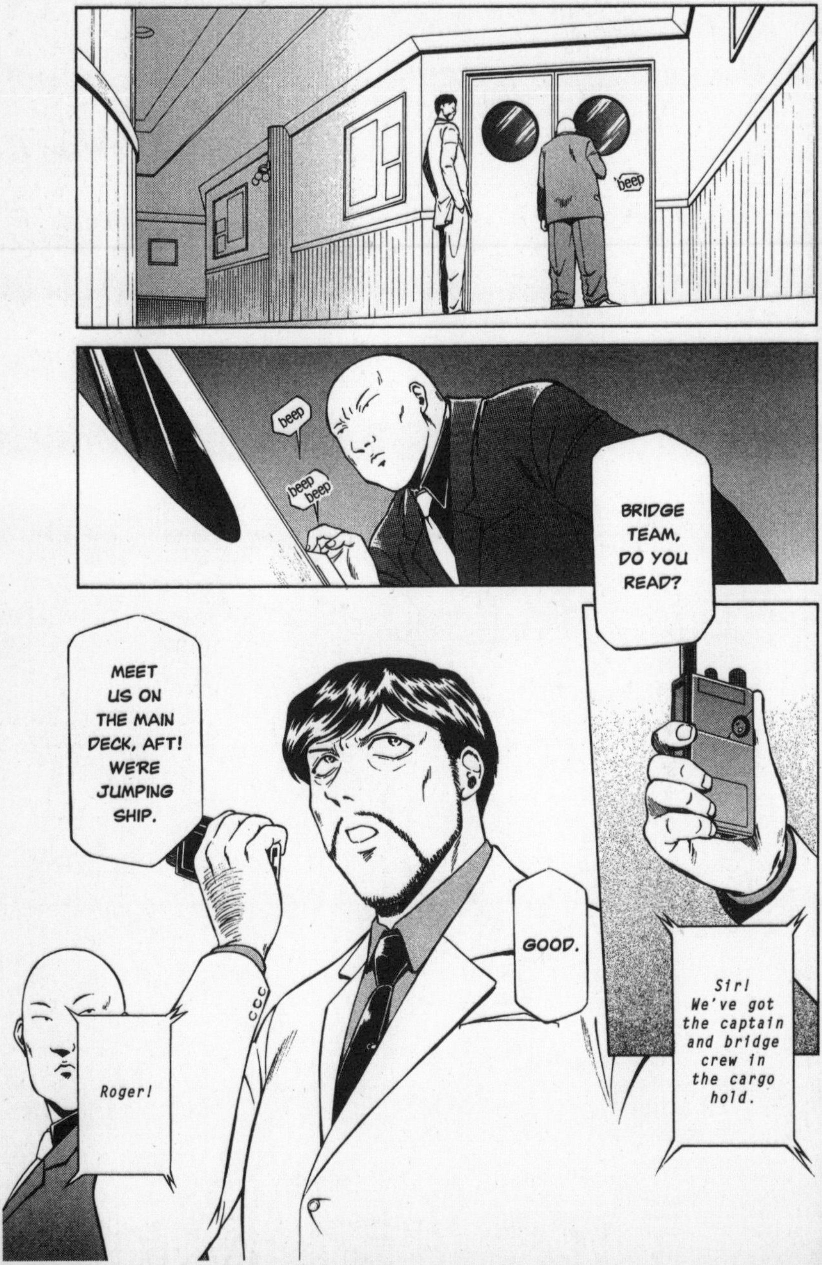

beep
beep
beep beep
BRIDGE TEAM, DO YOU READ?
Sir! We've got the captain and bridge crew in the cargo hold.
GOOD.
MEET US ON THE MAIN DECK, AFT! WE'RE JUMPING SHIP.
Roger!

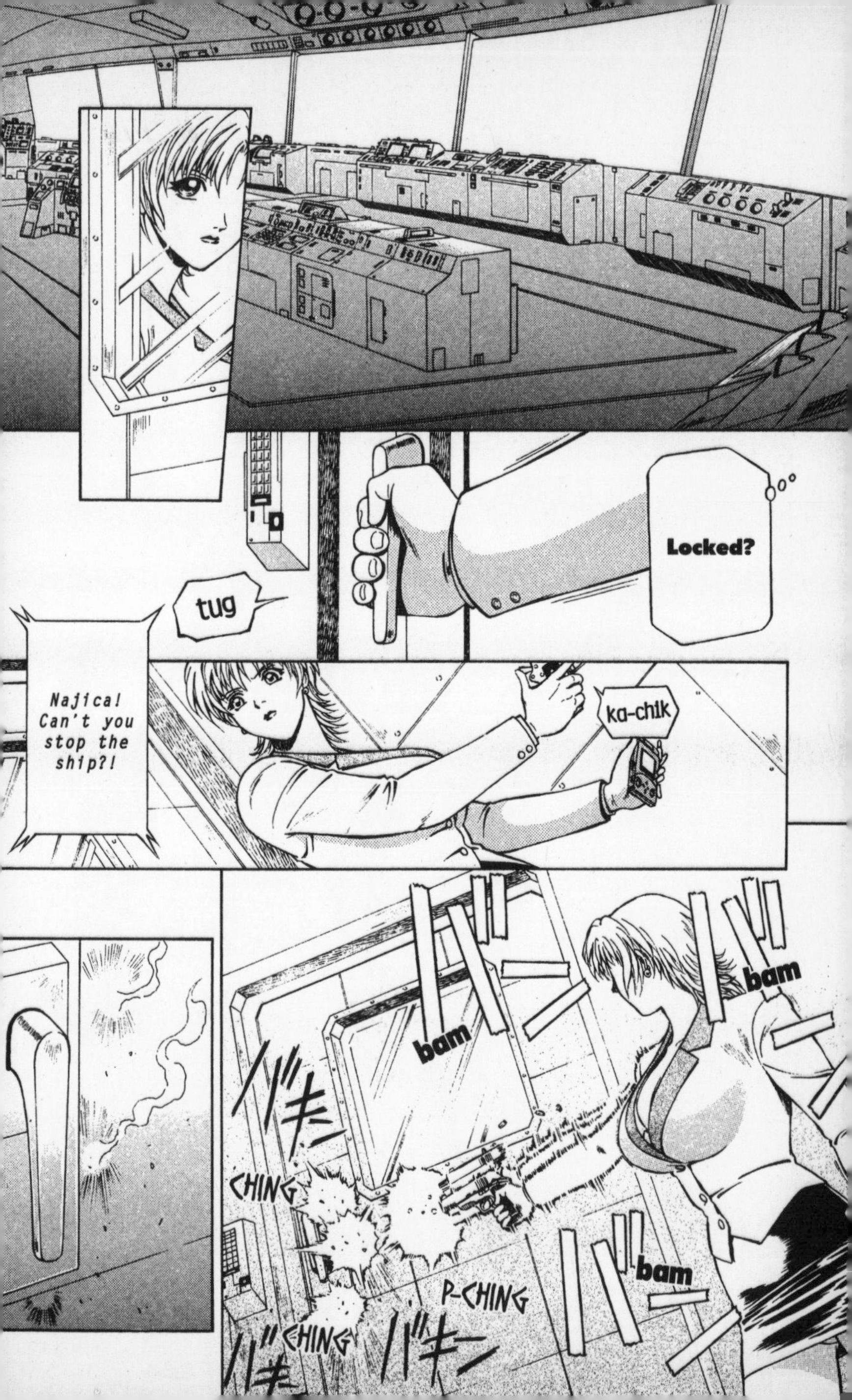

Locked?
tug
ka-chik
Najica! Can't you stop the ship?!
bam
bam
バキ
CHING
bam
P-CHING
バキー
CHING
バキ

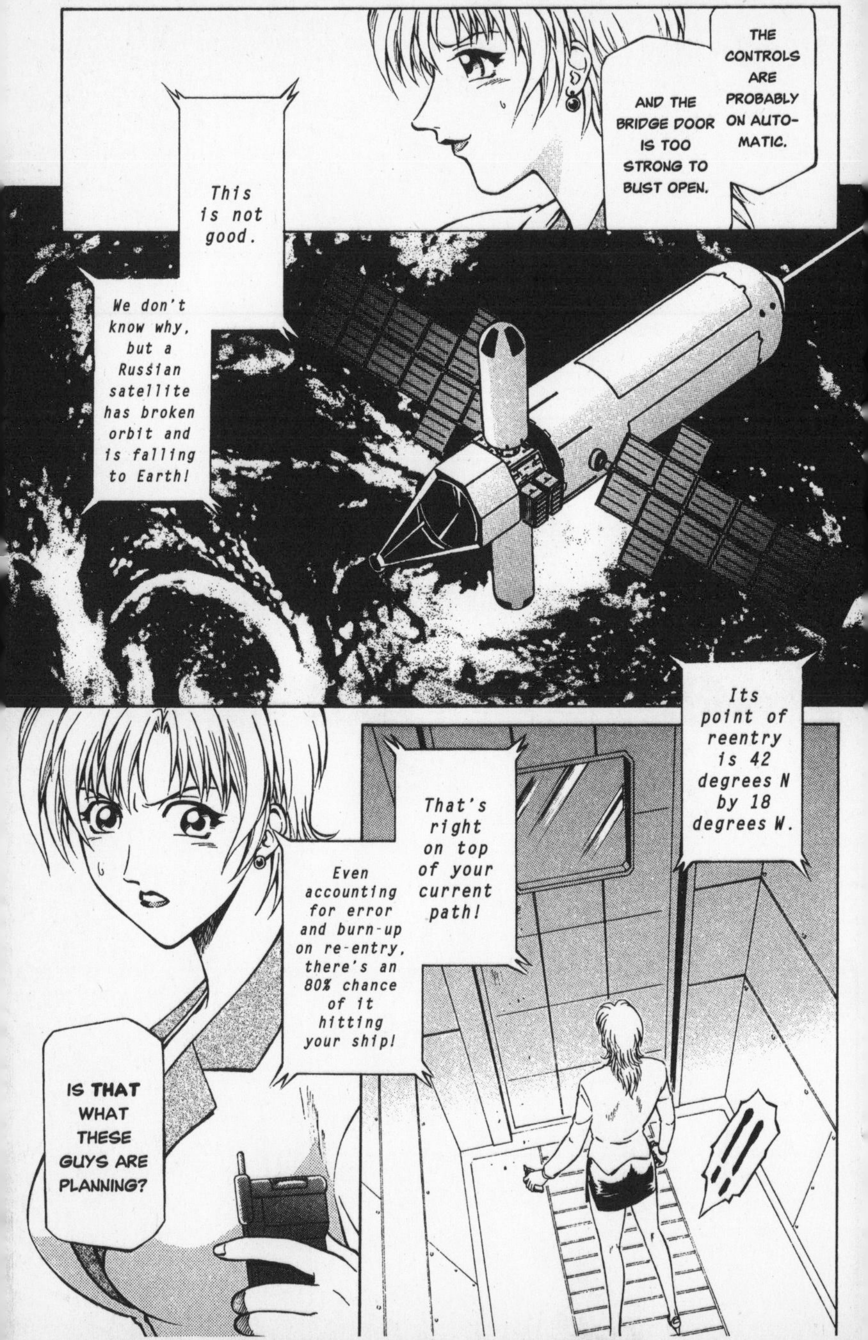
THE CONTROLS ARE PROBABLY ON AUTO-MATIC.
AND THE BRIDGE DOOR IS TOO STRONG TO BUST OPEN.
This is not good.
We don't know why, but a Russian satellite has broken orbit and is falling to Earth!
Its point of reentry is 42 degrees N by 18 degrees W.
That's right on top of your current path!
Even accounting for error and burn-up on re-entry, there's an 80% chance of it hitting your ship!
IS THAT WHAT THESE GUYS ARE PLANNING?

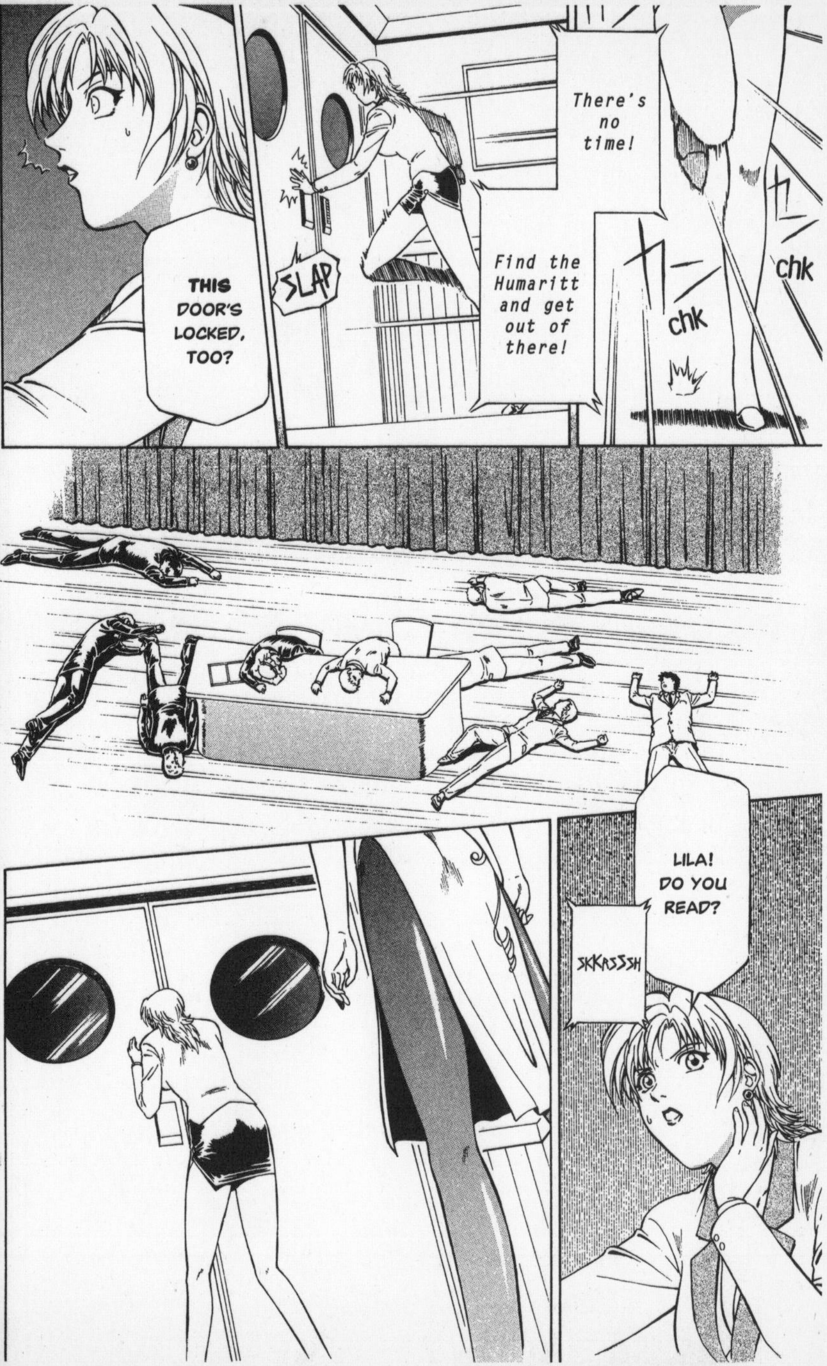
chk
chk
There's no time!
Find the Humaritt and get out of there!
SLAP
THIS DOOR'S LOCKED, TOO?
LILA! DO YOU READ?
SKKRSSSH

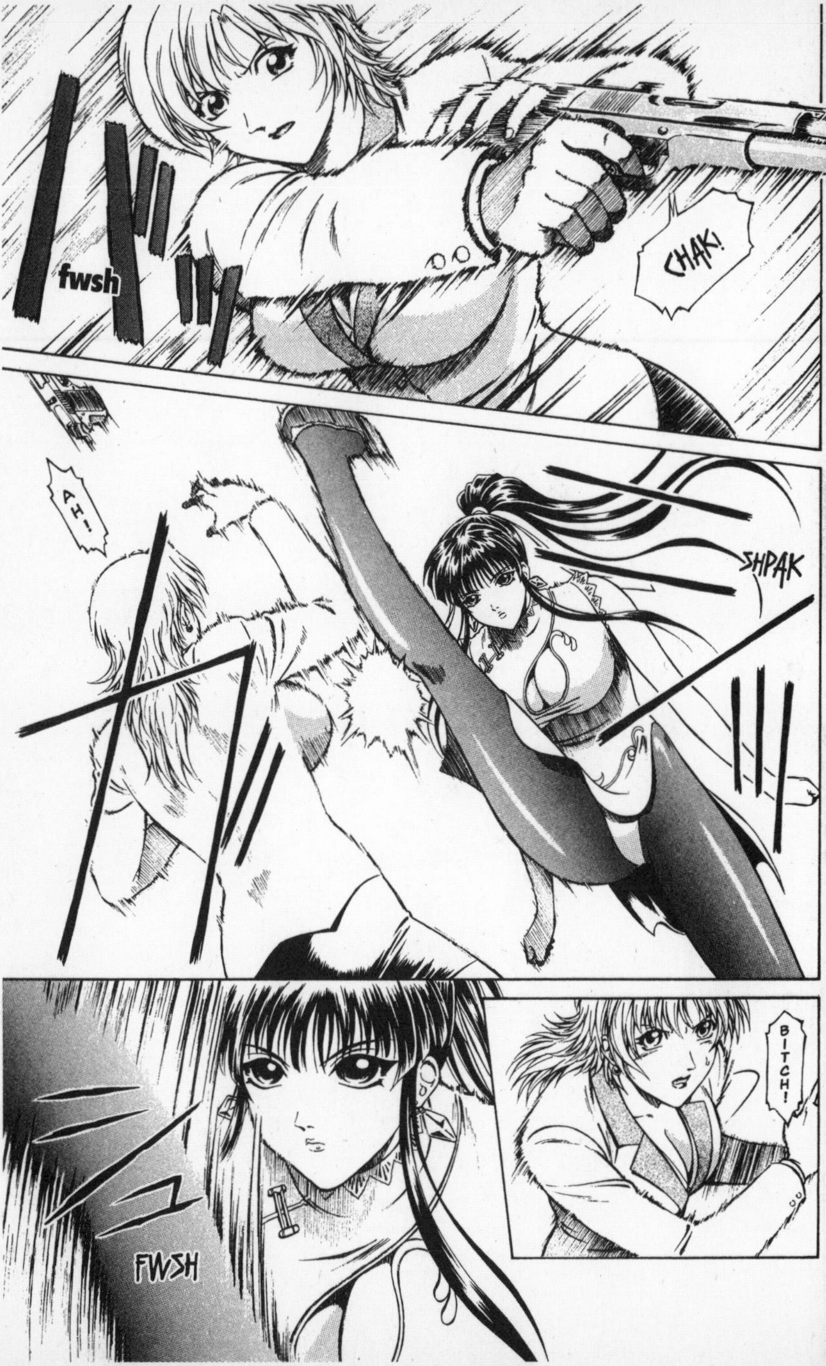
CHAK!
fwsh
SHPAK
AH!
BITCH!
FWSH

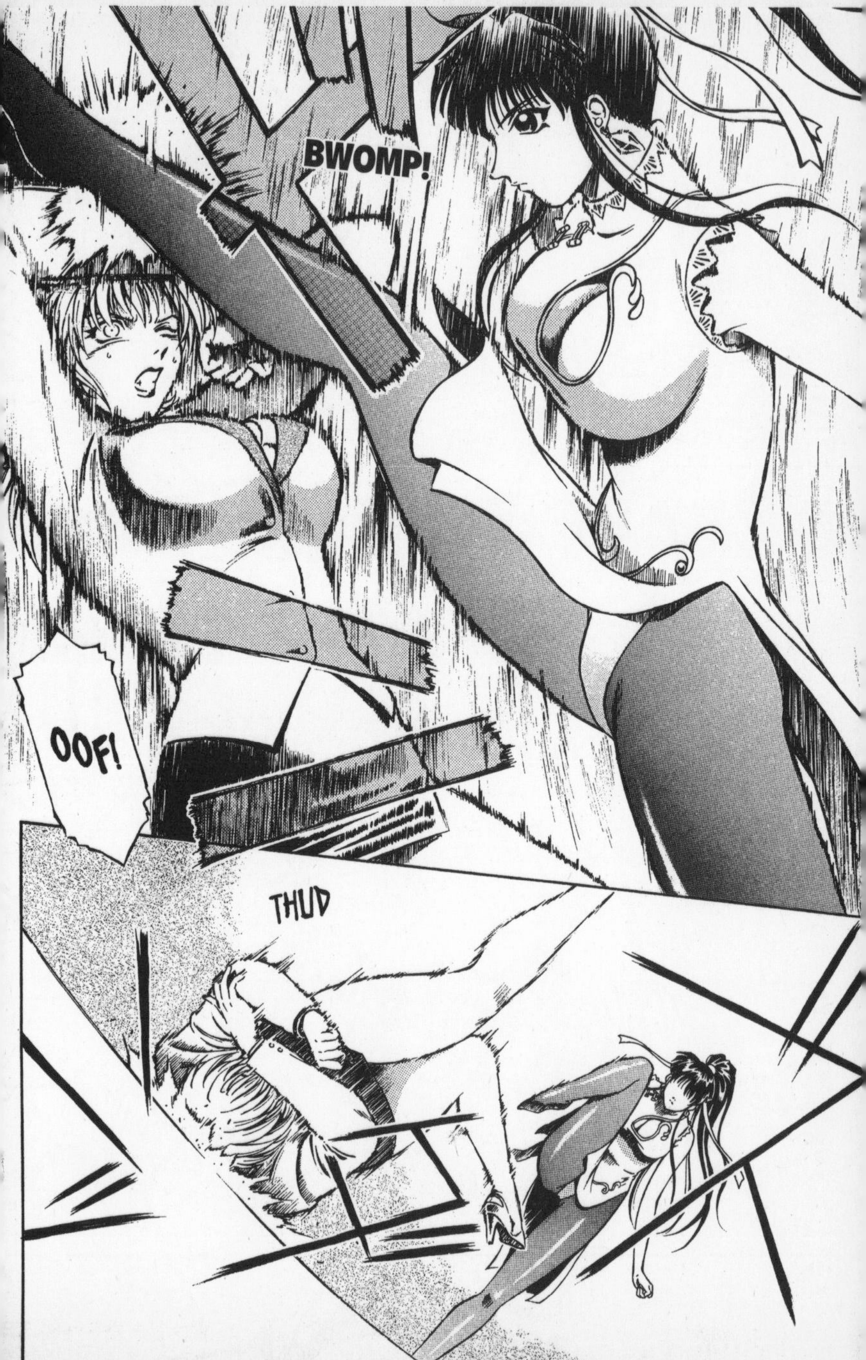
BWOMP!
OOF!
THUD

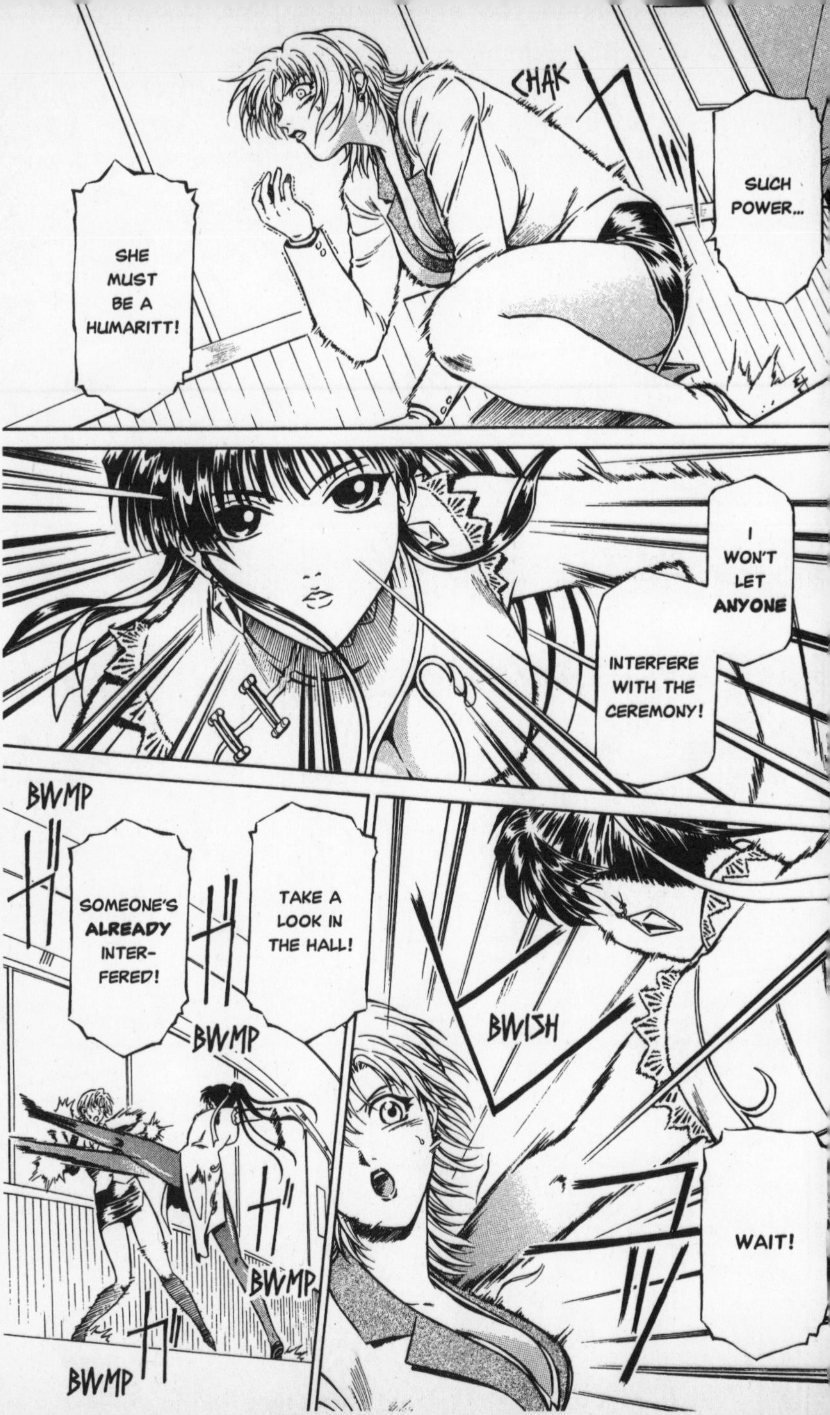
SUCH POWER...
CHAK
SHE MUST BE A HUMARITT!
I WON'T LET ANYONE
INTERFERE WITH THE CEREMONY!
TAKE A LOOK IN THE HALL!
SOMEONE'S ALREADY INTER-FERED!
BWMP
BWISH
BWMP
WAIT!
BWMP
BWMP

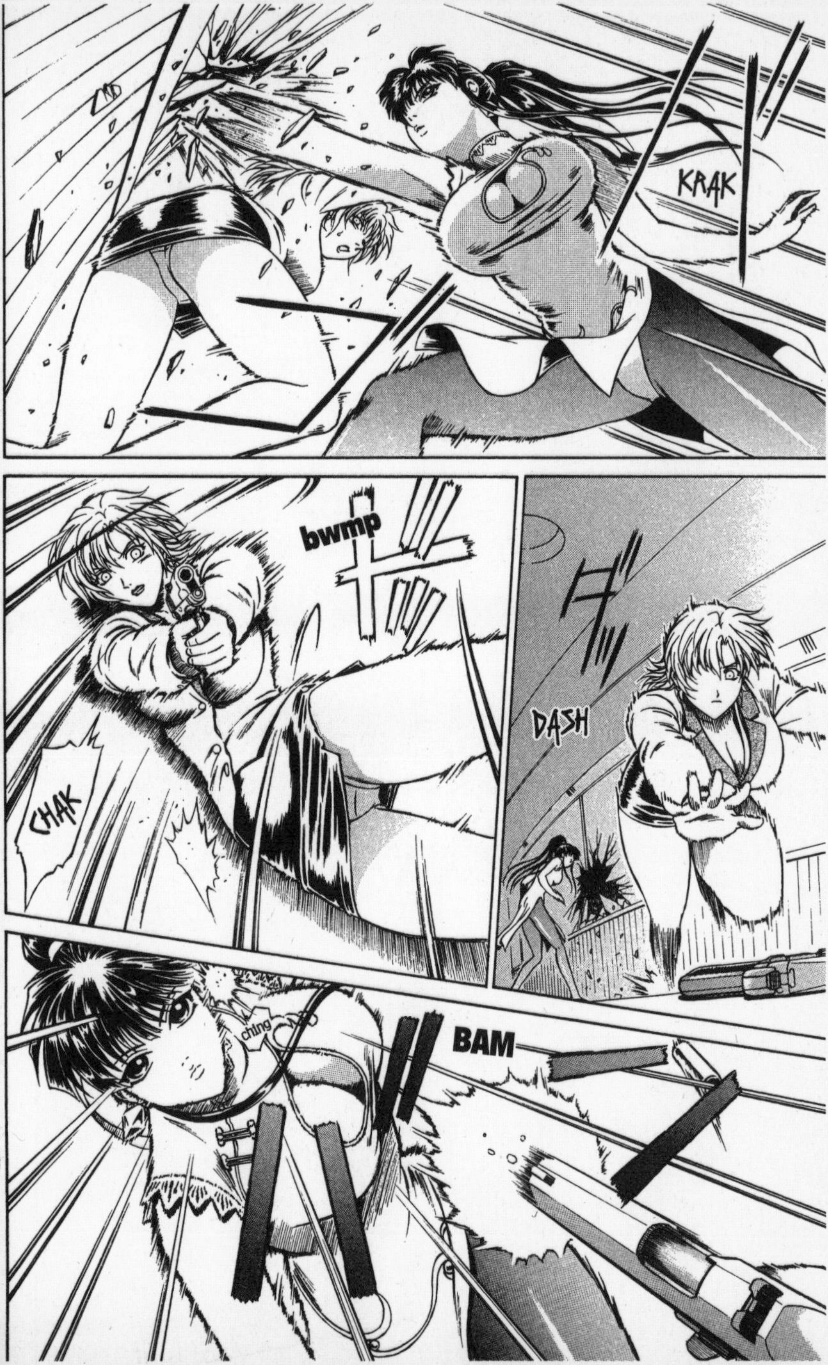
KRAK
DASH
bwmp
CHAK
BAM
ching

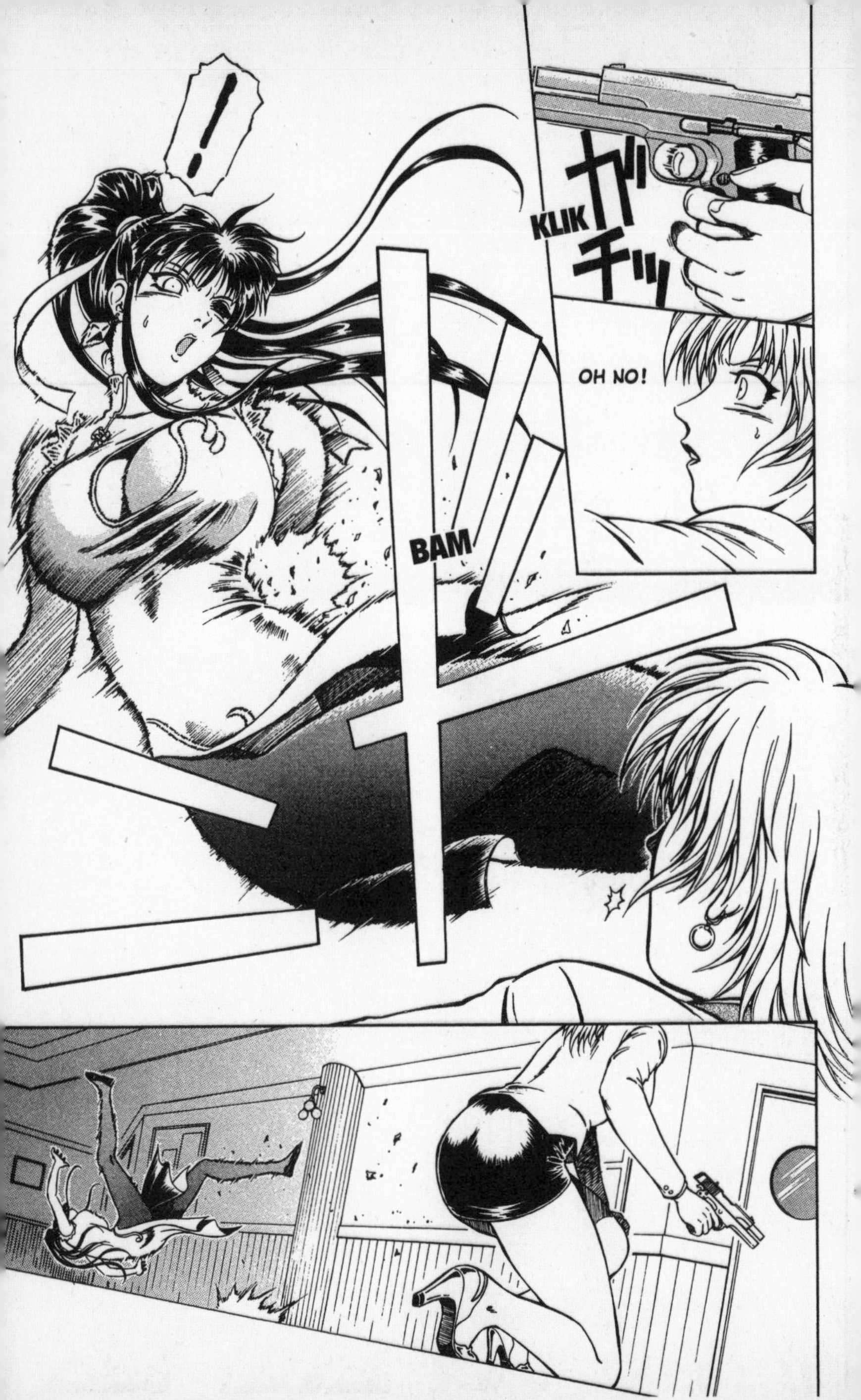
KLIK
カチッ
OH NO!
!
BAM

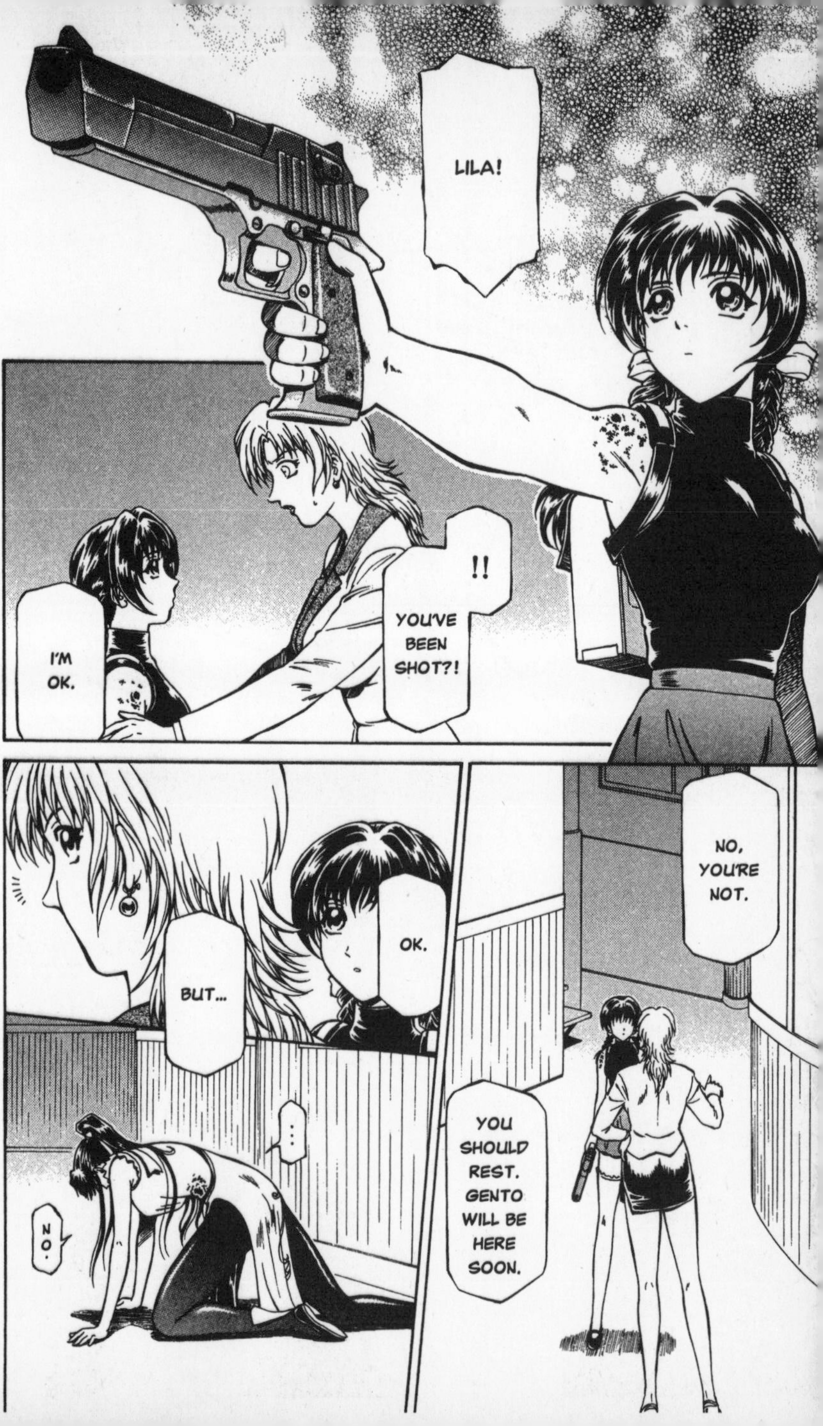
LILA!
!!
YOU'VE BEEN SHOT?!
I'M OK.
NO, YOU'RE NOT.
YOU SHOULD REST. GENTO WILL BE HERE SOON.
OK.
BUT...
...
NO.

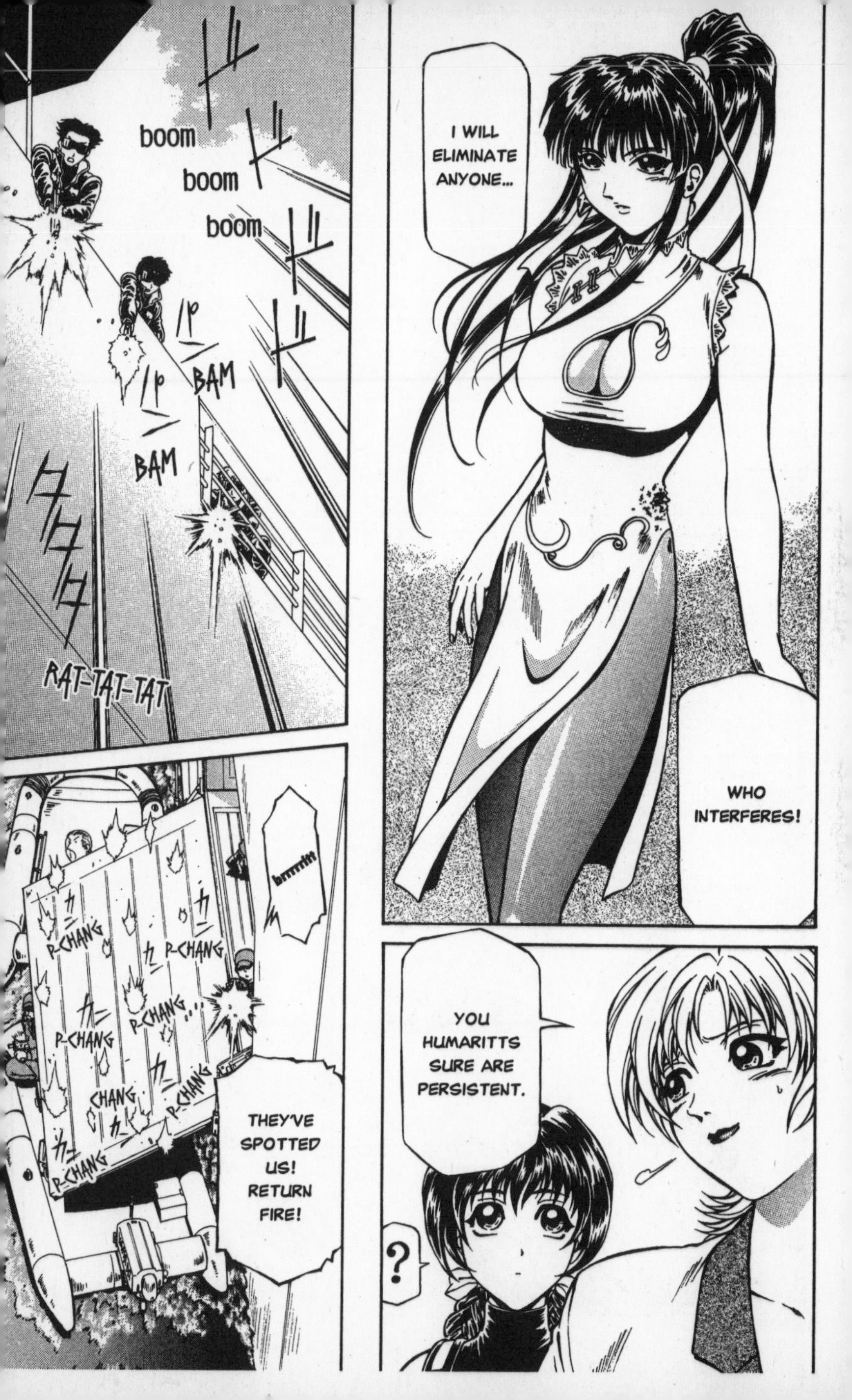
I WILL ELIMINATE ANYONE...
WHO INTERFERES!
boom
boom
boom
BAM
BAM
RAT-TAT-TAT
YOU HUMARITTS SURE ARE PERSISTENT.
?
brrrrrittt
P-CHANG
P-CHANG
P-CHANG...
P-CHANG
CHANG
P-CHANG
P-CHANG
THEY'VE SPOTTED US! RETURN FIRE!

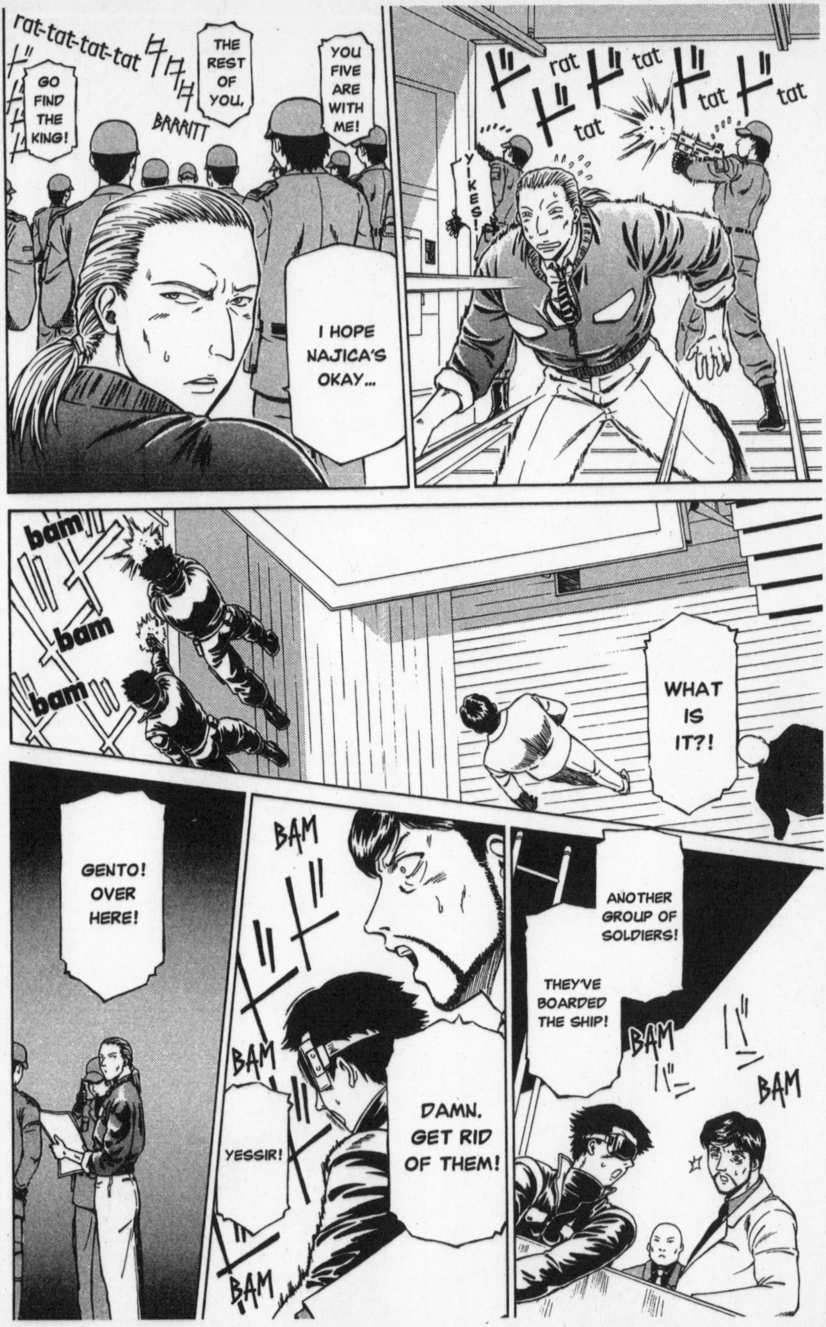
rat tat tat tat tat
YIKES!
YOU FIVE ARE WITH ME!
THE REST OF YOU,
GO FIND THE KING!
rat-tat-tat-tat
BRRRITT
I HOPE NAJICA'S OKAY...
bam
bam
bam
WHAT IS IT?!
ANOTHER GROUP OF SOLDIERS!
THEY'VE BOARDED THE SHIP!
BAM
BAM
BAM
DAMN. GET RID OF THEM!
BAM
YESSIR!
BAM
GENTO! OVER HERE!

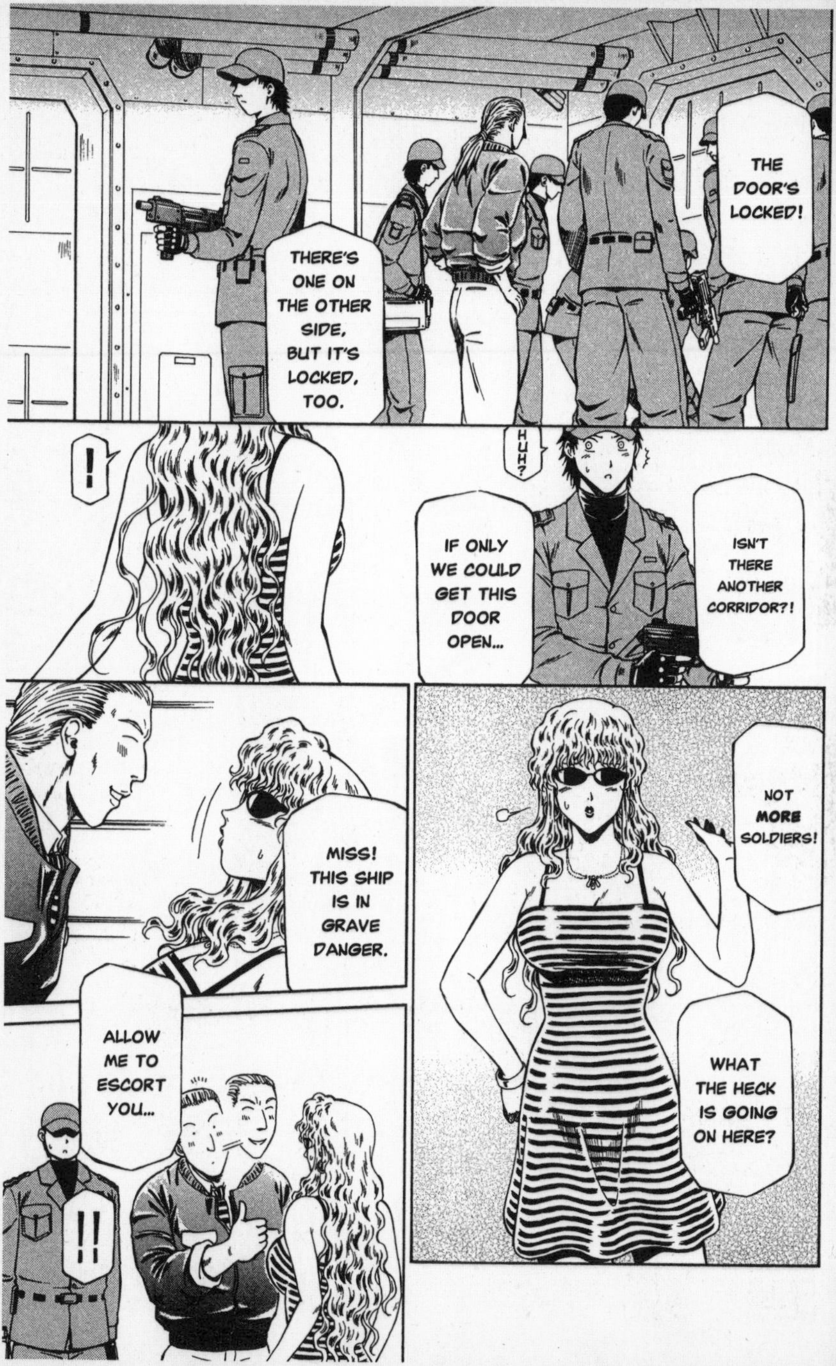
THE DOOR'S LOCKED!
THERE'S ONE ON THE OTHER SIDE, BUT IT'S LOCKED, TOO.
ISN'T THERE ANOTHER CORRIDOR?!
IF ONLY WE COULD GET THIS DOOR OPEN...
HUH?
!
NOT MORE SOLDIERS!
WHAT THE HECK IS GOING ON HERE?
MISS! THIS SHIP IS IN GRAVE DANGER.
ALLOW ME TO ESCORT YOU...
!!

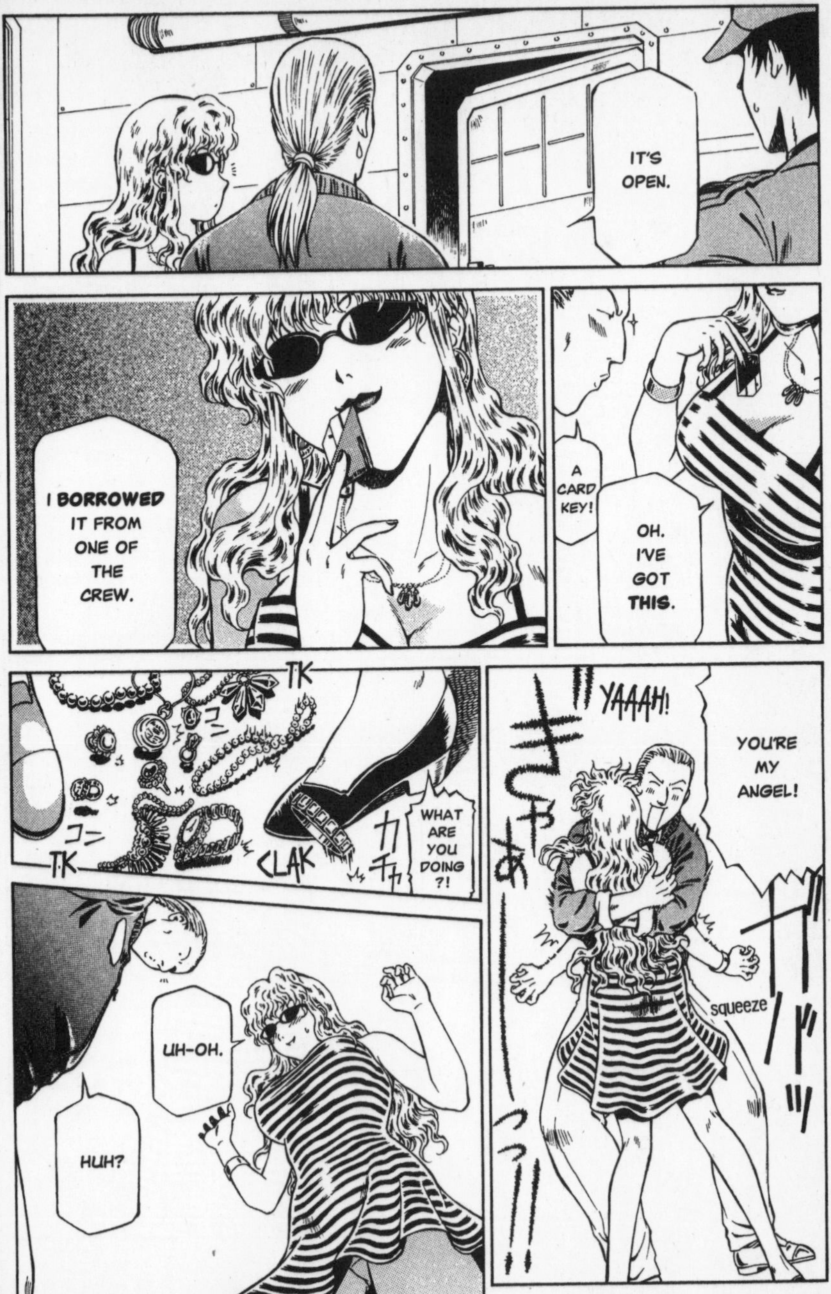

IT'S OPEN.
A CARD KEY!
OH. I'VE GOT THIS.
I BORROWED IT FROM ONE OF THE CREW.
YAAAH!
YOU'RE MY ANGEL!
squeeze
WHAT ARE YOU DOING?!
TK
TK
CLAK
UH-OH.
HUH?

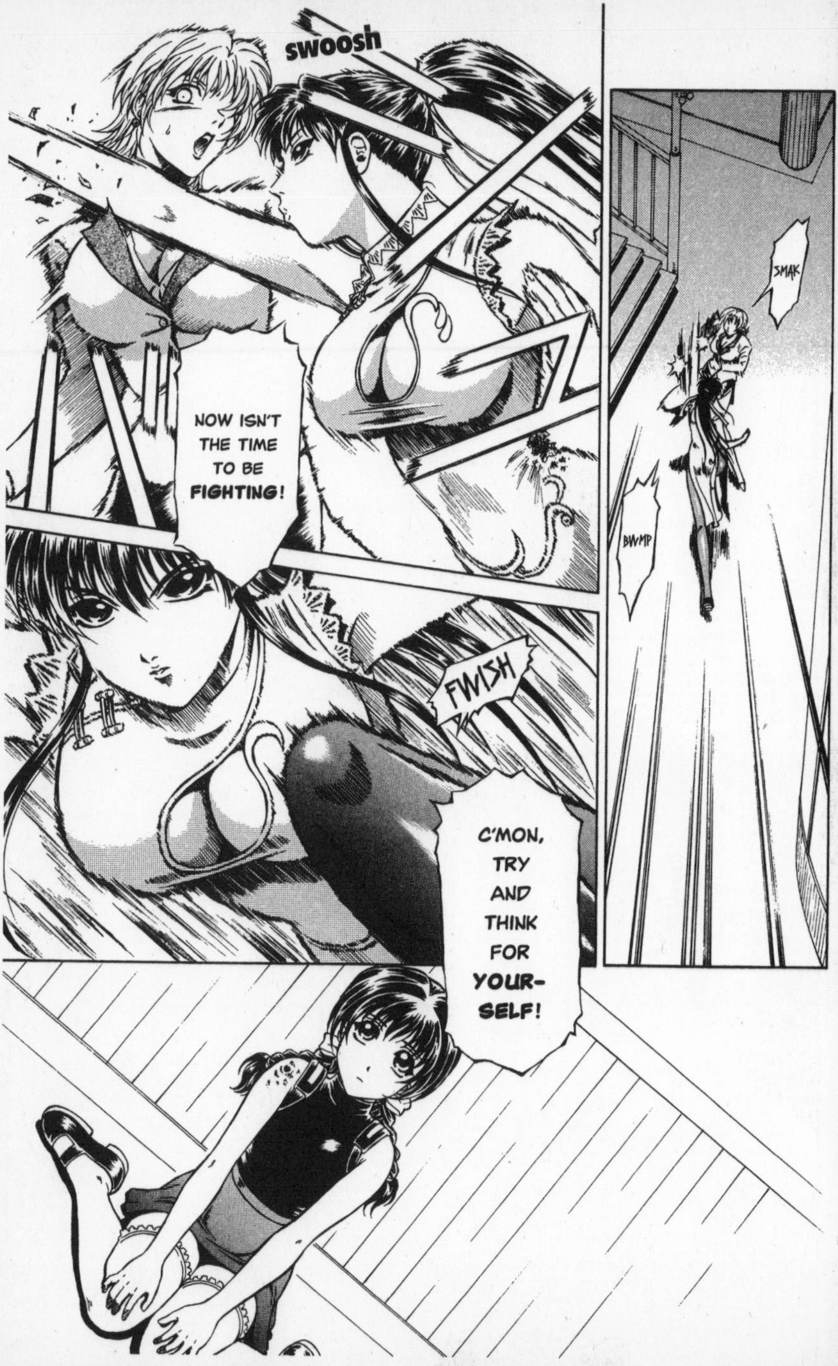
SMAK
BWMP
swoosh
NOW ISN'T THE TIME TO BE FIGHTING!
FWISH
C'MON, TRY AND THINK FOR YOURSELF!

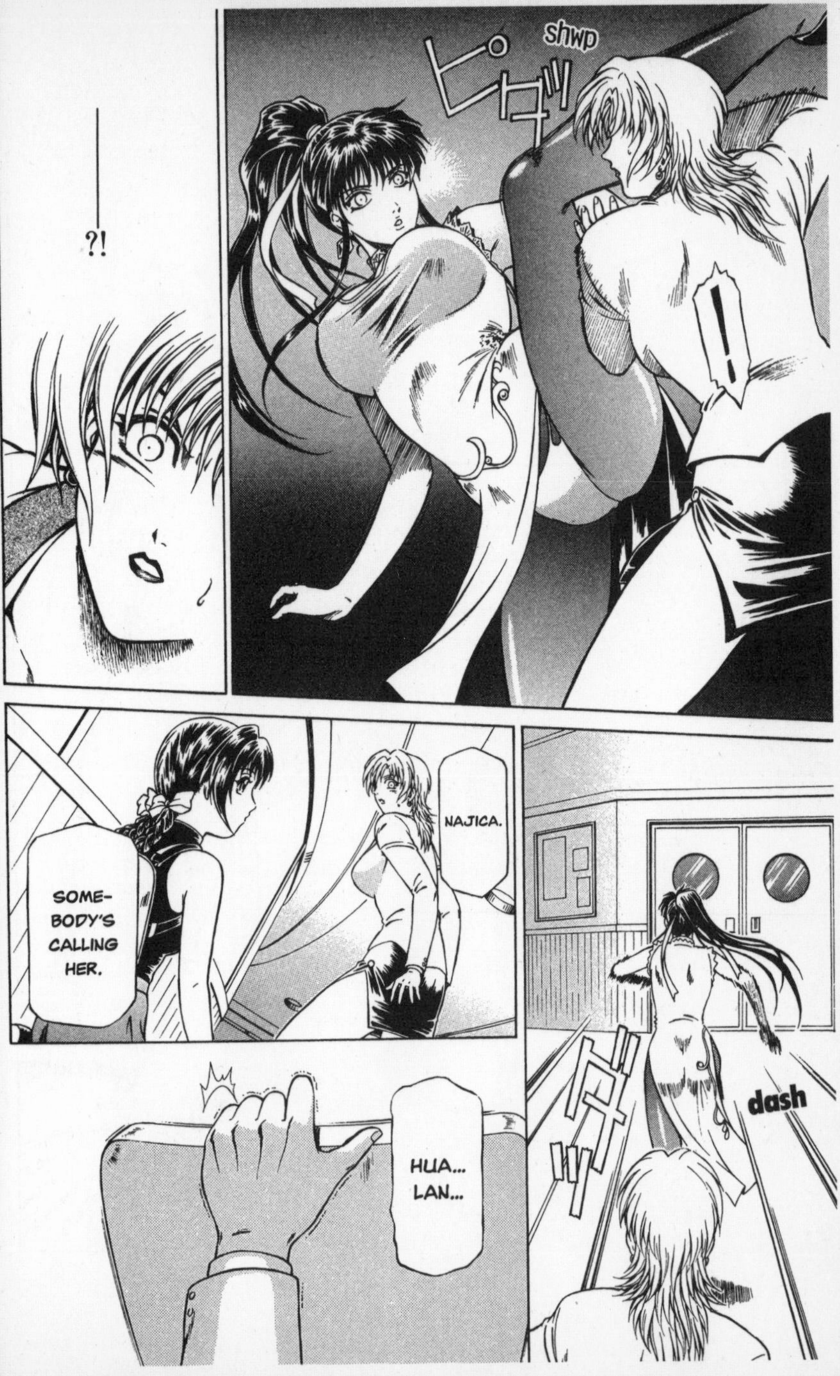

shwp
ピダッ
!
—
?!
dash
ダダッ
NAJICA.
SOME-BODY'S CALLING HER.
HUA... LAN...

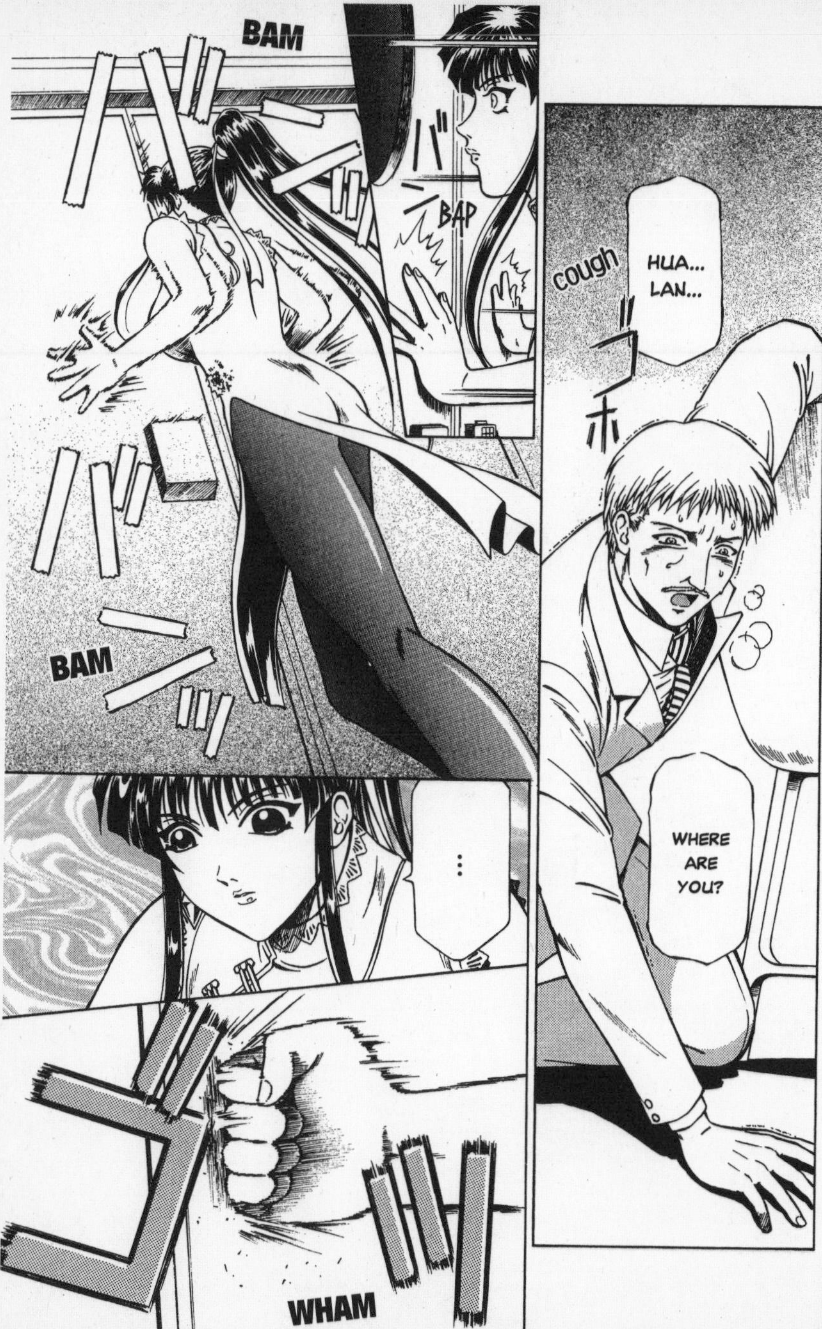
BAM
BAP
BAM
cough
HUA... LAN...
WHERE ARE YOU?
...
WHAM

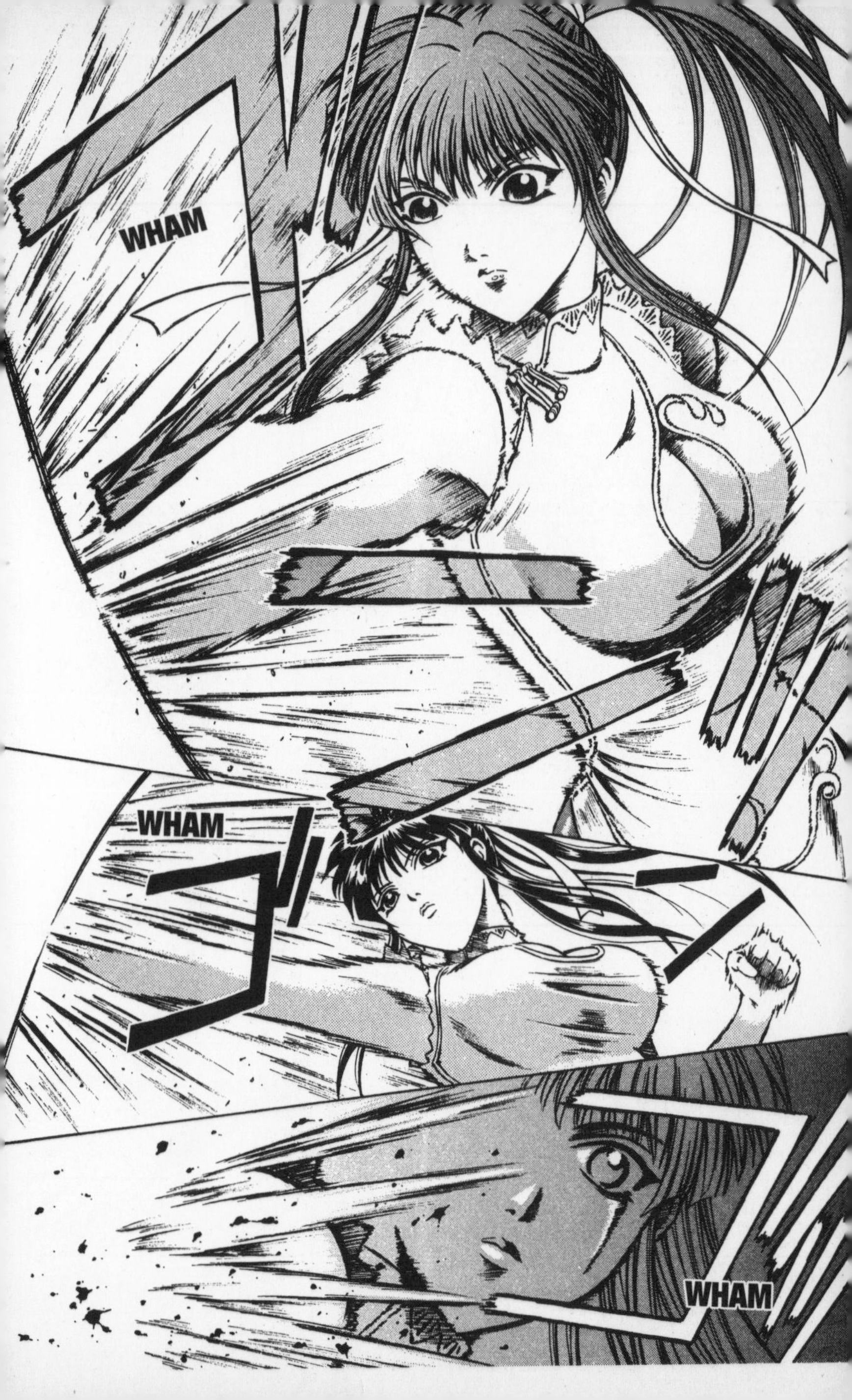
WHAM
WHAM
WHAM

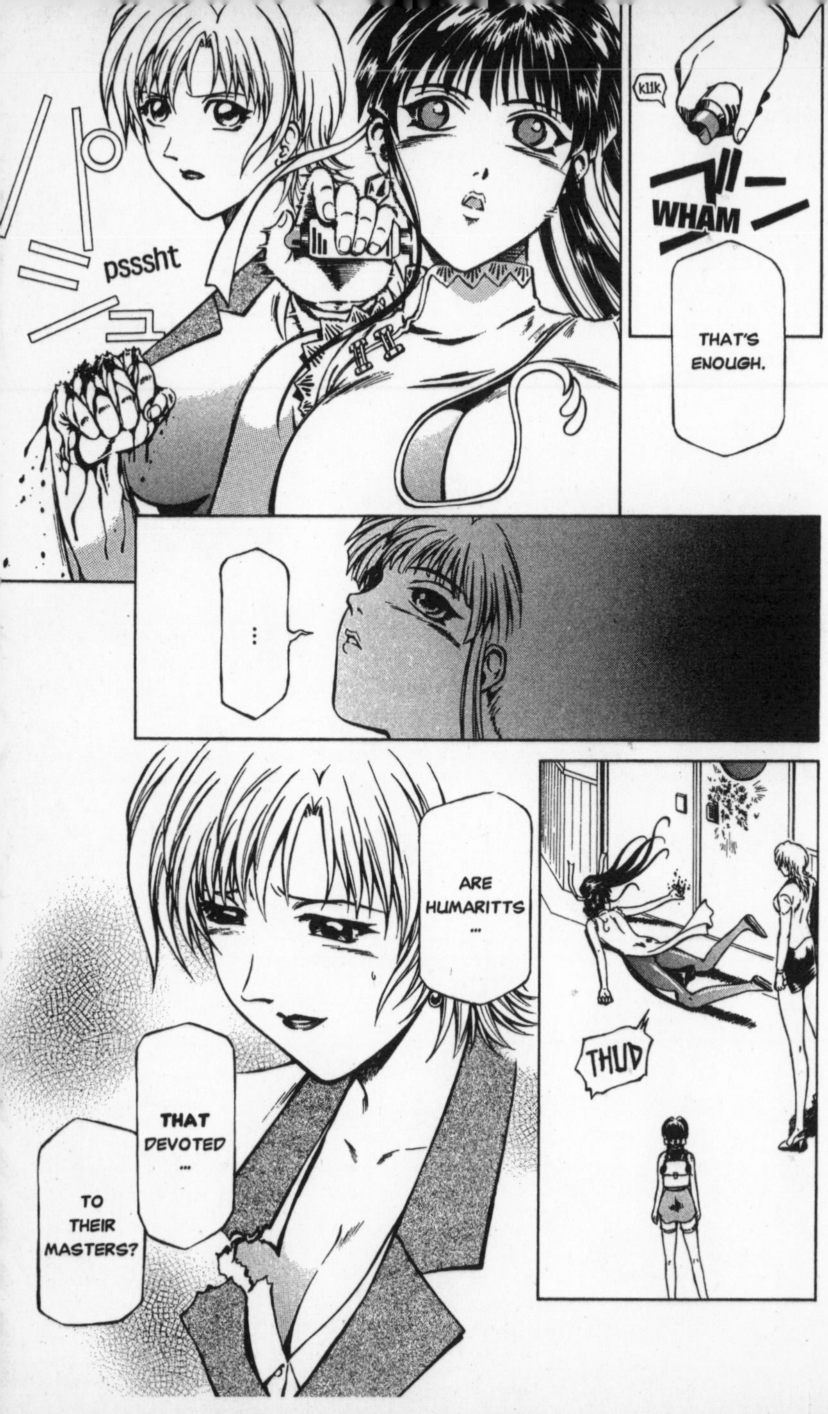

klik
WHAM
THAT'S ENOUGH.
psssht
...
THUD
ARE HUMARITTS ...
THAT DEVOTED ...
TO THEIR MASTERS?

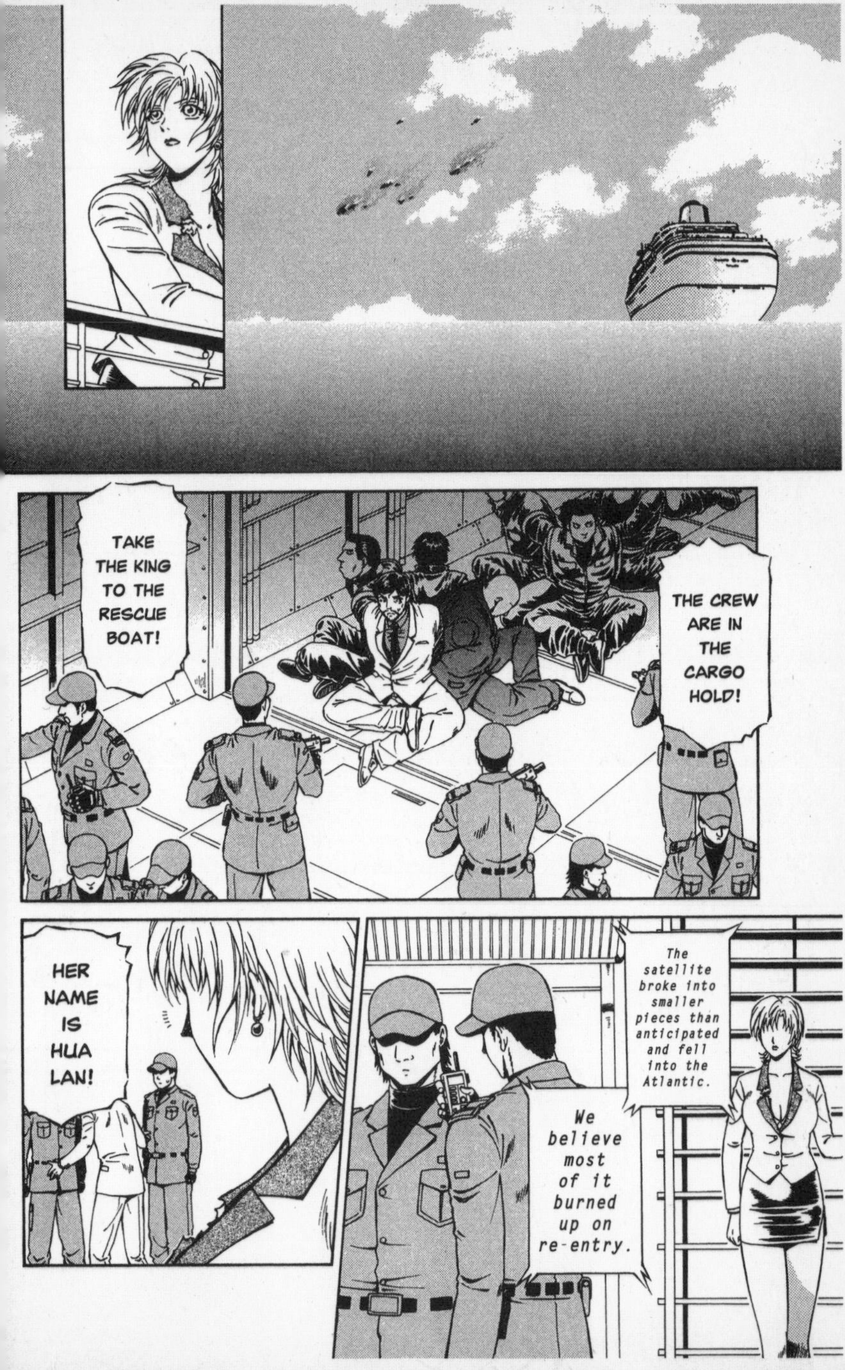
THE CREW ARE IN THE CARGO HOLD!
TAKE THE KING TO THE RESCUE BOAT!
The satellite broke into smaller pieces than anticipated and fell into the Atlantic.
We believe most of it burned up on re-entry.
HER NAME IS HUA LAN!

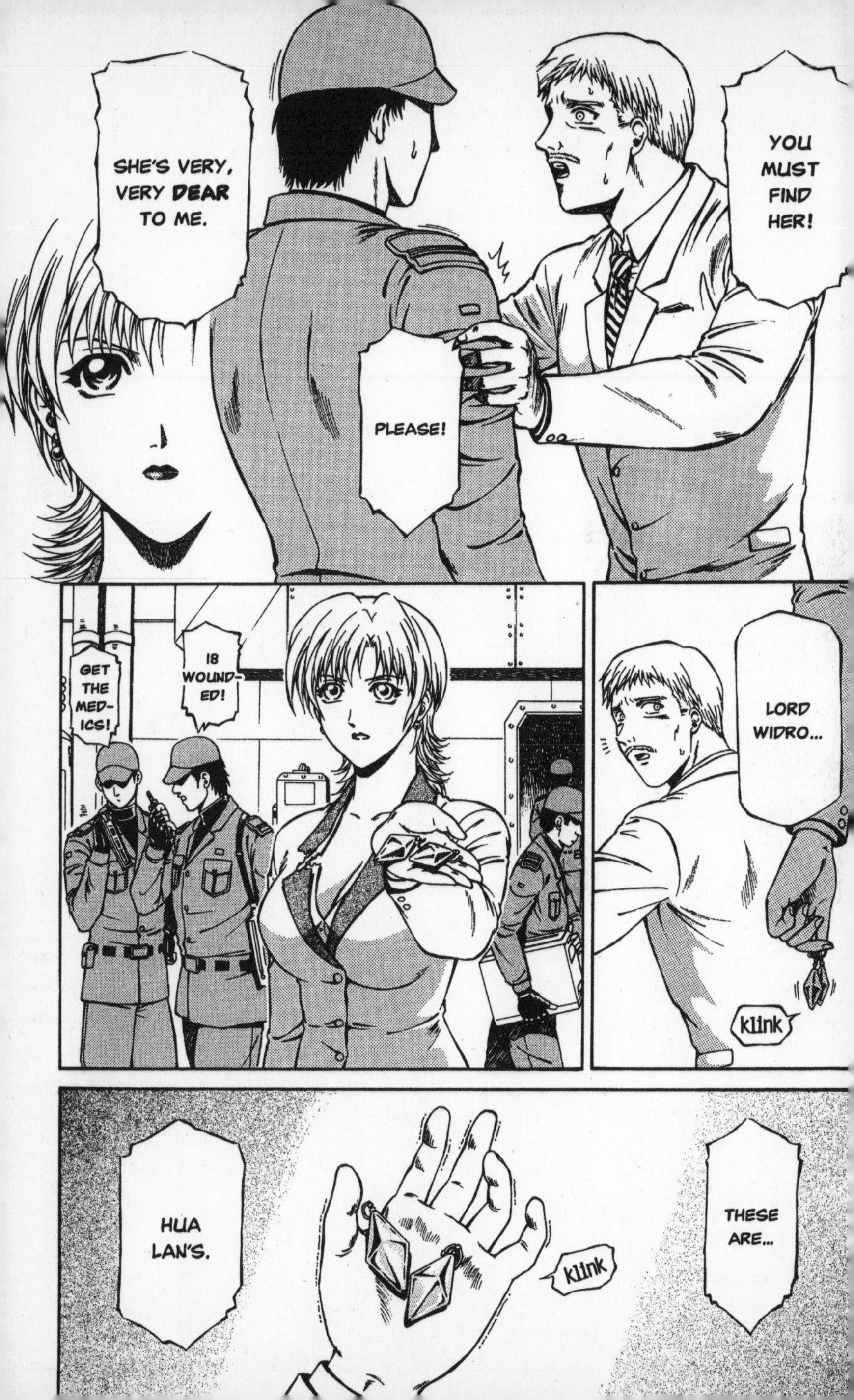
YOU MUST FIND HER!
SHE'S VERY, VERY **DEAR** TO ME.
PLEASE!
LORD WIDRO...
klink
18 WOUNDED!
GET THE MEDICS!
THESE ARE...
klink
HUA LAN'S.

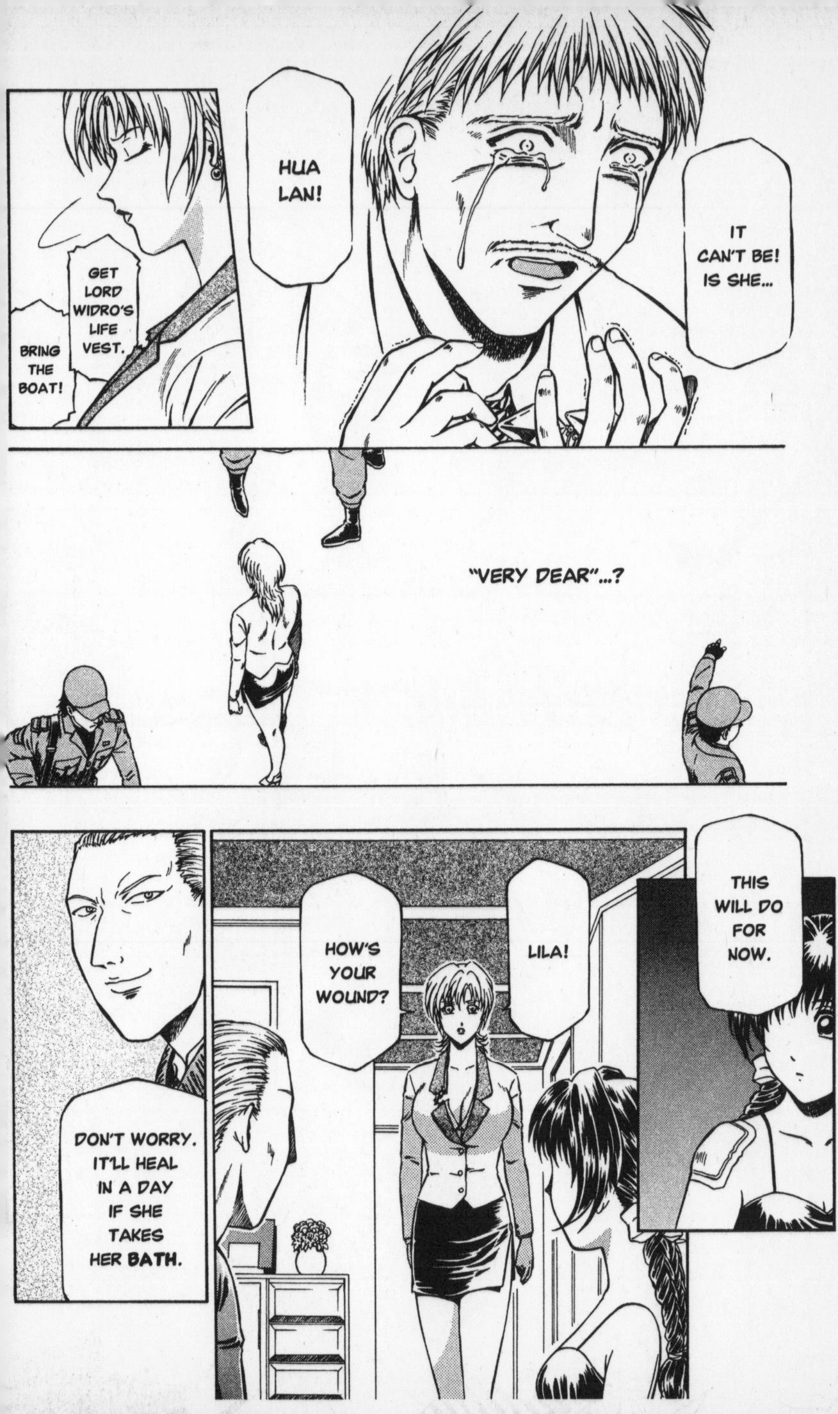
IT CAN'T BE! IS SHE...
HUA LAN!
GET LORD WIDRO'S LIFE VEST.
BRING THE BOAT!
"VERY DEAR"...?
THIS WILL DO FOR NOW.
LILA!
HOW'S YOUR WOUND?
DON'T WORRY. IT'LL HEAL IN A DAY IF SHE TAKES HER BATH.

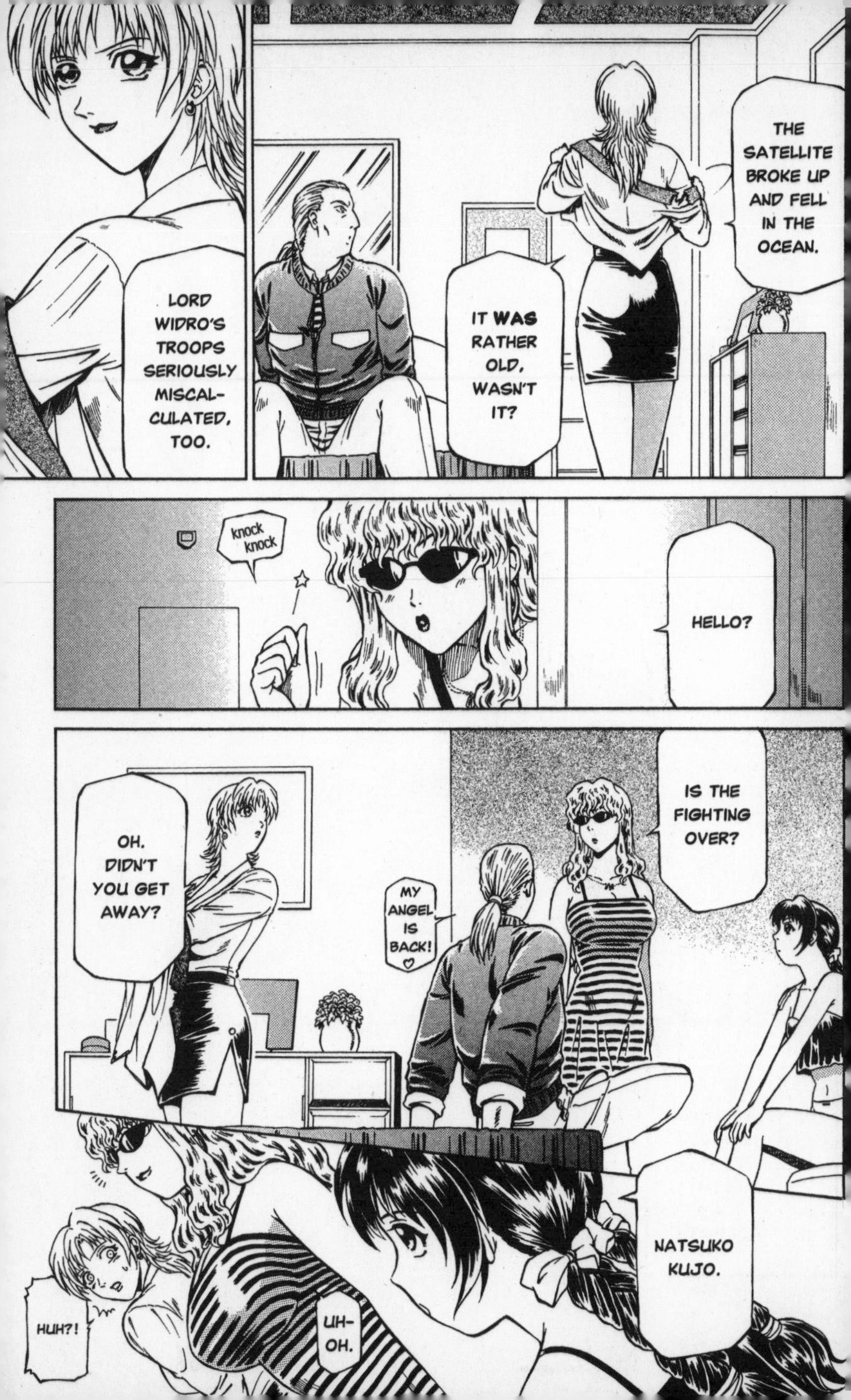
THE SATELLITE BROKE UP AND FELL IN THE OCEAN.
IT WAS RATHER OLD, WASN'T IT?
LORD WIDRO'S TROOPS SERIOUSLY MISCALCULATED, TOO.
HELLO?
knock knock
IS THE FIGHTING OVER?
MY ANGEL IS BACK! ♡
OH. DIDN'T YOU GET AWAY?
NATSUKO KUJO.
UH-OH.
HUH?!

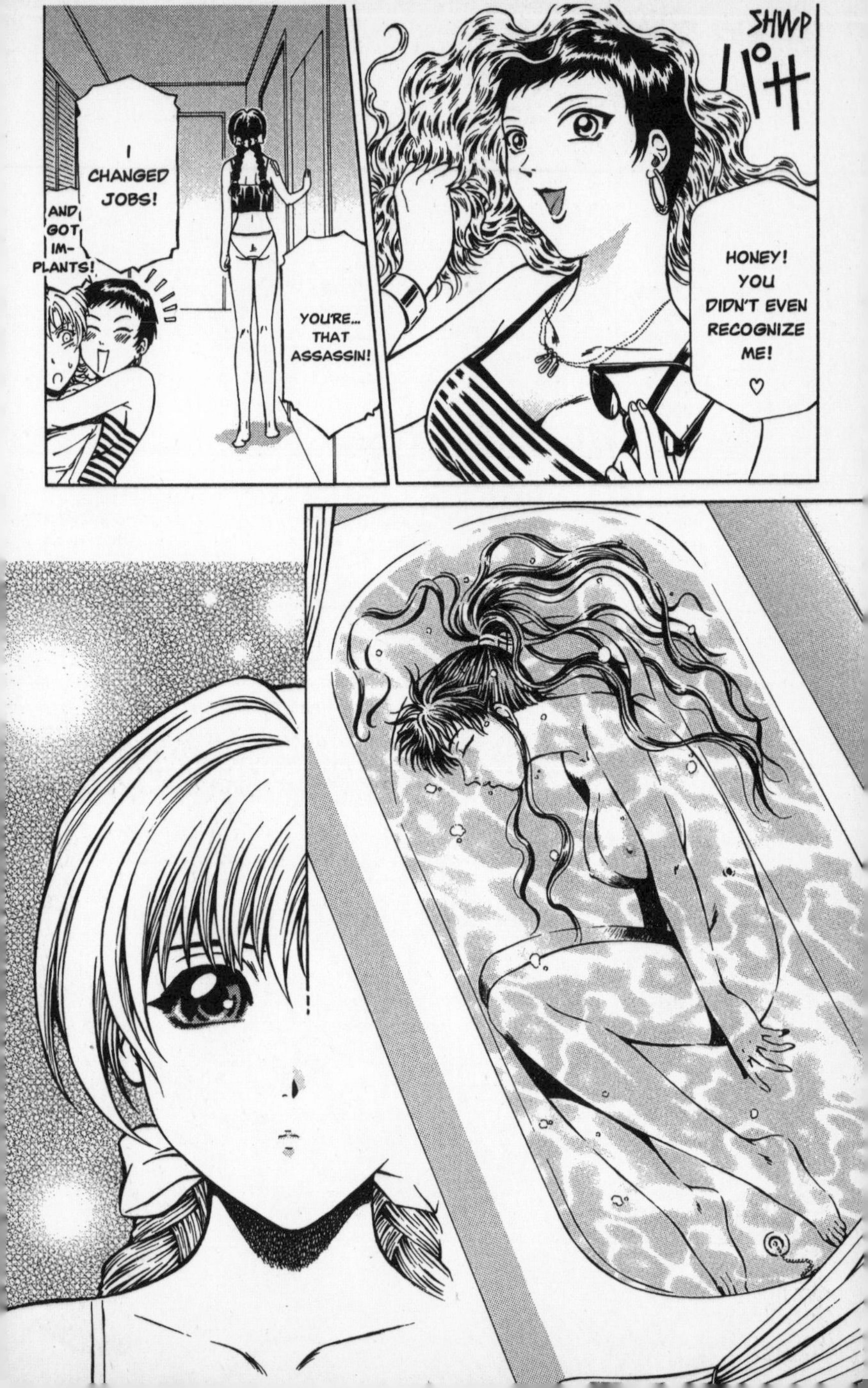
SHWP
パサ
HONEY! YOU DIDN'T EVEN RECOGNIZE ME! ♡
YOU'RE... THAT ASSASSIN!
I CHANGED JOBS!
AND GOT IM-PLANTS!

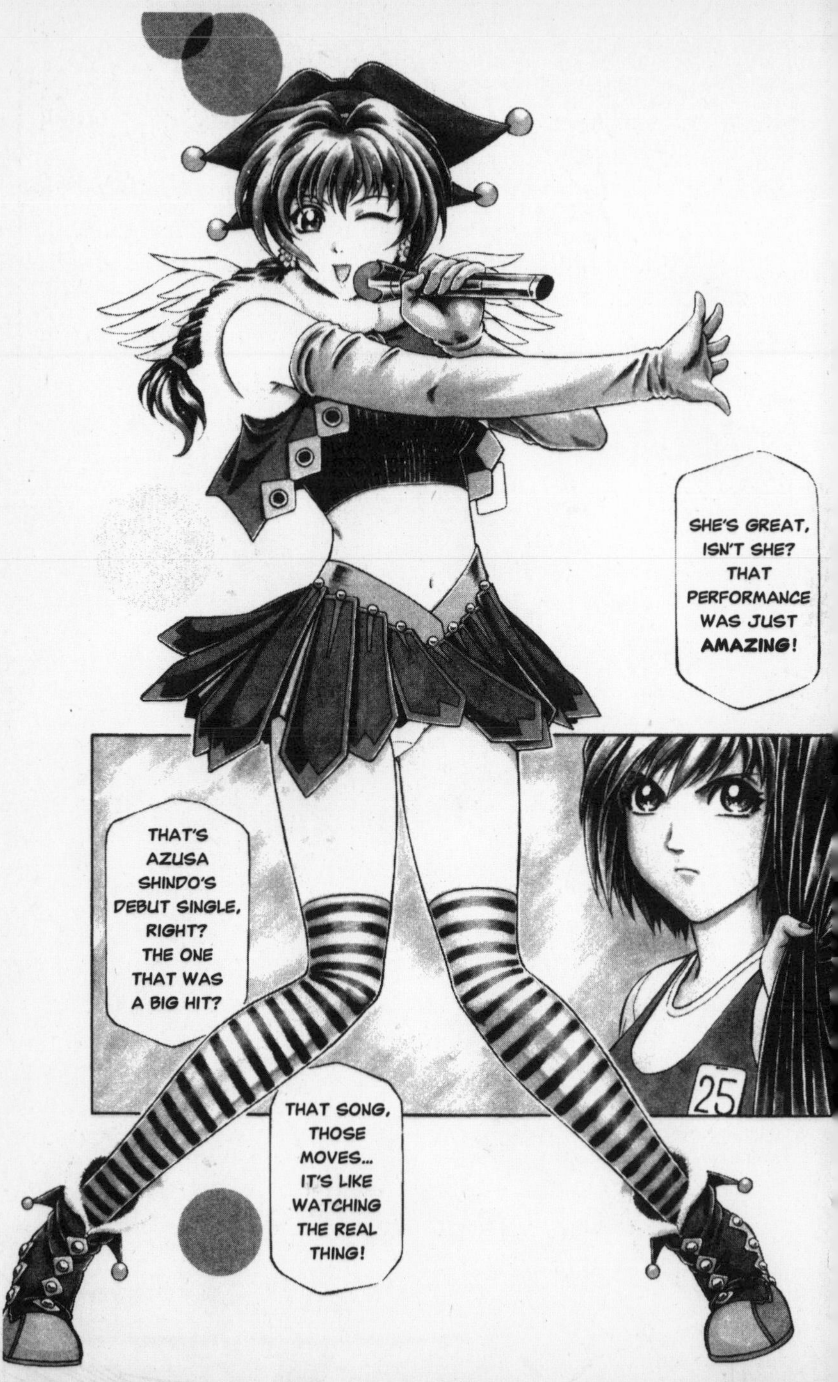
SHE'S GREAT, ISN'T SHE? THAT PERFORMANCE WAS JUST AMAZING!
THAT'S AZUSA SHINDO'S DEBUT SINGLE, RIGHT? THE ONE THAT WAS A BIG HIT?
THAT SONG, THOSE MOVES... IT'S LIKE WATCHING THE REAL THING!

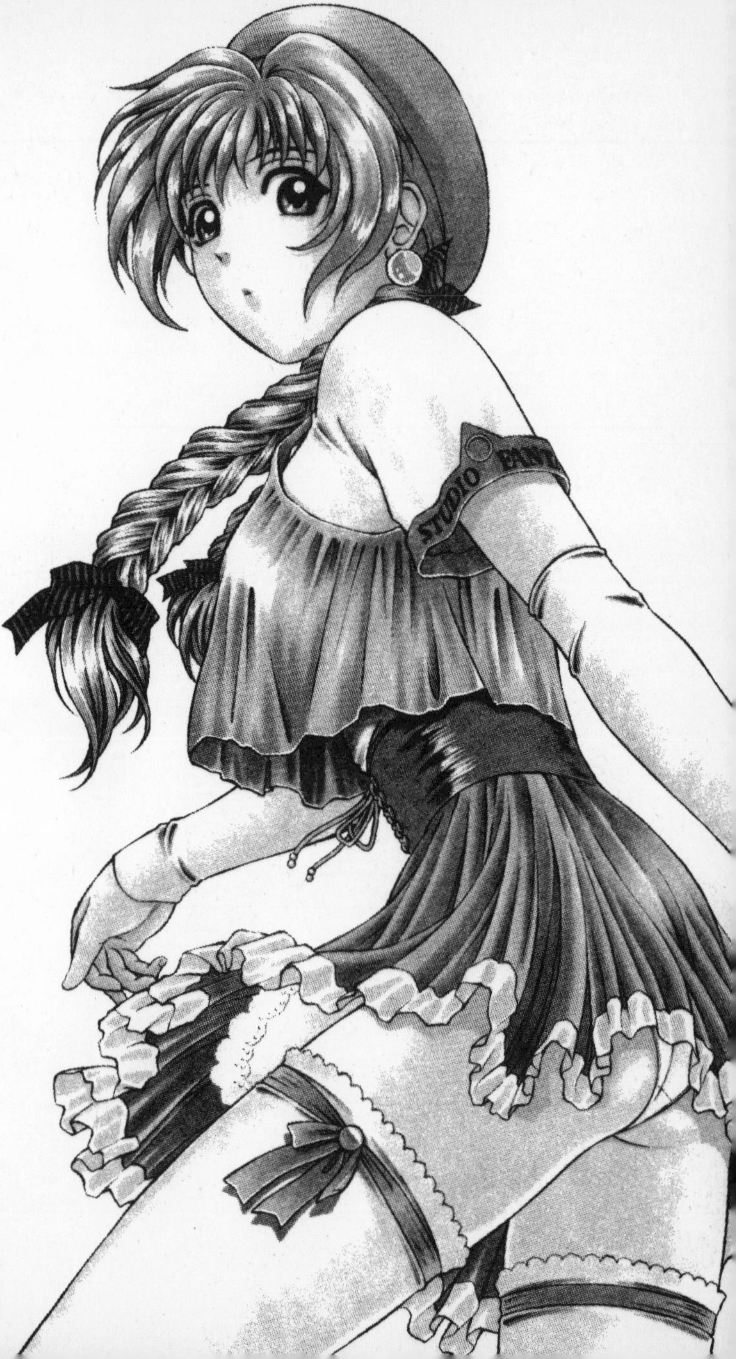
STUDIO

Operation. 10
TOP IDOL

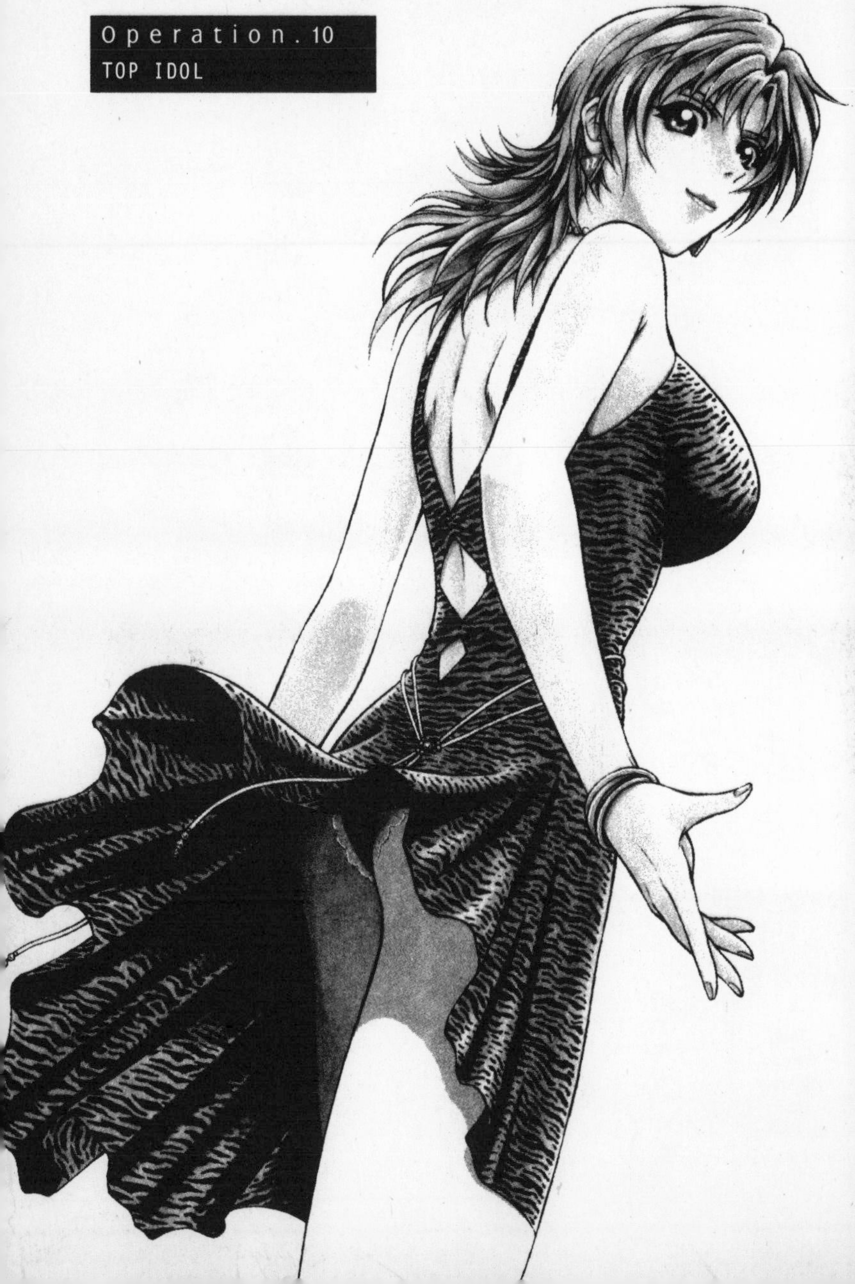

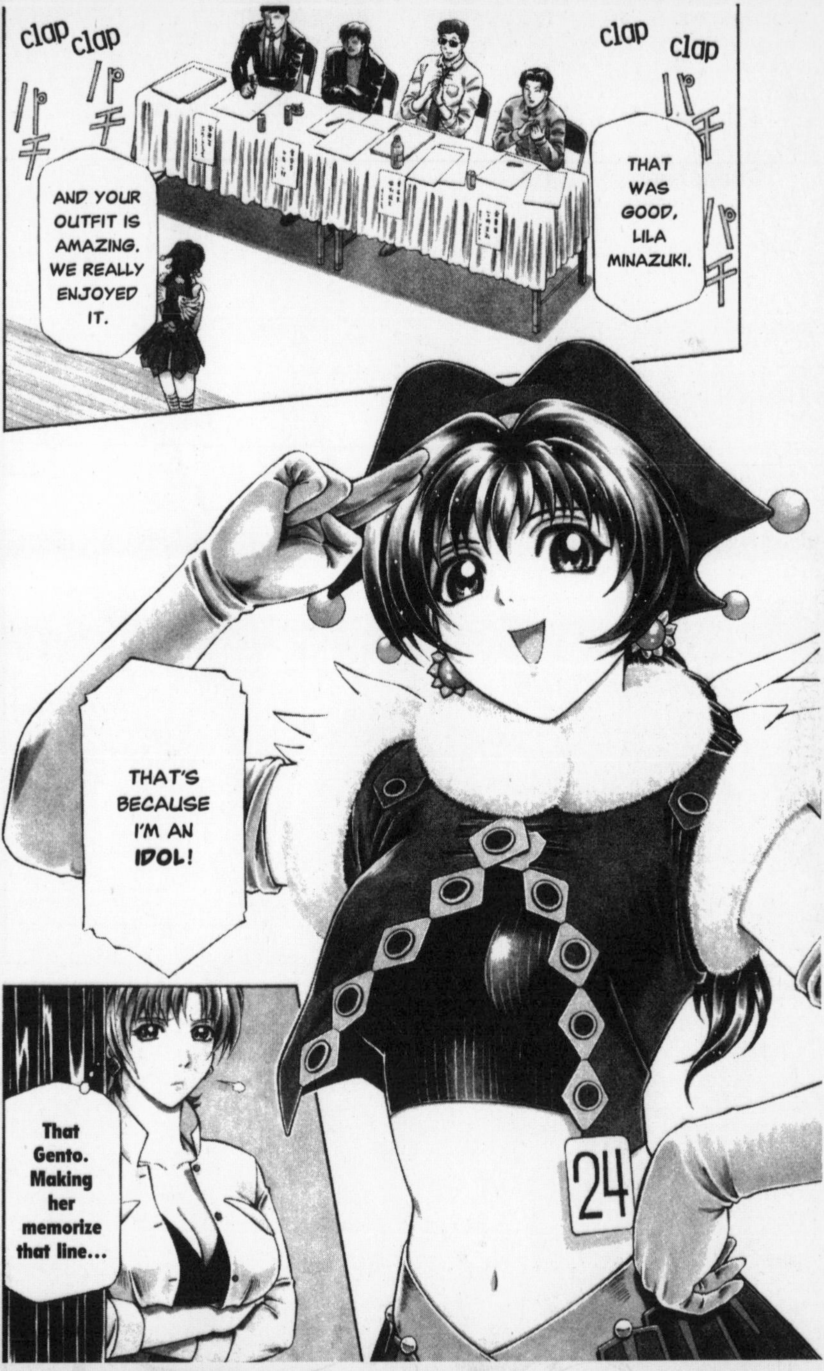

clap
clap
パチ
パチ
THAT WAS GOOD, LILA MINAZUKI.
AND YOUR OUTFIT IS AMAZING. WE REALLY ENJOYED IT.
clap
clap
パチ
パチ
THAT'S BECAUSE I'M AN IDOL!
24
That Gento. Making her memorize that line...

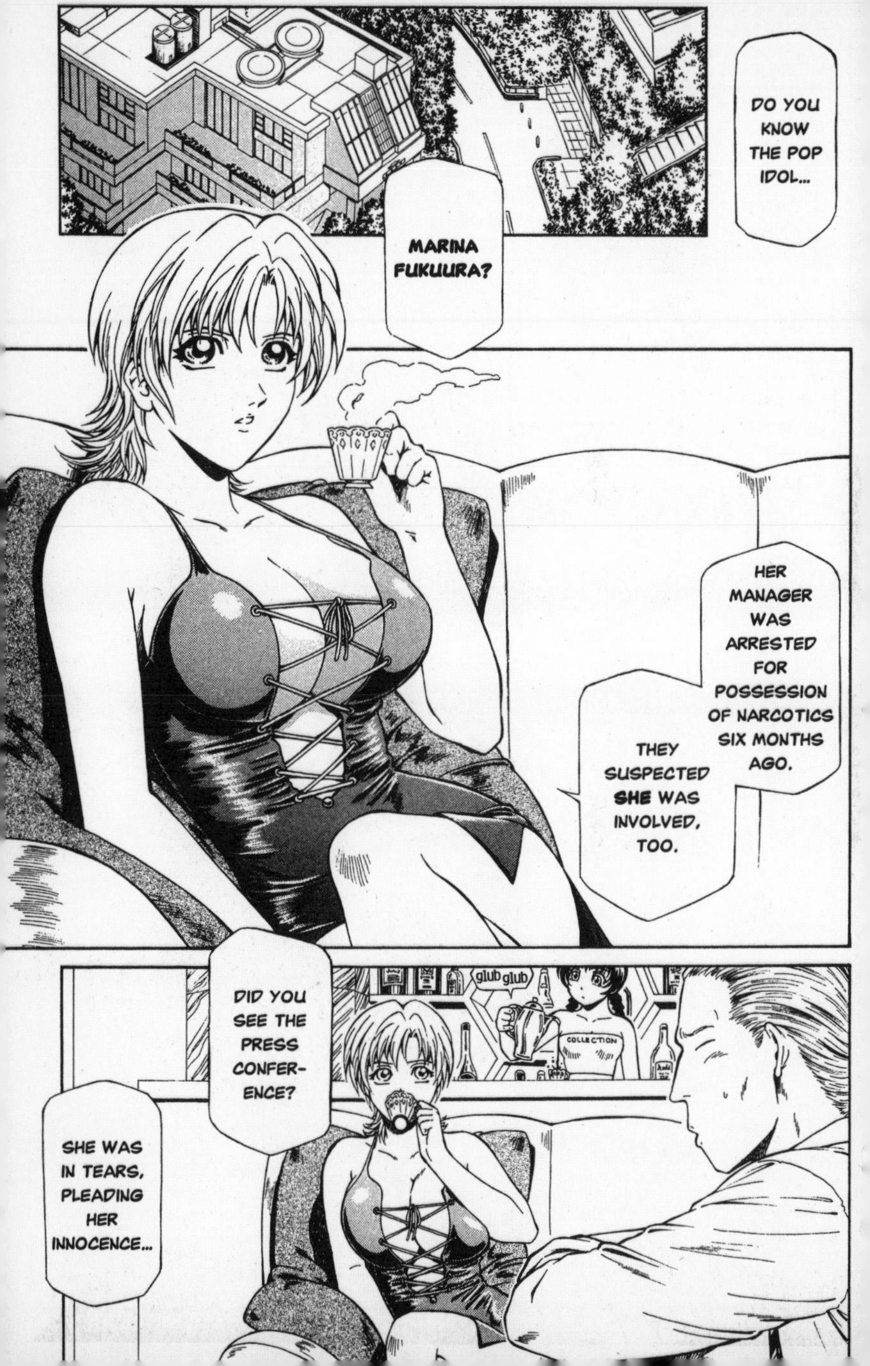
DO YOU KNOW THE POP IDOL...
MARINA FUKUURA?
HER MANAGER WAS ARRESTED FOR POSSESSION OF NARCOTICS SIX MONTHS AGO.
THEY SUSPECTED **SHE** WAS INVOLVED, TOO.
glub glub
COLLECTION
DID YOU SEE THE PRESS CONFERENCE?
SHE WAS IN TEARS, PLEADING HER INNOCENCE...

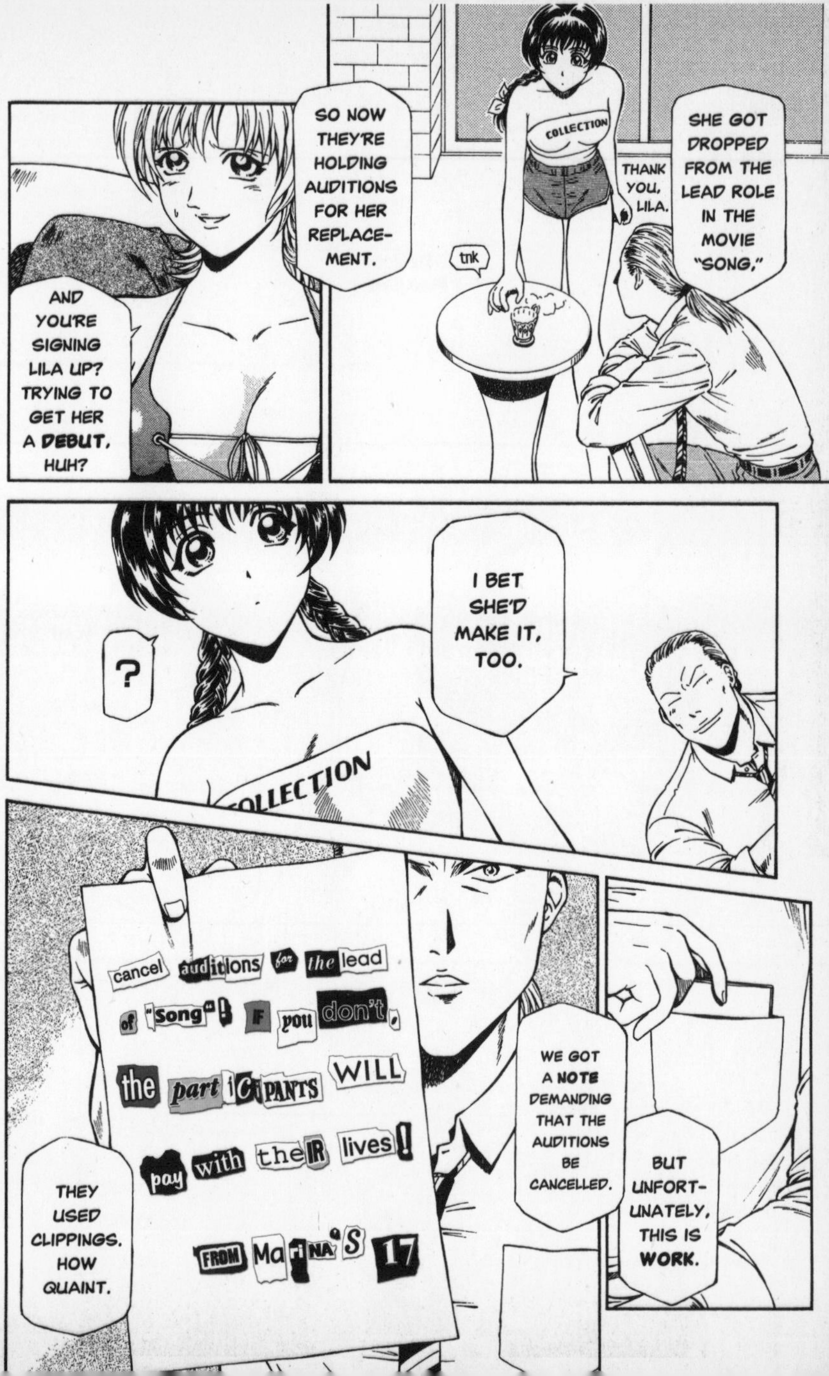
SHE GOT DROPPED FROM THE LEAD ROLE IN THE MOVIE "SONG,"
THANK YOU, LILA.
tnk
SO NOW THEY'RE HOLDING AUDITIONS FOR HER REPLACE-MENT.
AND YOU'RE SIGNING LILA UP? TRYING TO GET HER A **DEBUT**, HUH?
I BET SHE'D MAKE IT, TOO.
?
COLLECTION
WE GOT A **NOTE** DEMANDING THAT THE AUDITIONS BE CANCELLED.
BUT UNFORT-UNATELY, THIS IS **WORK**.
cancel auditions for the lead
of "Song"! If you don't,
the participants WILL
pay with theIR lives!
FROM Marina'S 17
THEY USED CLIPPINGS. HOW QUAINT.

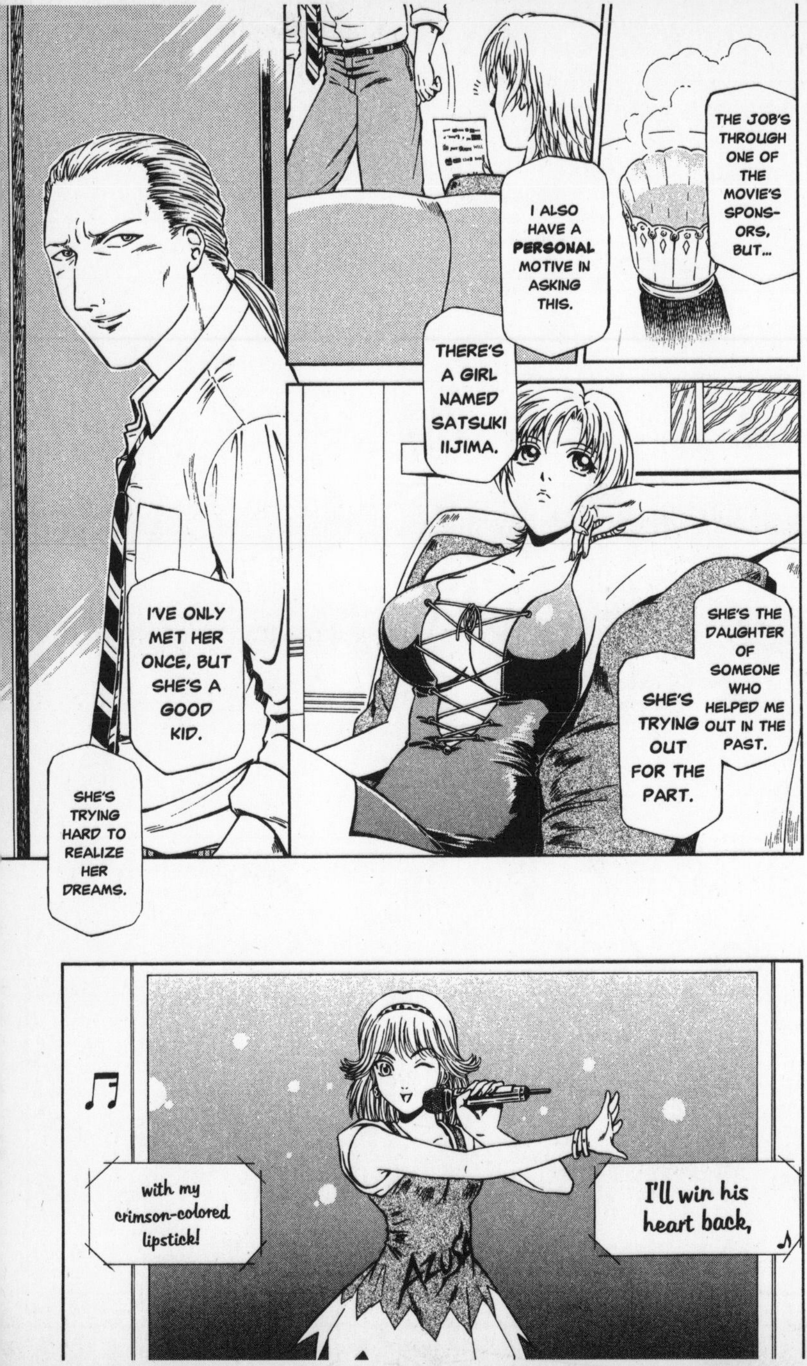
THE JOB'S THROUGH ONE OF THE MOVIE'S SPONSORS, BUT...
I ALSO HAVE A **PERSONAL** MOTIVE IN ASKING THIS.
THERE'S A GIRL NAMED SATSUKI IIJIMA.
SHE'S THE DAUGHTER OF SOMEONE WHO HELPED ME OUT IN THE PAST.
SHE'S TRYING OUT FOR THE PART.
I'VE ONLY MET HER ONCE, BUT SHE'S A GOOD KID.
SHE'S TRYING HARD TO REALIZE HER DREAMS.
I'll win his heart back,
with my crimson-colored lipstick!
AZUSA

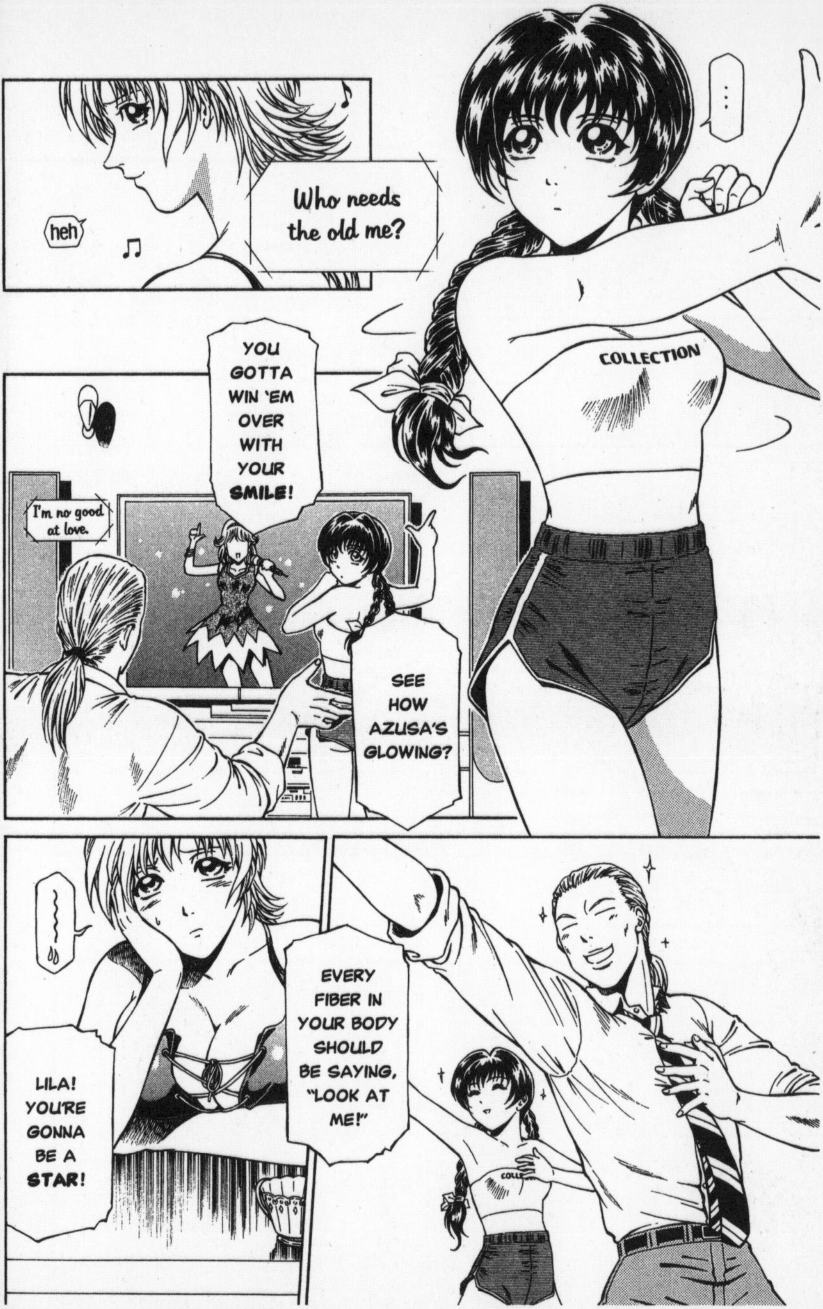
...
COLLECTION
Who needs the old me?
heh
YOU GOTTA WIN 'EM OVER WITH YOUR **SMILE!**
SEE HOW AZUSA'S GLOWING?
I'm no good at love.
EVERY FIBER IN YOUR BODY SHOULD BE SAYING, "LOOK AT ME!"
LILA! YOU'RE GONNA BE A **STAR!**

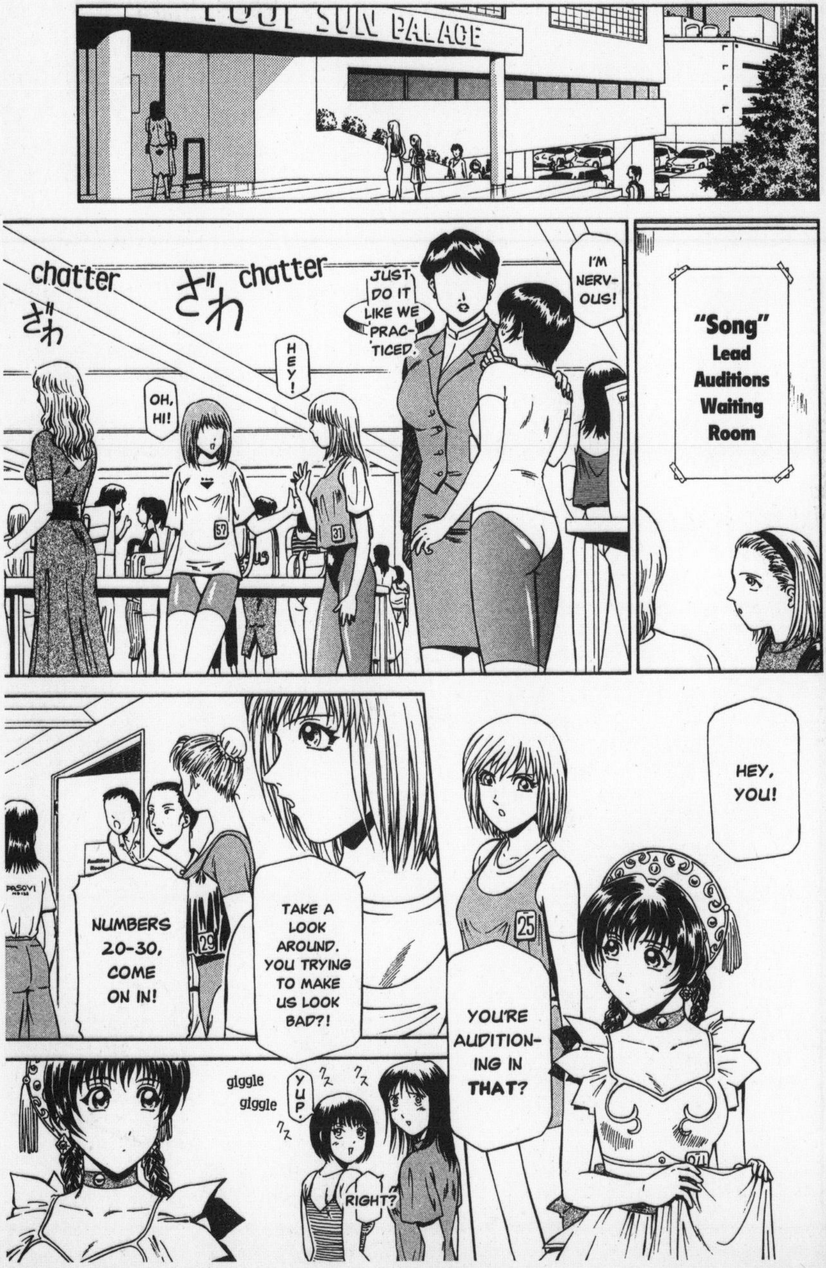
SUN PALACE
"Song" Lead Auditions Waiting Room
I'M NERV-OUS!
JUST DO IT LIKE WE PRAC-TICED.
HEY!
OH, HI!
chatter ざわ
chatter ざわ
HEY, YOU!
YOU'RE AUDITION-ING IN THAT?
TAKE A LOOK AROUND. YOU TRYING TO MAKE US LOOK BAD?!
NUMBERS 20-30, COME ON IN!
YUP.
クス クス
giggle giggle
クス
RIGHT?

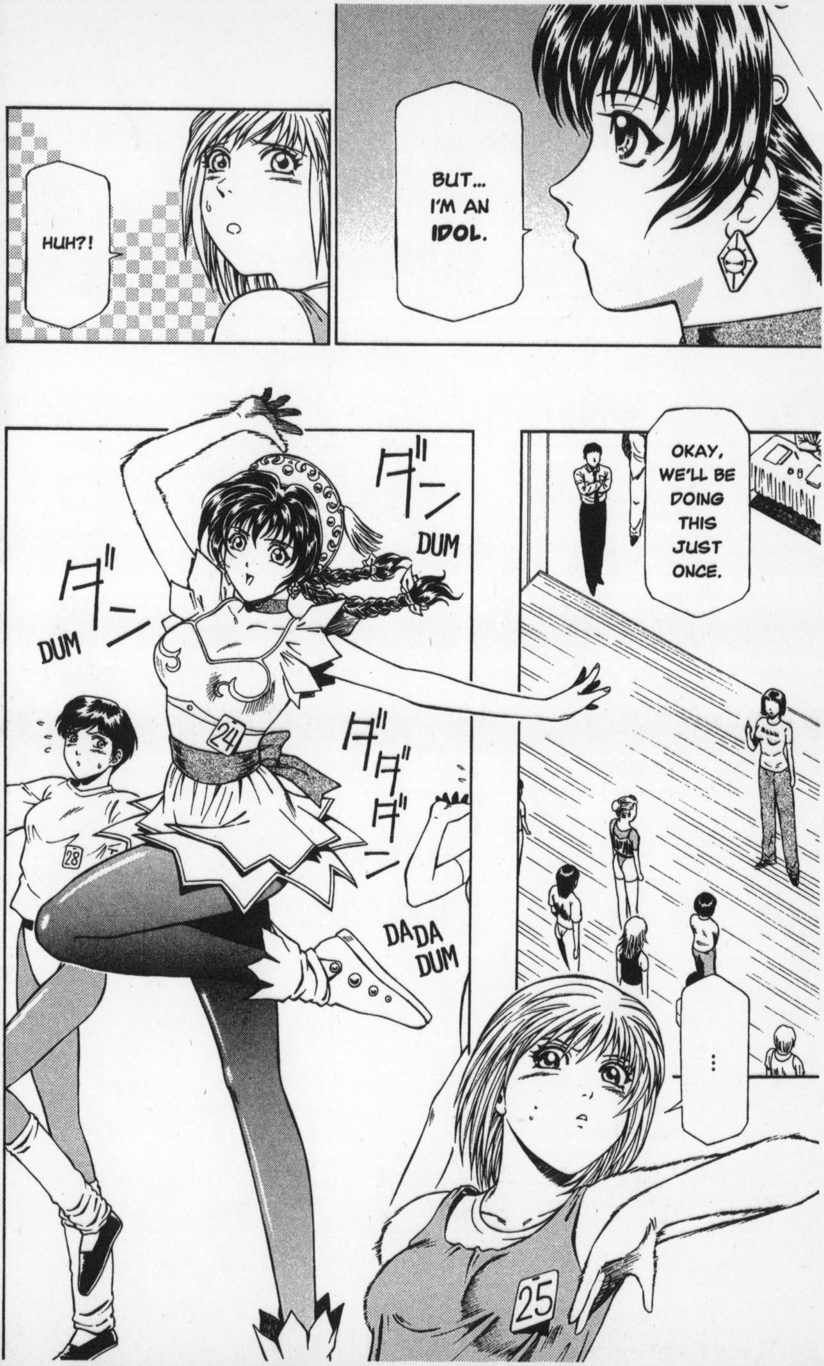
BUT... I'M AN IDOL.
HUH?!
OKAY, WE'LL BE DOING THIS JUST ONCE.
...
ダン
DUM
ダン
DUM
ダダダン
DADA DUM

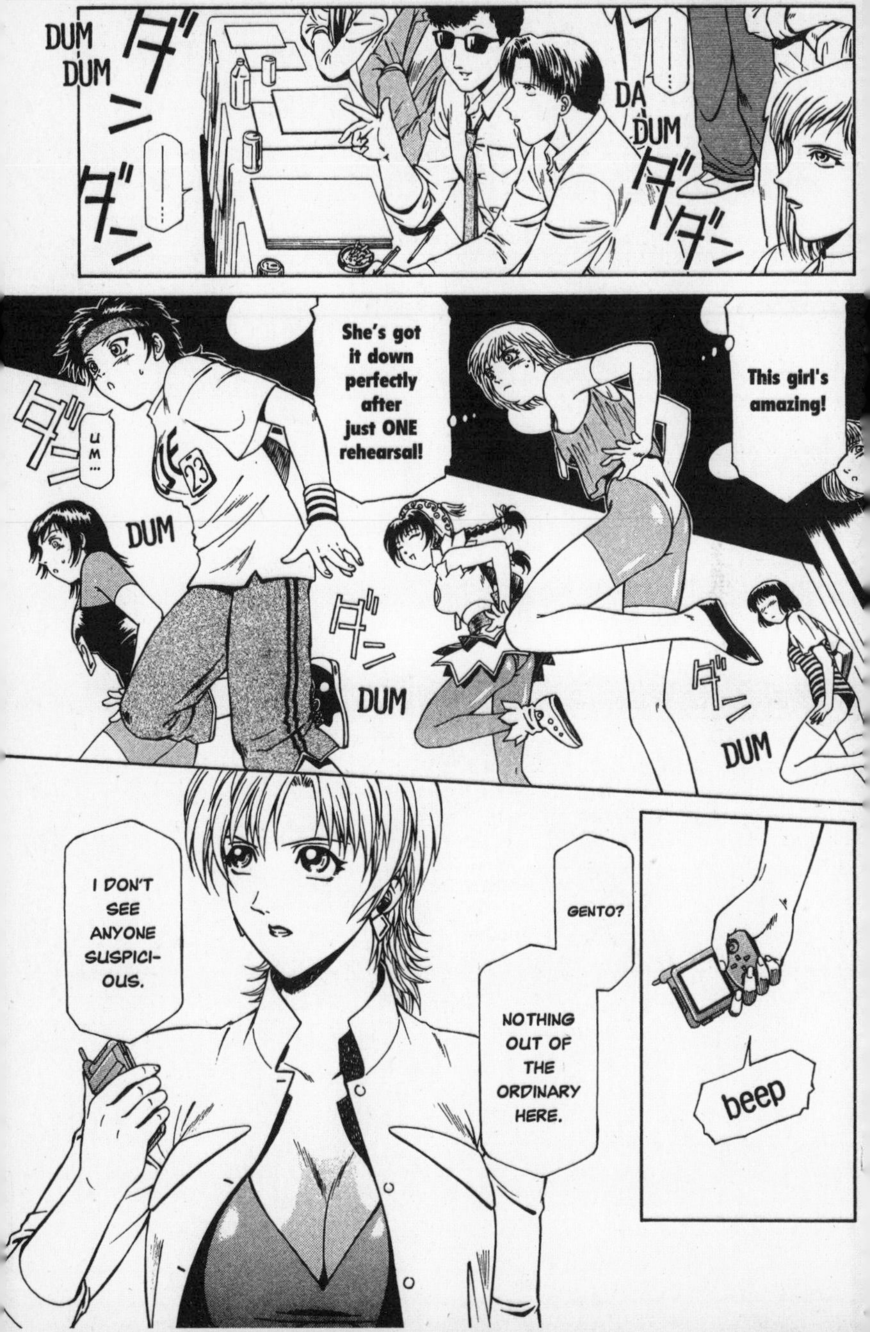
DA DUM
ダダン
DUM DUM
ダンダン
This girl's amazing!
She's got it down perfectly after just ONE rehearsal!
ダン
UM...
DUM
ダン
DUM
ダン
DUM
beep
GENTO?
NOTHING OUT OF THE ORDINARY HERE.
I DON'T SEE ANYONE SUSPICI-OUS.

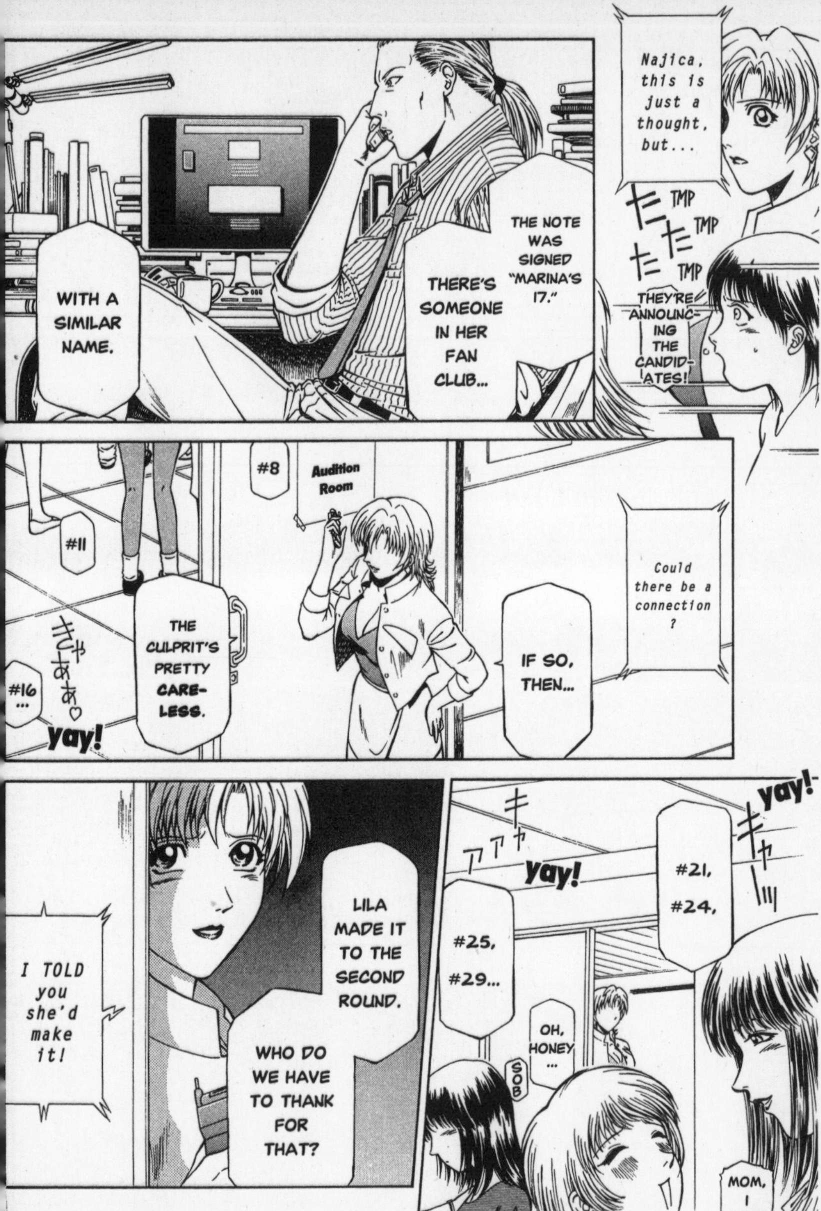
Najica, this is just a thought, but...
たたた
TMP TMP TMP
THEY'RE ANNOUNC-ING THE CANDID-ATES!
THE NOTE WAS SIGNED "MARINA'S 17."
THERE'S SOMEONE IN HER FAN CLUB...
WITH A SIMILAR NAME.
Could there be a connection ?
IF SO, THEN...
#8
Audition Room
THE CULPRIT'S PRETTY CARE-LESS.
#11
#16 ...
きゃあぁ♡
yay!
yay!
#21, #24,
yay!
#25, #29...
OH, HONEY ...
SOB
MOM, I MADE IT!
13
LILA MADE IT TO THE SECOND ROUND.
WHO DO WE HAVE TO THANK FOR THAT?
I TOLD you she'd make it!

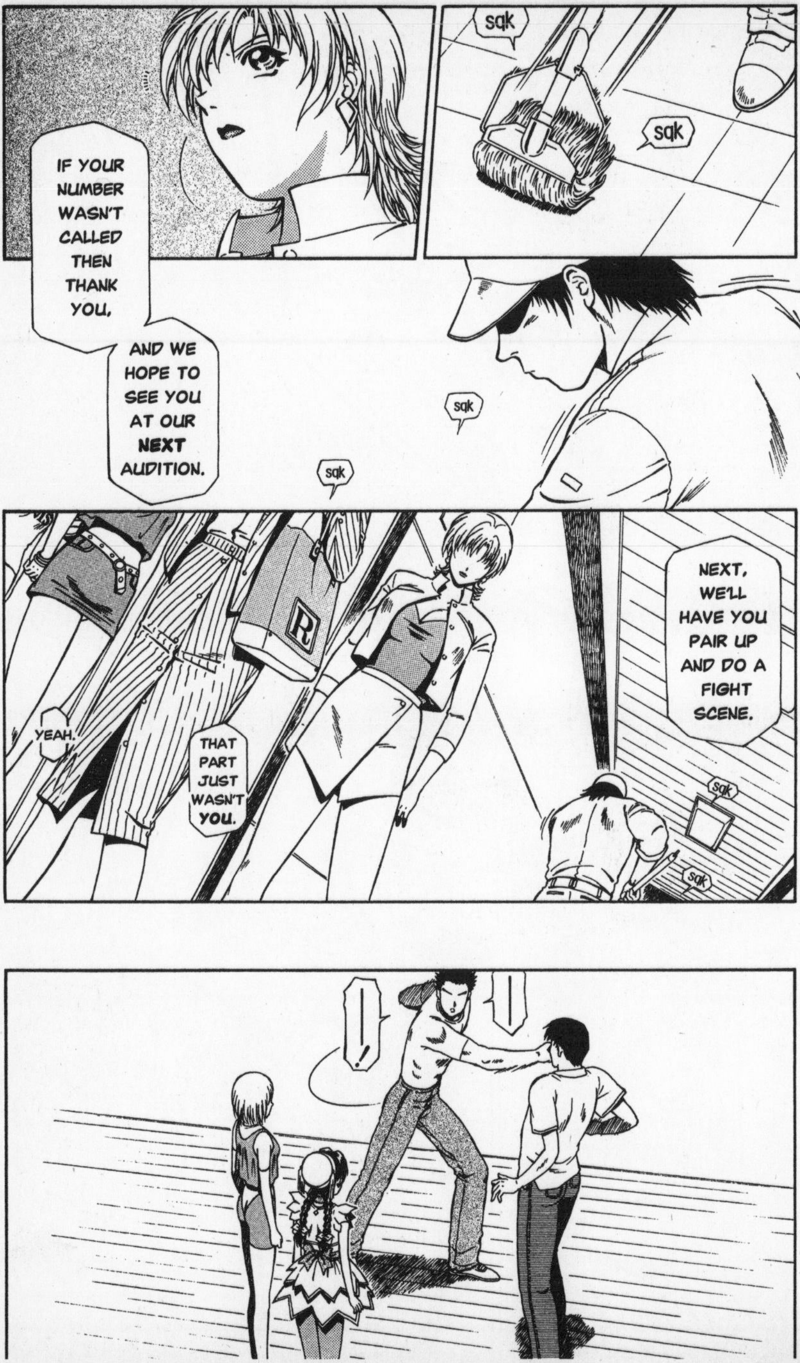
sqk
sqk
IF YOUR NUMBER WASN'T CALLED THEN THANK YOU,
AND WE HOPE TO SEE YOU AT OUR NEXT AUDITION.
sqk
sqk
NEXT, WE'LL HAVE YOU PAIR UP AND DO A FIGHT SCENE.
sqk
sqk
THAT PART JUST WASN'T YOU.
YEAH.
!
!

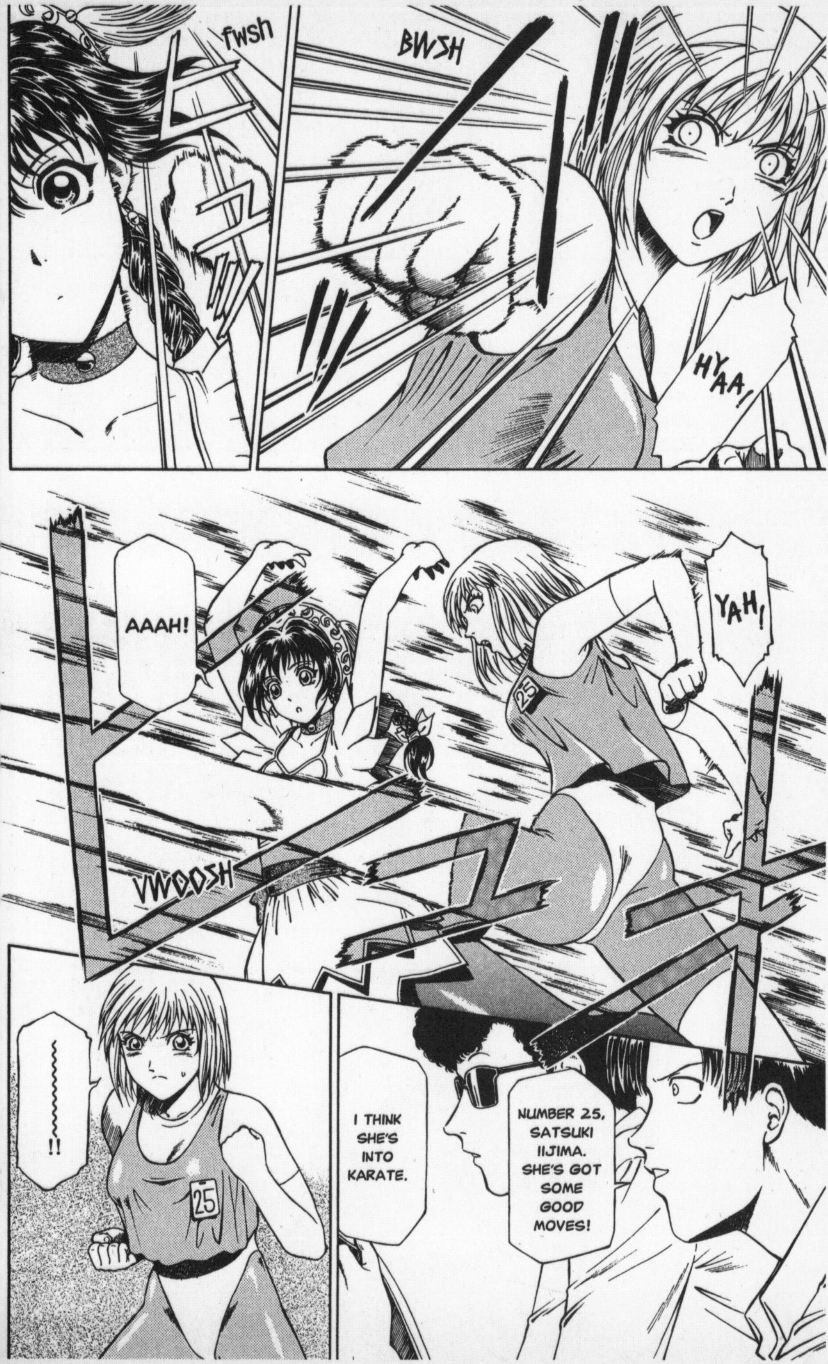
BWSH
fwsh
HYAA!
YAH!
AAAH!
VWOOSH
NUMBER 25, SATSUKI IIJIMA. SHE'S GOT SOME GOOD MOVES!
I THINK SHE'S INTO KARATE.
~~~~~!!
~~~~~

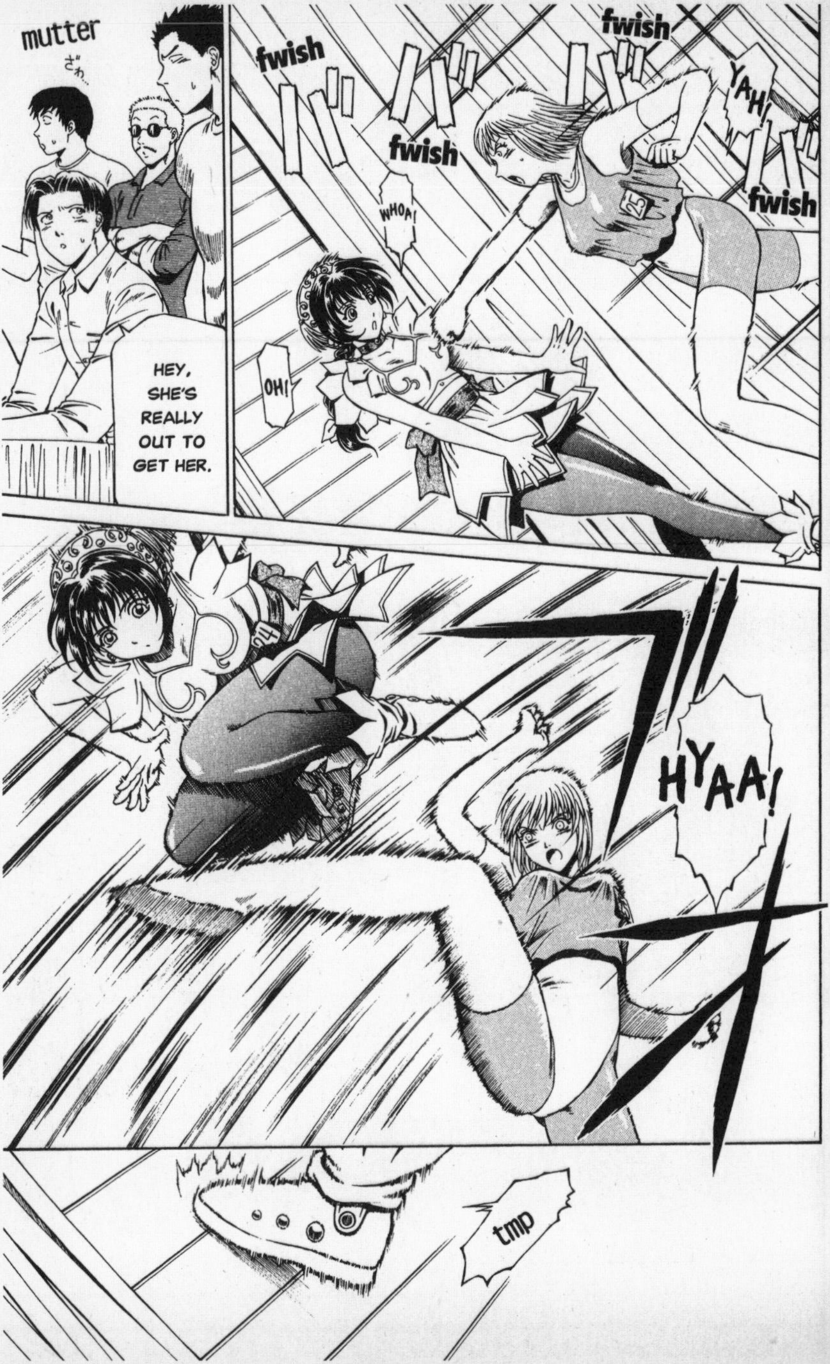
fwish
YAH!
fwish
fwish
fwish
WHOA!
OH!
mutter
ざわ…
HEY, SHE'S REALLY OUT TO GET HER.
HYAA!
tmp

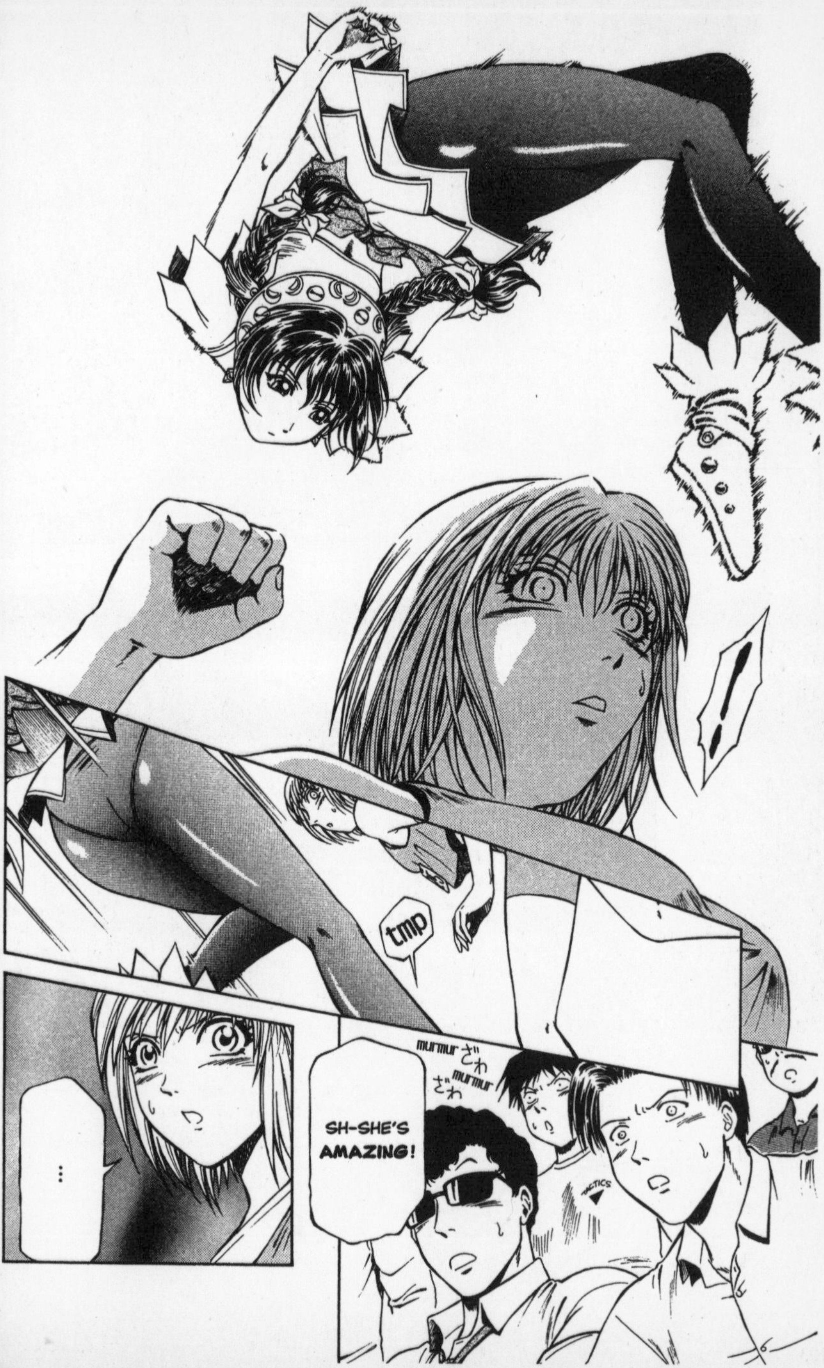

tmp
murmur ざわ murmur ざわ
SH-SHE'S AMAZING!
...

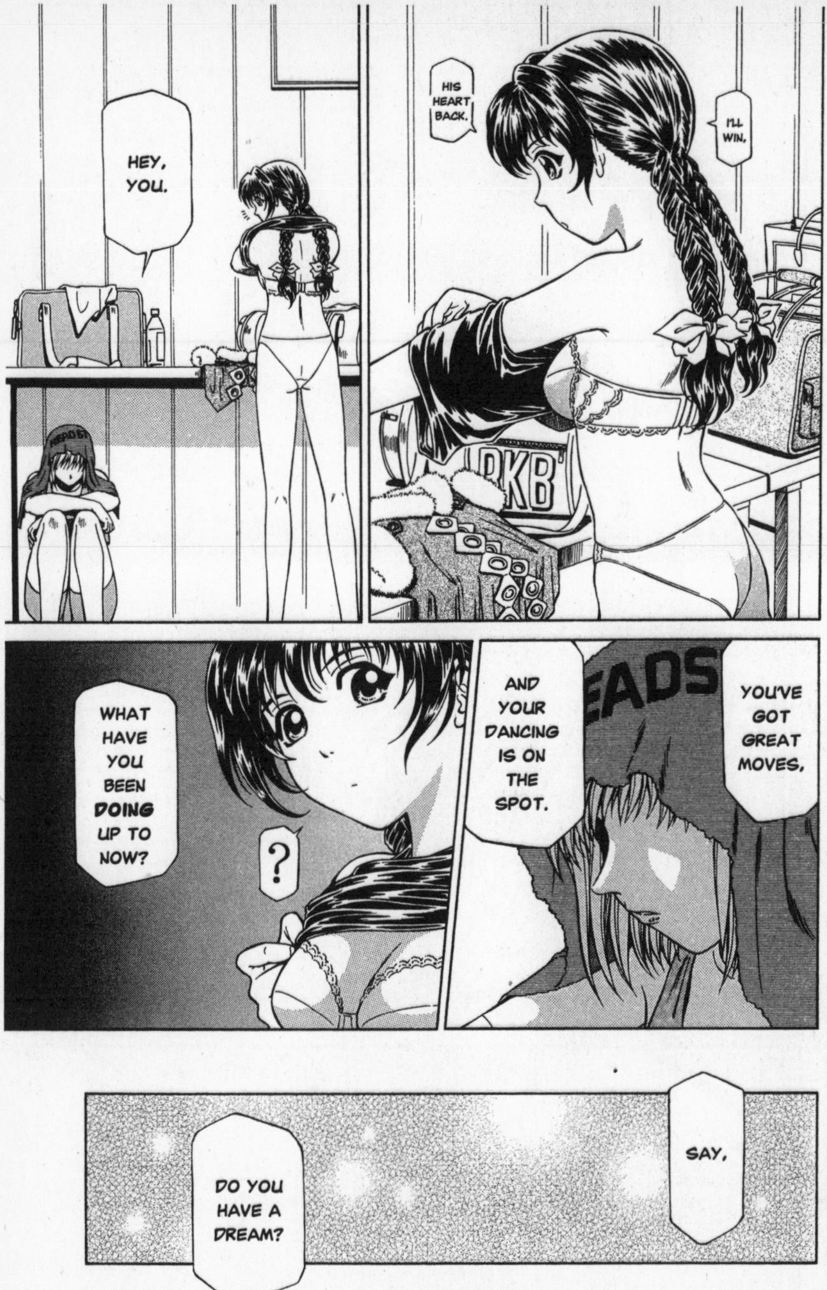
I'LL WIN,
HIS HEART BACK.
HEY, YOU.
YOU'VE GOT GREAT MOVES,
AND YOUR DANCING IS ON THE SPOT.
WHAT HAVE YOU BEEN DOING UP TO NOW?
?
RKB
SAY,
DO YOU HAVE A DREAM?

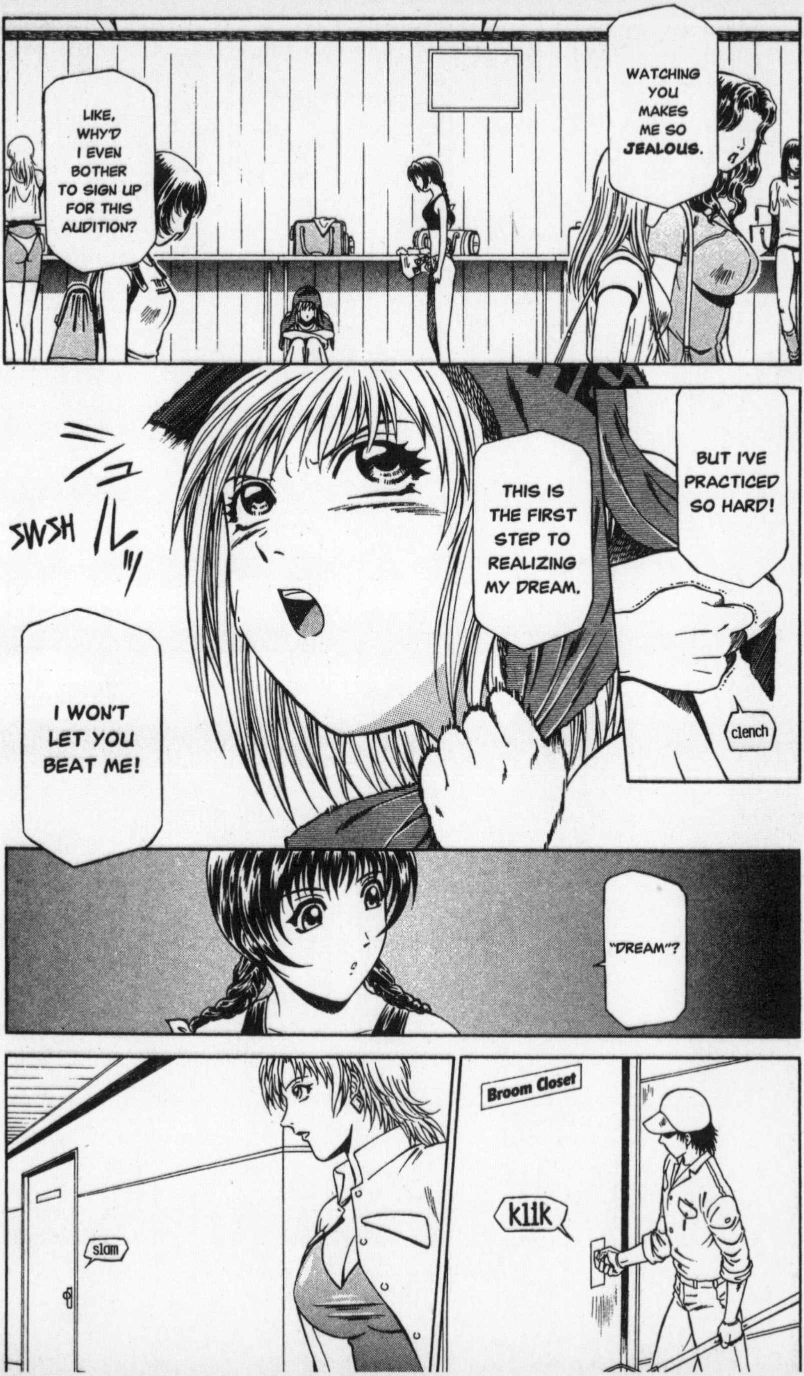
WATCHING YOU MAKES ME SO JEALOUS.
LIKE, WHY'D I EVEN BOTHER TO SIGN UP FOR THIS AUDITION?
BUT I'VE PRACTICED SO HARD!
clench
THIS IS THE FIRST STEP TO REALIZING MY DREAM.
SWSH
I WON'T LET YOU BEAT ME!
"DREAM"?
Broom Closet
klik
slam

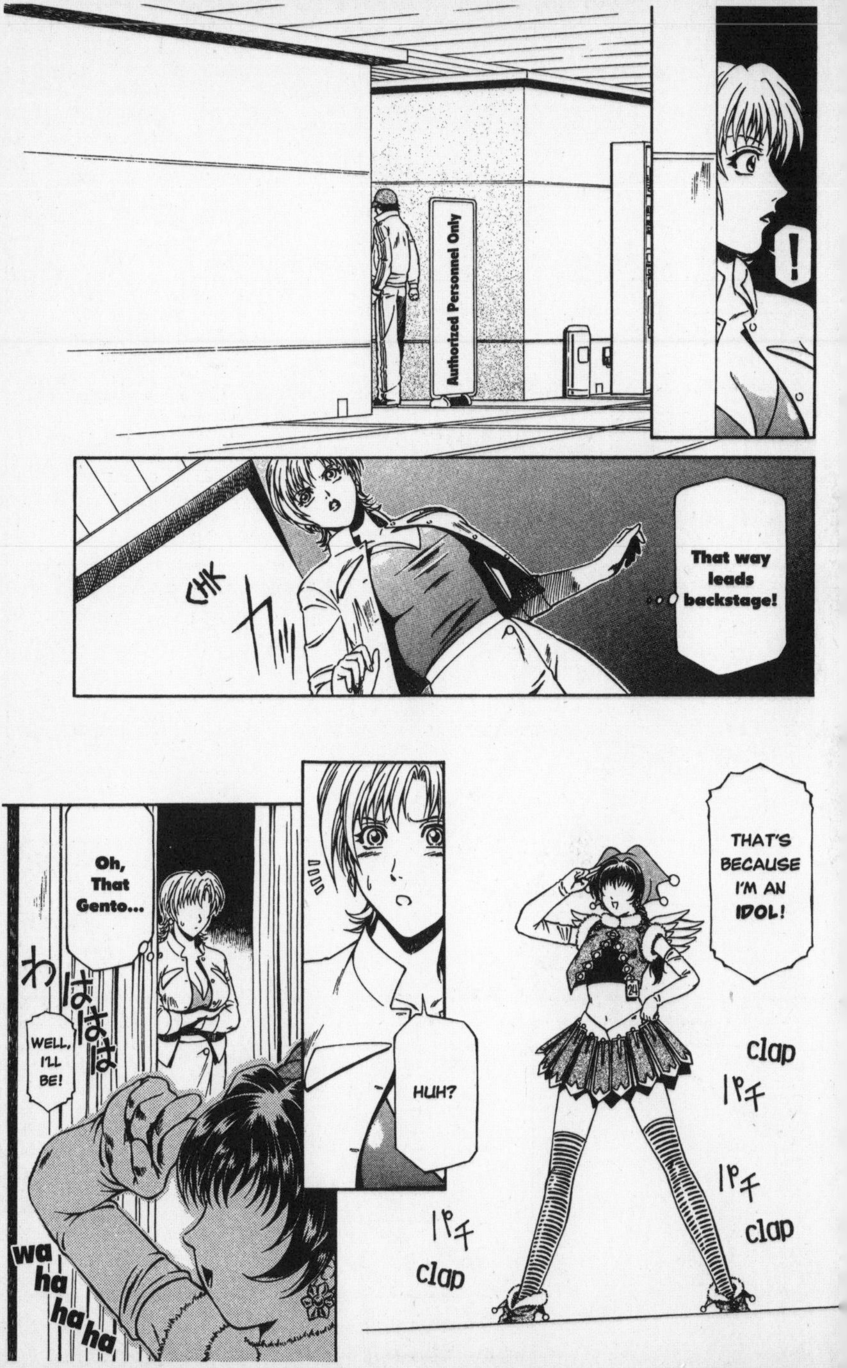
!
Authorized Personnel Only
That way leads backstage!
CHK
カッ
THAT'S BECAUSE I'M AN IDOL!
clap
パチ
パチ
clap
パチ
clap
HUH?
Oh, That Gento...
わははは
WELL, I'LL BE!
wa ha ha ha

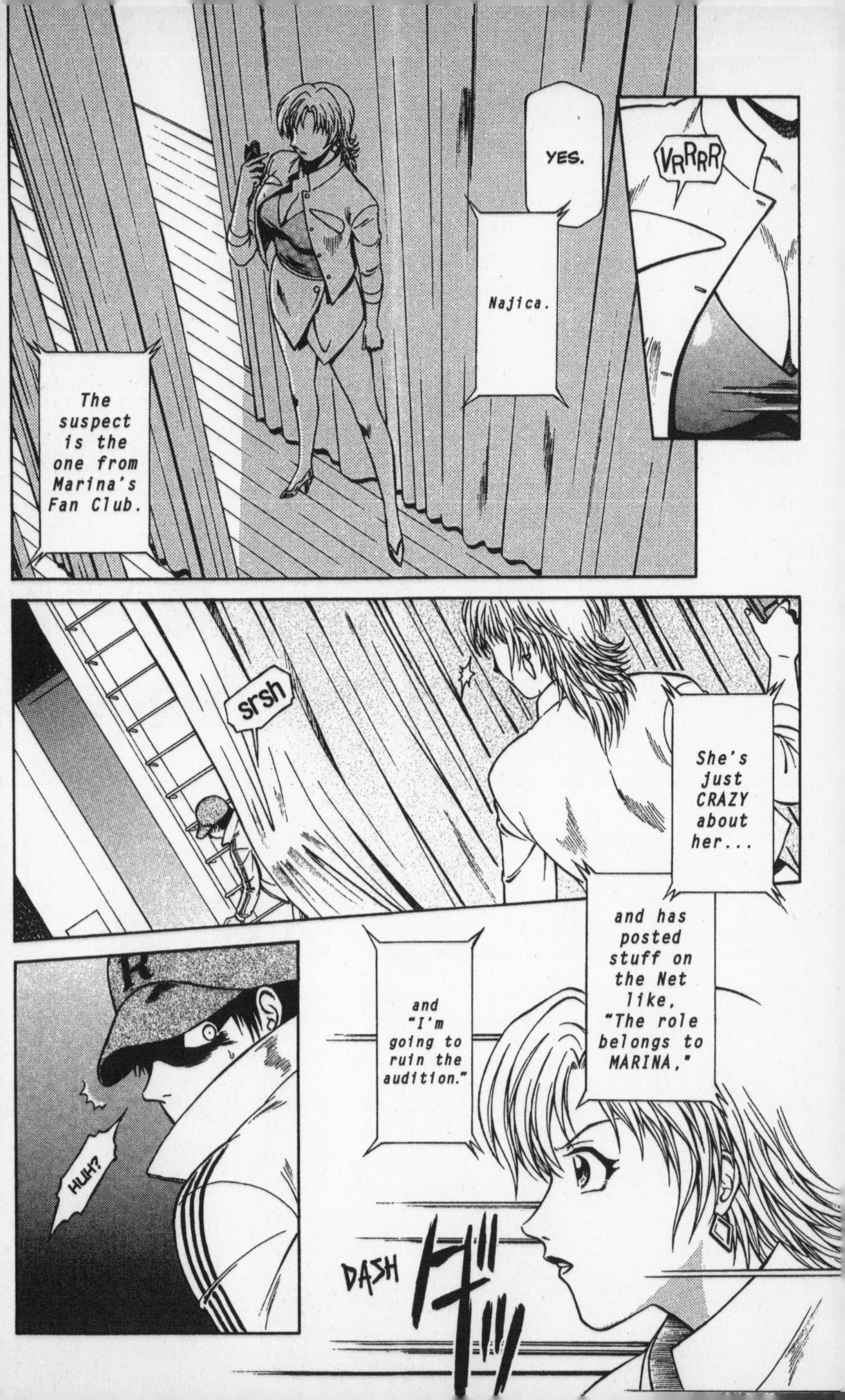
VRRRR
YES.
Najica.
The suspect is the one from Marina's Fan Club.
She's just CRAZY about her...
srsh
and has posted stuff on the Net like, "The role belongs to MARINA,"
and "I'm going to ruin the audition."
DASH
HUH?

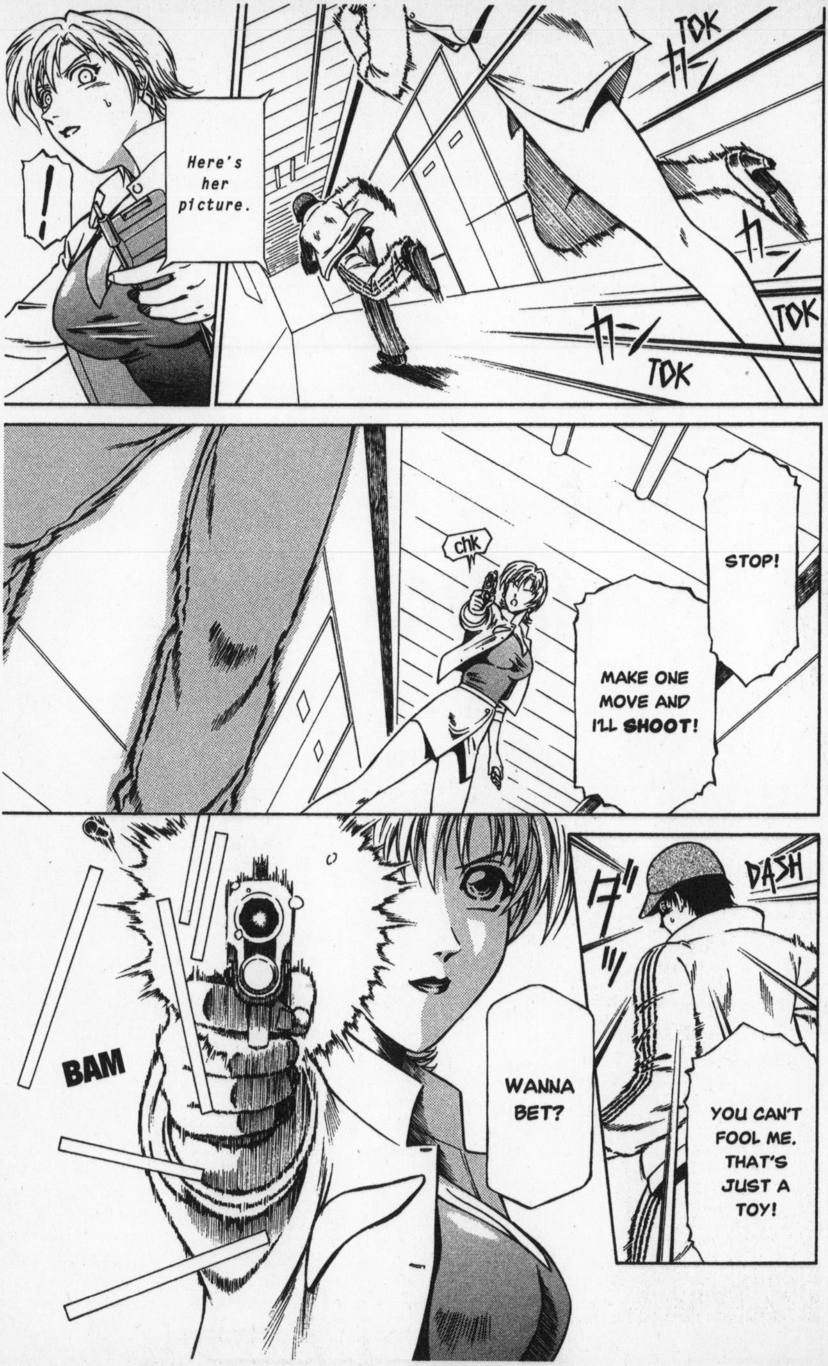
TOK
TOK
TOK
Here's her picture.
!
STOP!
MAKE ONE MOVE AND I'LL SHOOT!
chk
DASH
YOU CAN'T FOOL ME. THAT'S JUST A TOY!
WANNA BET?
BAM

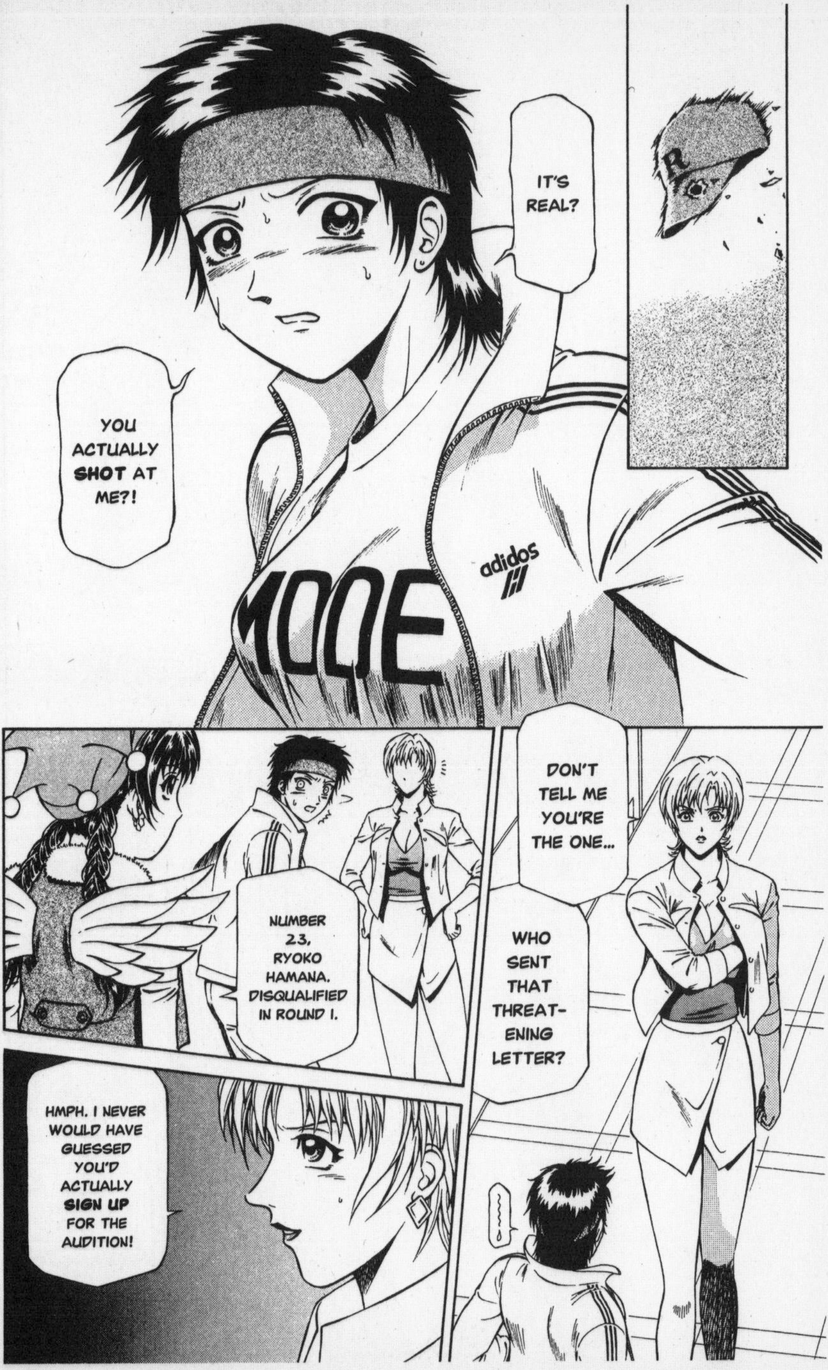

IT'S REAL?
YOU ACTUALLY SHOT AT ME?!
adidos
MOQE
DON'T TELL ME YOU'RE THE ONE...
WHO SENT THAT THREAT-ENING LETTER?
NUMBER 23, RYOKO HAMANA. DISQUALIFIED IN ROUND 1.
HMPH. I NEVER WOULD HAVE GUESSED YOU'D ACTUALLY SIGN UP FOR THE AUDITION!

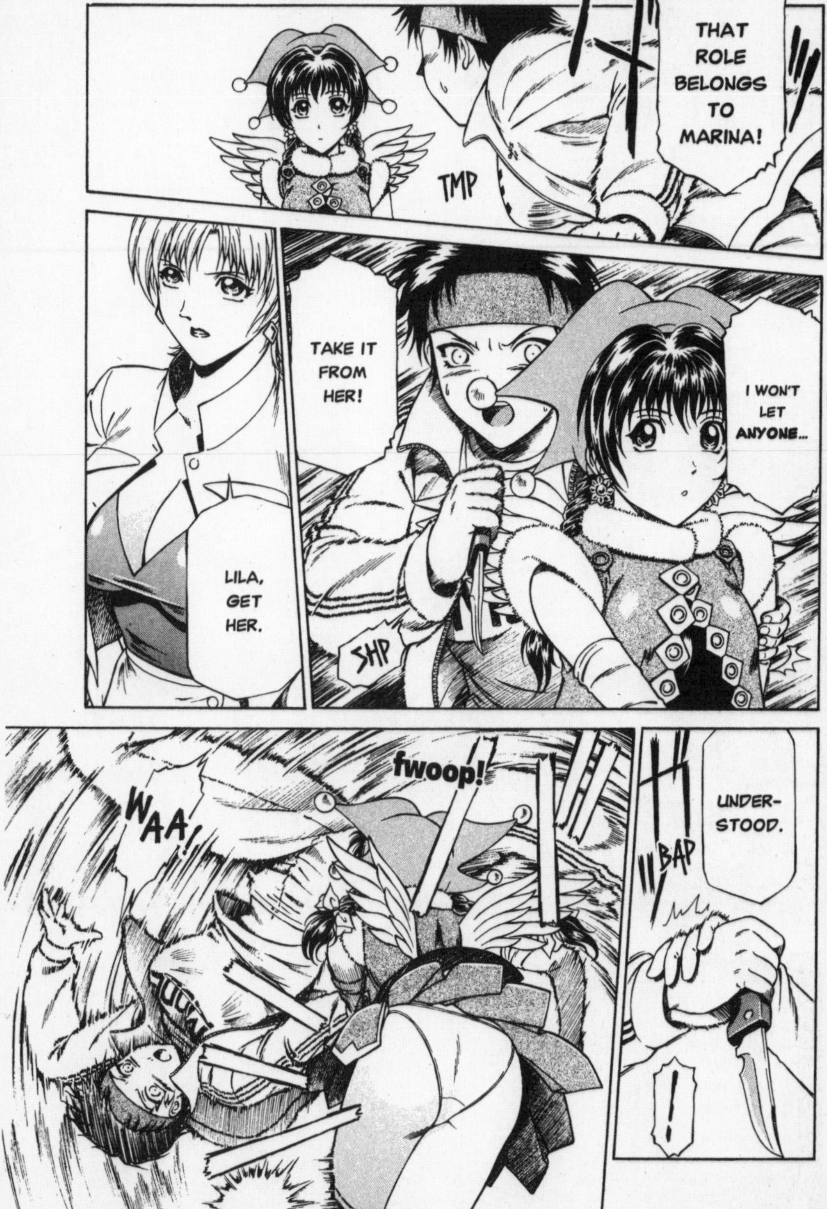
THAT ROLE BELONGS TO MARINA!
TMP
I WON'T LET ANYONE...
TAKE IT FROM HER!
SHP
LILA, GET HER.
UNDER-STOOD.
BAP
!
fwoop!
WAA!

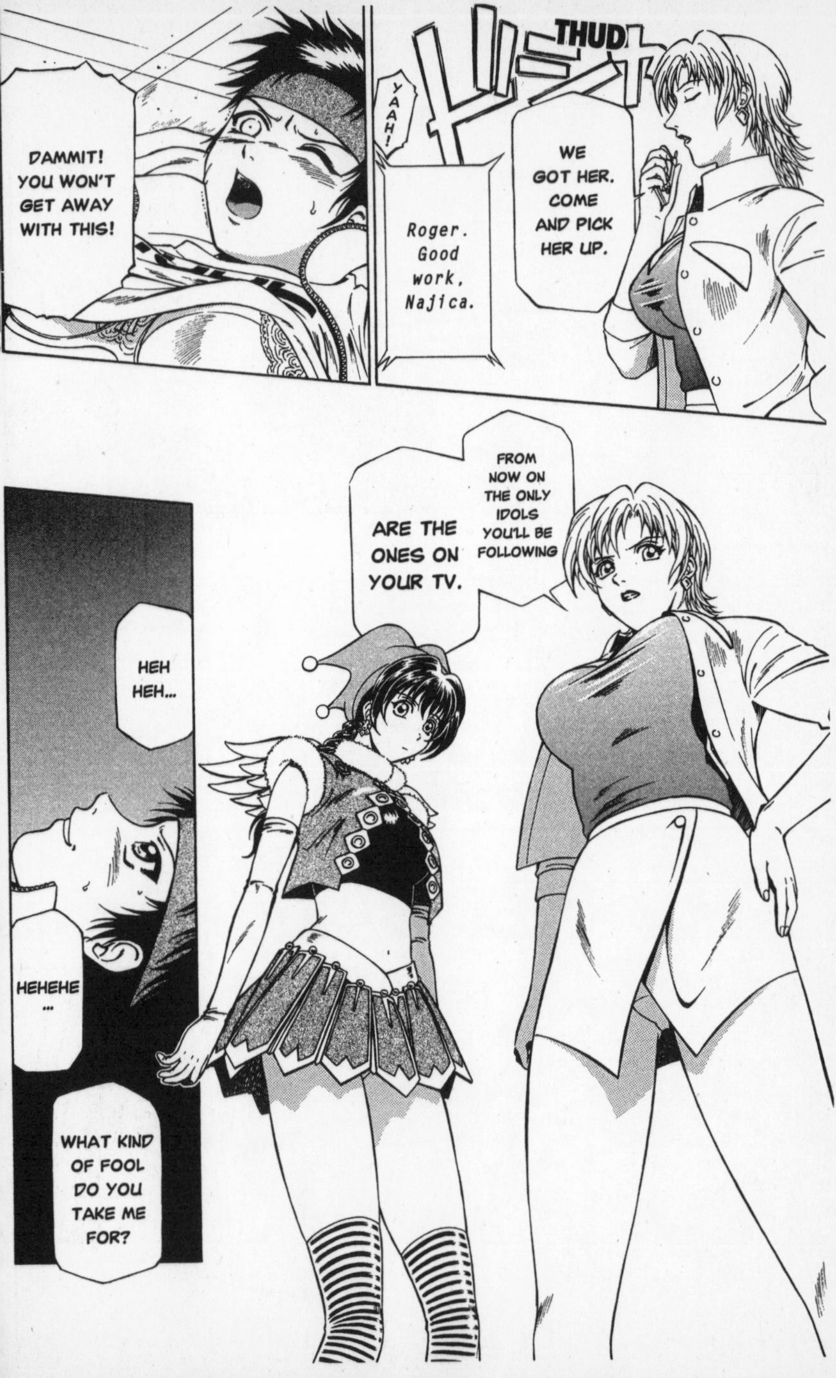
THUD
YAAH!
WE GOT HER. COME AND PICK HER UP.
Roger. Good work, Najica.
DAMMIT! YOU WON'T GET AWAY WITH THIS!
FROM NOW ON THE ONLY IDOLS YOU'LL BE FOLLOWING
ARE THE ONES ON YOUR TV.
HEH HEH...
HEHEHE ...
WHAT KIND OF FOOL DO YOU TAKE ME FOR?

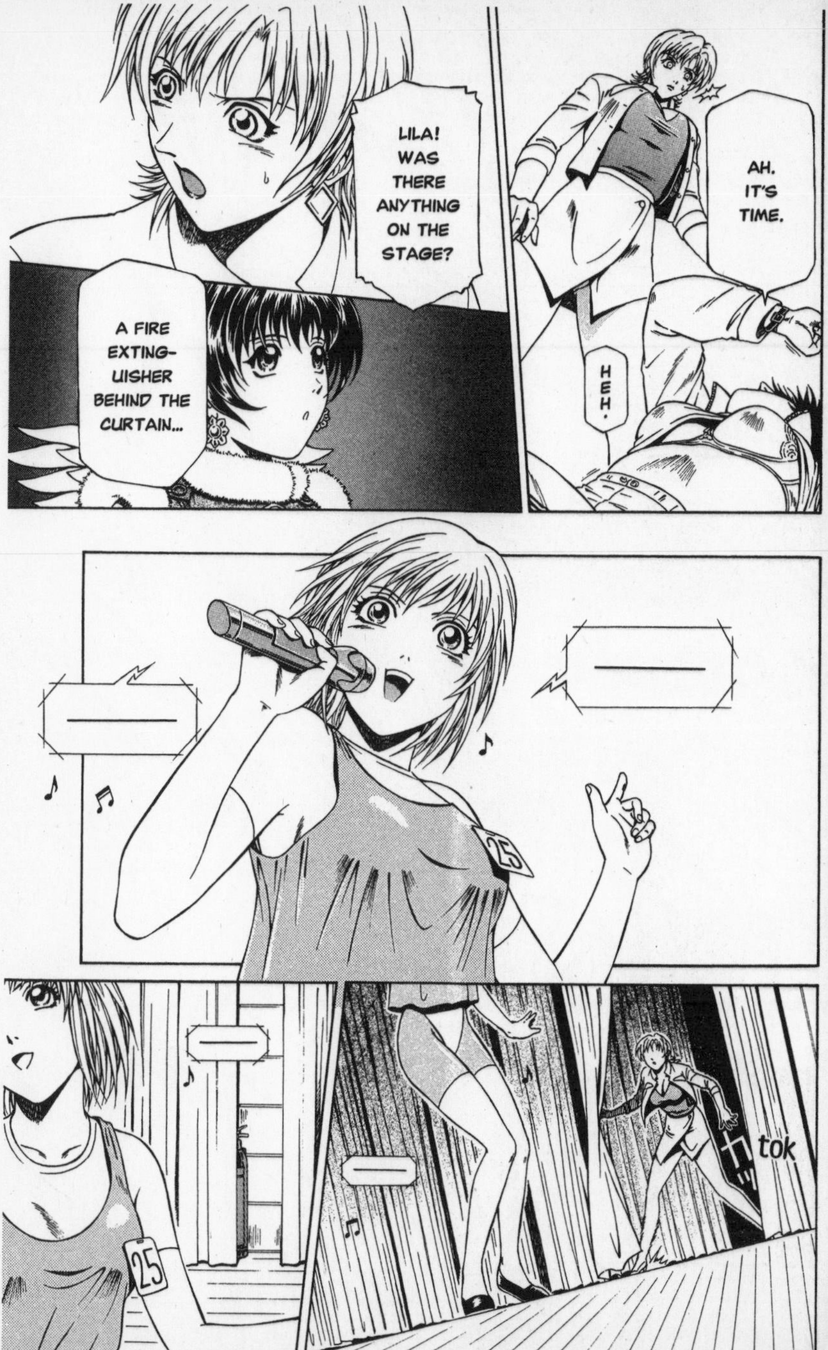
AH. IT'S TIME.
HEH.
LILA! WAS THERE ANYTHING ON THE STAGE?
A FIRE EXTING-UISHER BEHIND THE CURTAIN...
tok

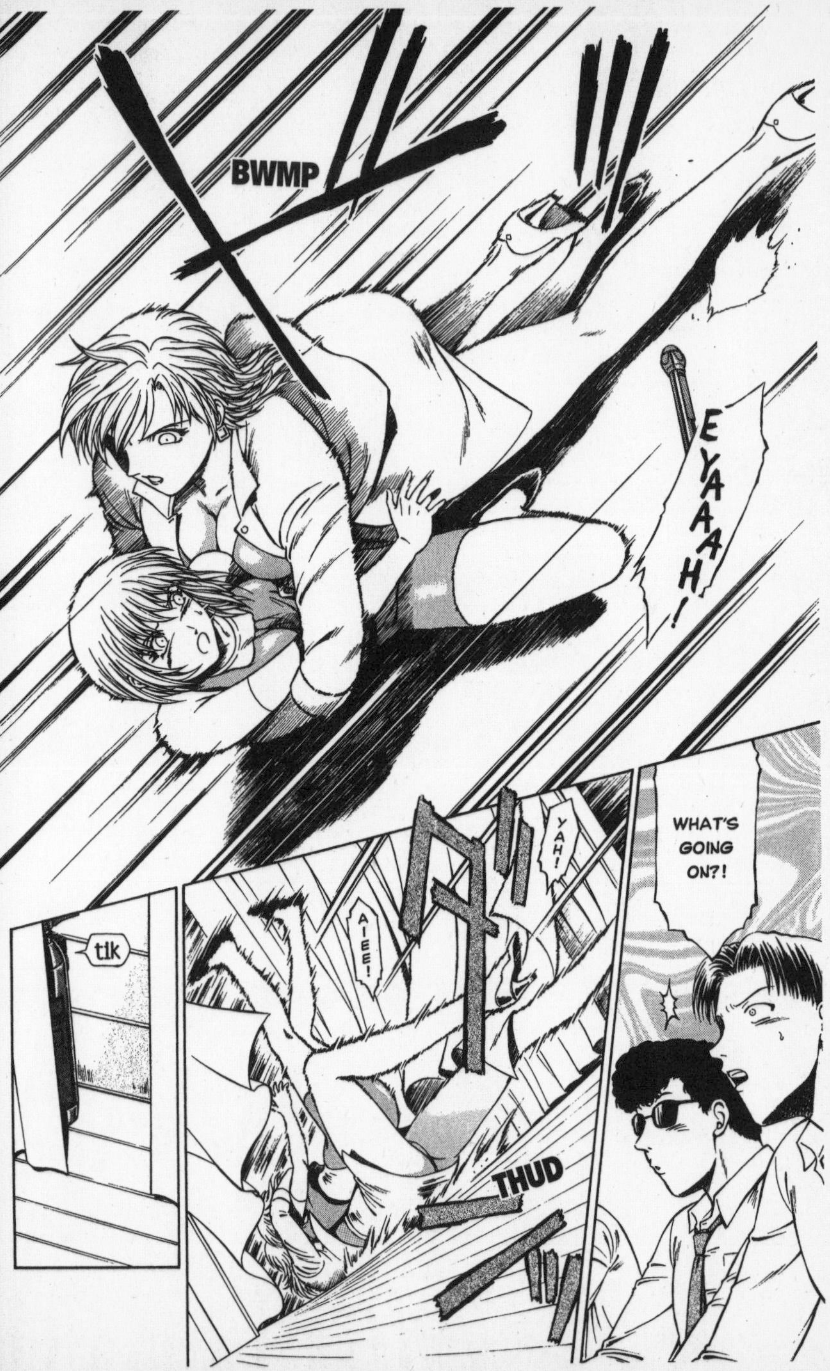
BWMP
EYAAAH!
WHAT'S GOING ON?!
YAH!
AIEEE!
THUD
tik

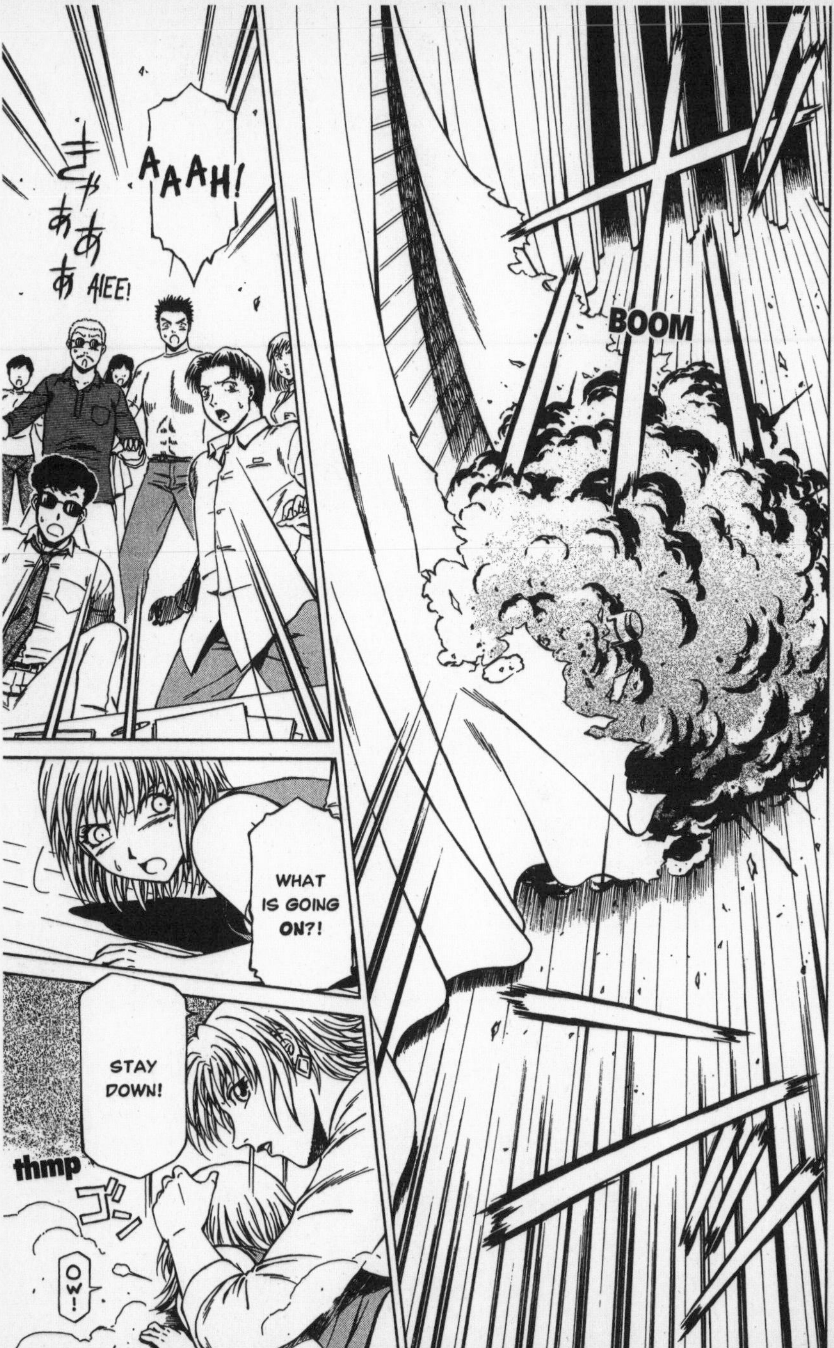
BOOM
AAAH!
きゃあああ
AIEE!
WHAT IS GOING ON?!
STAY DOWN!
thmp
ゴン
OW!

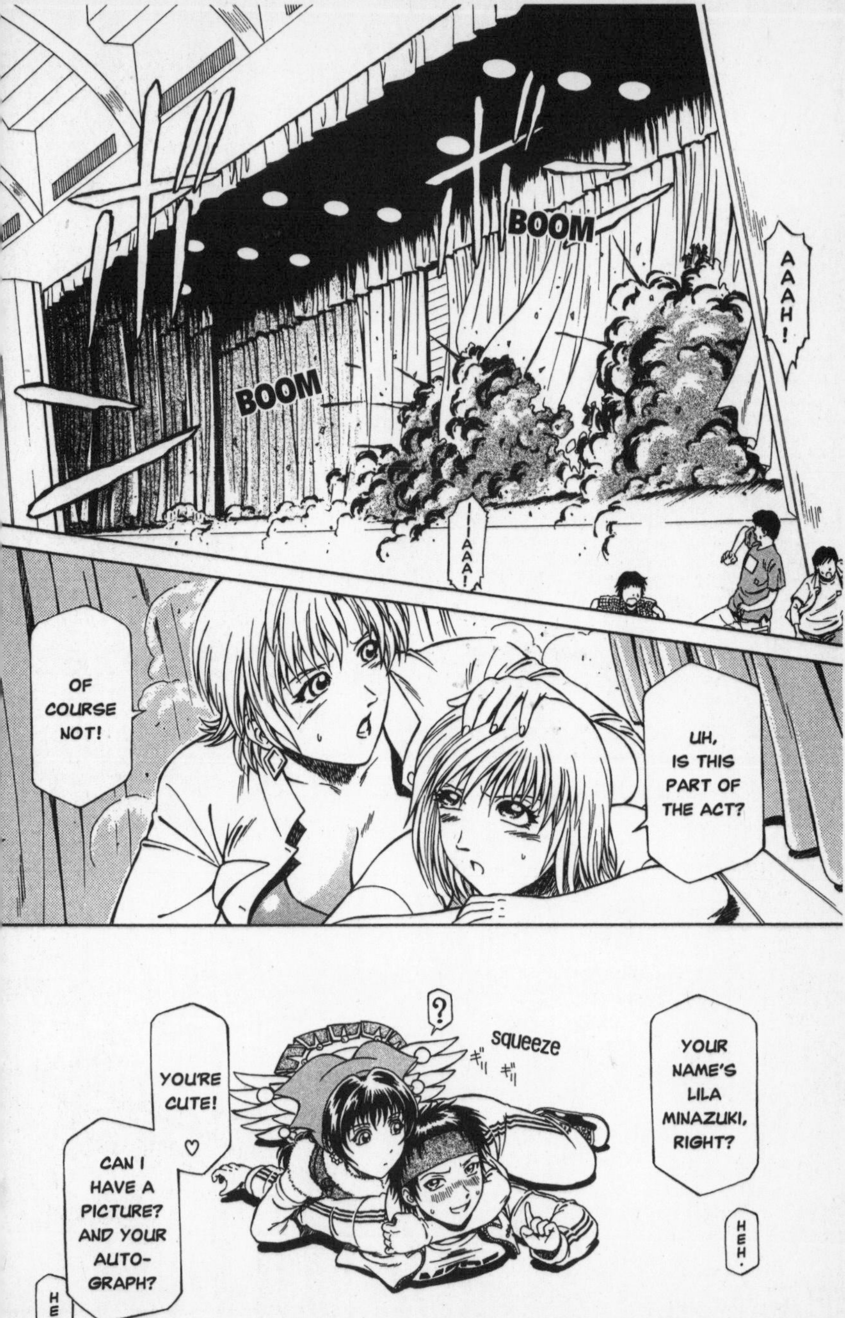

AAAH!
BOOM
BOOM
AAA!!
UH, IS THIS PART OF THE ACT?
OF COURSE NOT!
YOUR NAME'S LILA MINAZUKI, RIGHT?
HEH.
?
squeeze
YOU'RE CUTE! ♡
CAN I HAVE A PICTURE? AND YOUR AUTO-GRAPH?
HEH.

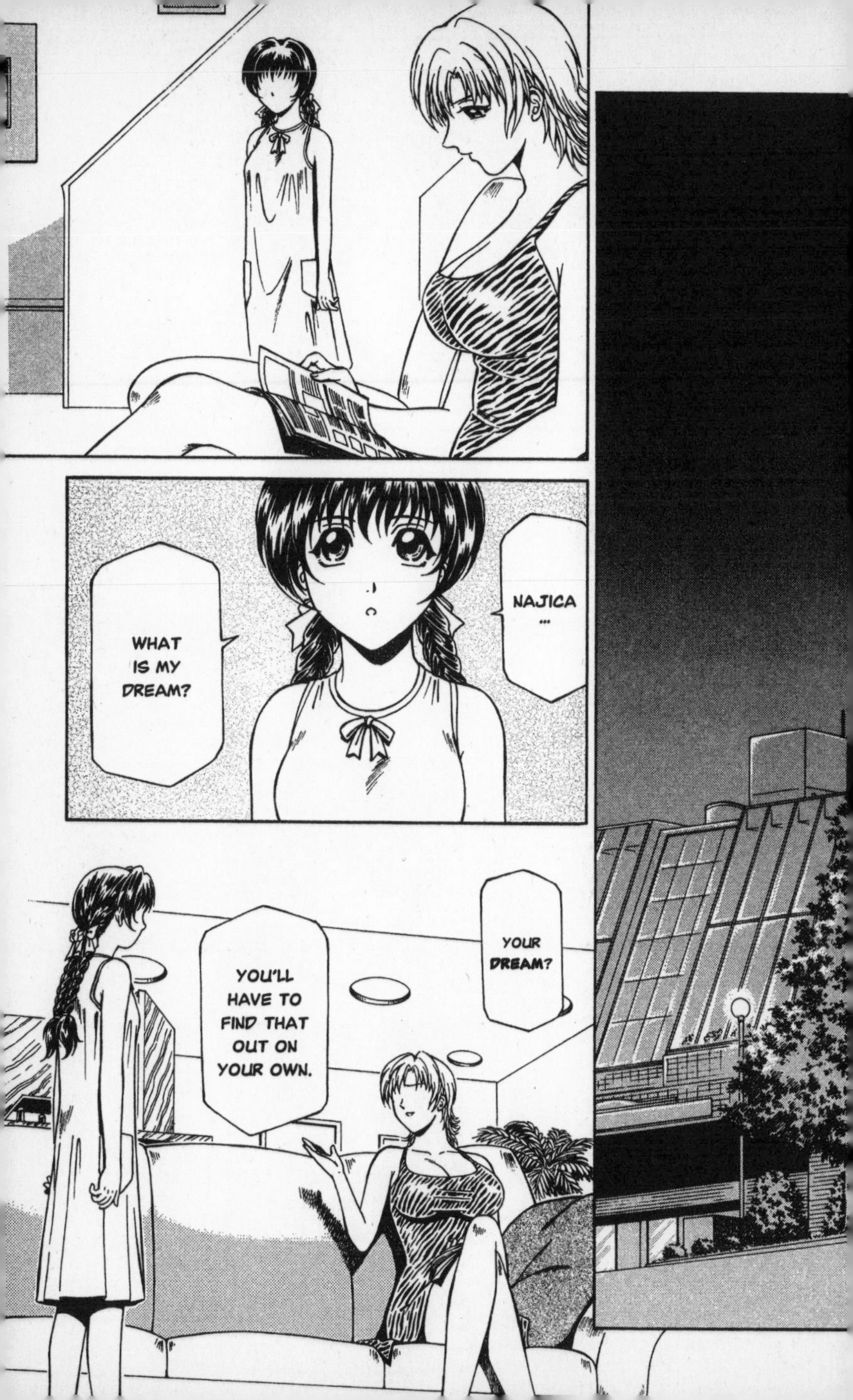
NAJICA ...
WHAT IS MY DREAM?
YOUR DREAM?
YOU'LL HAVE TO FIND THAT OUT ON YOUR OWN.

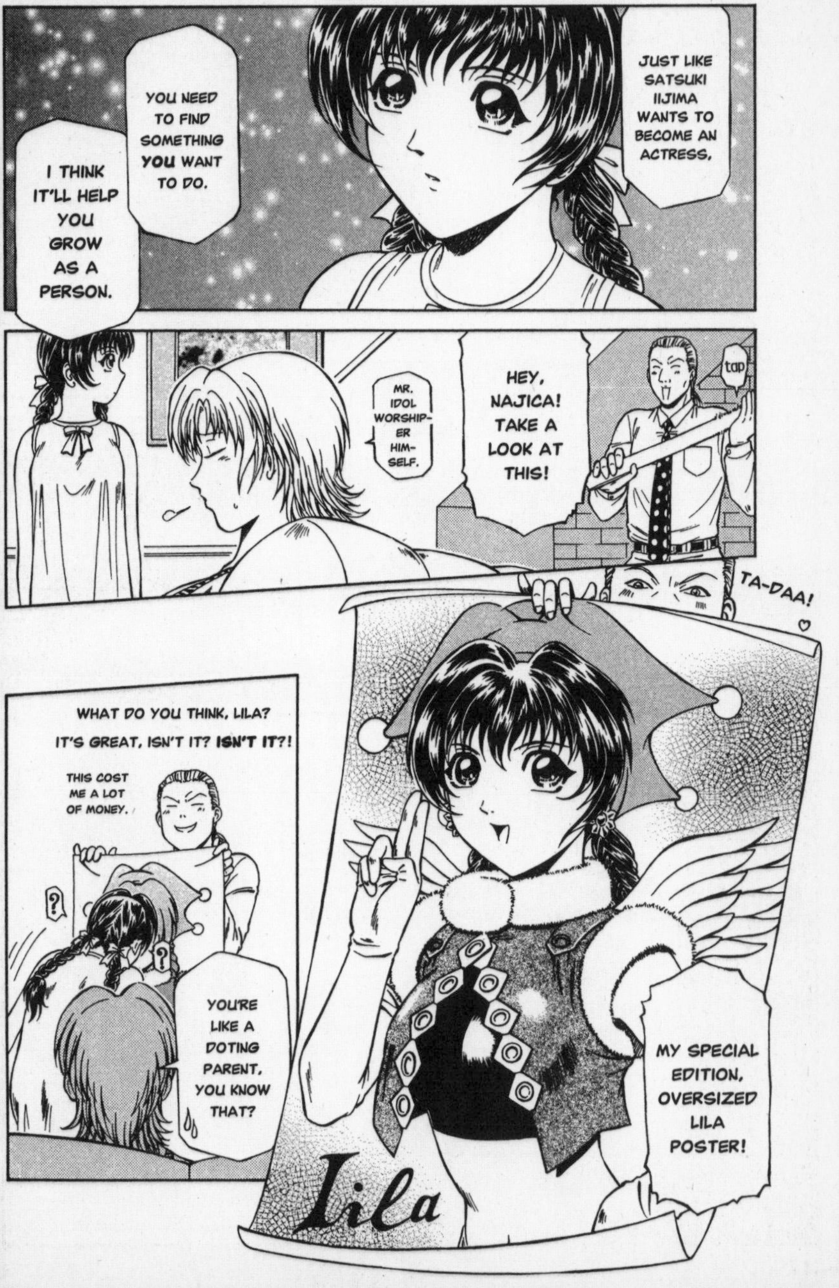
JUST LIKE SATSUKI IIJIMA WANTS TO BECOME AN ACTRESS,
YOU NEED TO FIND SOMETHING YOU WANT TO DO.
I THINK IT'LL HELP YOU GROW AS A PERSON.
tap
HEY, NAJICA! TAKE A LOOK AT THIS!
MR. IDOL WORSHIPER HIMSELF.
TA-DAA!
MY SPECIAL EDITION, OVERSIZED LILA POSTER!
Lila
WHAT DO YOU THINK, LILA?
IT'S GREAT, ISN'T IT? ISN'T IT?!
THIS COST ME A LOT OF MONEY.
?
?
YOU'RE LIKE A DOTING PARENT, YOU KNOW THAT?

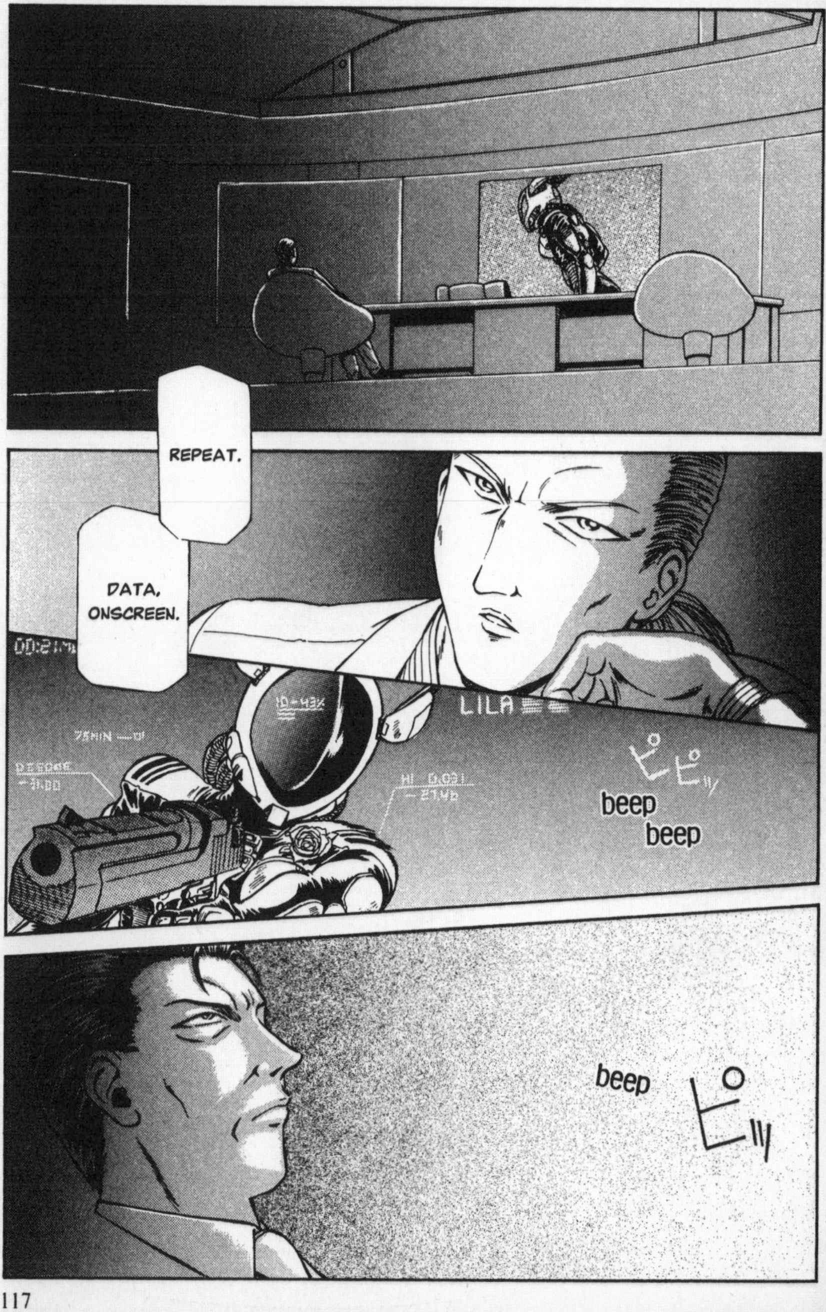
REPEAT.
DATA, ONSCREEN.
LILA
ピピッ
beep beep
beep
ピッ

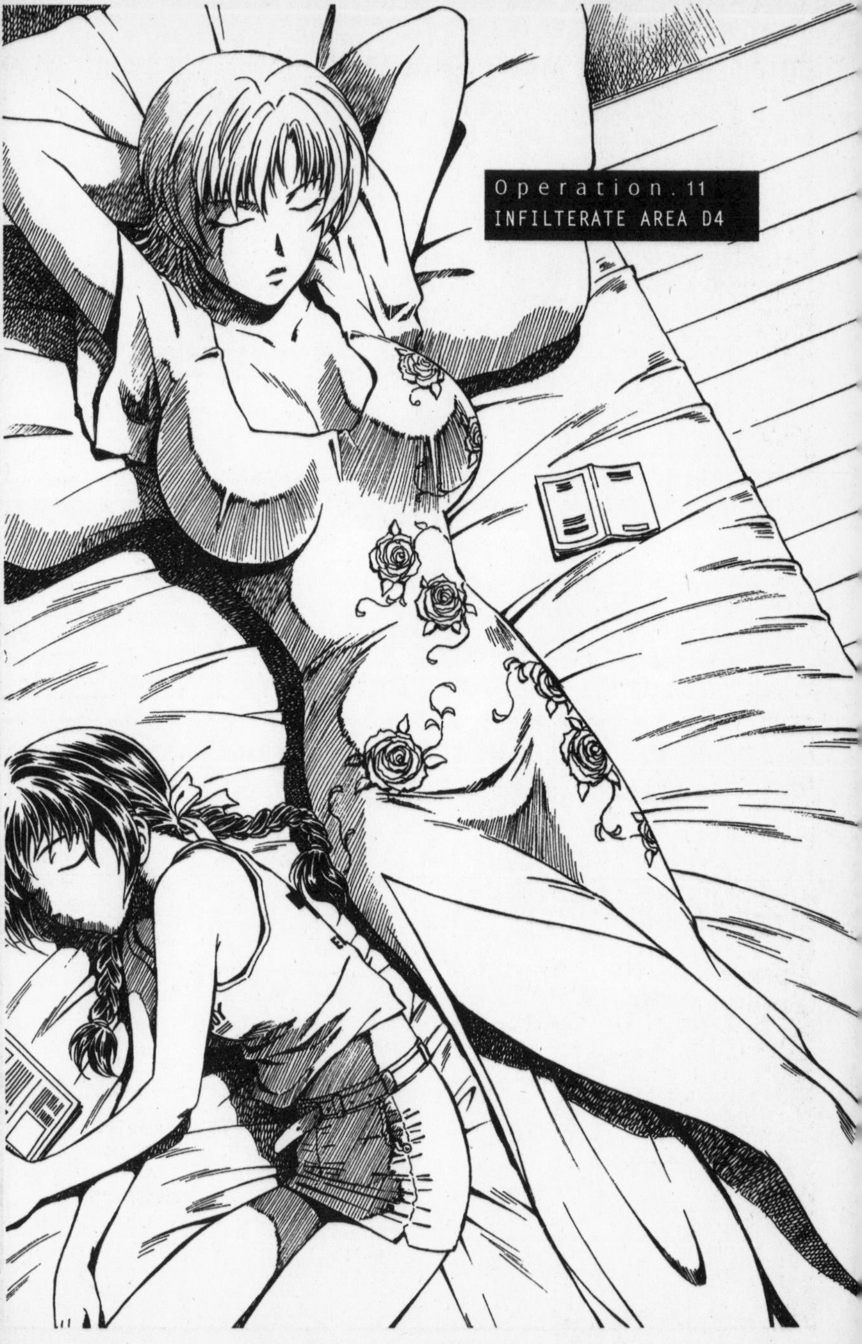
Operation.11
INFILTERATE AREA D4

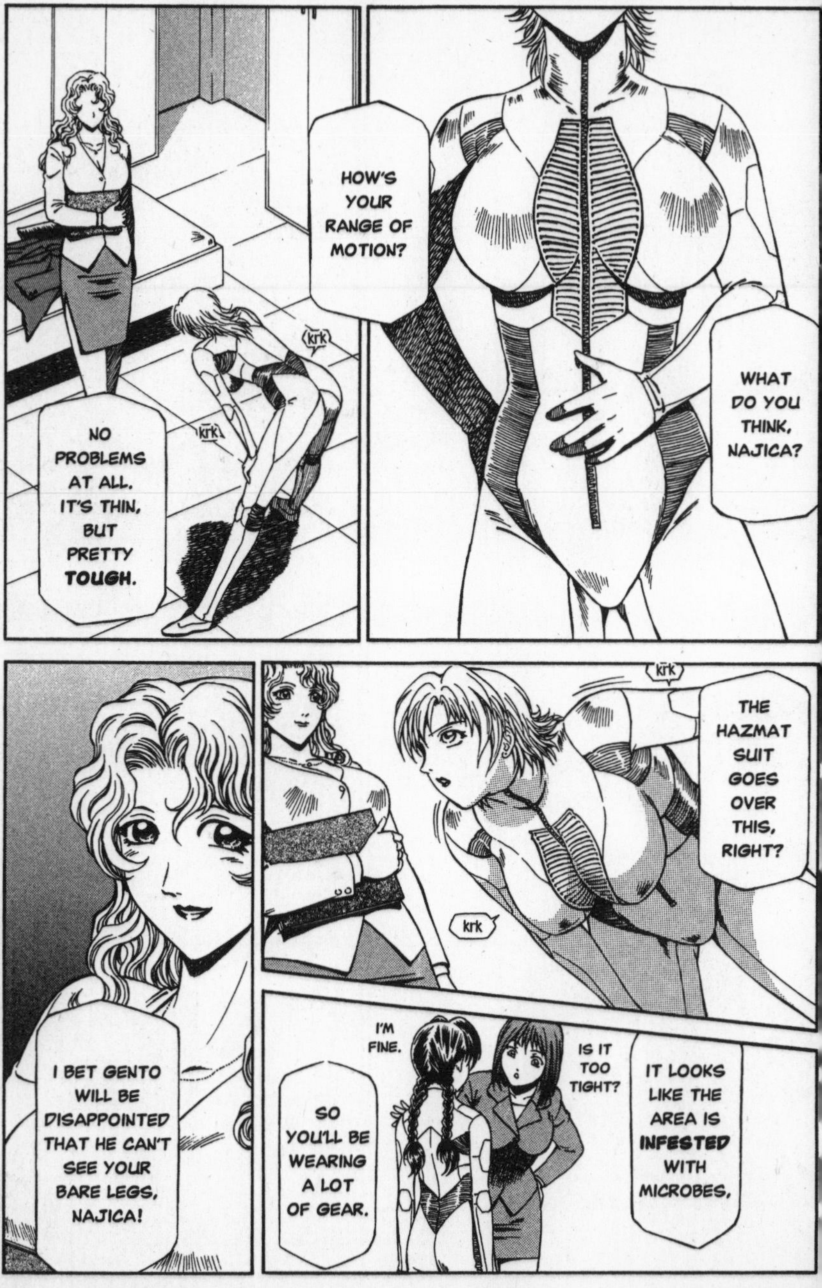
WHAT DO YOU THINK, NAJICA?
HOW'S YOUR RANGE OF MOTION?
krk
krk
NO PROBLEMS AT ALL. IT'S THIN, BUT PRETTY **TOUGH**.
krk
THE HAZMAT SUIT GOES OVER THIS, RIGHT?
krk
IT LOOKS LIKE THE AREA IS **INFESTED** WITH MICROBES.
IS IT TOO TIGHT?
I'M FINE.
SO YOU'LL BE WEARING A LOT OF GEAR.
I BET GENTO WILL BE DISAPPOINTED THAT HE CAN'T SEE YOUR BARE LEGS, NAJICA!

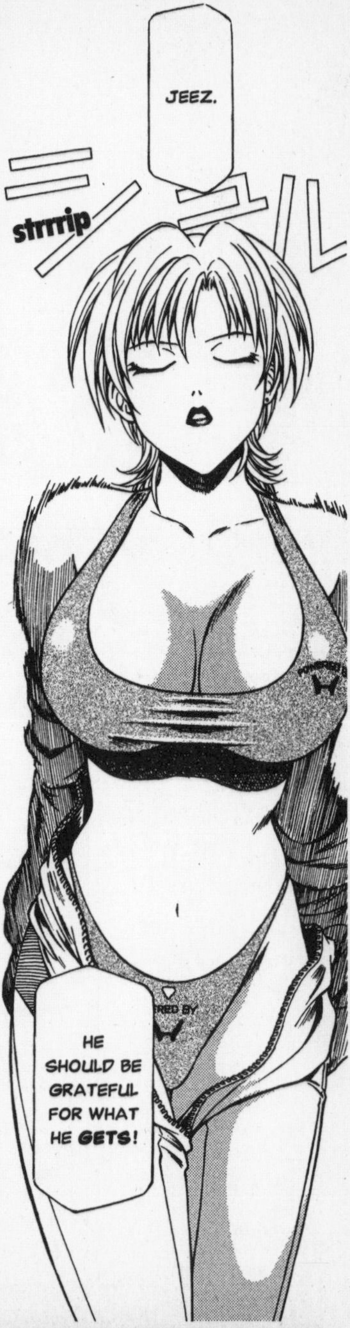
JEEZ.
strrrip
HE SHOULD BE GRATEFUL FOR WHAT HE GETS!

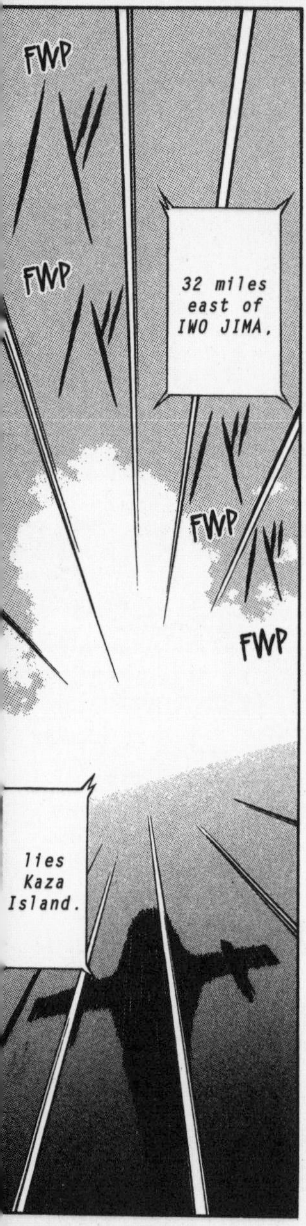
32 miles east of IWO JIMA,
FWP
FWP
FWP
FWP
lies Kaza Island.

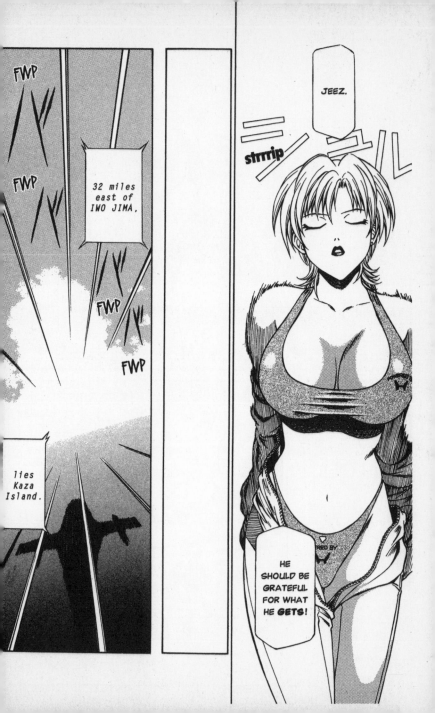

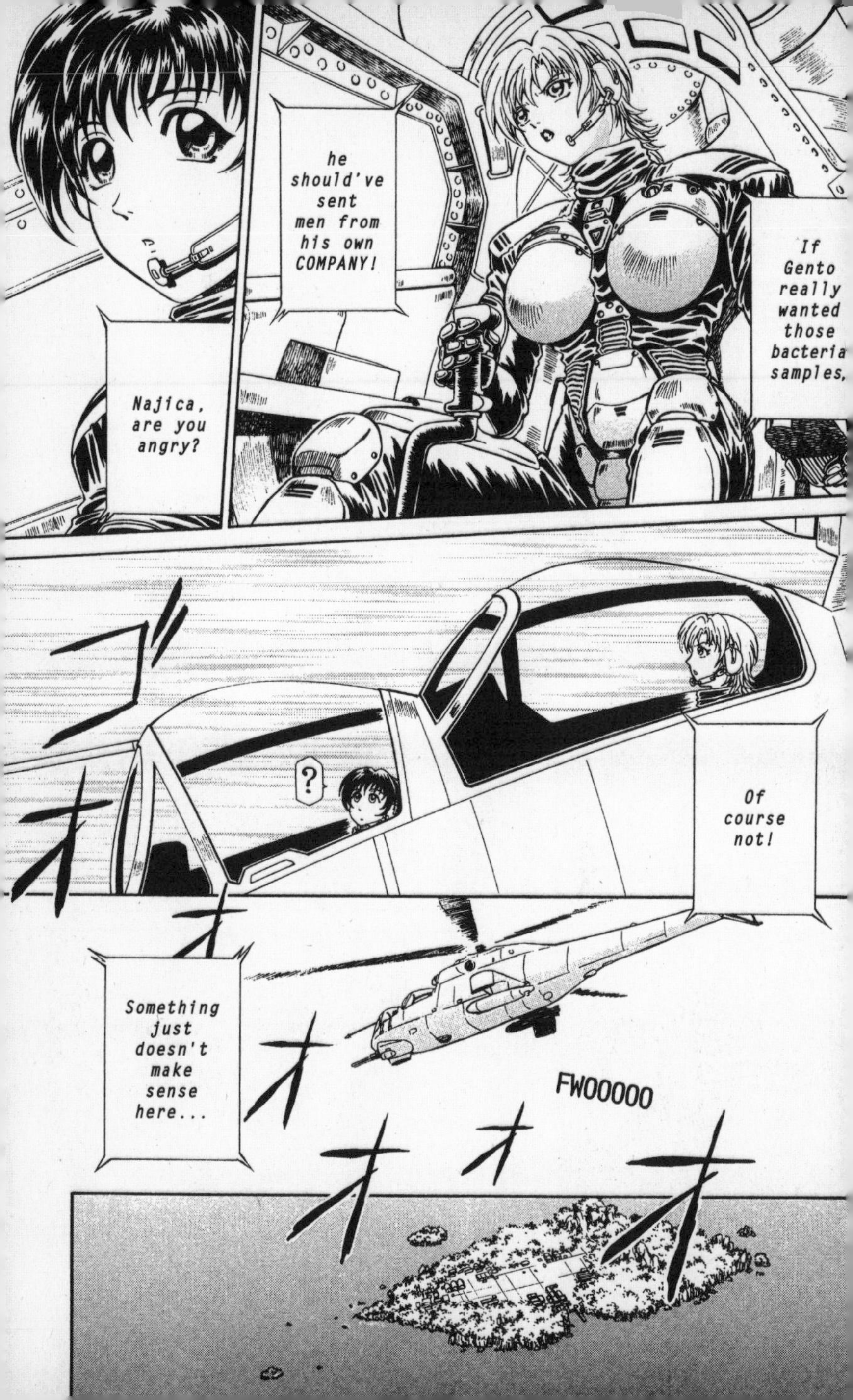
If Gento really wanted those bacteria samples,
he should've sent men from his own COMPANY!
Najica, are you angry?
Of course not!
?
Something just doesn't make sense here...
FWOOOOO

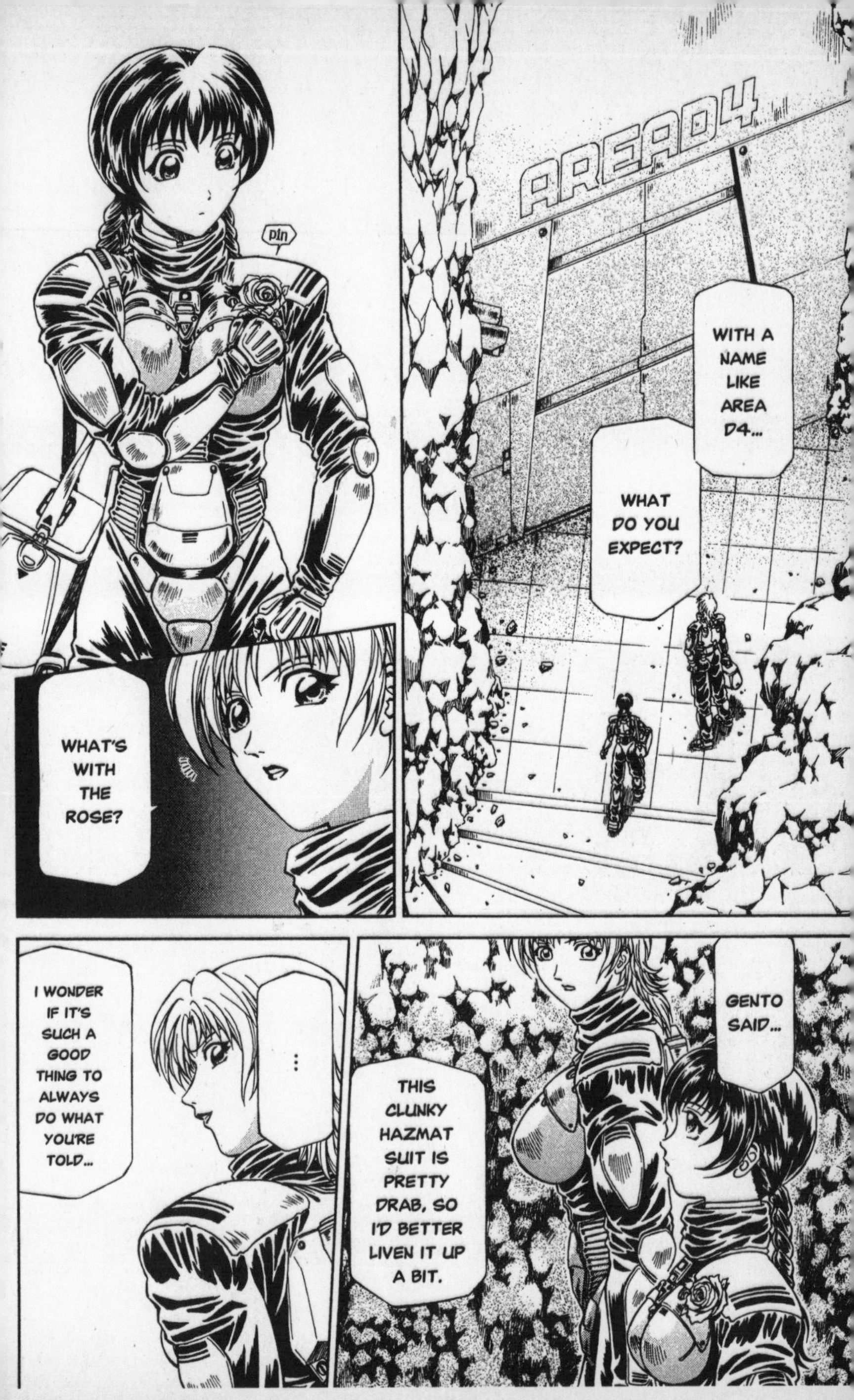
AREA D4
WITH A NAME LIKE AREA D4...
WHAT DO YOU EXPECT?
pin
WHAT'S WITH THE ROSE?
GENTO SAID...
THIS CLUNKY HAZMAT SUIT IS PRETTY DRAB, SO I'D BETTER LIVEN IT UP A BIT.
...
I WONDER IF IT'S SUCH A GOOD THING TO ALWAYS DO WHAT YOU'RE TOLD...

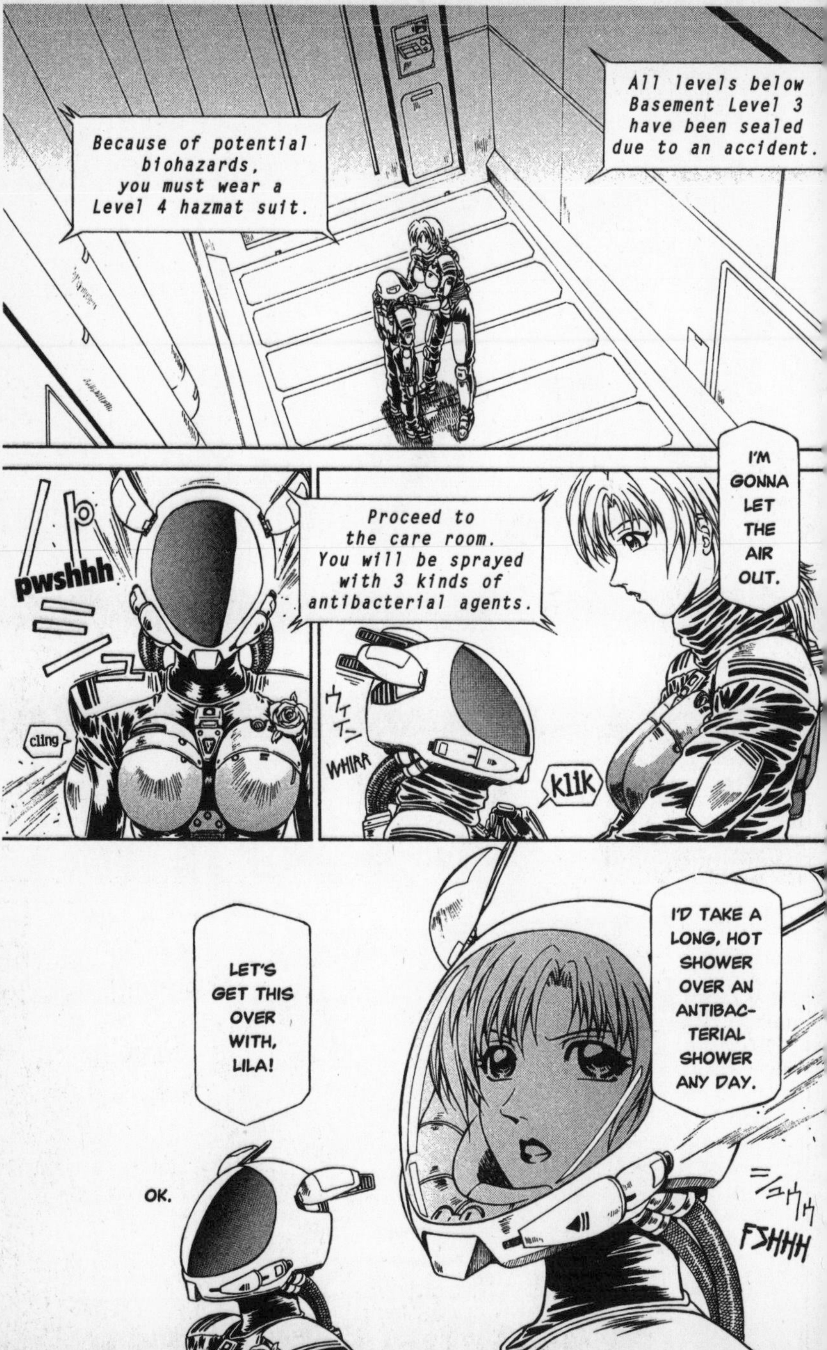
All levels below Basement Level 3 have been sealed due to an accident.
Because of potential biohazards, you must wear a Level 4 hazmat suit.
I'M GONNA LET THE AIR OUT.
Proceed to the care room. You will be sprayed with 3 kinds of antibacterial agents.
WHIRR
klik
pwshhh
cling
I'D TAKE A LONG, HOT SHOWER OVER AN ANTIBACTERIAL SHOWER ANY DAY.
FSHHH
LET'S GET THIS OVER WITH, LILA!
OK.

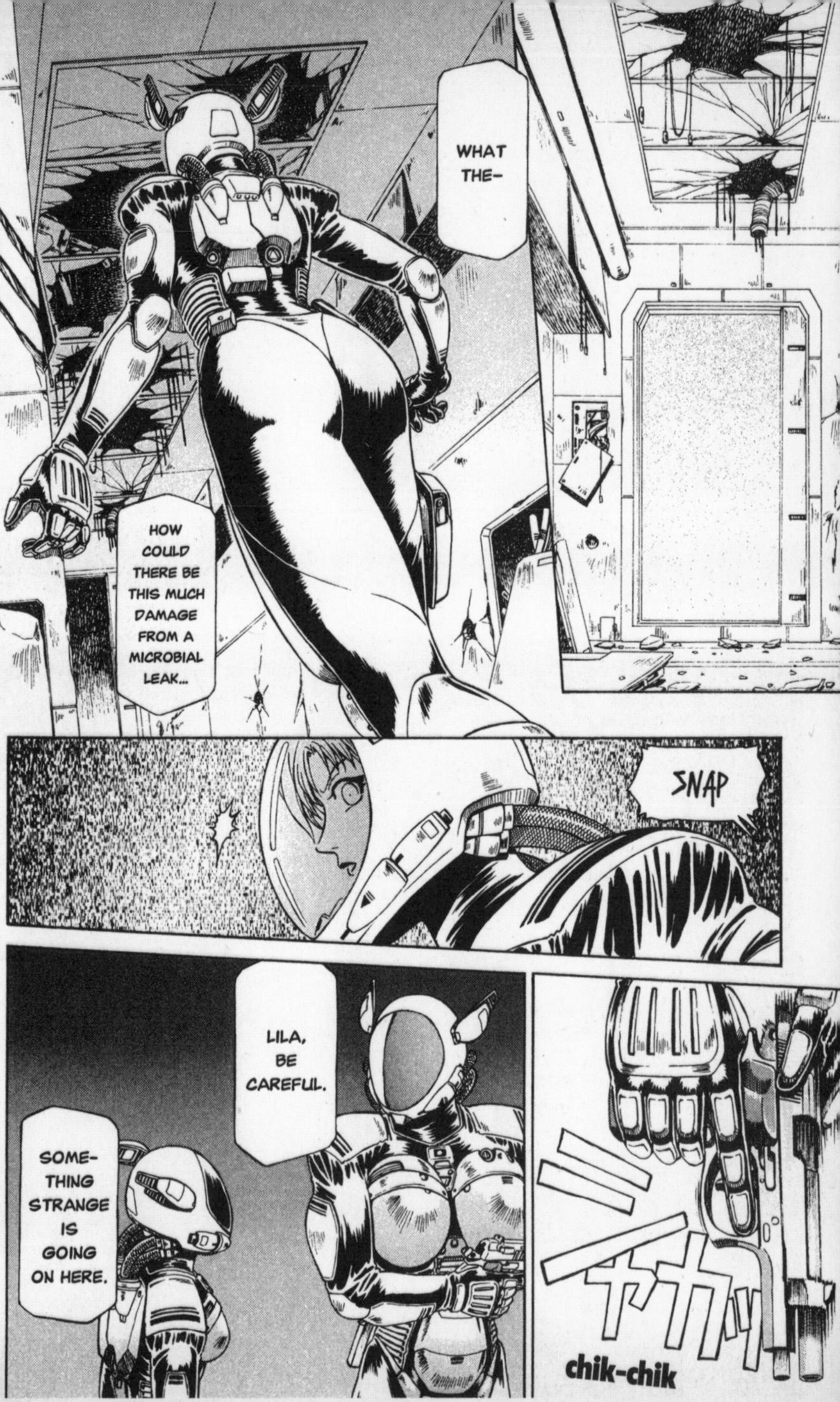
WHAT THE-
HOW COULD THERE BE THIS MUCH DAMAGE FROM A MICROBIAL LEAK...
SNAP
chik-chik
LILA, BE CAREFUL.
SOME-THING STRANGE IS GOING ON HERE.

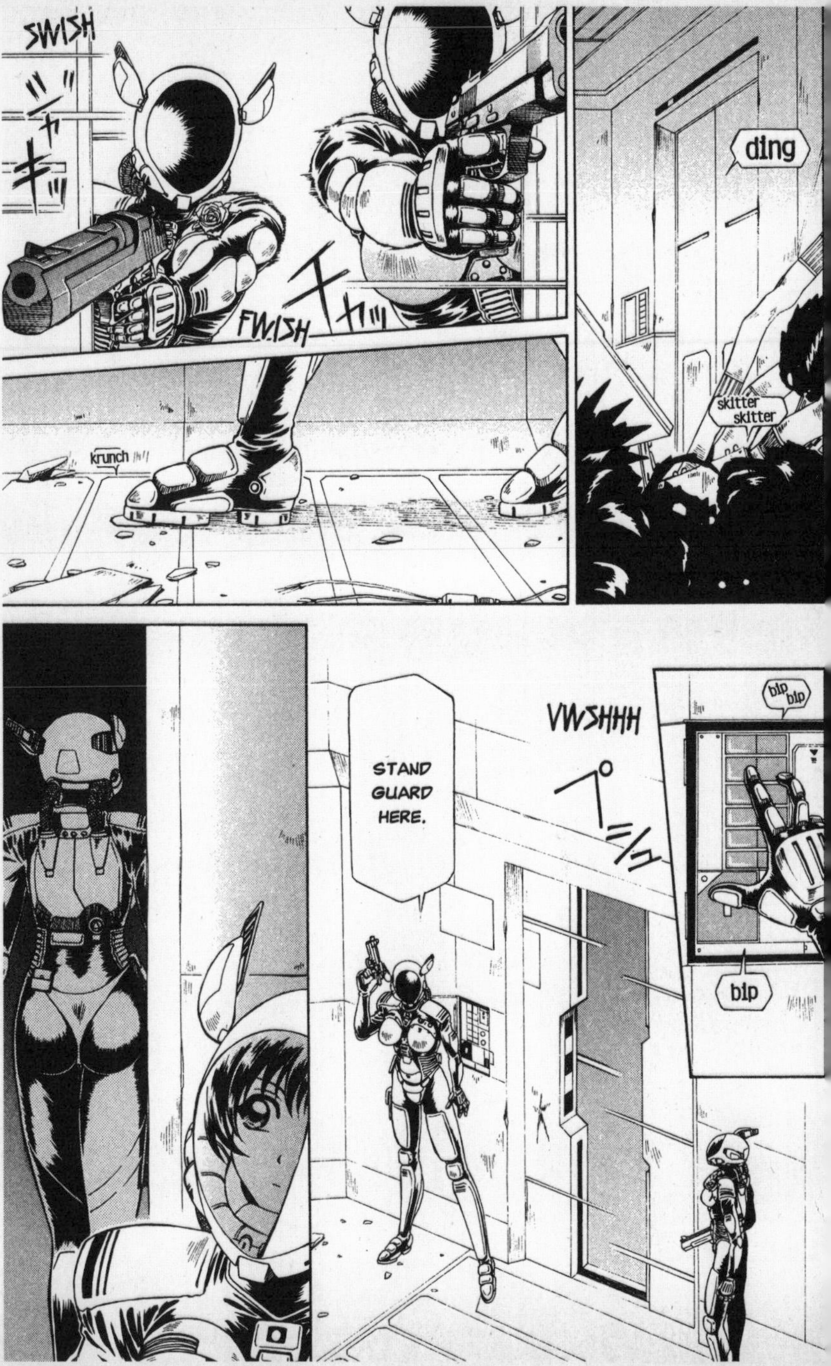
ding
skitter skitter
SWISH
FWISH
krunch
bip bip
bip
VWSHHH
STAND GUARD HERE.

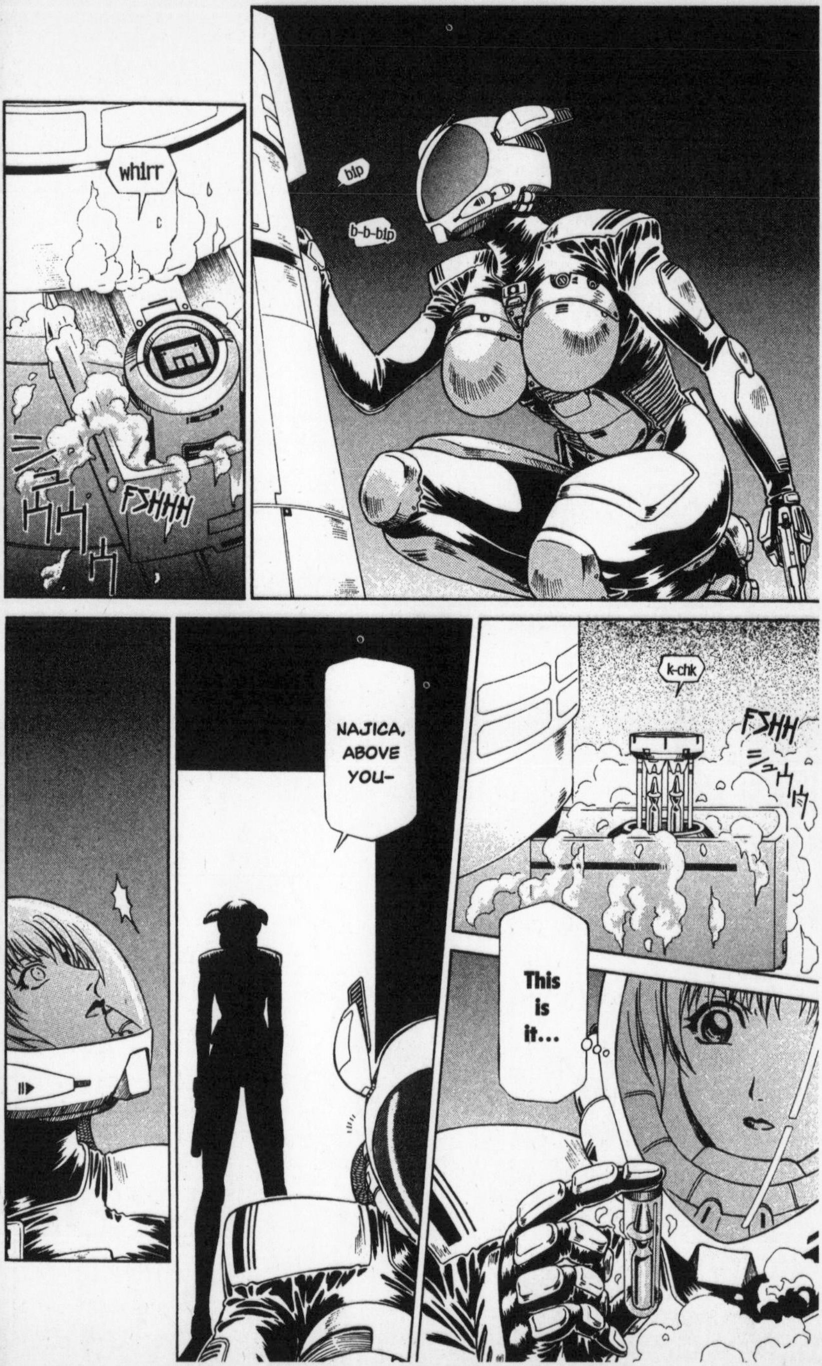
bip
b-b-bip
whirr
FSHHH
k-chk
FSHH
This is it...
NAJICA, ABOVE YOU-

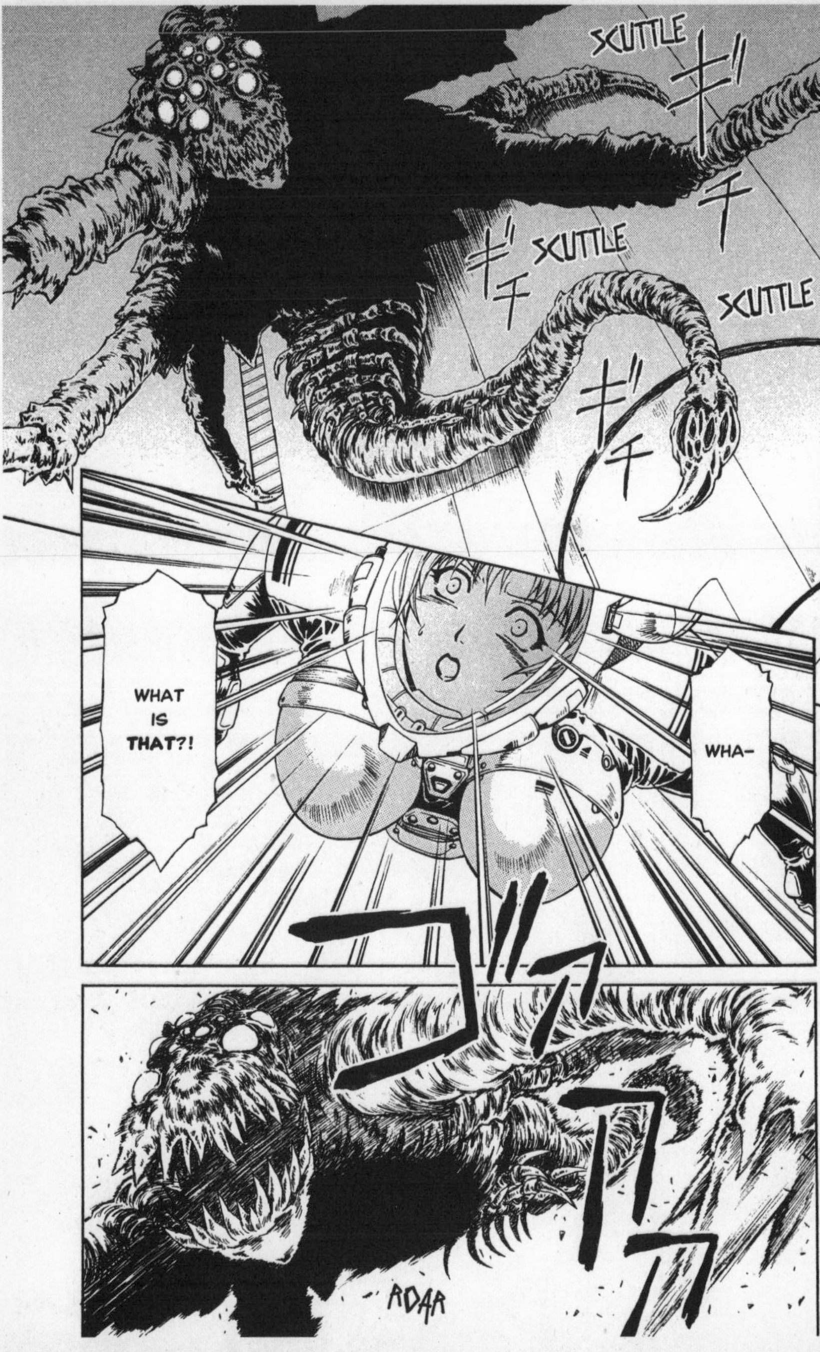
SCUTTLE
ギチ
SCUTTLE
ギチ
SCUTTLE
ギチ
WHA-
WHAT IS THAT?!
ゴァァ
ROAR

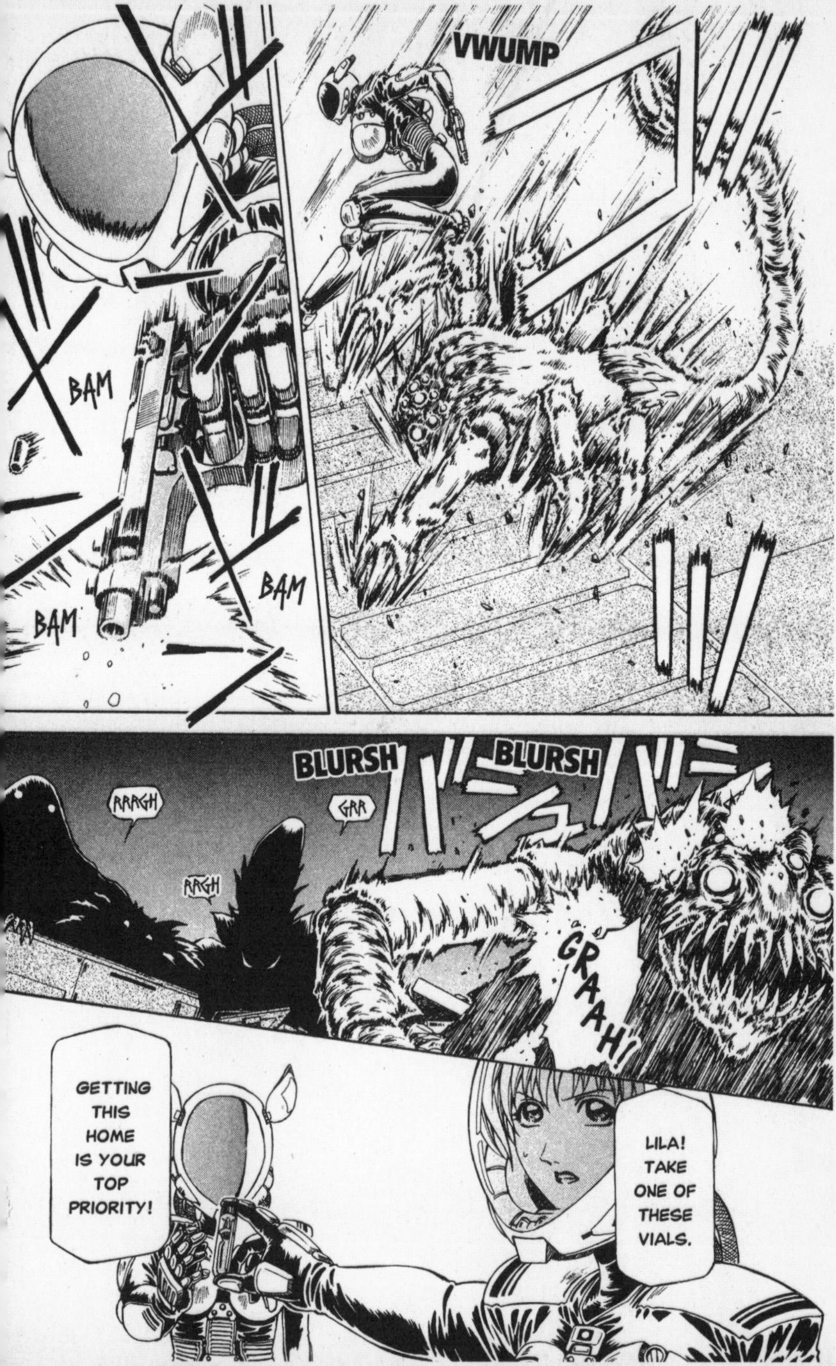
VWUMP
BAM
BAM
BAM
BLURSH
BLURSH
GRR
RRRAGH
RRAGH
GRAAAH!
LILA! TAKE ONE OF THESE VIALS.
GETTING THIS HOME IS YOUR TOP PRIORITY!

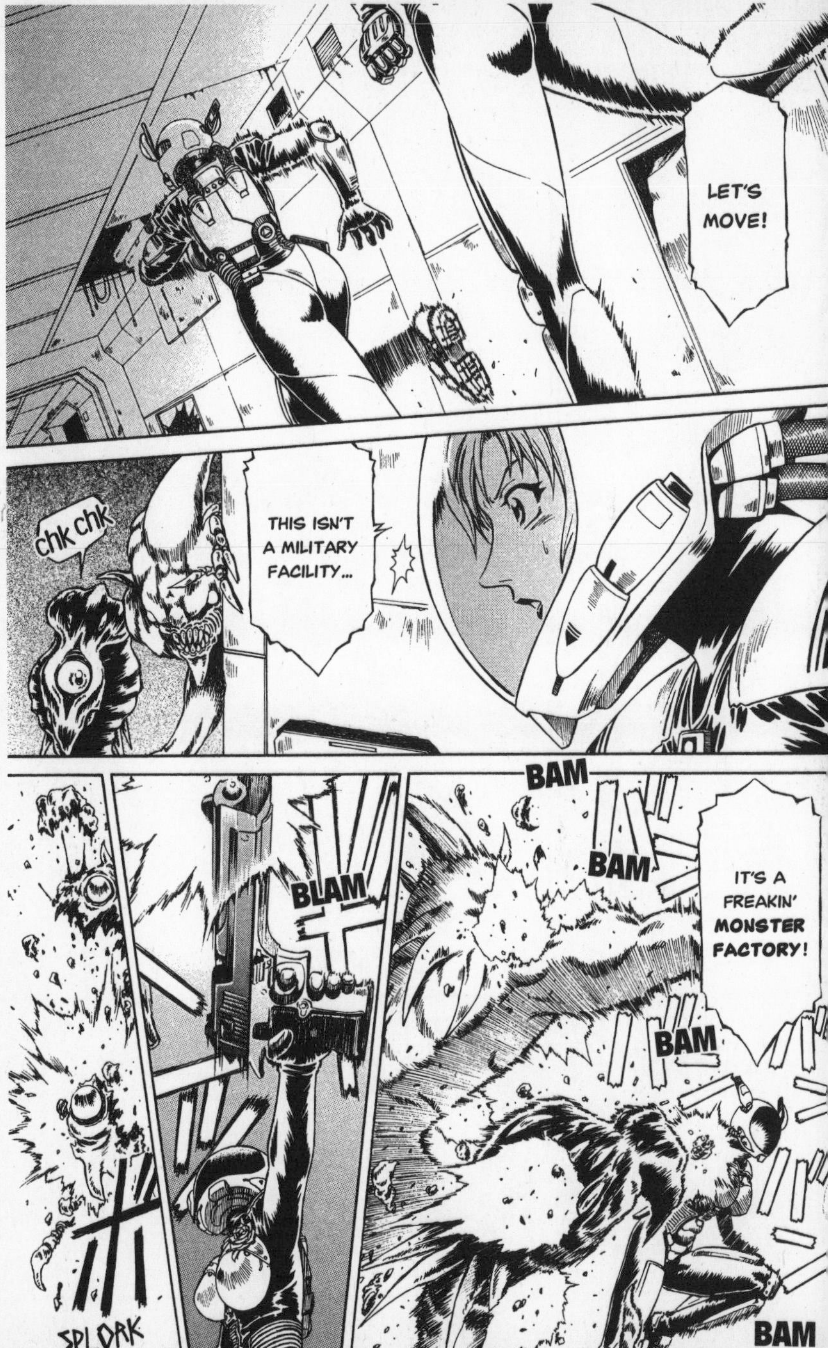
LET'S MOVE!
THIS ISN'T A MILITARY FACILITY...
chk chk
BAM
IT'S A FREAKIN' **MONSTER FACTORY**!
BAM
BAM
BAM
BLAM
SPLORK

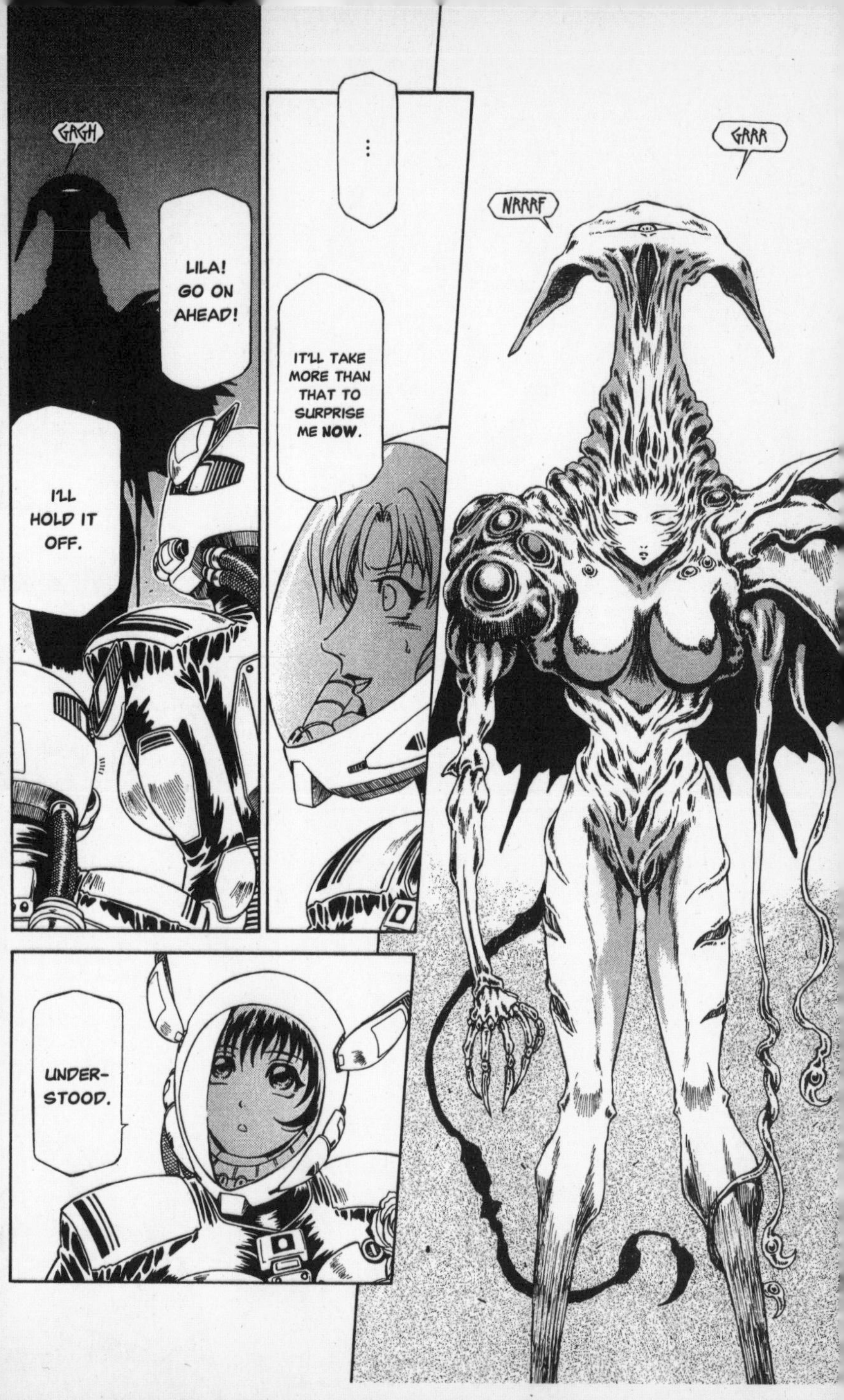
GRRR
NRRRF
...
IT'LL TAKE MORE THAN THAT TO SURPRISE ME **NOW**.
GRGH
LILA! GO ON AHEAD!
I'LL HOLD IT OFF.
UNDER-STOOD.

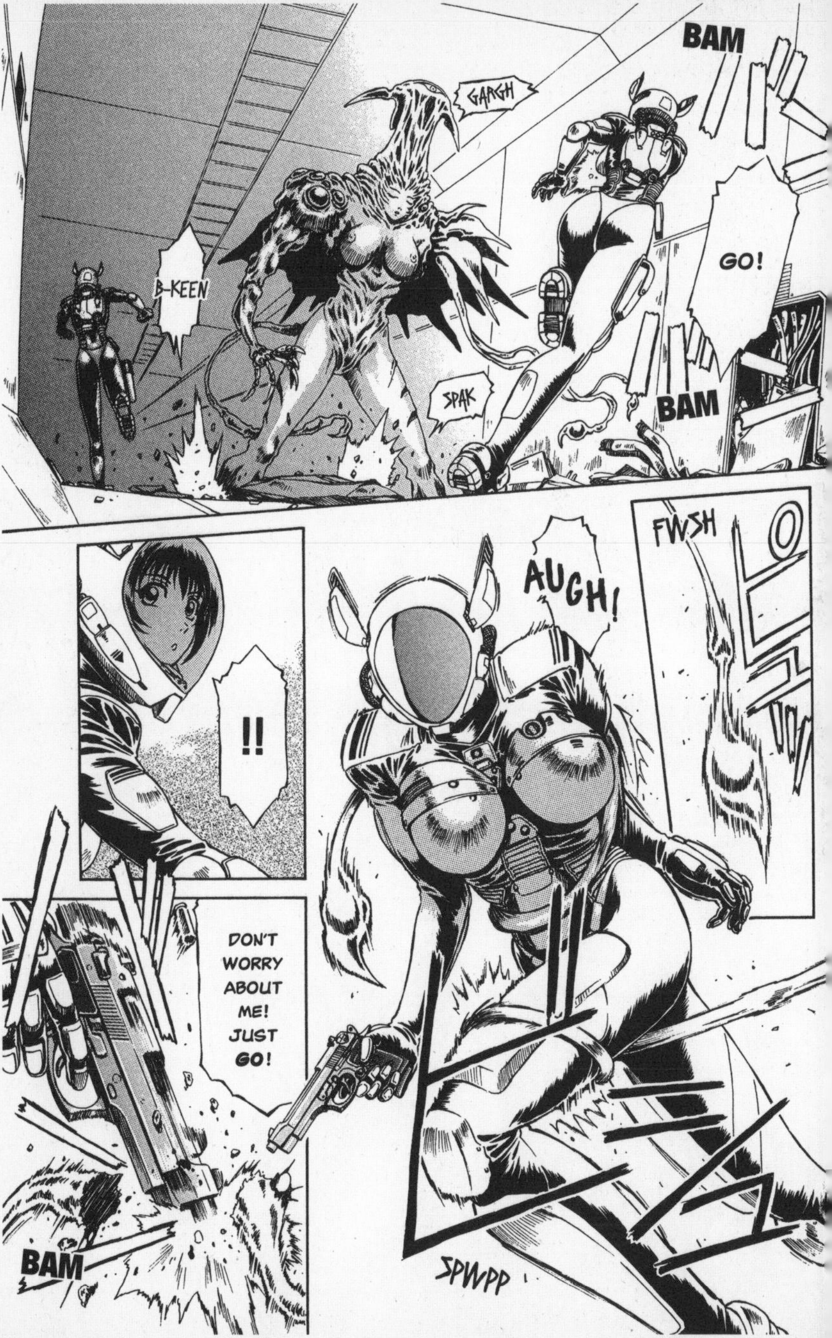
BAM
GARGH
GO!
BAM
SPAK
B-KEEN
FWSH
AUGH!
SPWPP
!!
DON'T WORRY ABOUT ME! JUST GO!
BAM

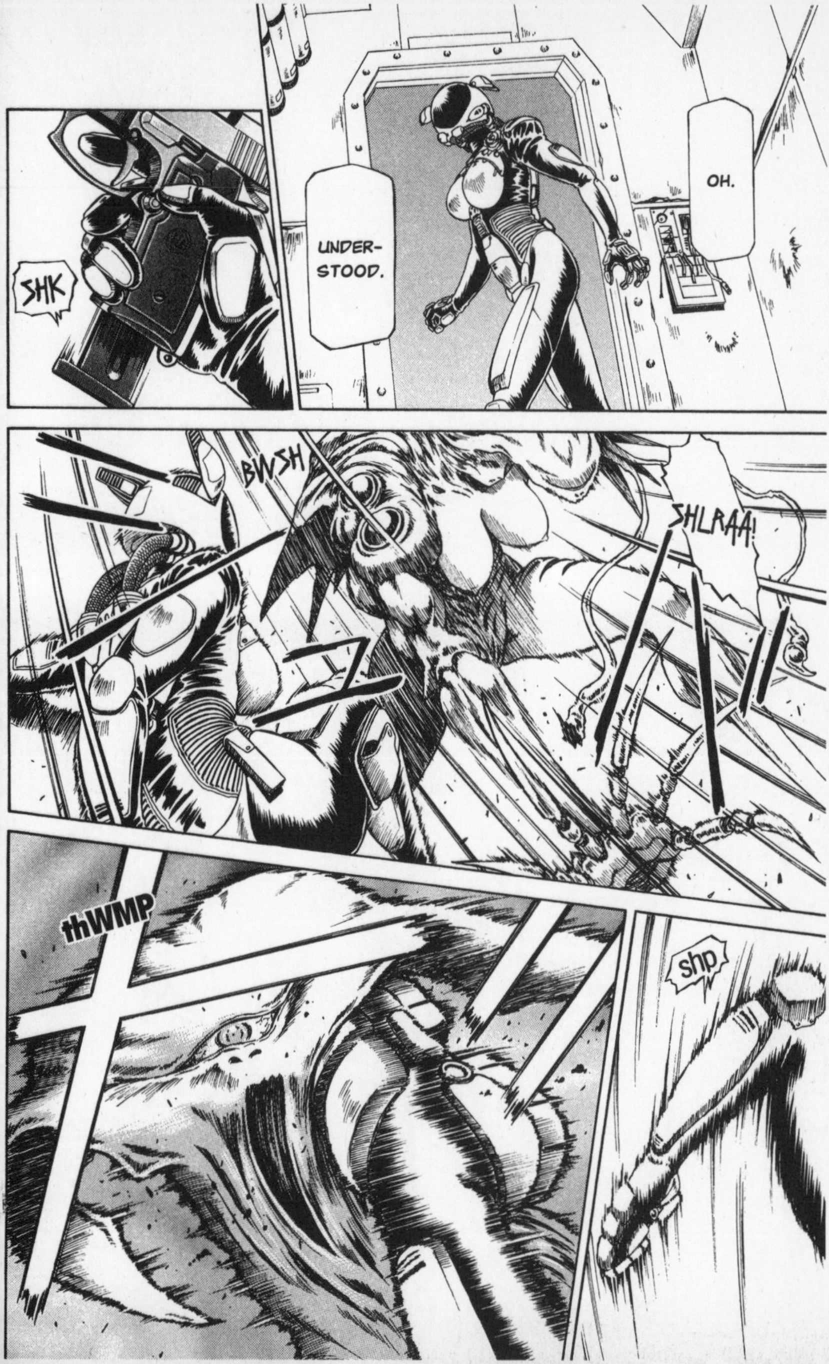
OH.
UNDER-STOOD.
SHK
SHLRAA!
BWSH
shp
thWMP

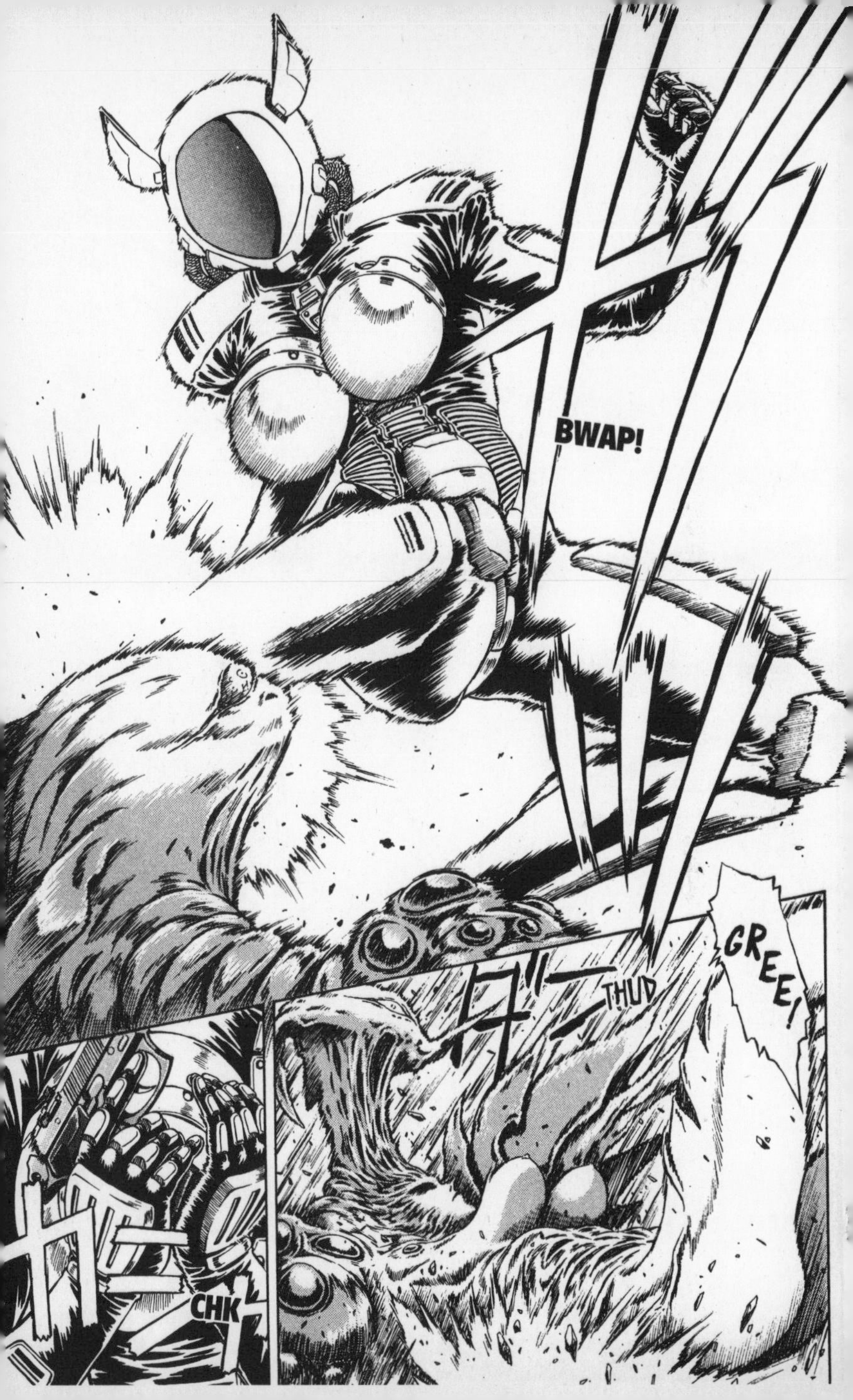
BWAP!
GREEE!
THUD
CHK

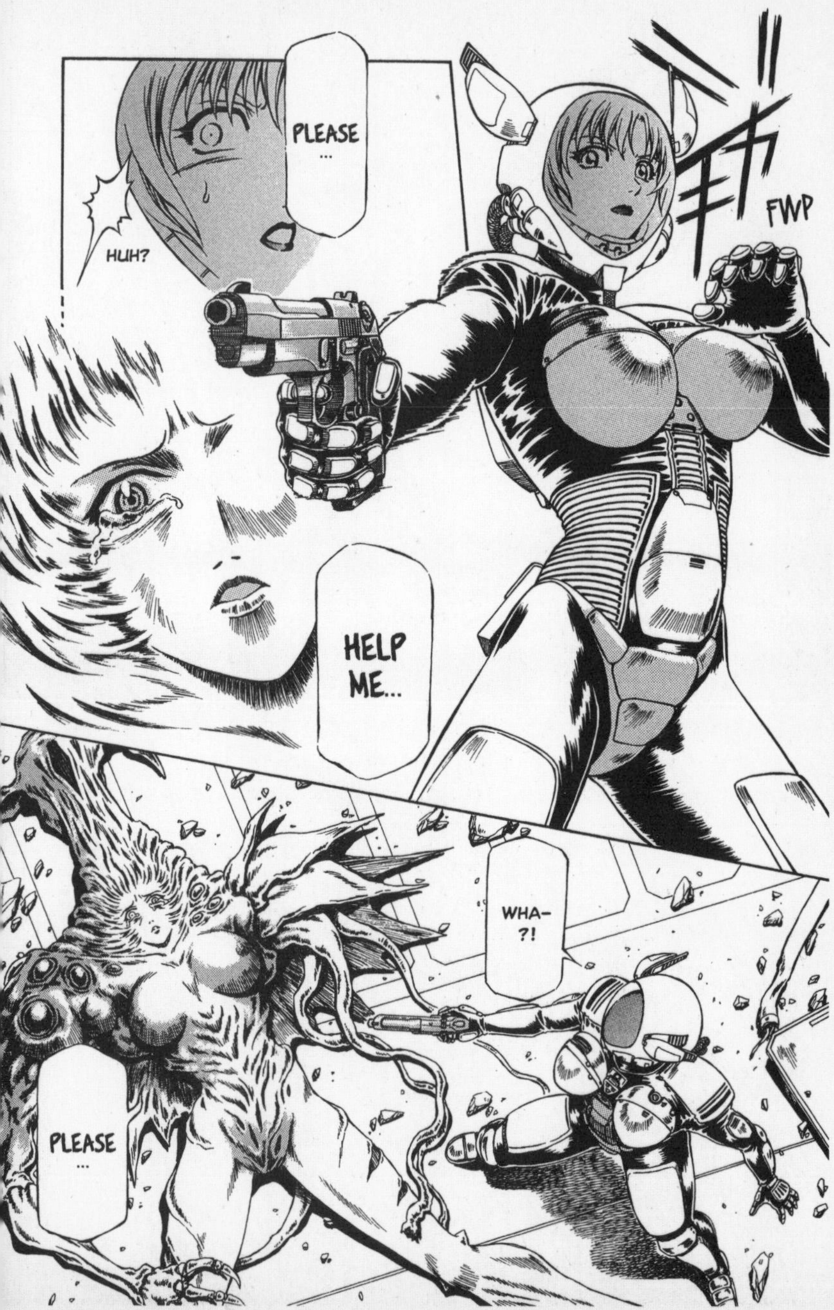
FWP
PLEASE ...
HUH?
HELP ME...
WHA- ?!
PLEASE ...

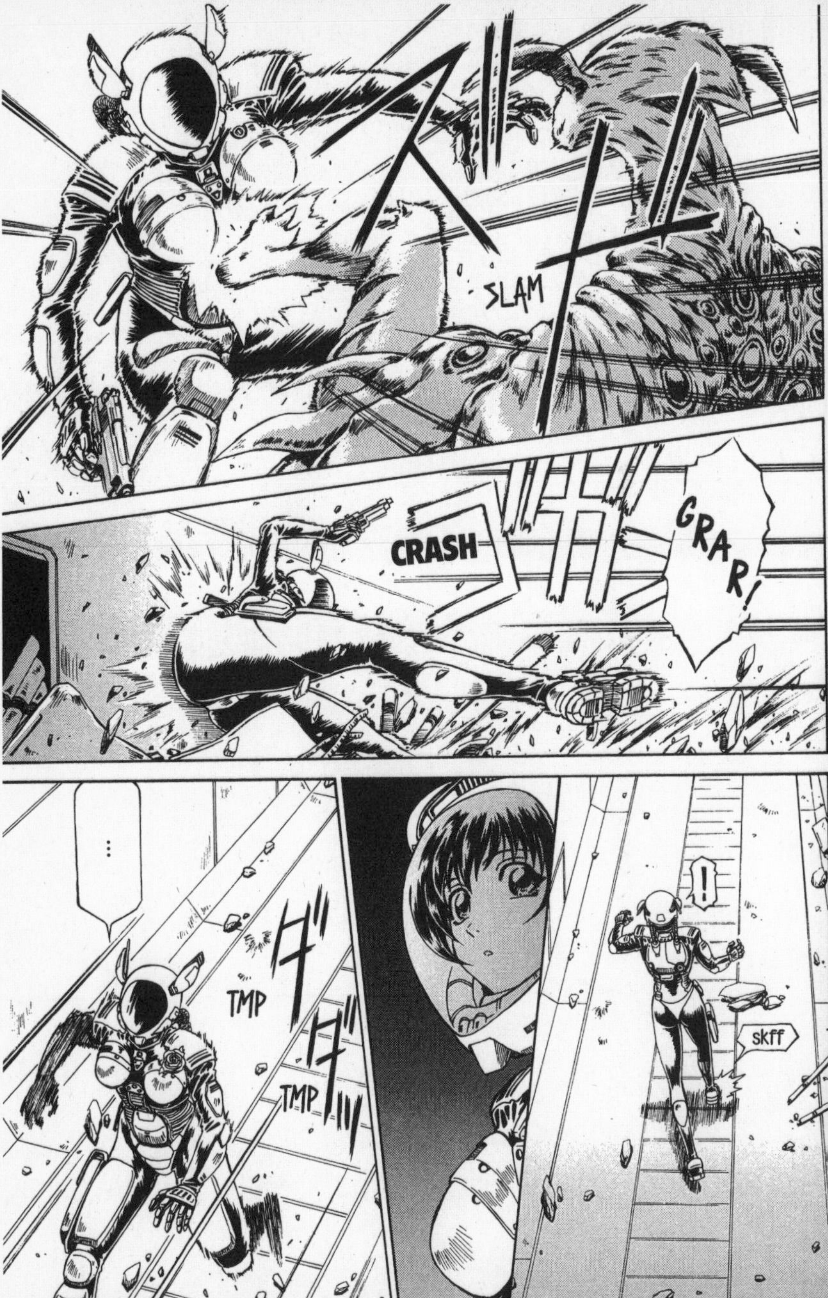
SLAM
GRAR!
CRASH
!
SKFF
...
TMP
TMP

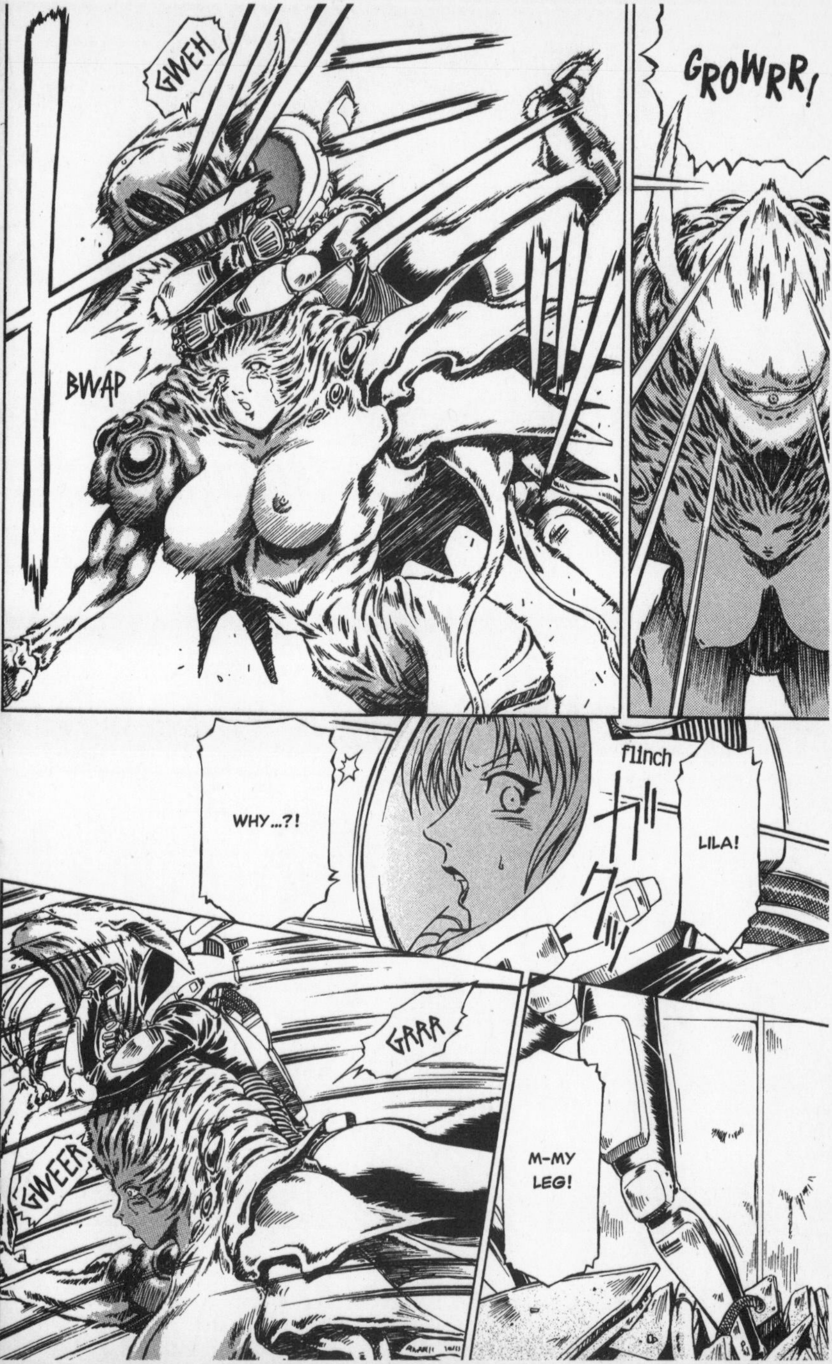
GROWRR!
GWEH
BWAP
flinch
LILA!
WHY...?!
M-MY LEG!
GRRR
GWEER

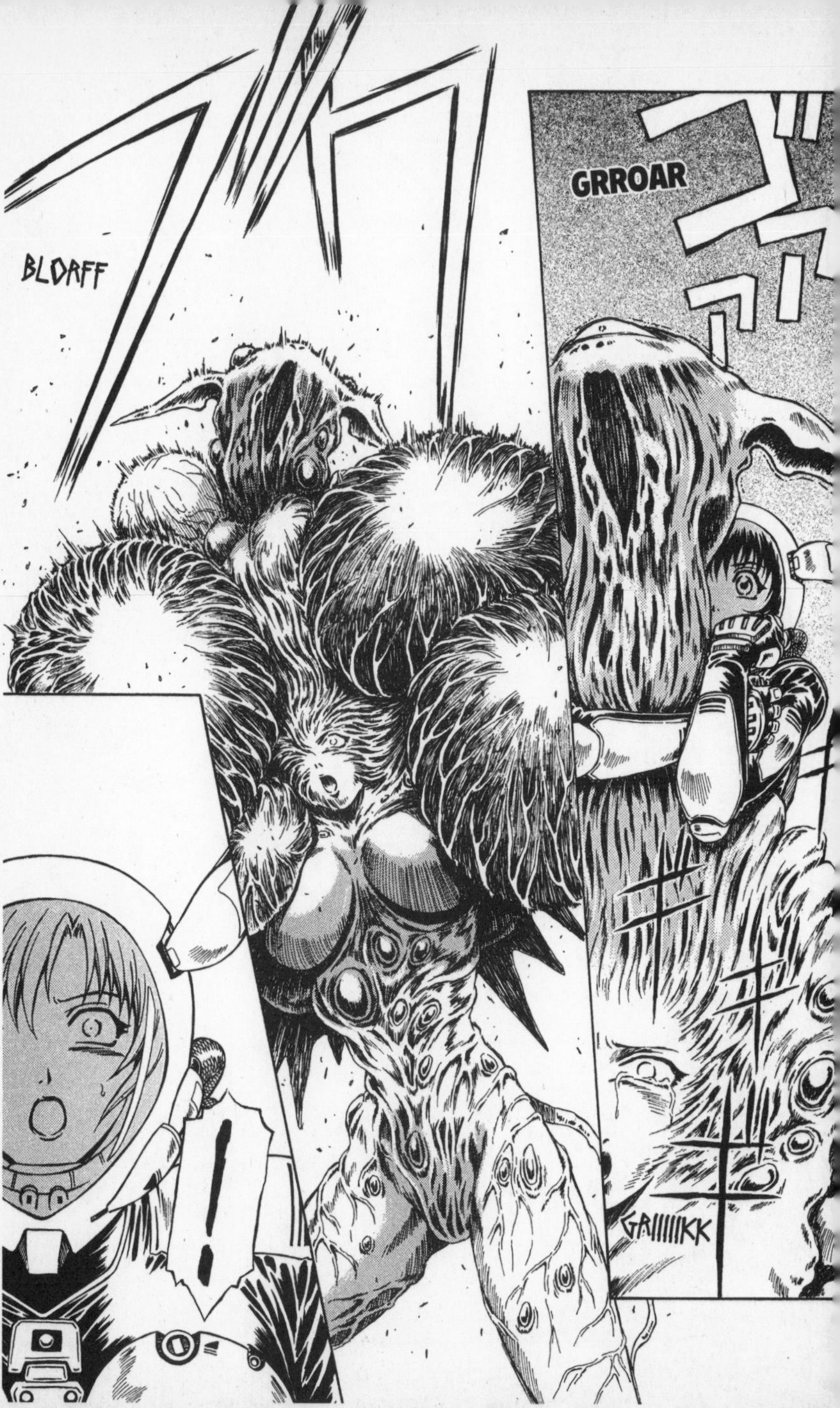
GRROAR
GRIIIIIKK
BLORFF
!

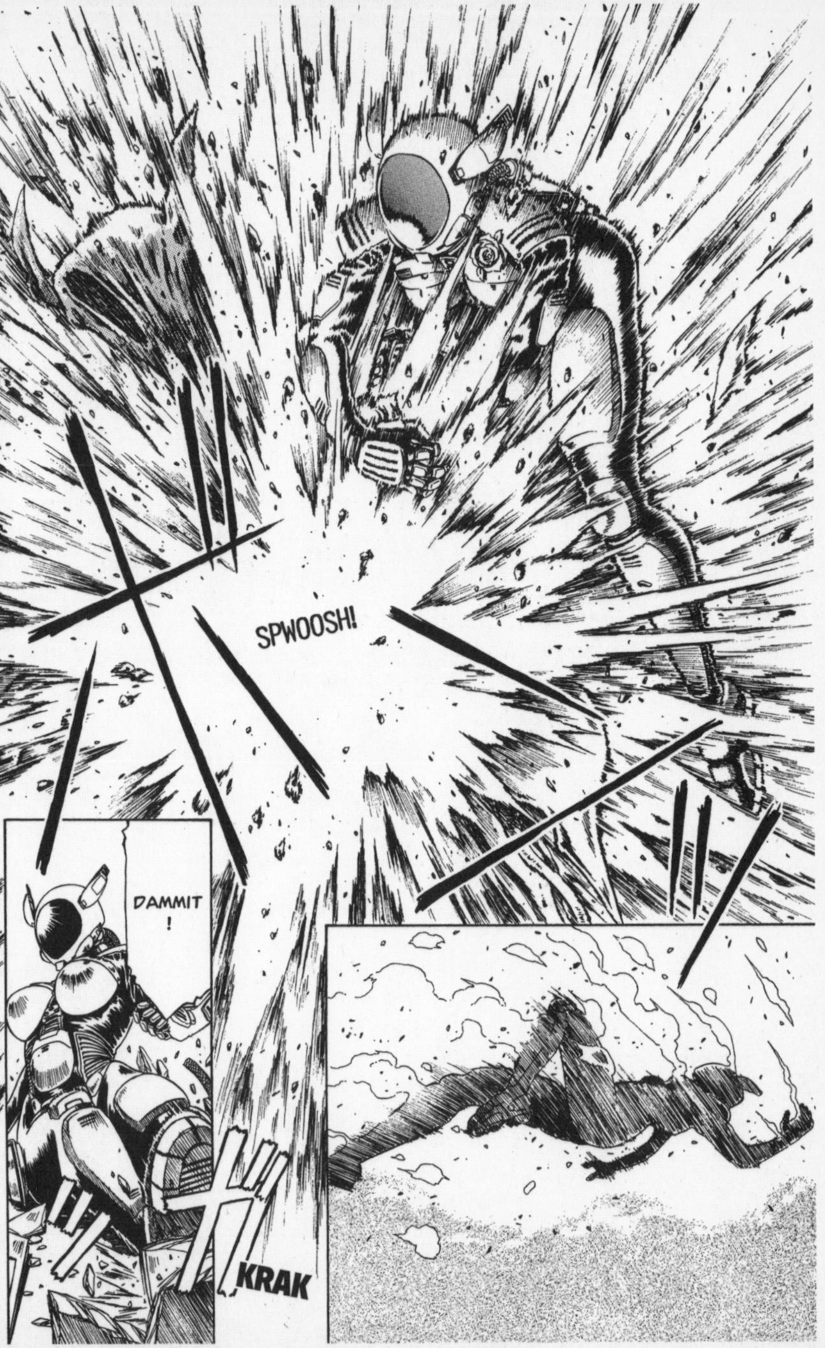
SPWOOSH!
DAMMIT !
KRAK

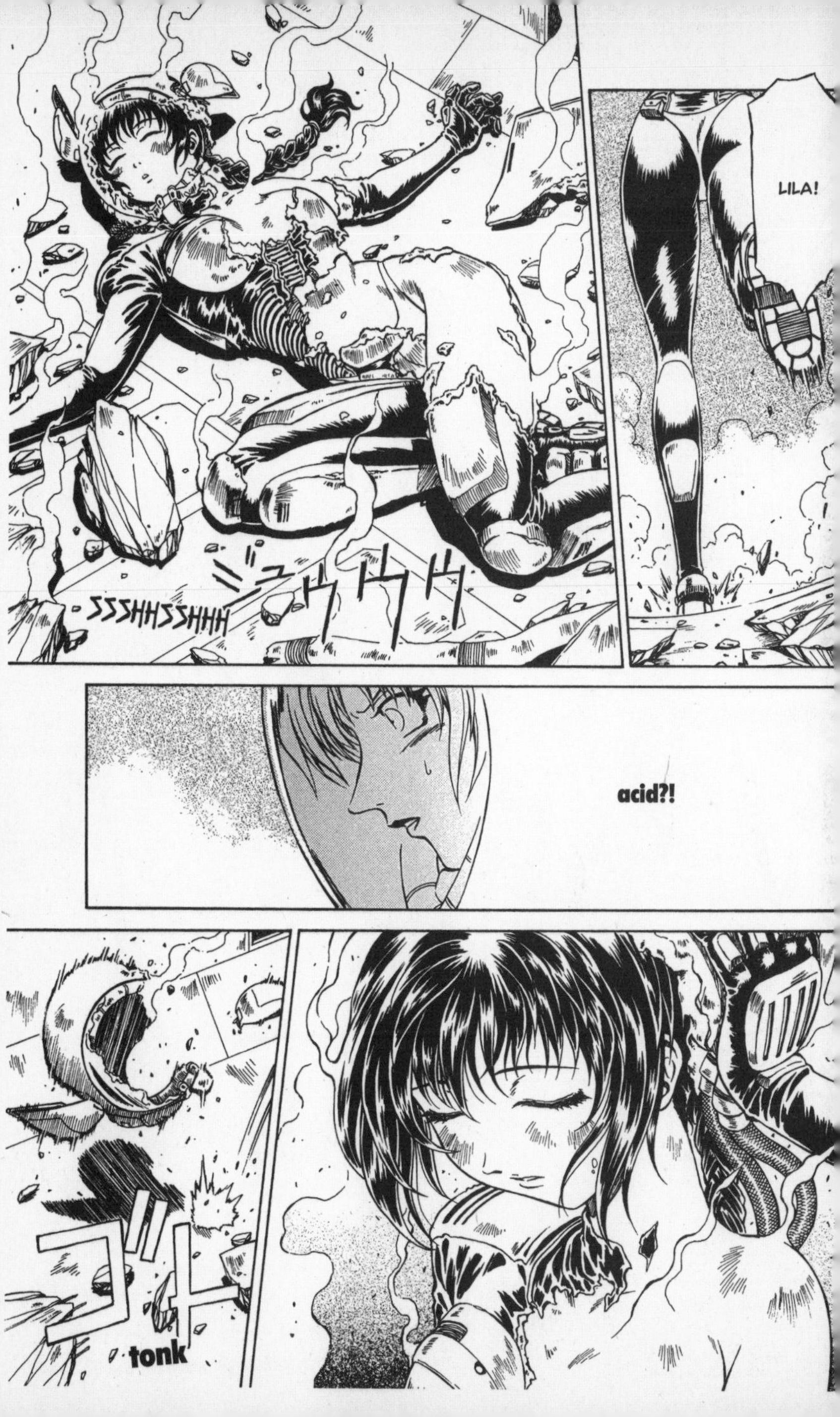
LILA!
ジュウウウ
SSSHHSSHHH
acid?!
ゴト
tonk

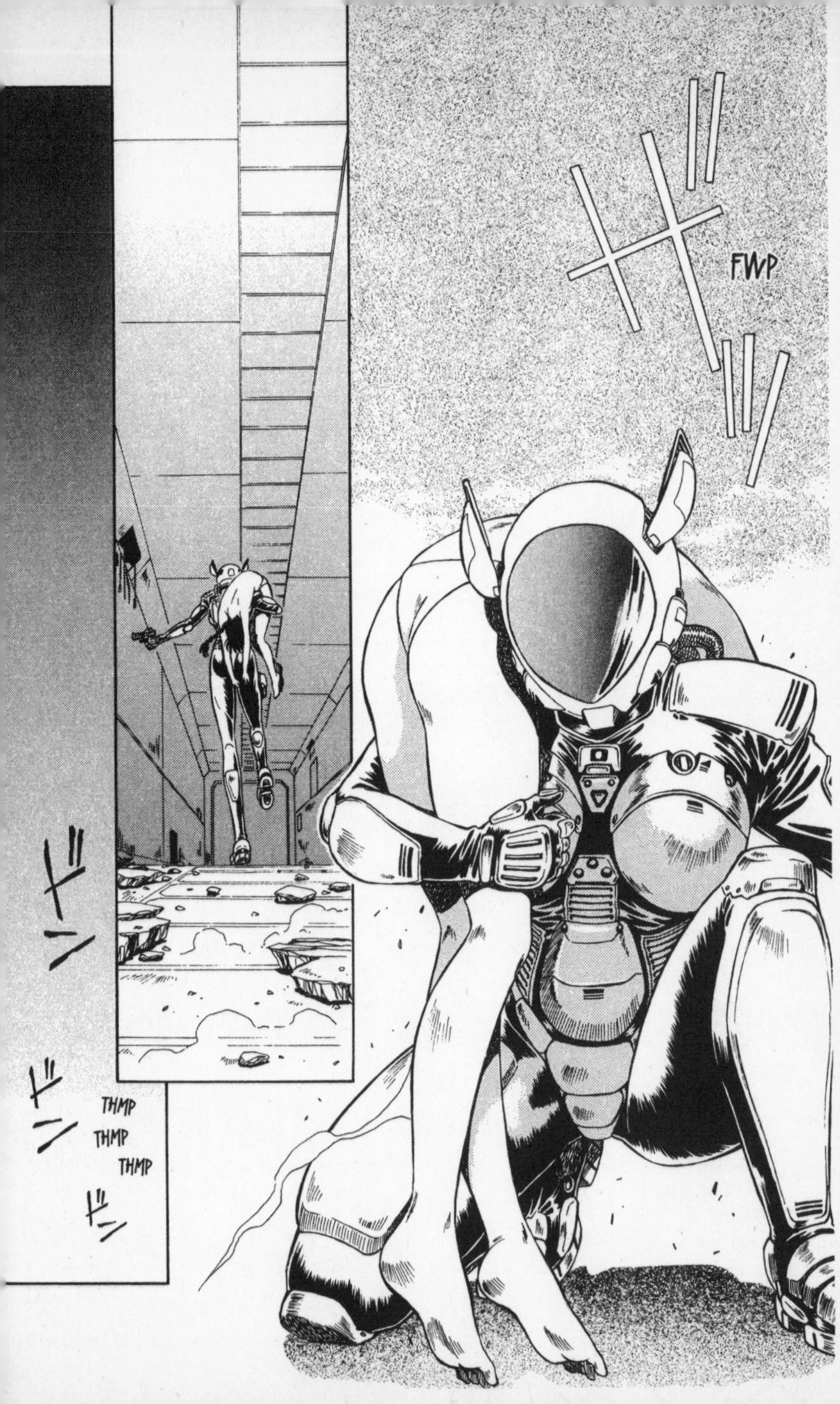
FWP
ドン
ドン
THMP
THMP
THMP
ドン

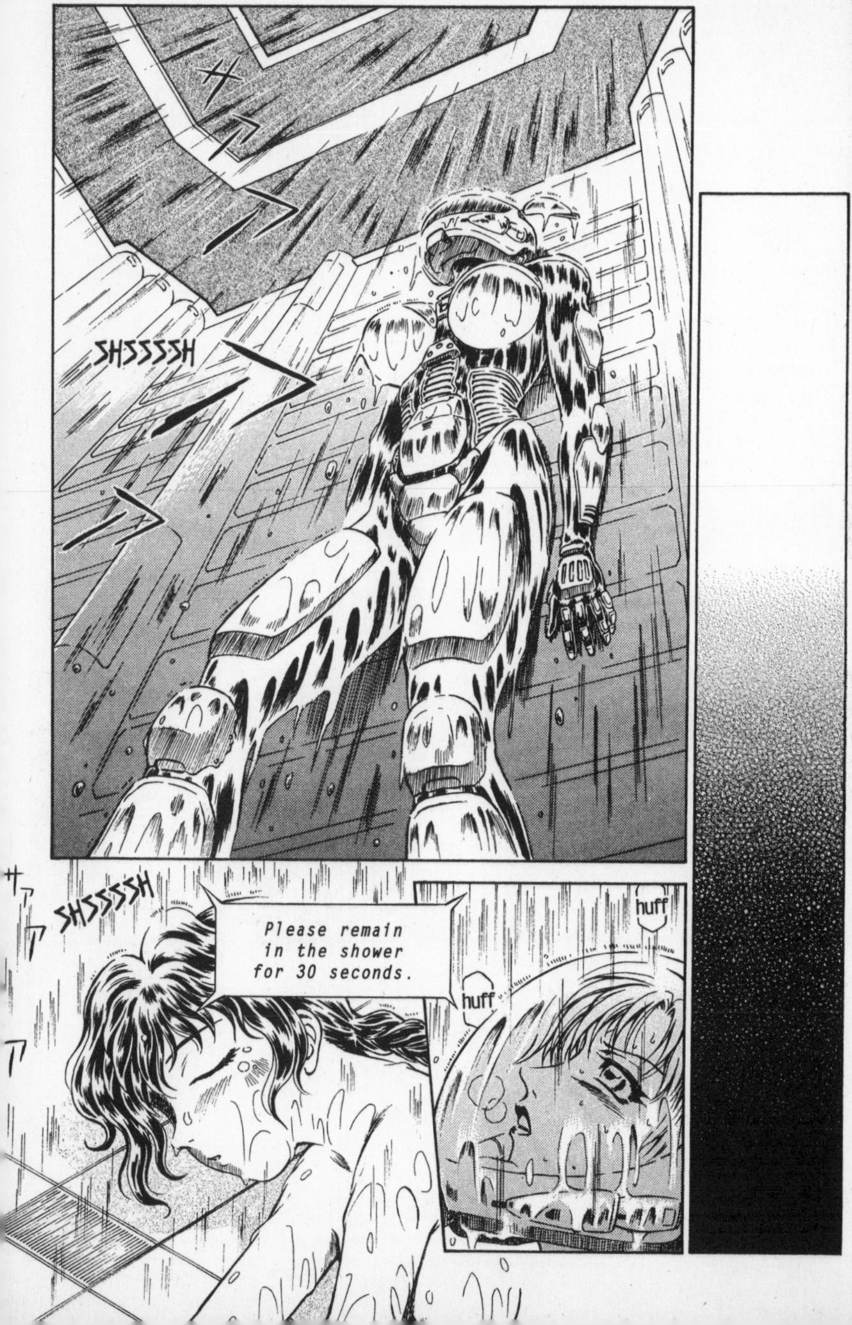
SHSSSSH
huff
huff
SHSSSSH
Please remain in the shower for 30 seconds.

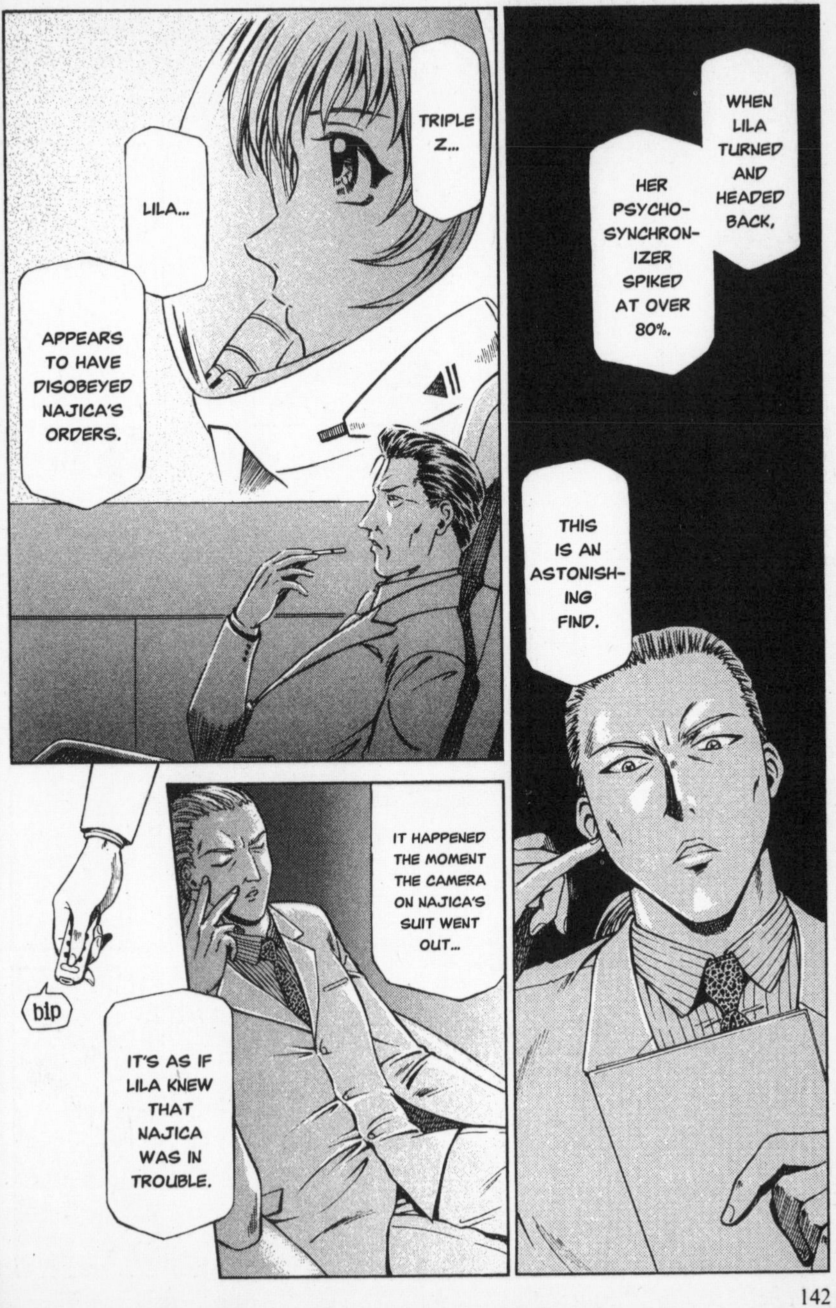
WHEN LILA TURNED AND HEADED BACK,
HER PSYCHO-SYNCHRONIZER SPIKED AT OVER 80%.
THIS IS AN ASTONISHING FIND.
TRIPLE Z...
LILA...
APPEARS TO HAVE DISOBEYED NAJICA'S ORDERS.
IT HAPPENED THE MOMENT THE CAMERA ON NAJICA'S SUIT WENT OUT...
IT'S AS IF LILA KNEW THAT NAJICA WAS IN TROUBLE.
bip

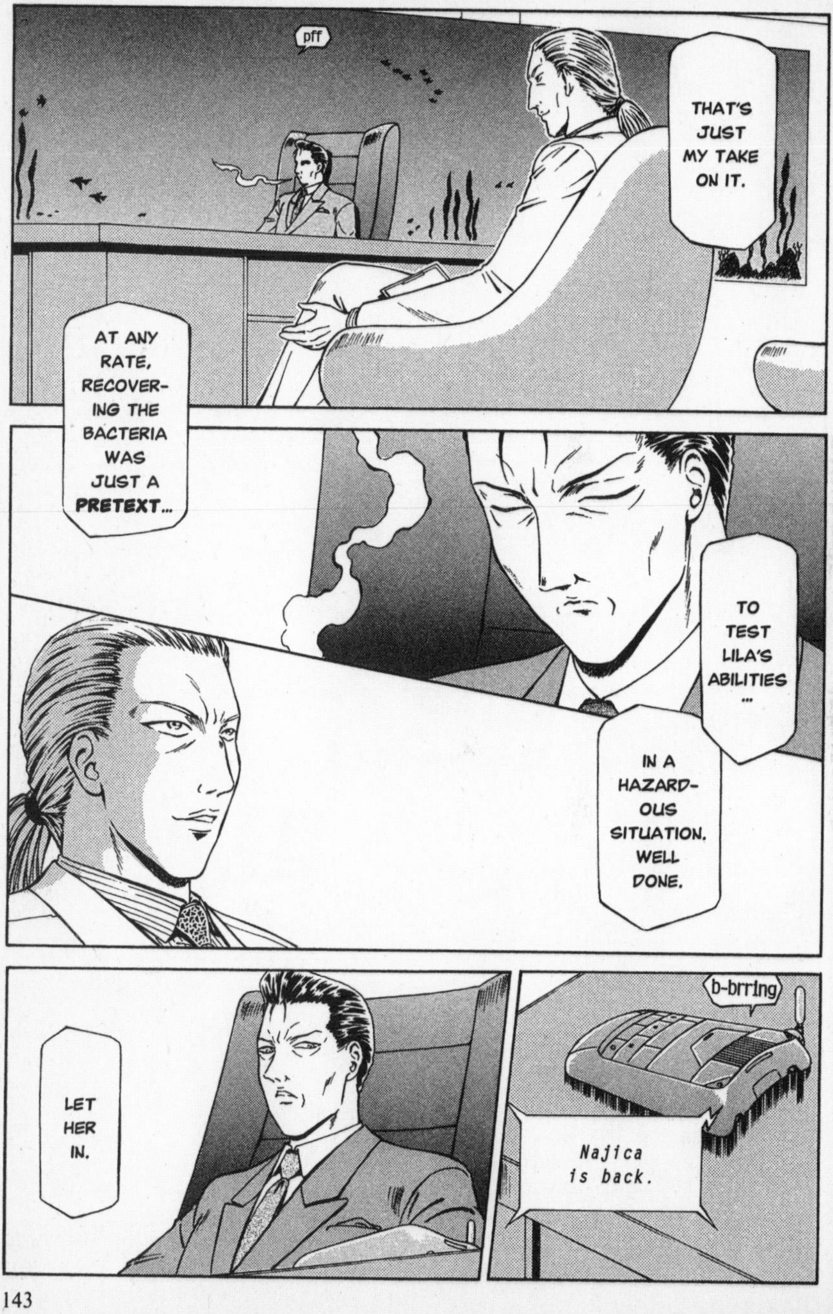
THAT'S JUST MY TAKE ON IT.
pff
AT ANY RATE, RECOVERING THE BACTERIA WAS JUST A **PRETEXT**...
TO TEST LILA'S ABILITIES ...
IN A HAZARDOUS SITUATION. WELL DONE.
b-brring
Najica is back.
LET HER IN.

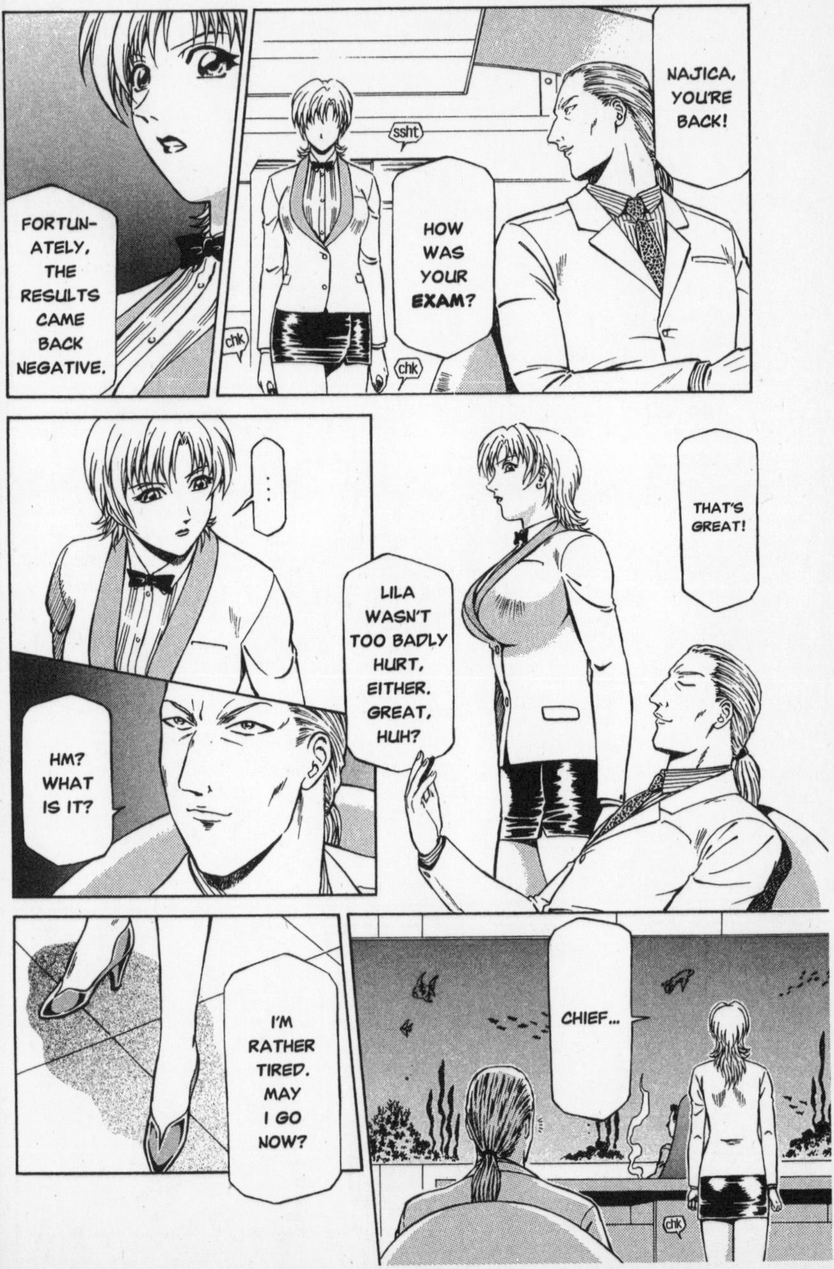
NAJICA, YOU'RE BACK!
sssht
HOW WAS YOUR EXAM?
chk
chk
FORTUN-ATELY, THE RESULTS CAME BACK NEGATIVE.
THAT'S GREAT!
LILA WASN'T TOO BADLY HURT, EITHER. GREAT, HUH?
...
HM? WHAT IS IT?
CHIEF...
chk
I'M RATHER TIRED. MAY I GO NOW?

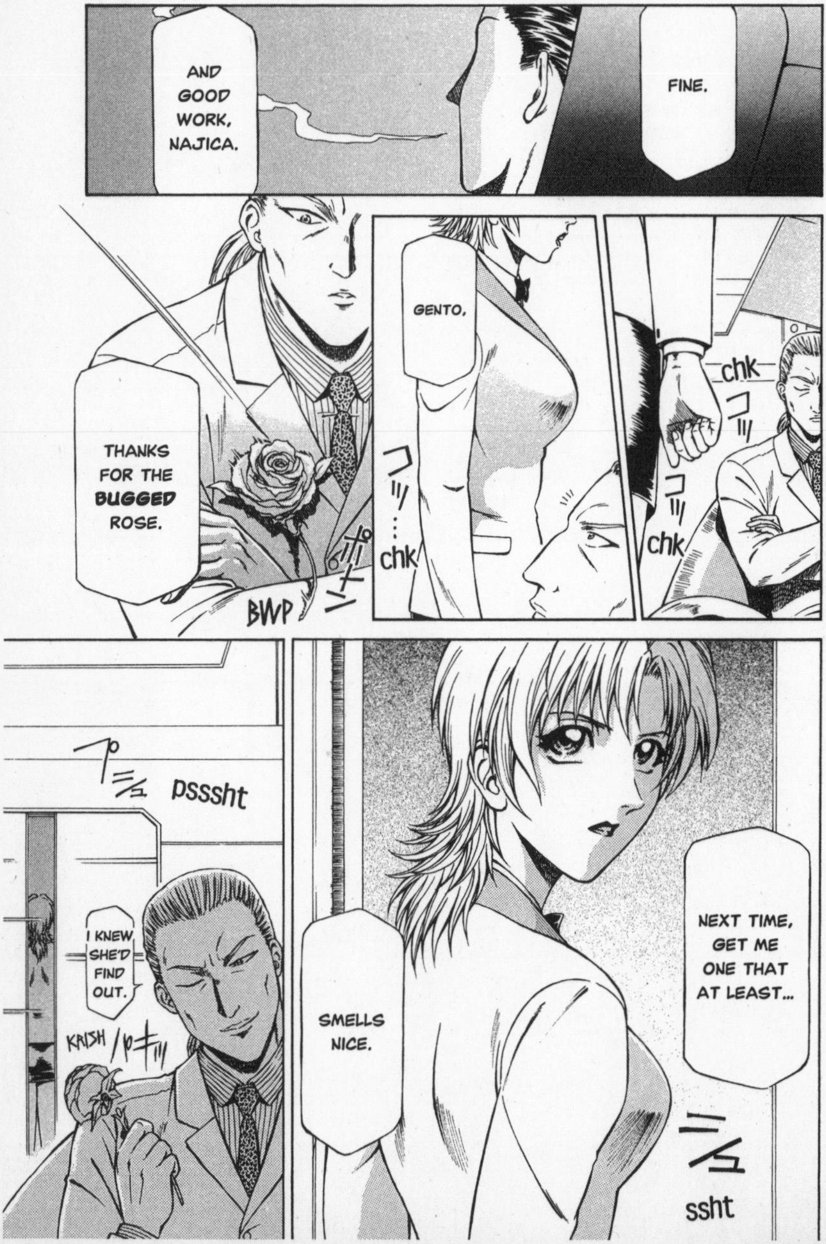
FINE.
AND GOOD WORK, NAJICA.
chk
chk
GENTO,
chk
THANKS FOR THE BUGGED ROSE.
BWP
NEXT TIME, GET ME ONE THAT AT LEAST...
SMELLS NICE.
ssht
psssht
I KNEW SHE'D FIND OUT.
KRISH

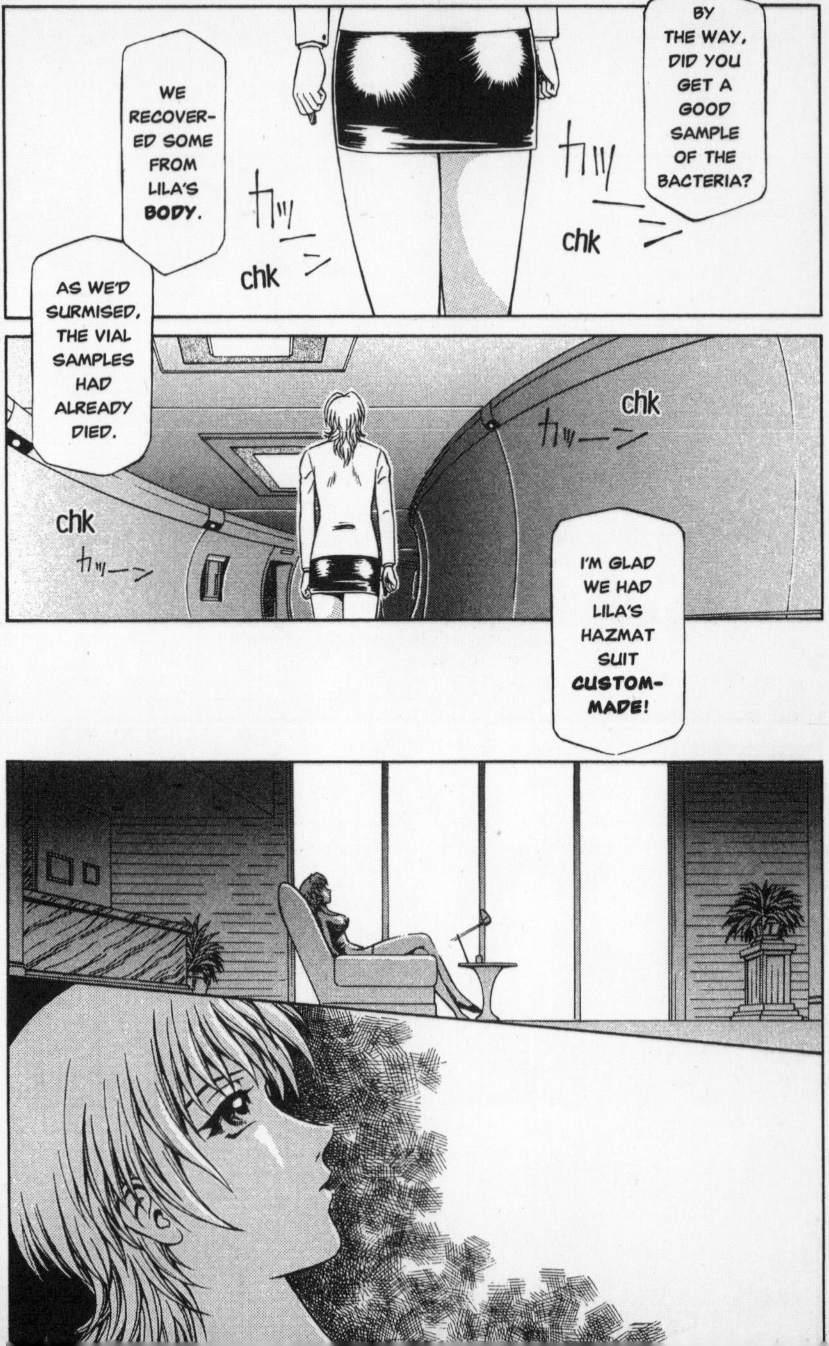
BY THE WAY, DID YOU GET A GOOD SAMPLE OF THE BACTERIA?
カッ
chk
WE RECOVERED-ED SOME FROM LILA'S **BODY**.
カッ
chk
AS WE'D SURMISED, THE VIAL SAMPLES HAD ALREADY DIED.
chk
カッーン
chk
カッーン
I'M GLAD WE HAD LILA'S HAZMAT SUIT **CUSTOM-MADE!**

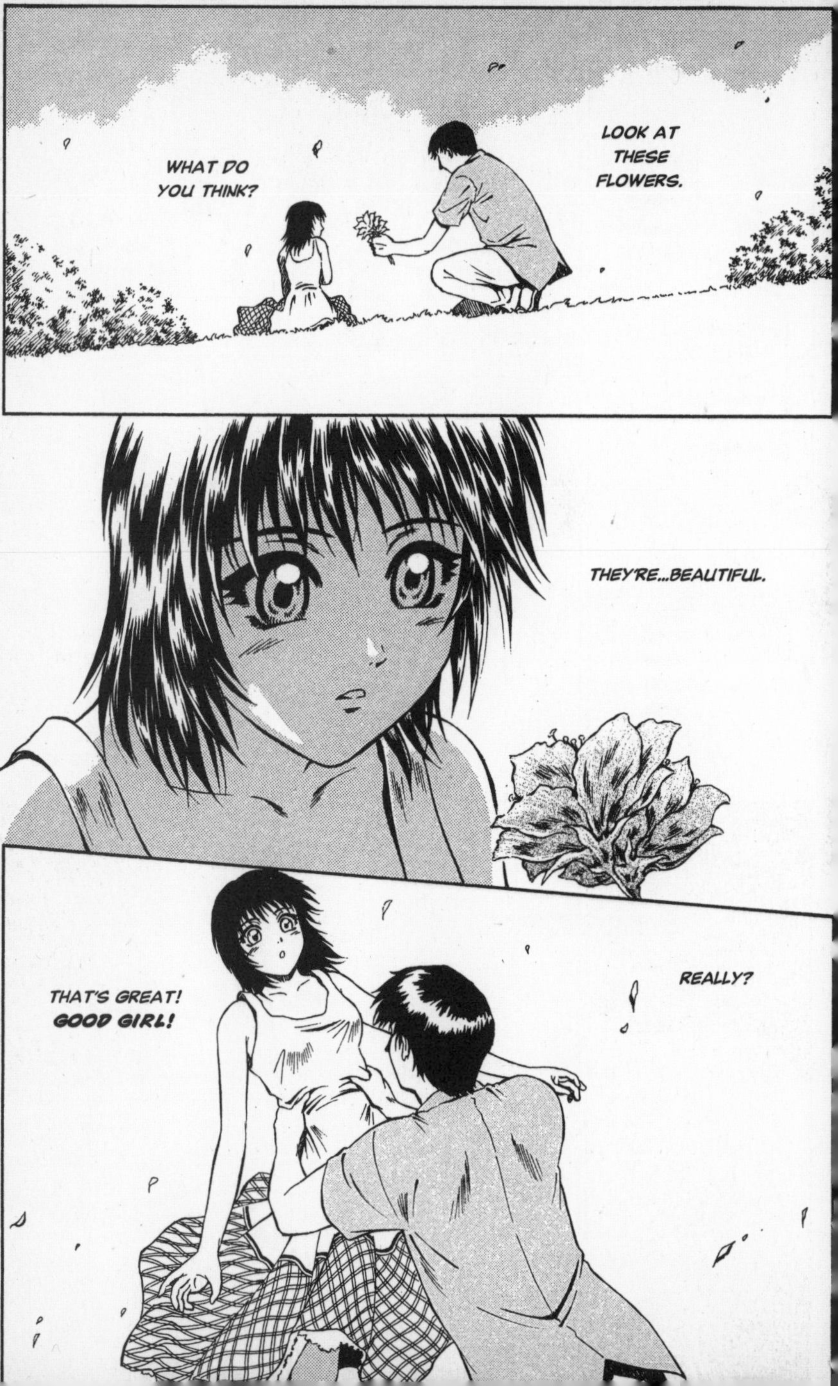
LOOK AT THESE FLOWERS.
WHAT DO YOU THINK?
THEY'RE...BEAUTIFUL.
REALLY?
THAT'S GREAT! GOOD GIRL!

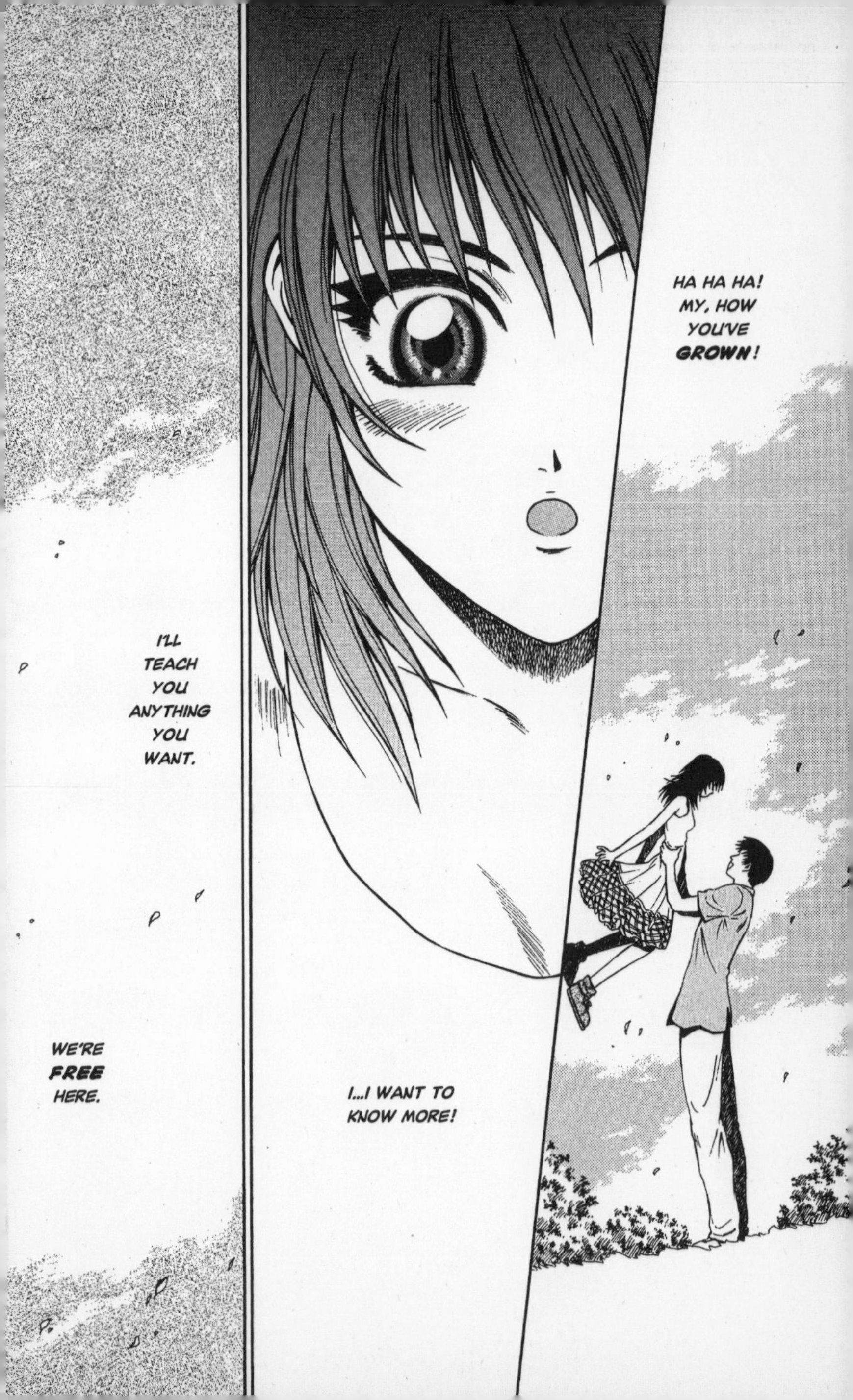
HA HA HA! MY, HOW YOU'VE GROWN!
I...I WANT TO KNOW MORE!
I'LL TEACH YOU ANYTHING YOU WANT.
WE'RE FREE HERE.

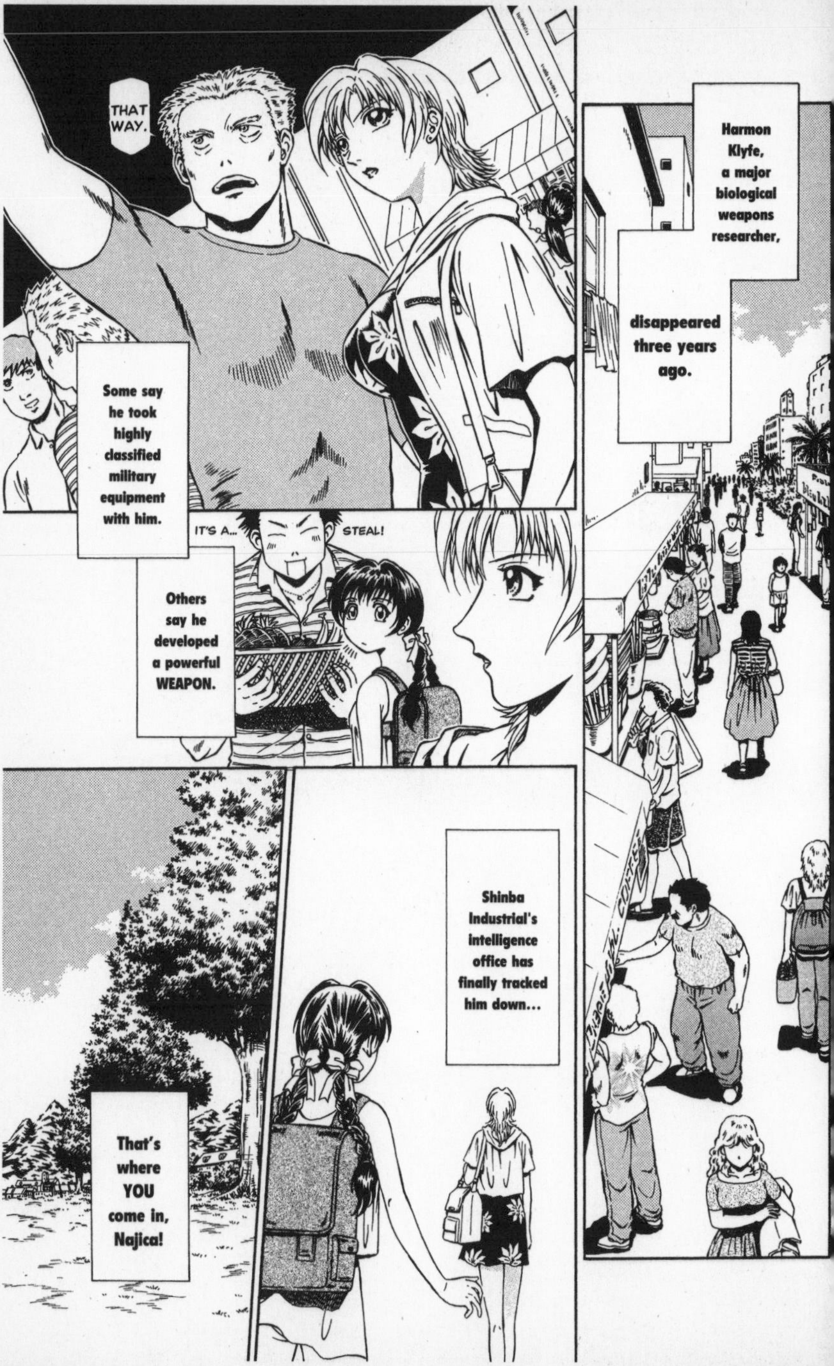
Harmon Klyfe, a major biological weapons researcher,
disappeared three years ago.
THAT WAY.
Some say he took highly classified military equipment with him.
IT'S A... STEAL!
Others say he developed a powerful WEAPON.
Shinba Industrial's intelligence office has finally tracked him down...
That's where YOU come in, Najica!

Operation. 12
RECOVER THE ISLAND HUMARITT

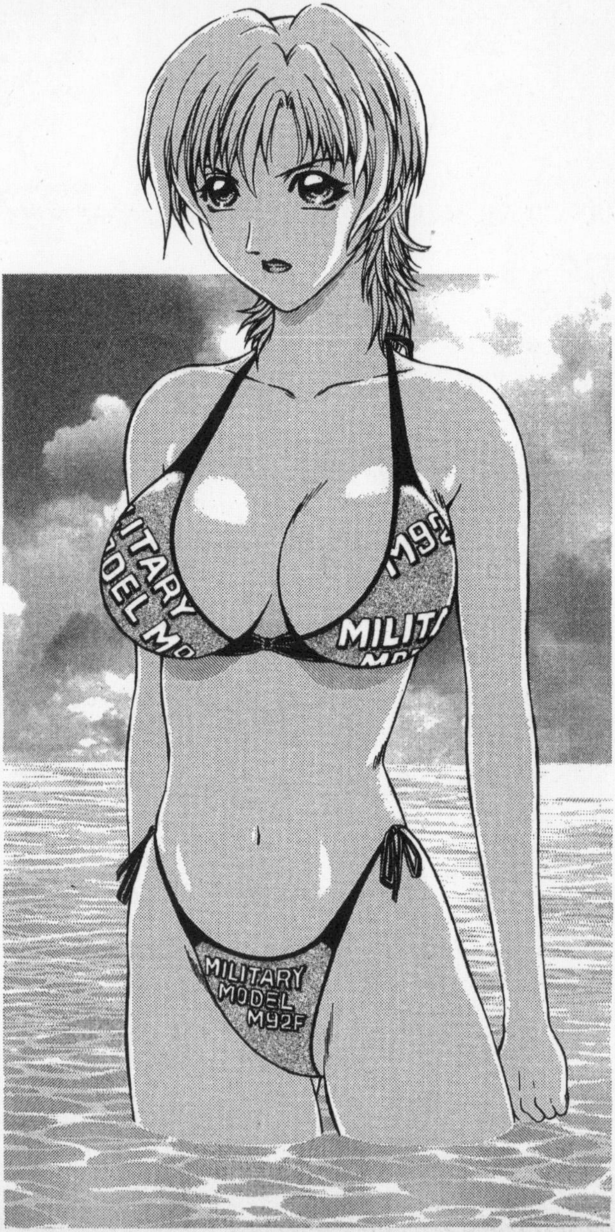
MILITARY
MODEL
M92F

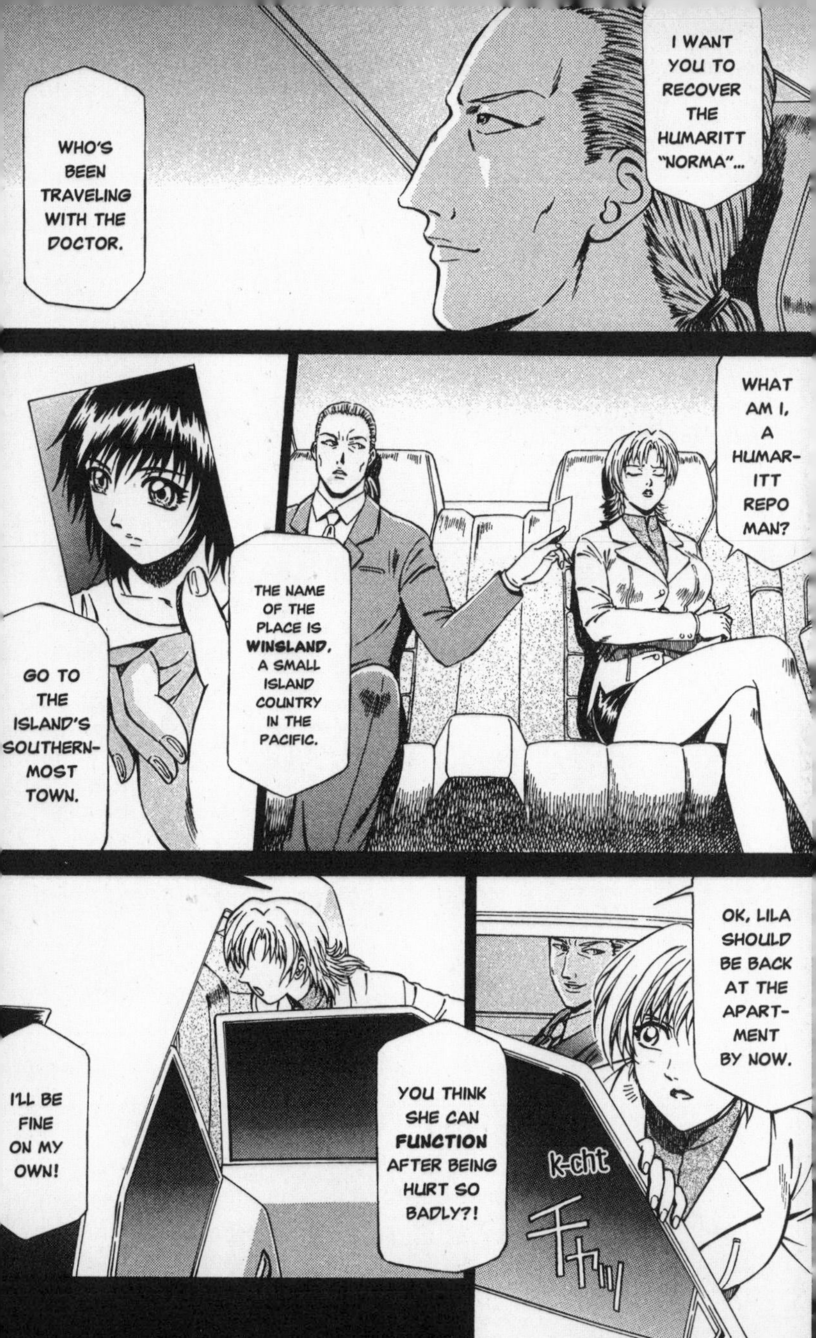
I WANT YOU TO RECOVER THE HUMARITT "NORMA"...
WHO'S BEEN TRAVELING WITH THE DOCTOR.
WHAT AM I, A HUMARITT REPO MAN?
THE NAME OF THE PLACE IS **WINSLAND**, A SMALL ISLAND COUNTRY IN THE PACIFIC.
GO TO THE ISLAND'S SOUTHERNMOST TOWN.
OK, LILA SHOULD BE BACK AT THE APARTMENT BY NOW.
k-cht
チャッ
YOU THINK SHE CAN **FUNCTION** AFTER BEING HURT SO BADLY?!
I'LL BE FINE ON MY OWN!

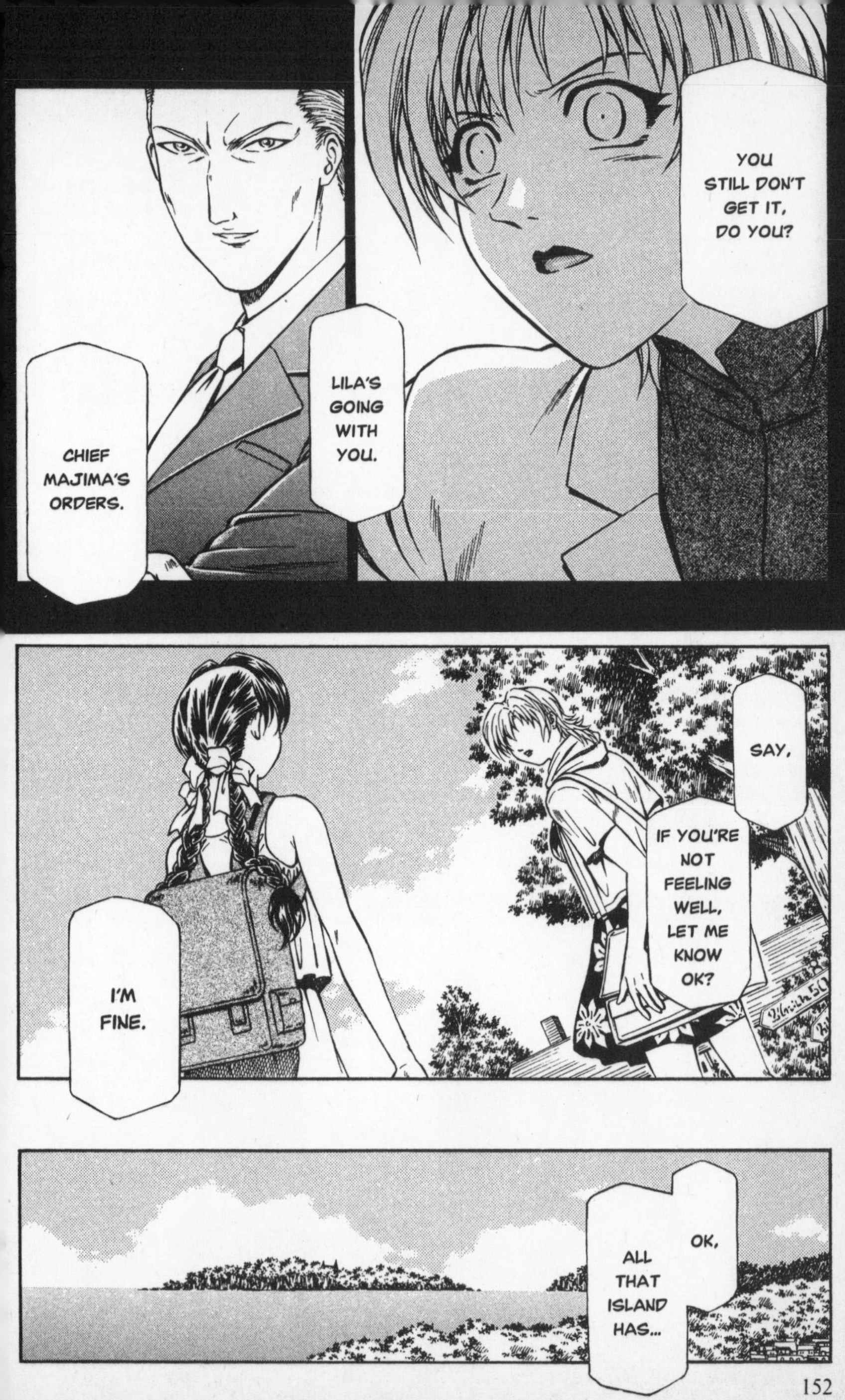
YOU STILL DON'T GET IT, DO YOU?
LILA'S GOING WITH YOU.
CHIEF MAJIMA'S ORDERS.
SAY,
IF YOU'RE NOT FEELING WELL, LET ME KNOW OK?
I'M FINE.
OK,
ALL THAT ISLAND HAS...

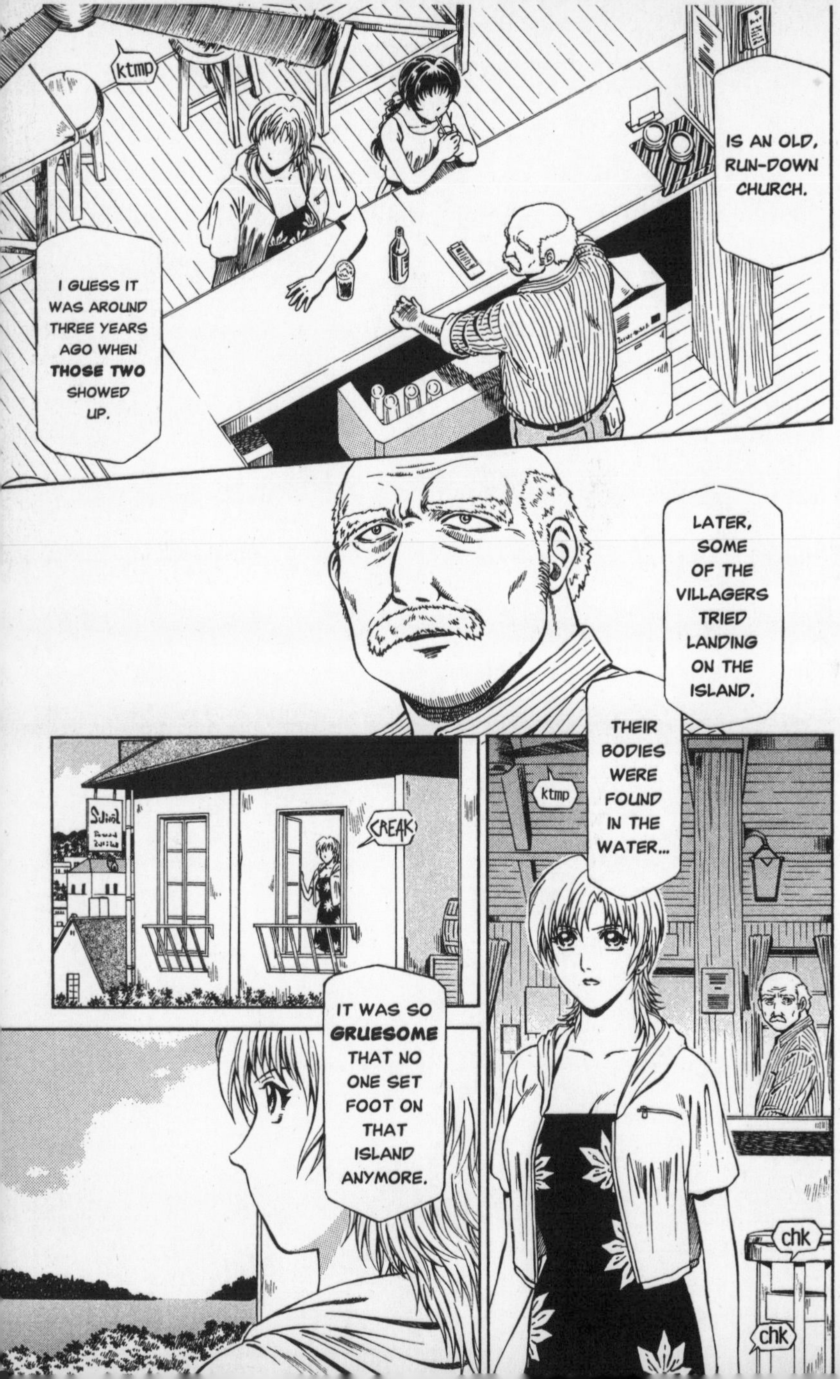
IS AN OLD, RUN-DOWN CHURCH.
ktmp
I GUESS IT WAS AROUND THREE YEARS AGO WHEN **THOSE TWO** SHOWED UP.
LATER, SOME OF THE VILLAGERS TRIED LANDING ON THE ISLAND.
THEIR BODIES WERE FOUND IN THE WATER...
ktmp
chk
chk
CREAK
IT WAS SO **GRUESOME** THAT NO ONE SET FOOT ON THAT ISLAND ANYMORE.

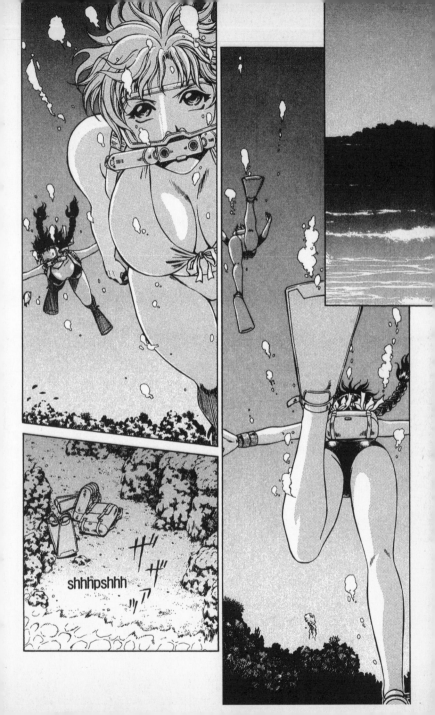

shhhpshhh

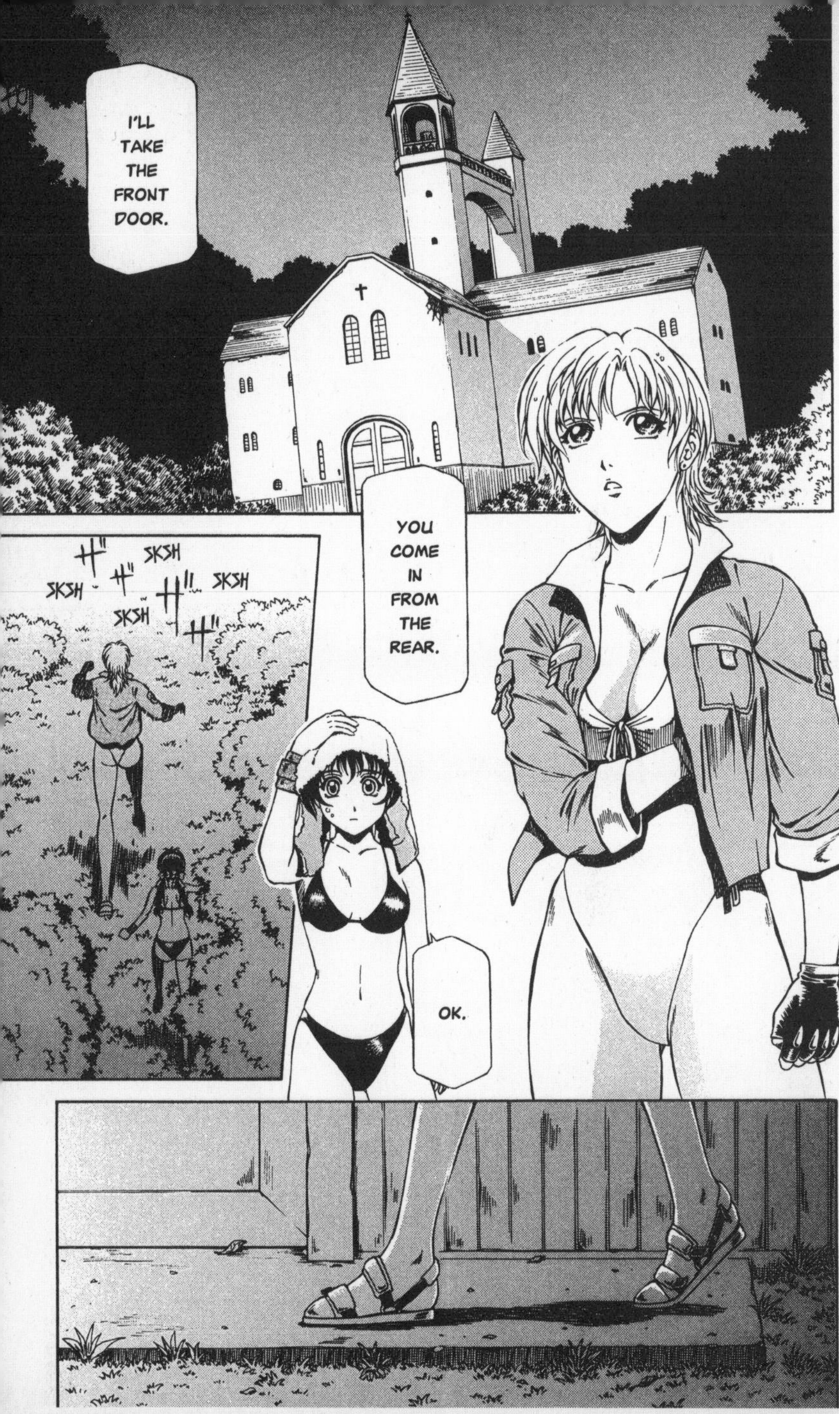
I'LL TAKE THE FRONT DOOR.
YOU COME IN FROM THE REAR.
OK.
SKSH
SKSH
SKSH
SKSH

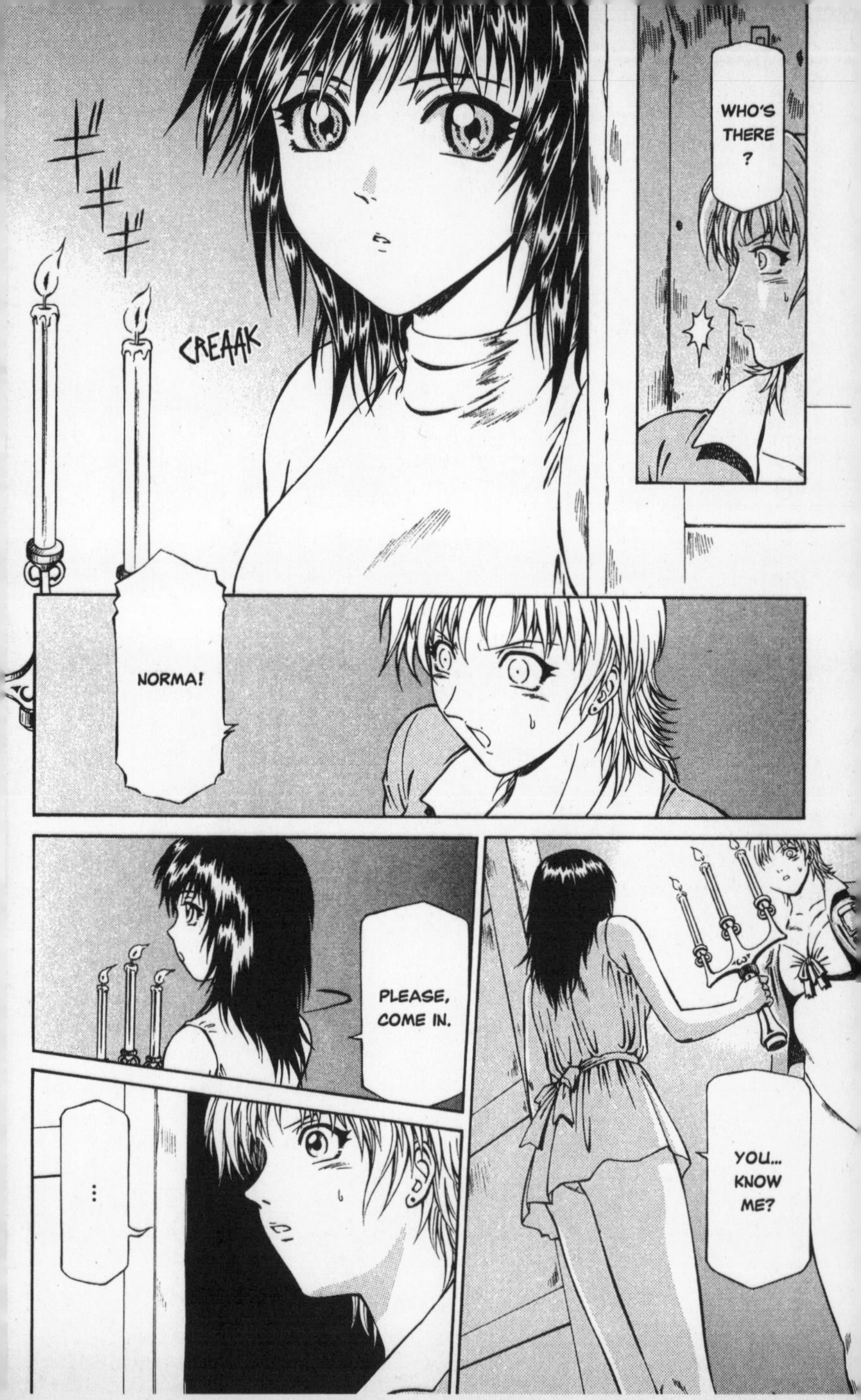
WHO'S THERE ?
ギギギ
CREAAK
NORMA!
YOU... KNOW ME?
PLEASE, COME IN.
...

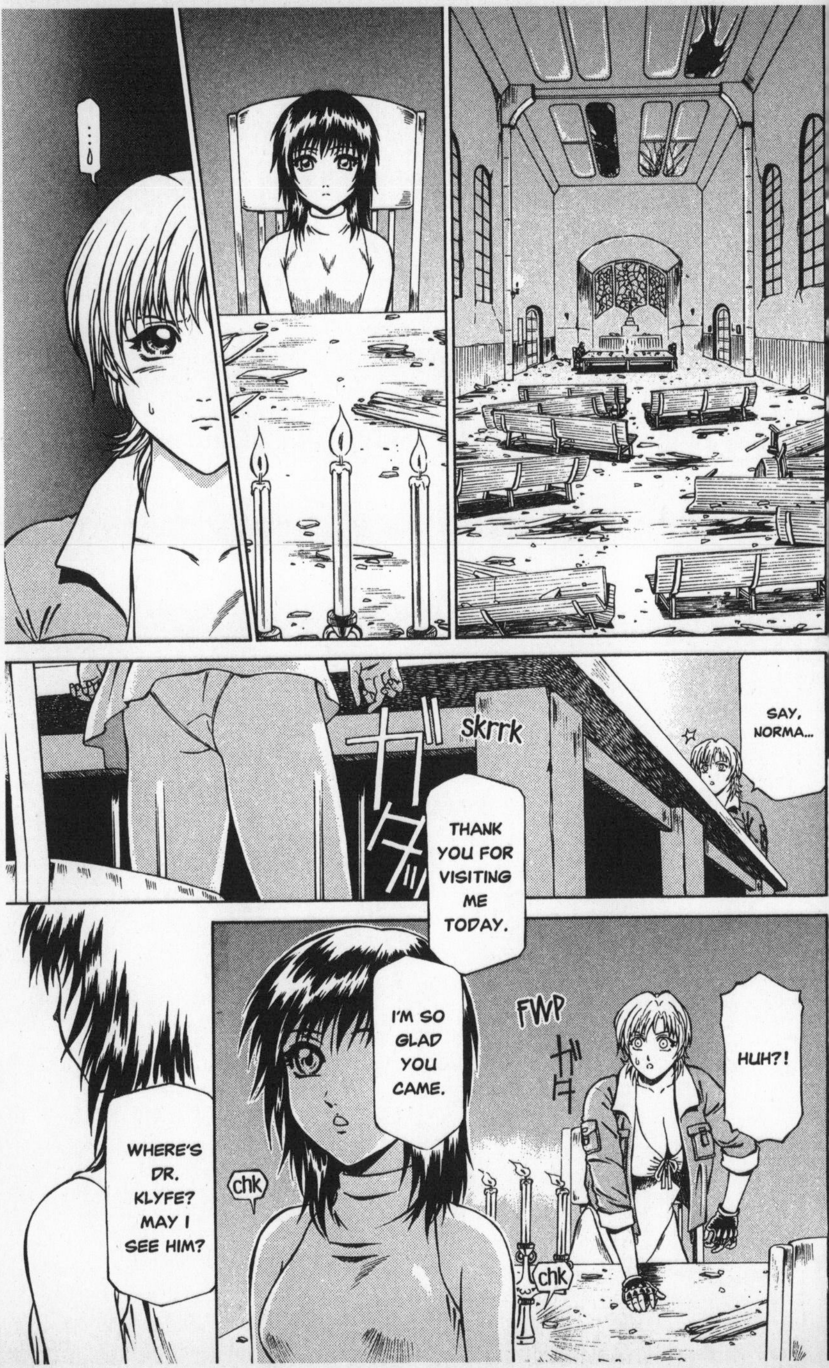
...
SAY, NORMA...
skrrk
THANK YOU FOR VISITING ME TODAY.
HUH?!
FWP
I'M SO GLAD YOU CAME.
chk
chk
WHERE'S DR. KLYFE? MAY I SEE HIM?

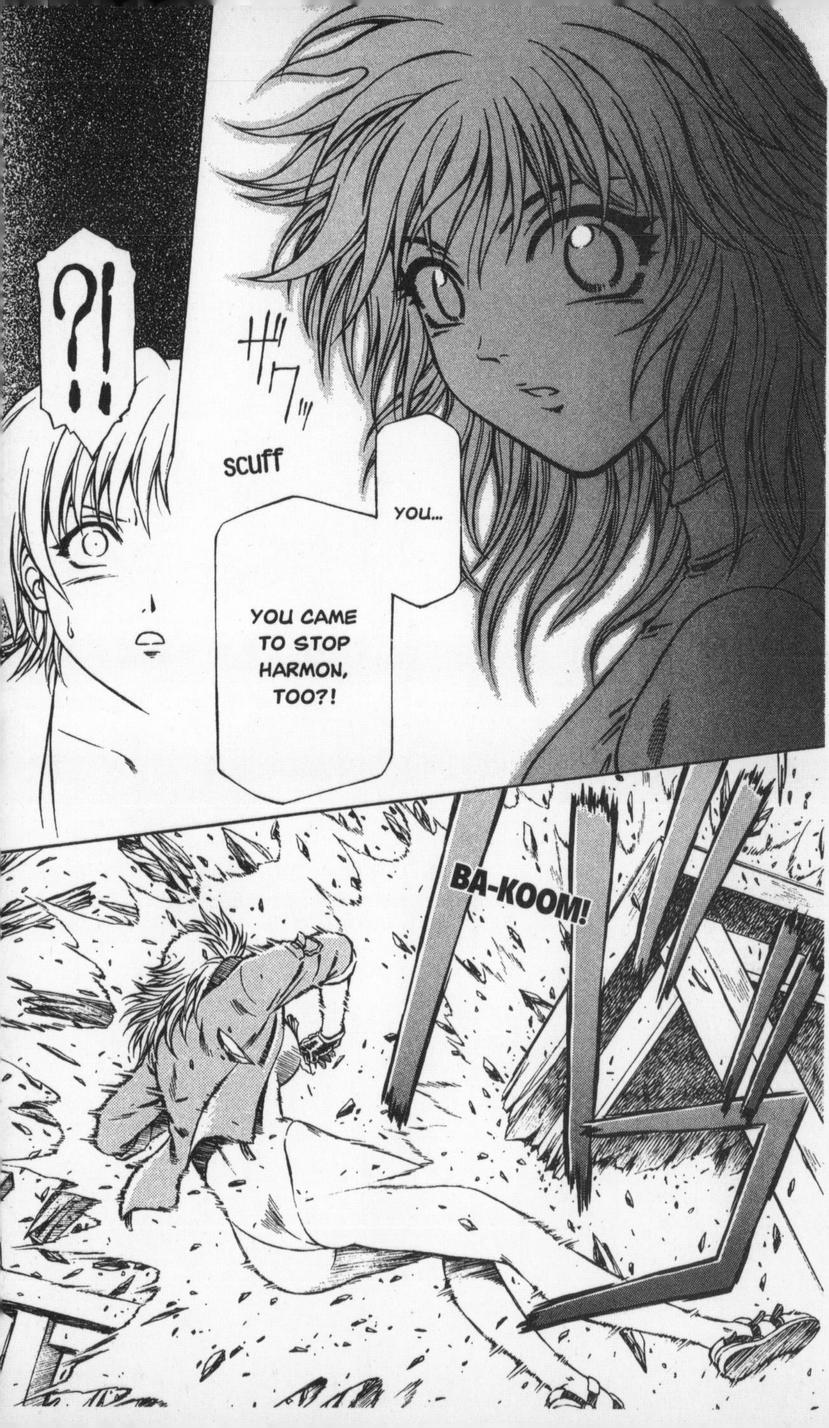
ザクッ
scuff
YOU...
YOU CAME TO STOP HARMON, TOO?!
?!
BA-KOOM!

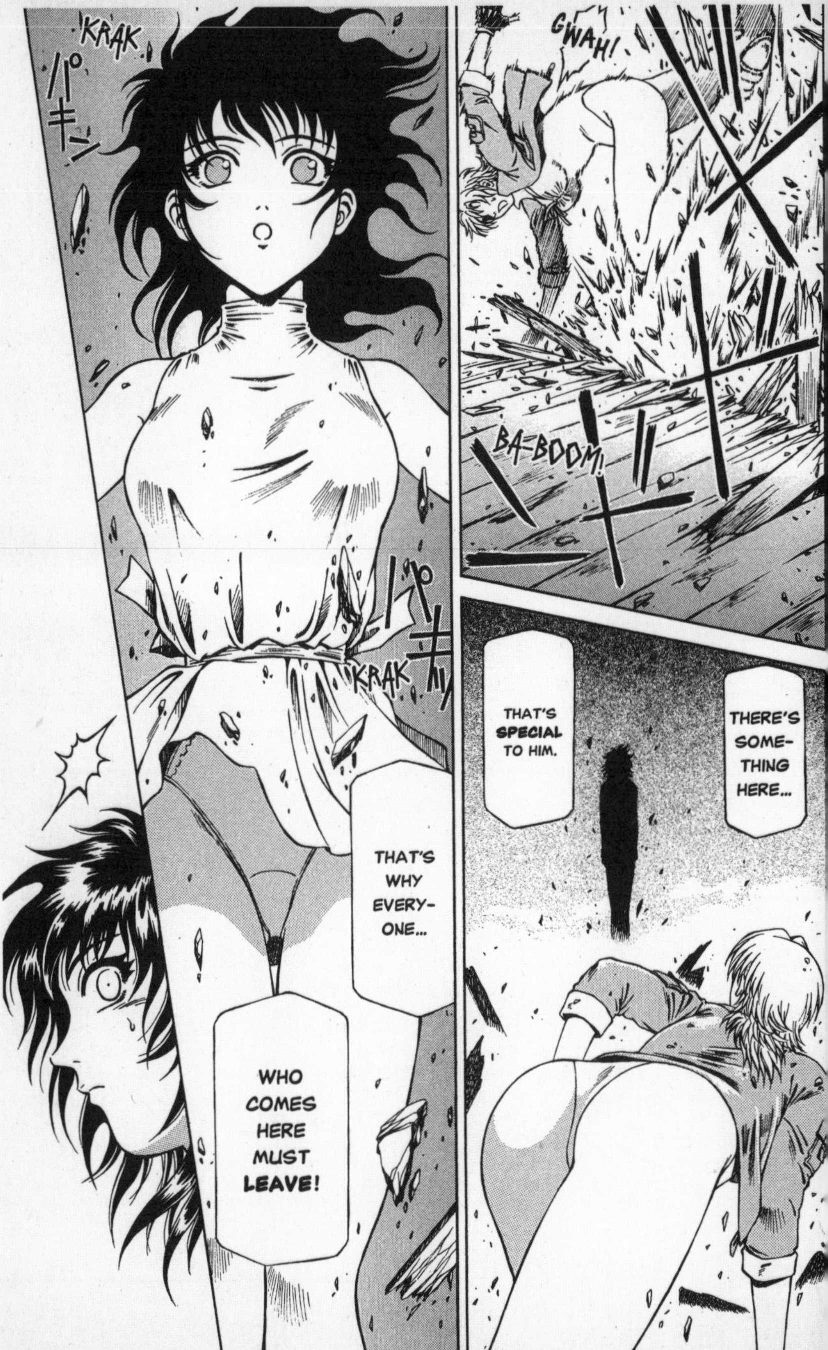
GWAH!
BA-BOOM!
THERE'S SOME-THING HERE...
THAT'S SPECIAL TO HIM.
KRAK
パキン
パキン
KRAK
THAT'S WHY EVERY-ONE...
WHO COMES HERE MUST LEAVE!

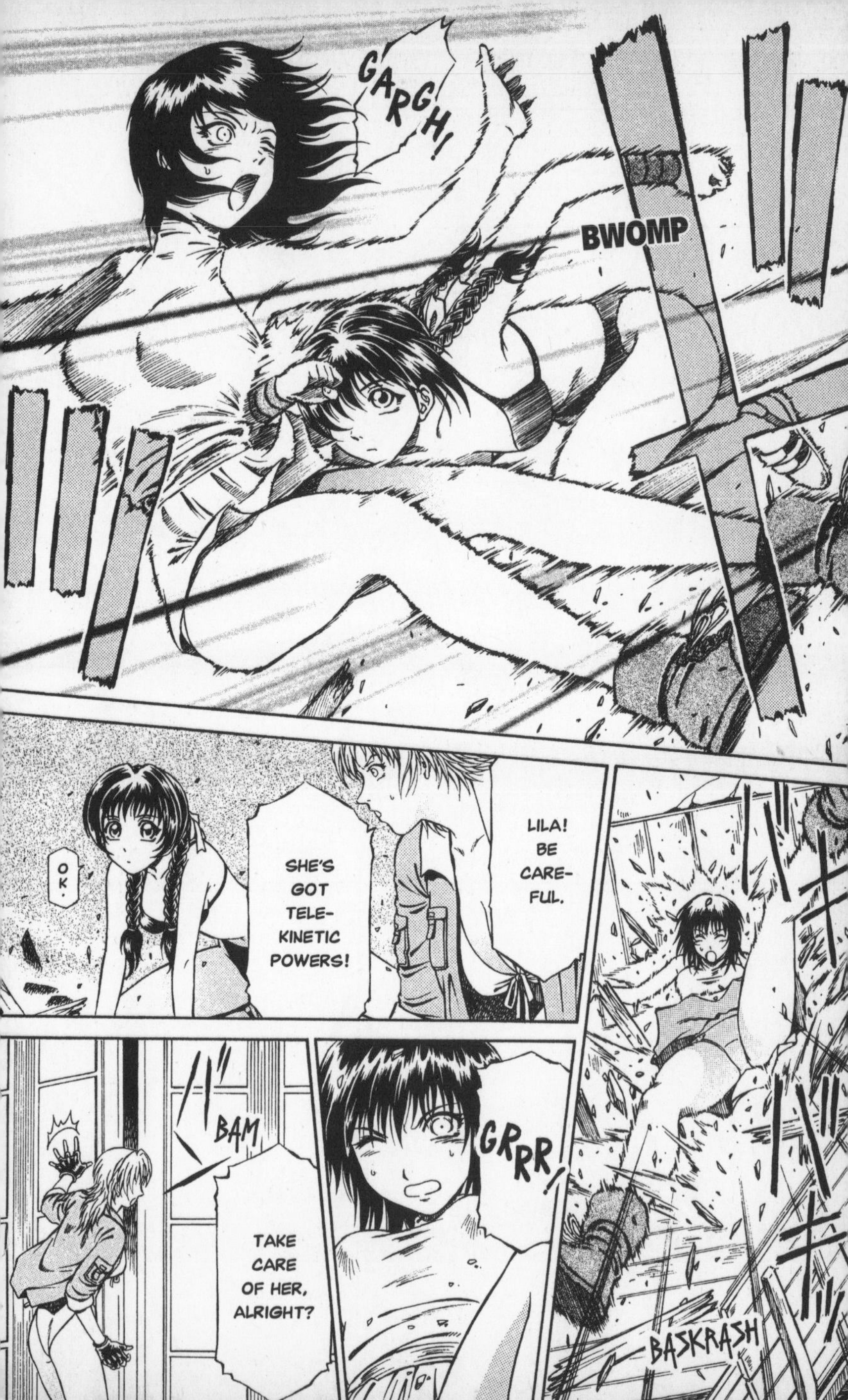
GARGH!
BWOMP
BASKRASH
LILA! BE CAREFUL.
SHE'S GOT TELEKINETIC POWERS!
OK.
GRRR!
BAM
TAKE CARE OF HER, ALRIGHT?

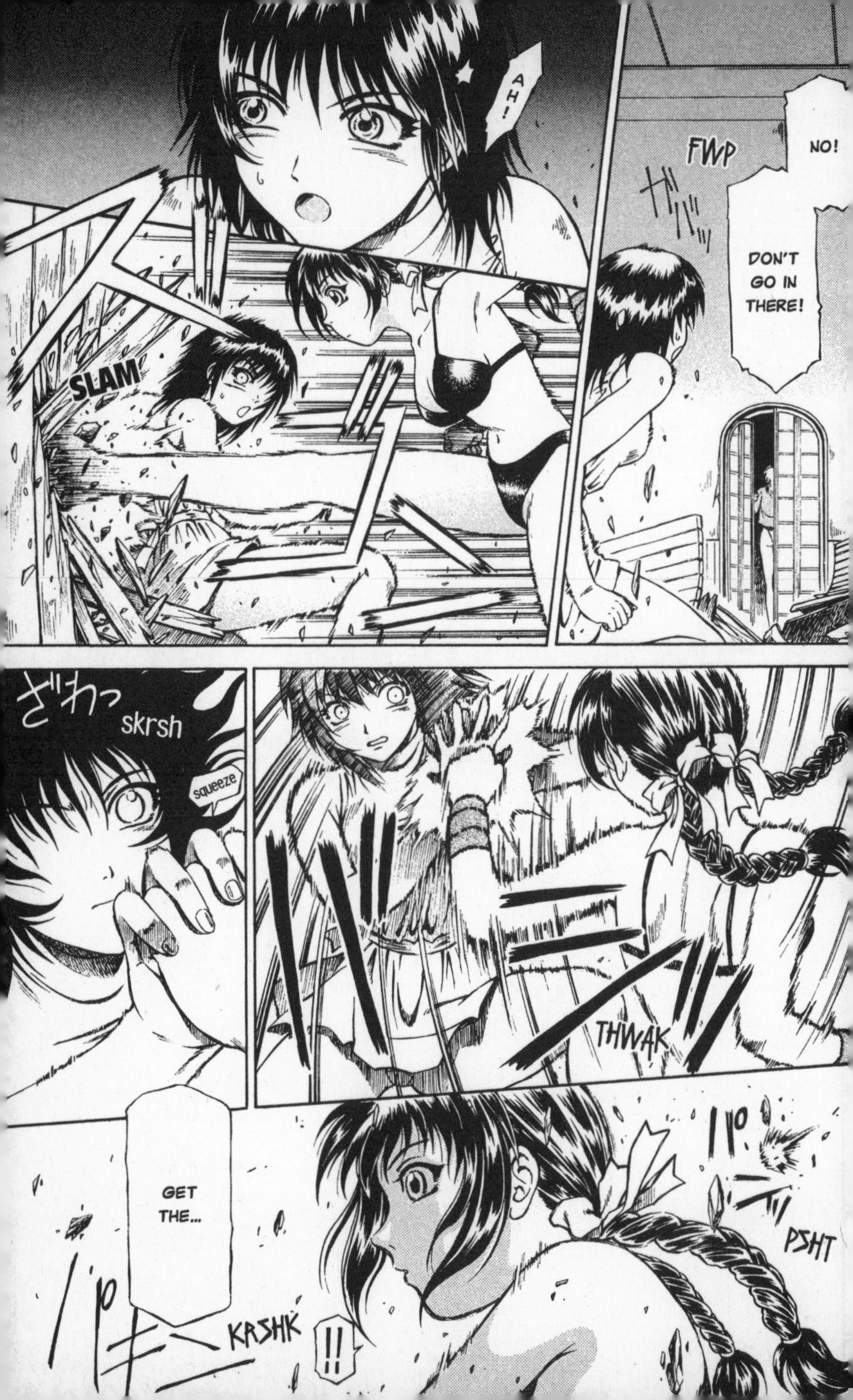
NO!
DON'T GO IN THERE!
FWP
AH!
SLAM
THWAK
ざわっ
skrsh
squeeze
PSHT
GET THE...
!!
KRSHK

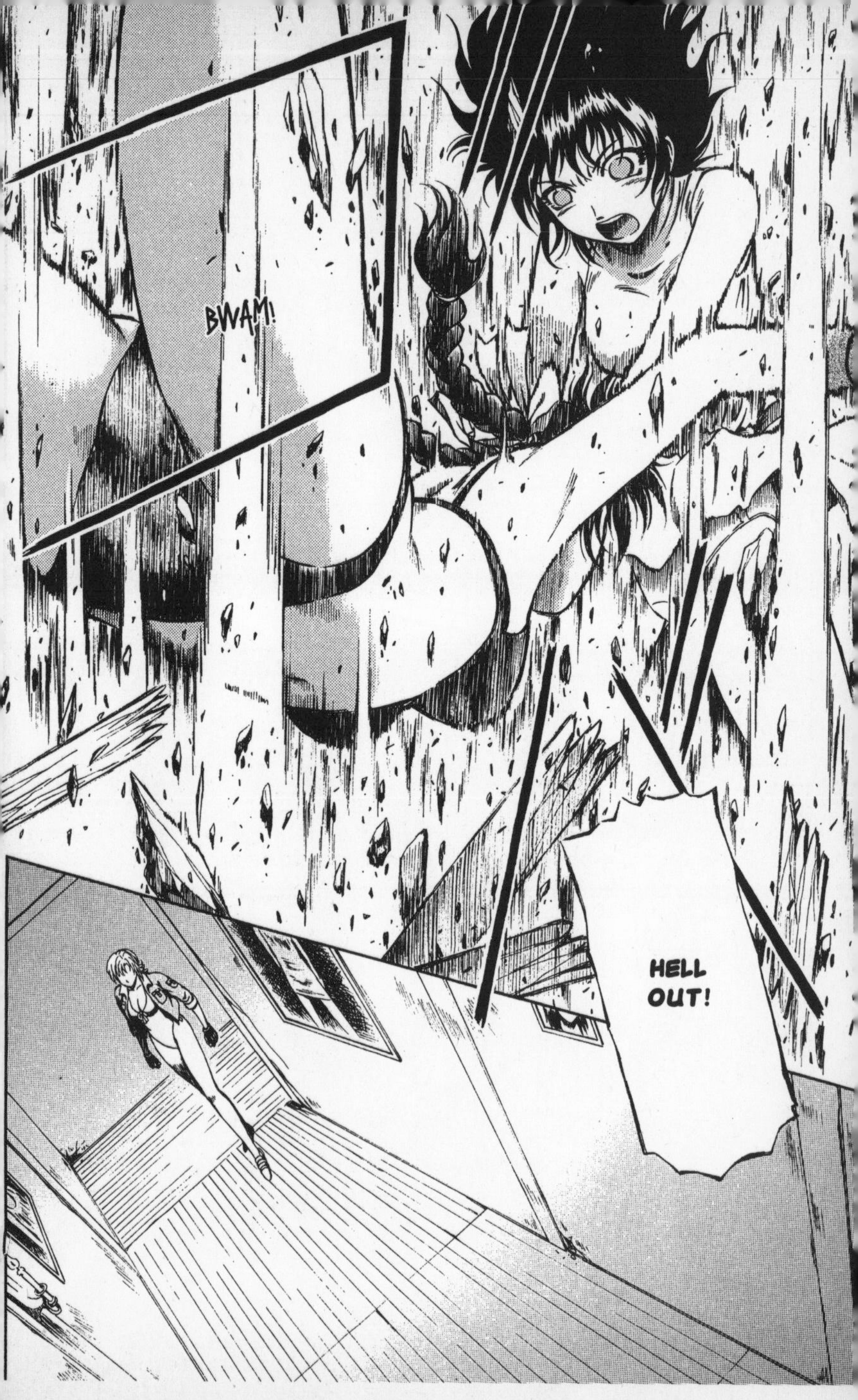
HELL OUT!
BWAM!

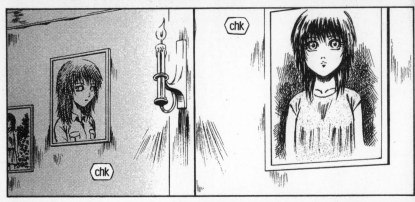

chk

chk

portraits of Norma.

They're all...

KREEE

chk

chk

163

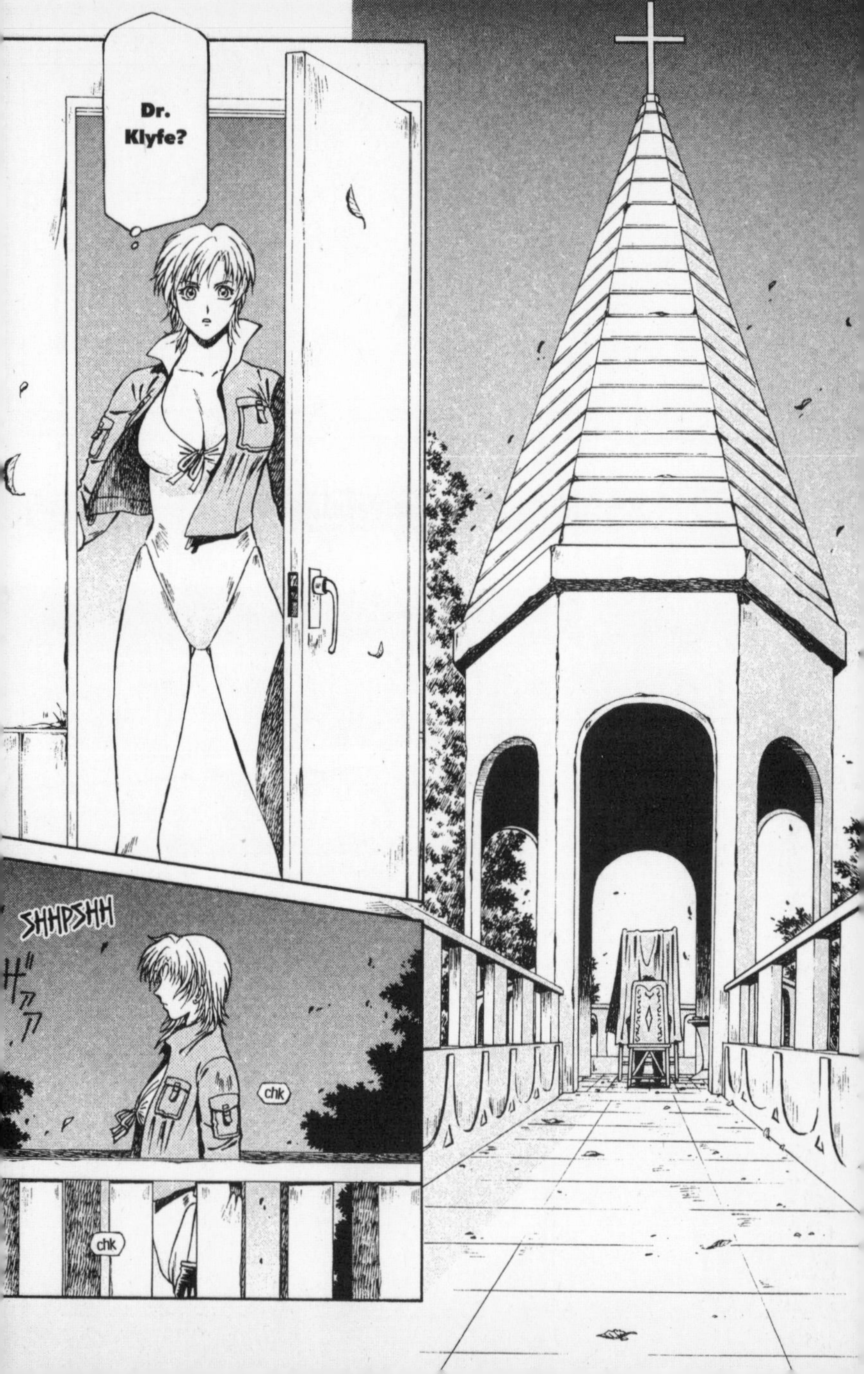
Dr. Klyfe?
SHHPSHH
ザァァ
chk
chk

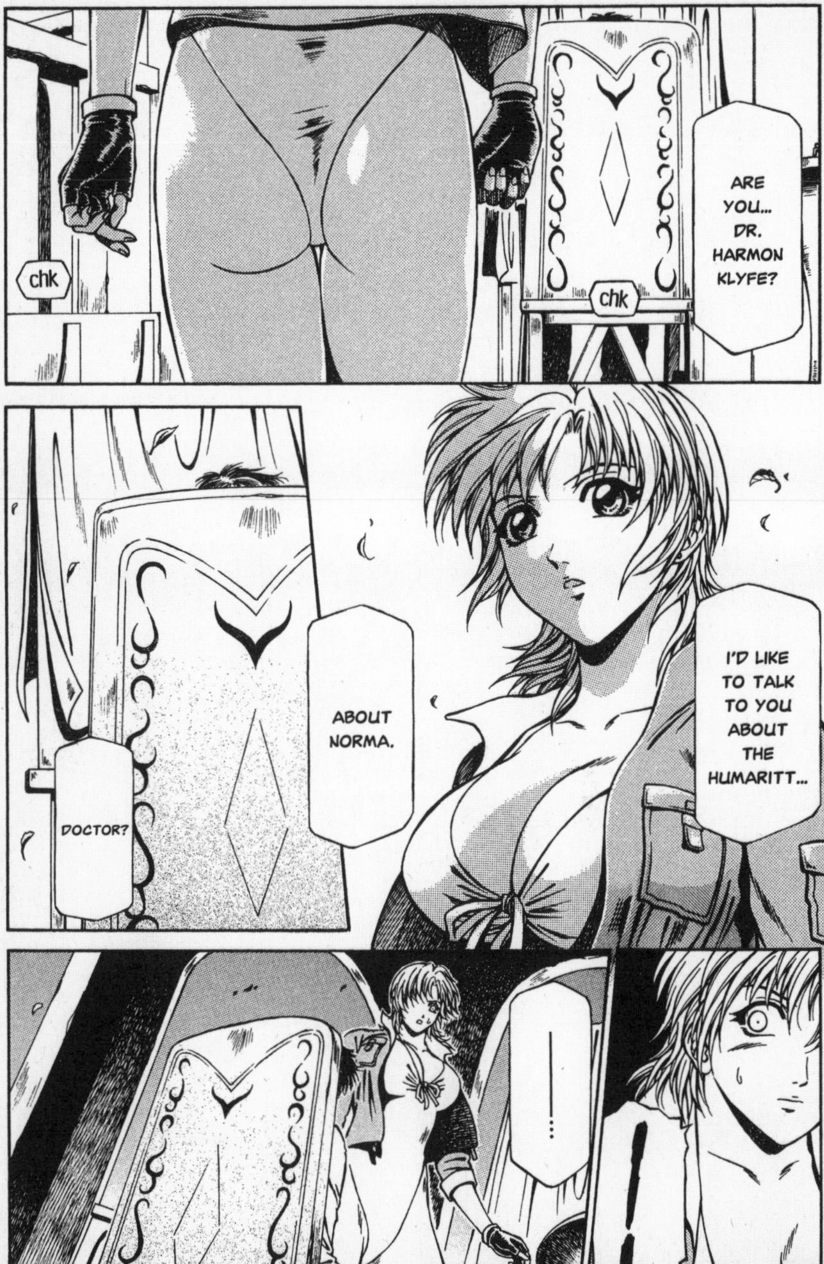

ARE YOU... DR. HARMON KLYFE?
chk
chk
I'D LIKE TO TALK TO YOU ABOUT THE HUMARITT...
ABOUT NORMA.
DOCTOR?
!
......

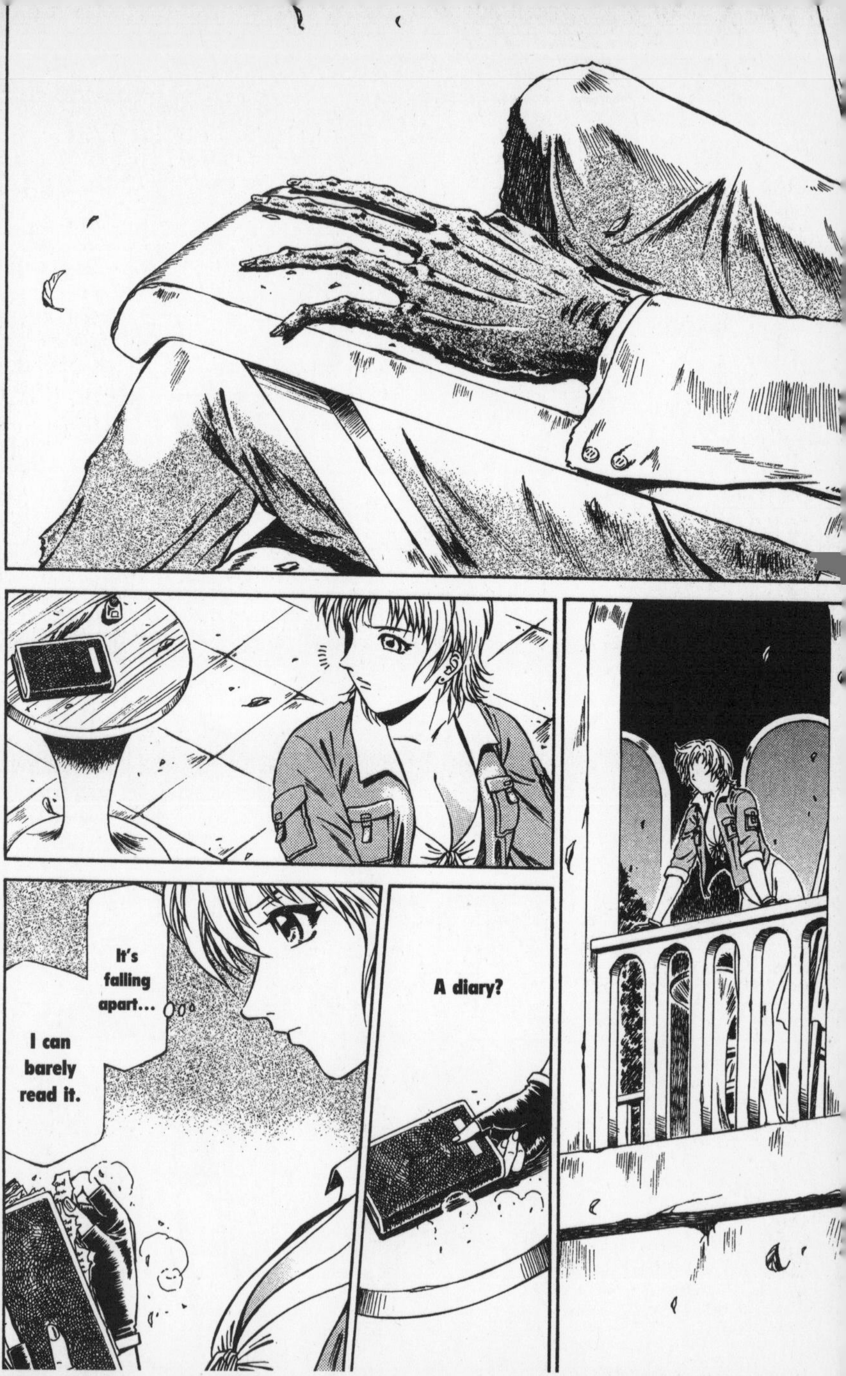
A diary?
It's falling apart...
I can barely read it.

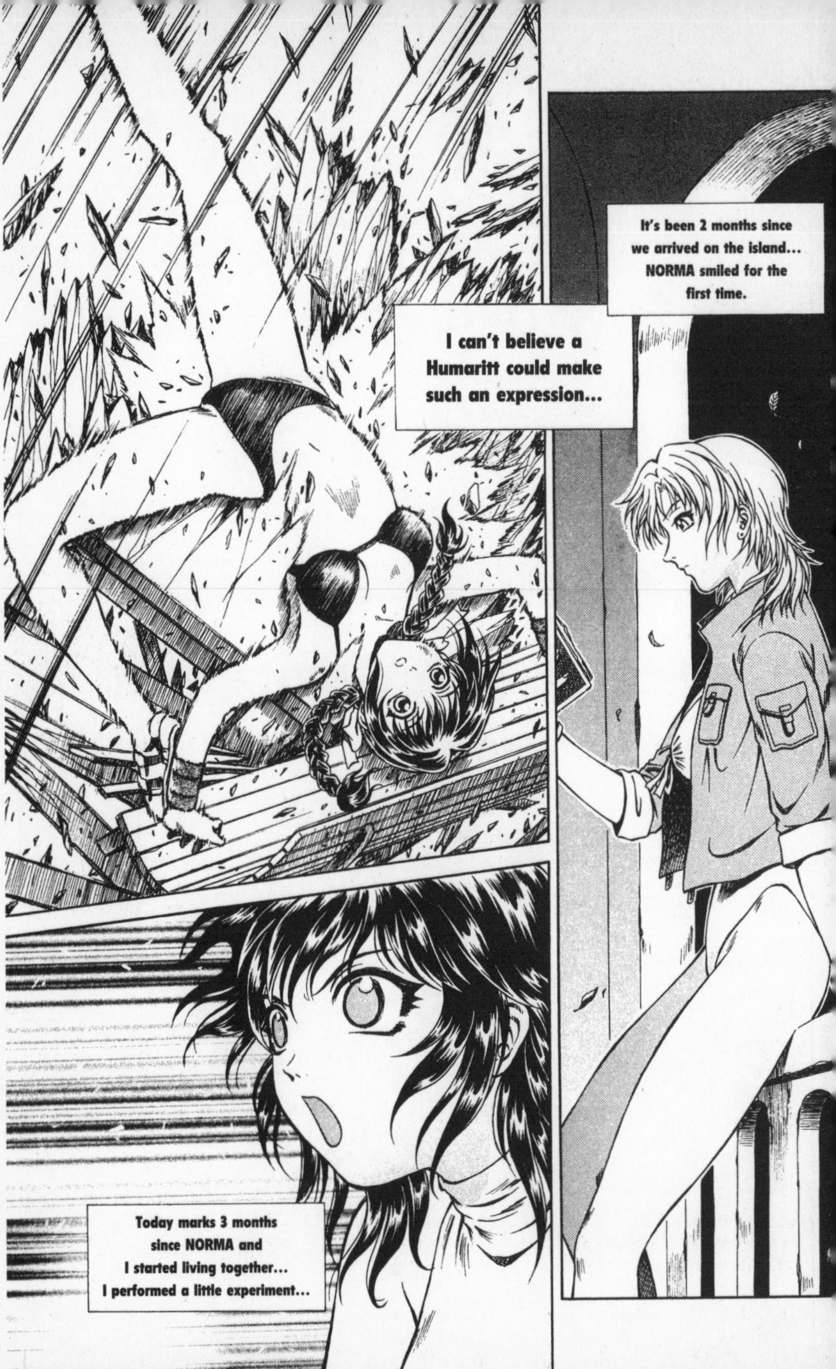
It's been 2 months since we arrived on the island... NORMA smiled for the first time.
I can't believe a Humaritt could make such an expression...
Today marks 3 months since NORMA and I started living together... I performed a little experiment...

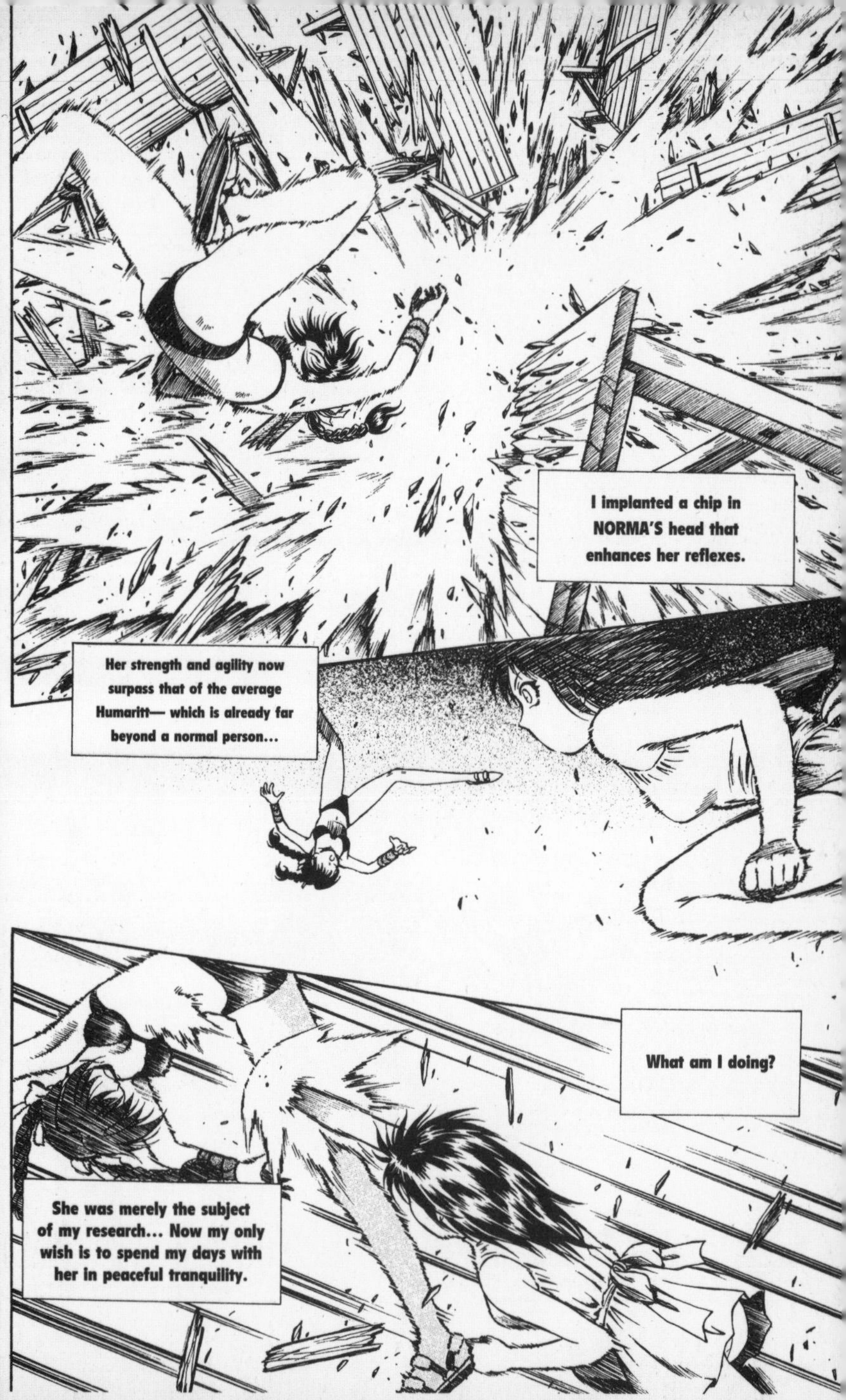
I implanted a chip in NORMA'S head that enhances her reflexes.
Her strength and agility now surpass that of the average Humaritt— which is already far beyond a normal person...
What am I doing?
She was merely the subject of my research... Now my only wish is to spend my days with her in peaceful tranquility.

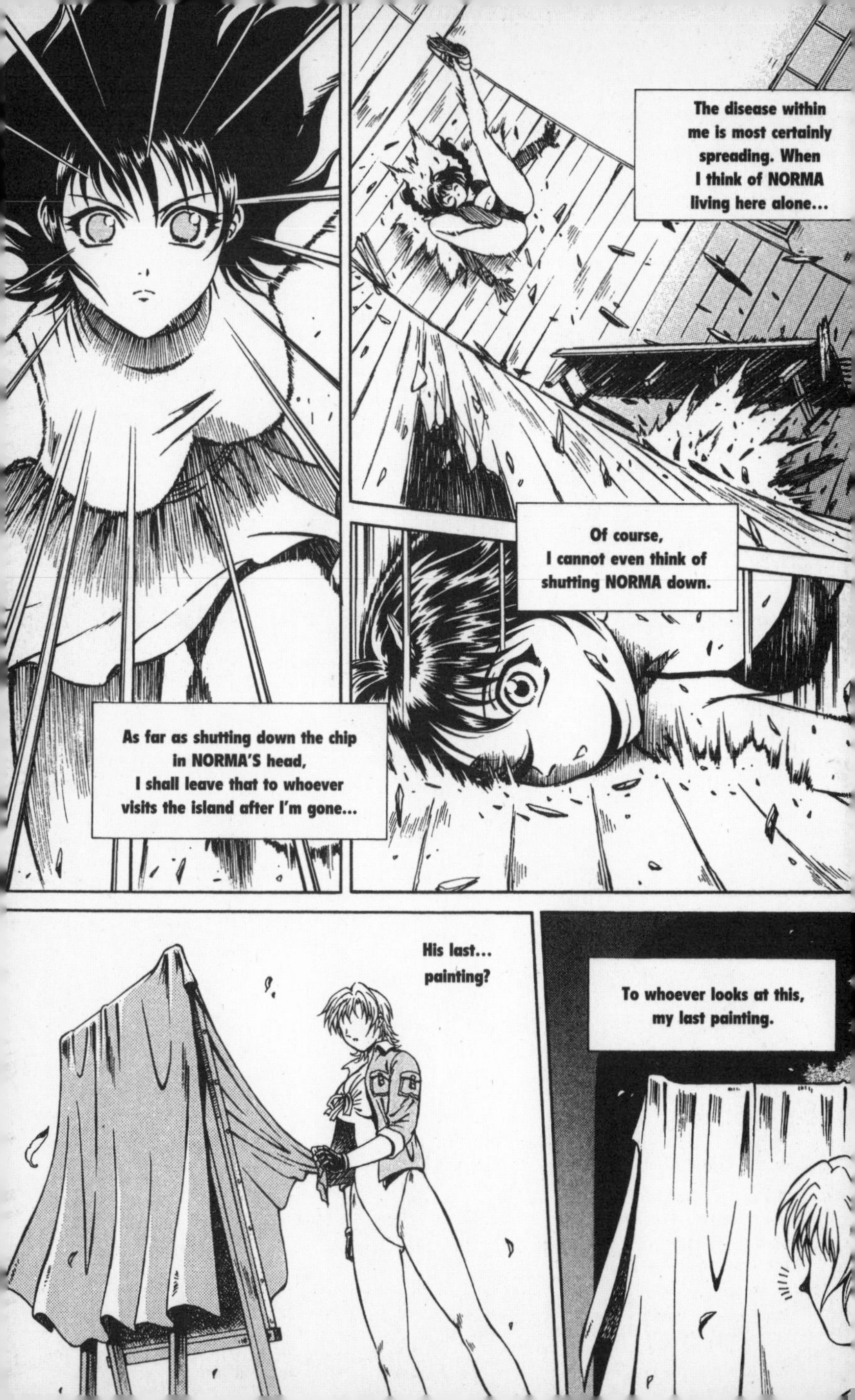
The disease within me is most certainly spreading. When I think of NORMA living here alone...
Of course, I cannot even think of shutting NORMA down.
As far as shutting down the chip in NORMA'S head, I shall leave that to whoever visits the island after I'm gone...
To whoever looks at this, my last painting.
His last... painting?

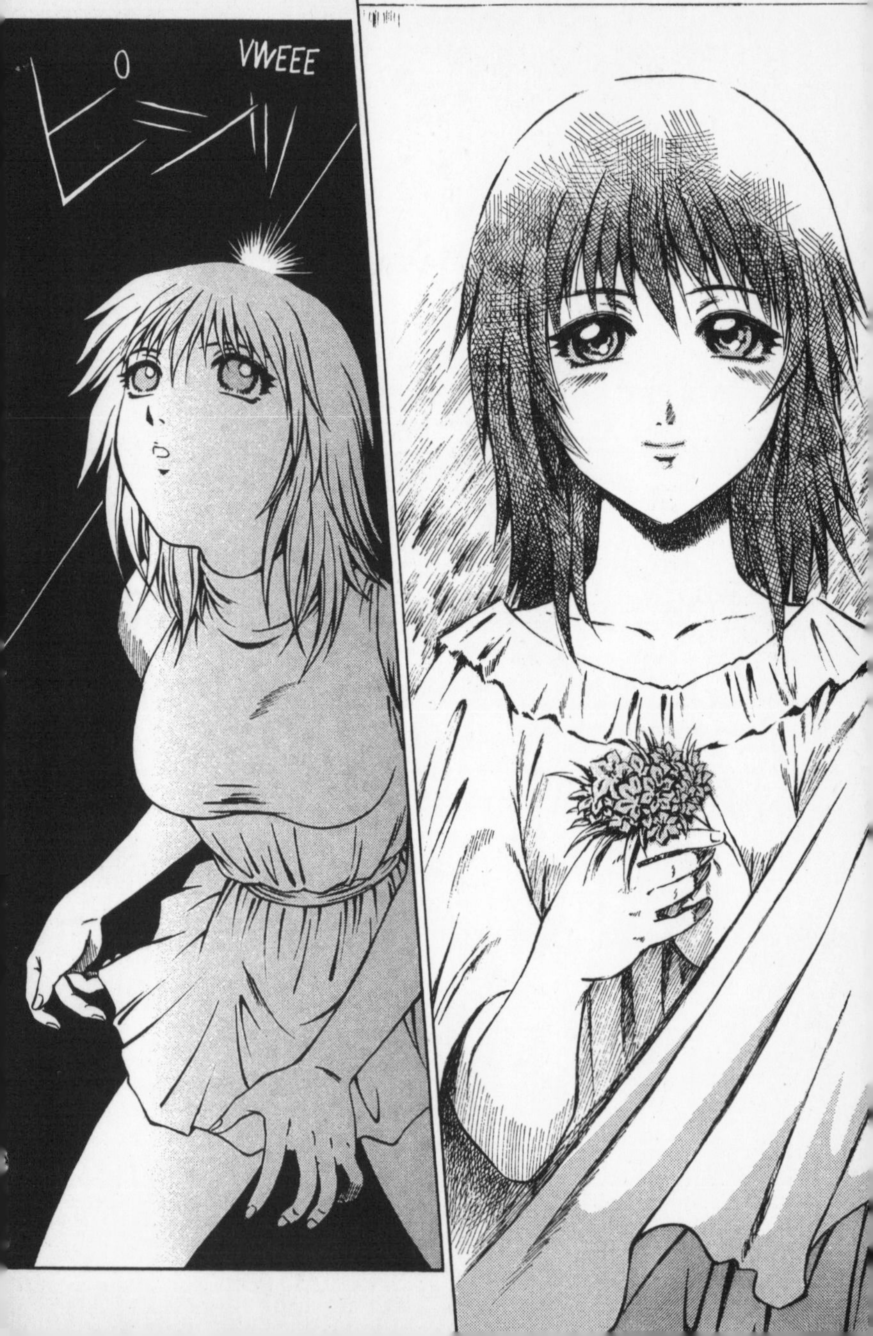
O
VWEEE

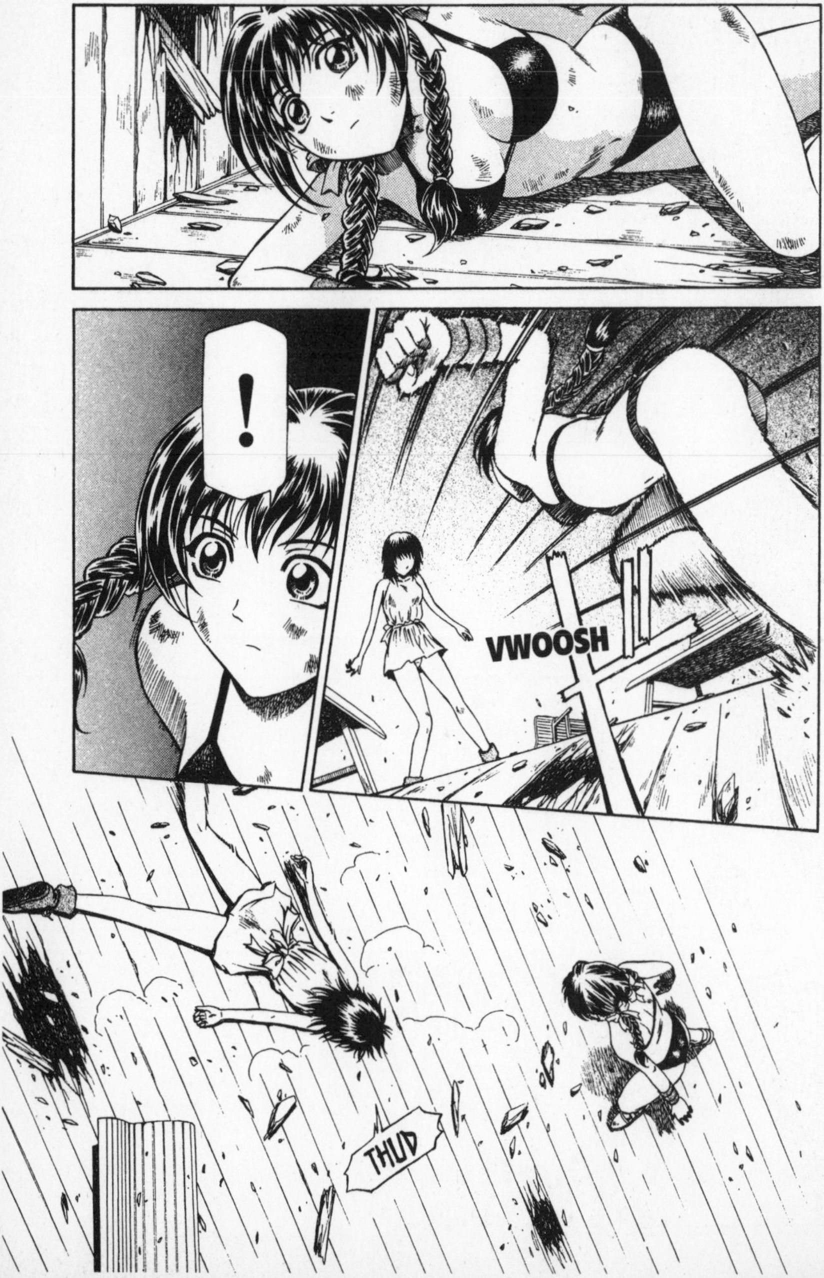
VWOOSH
!
THUD

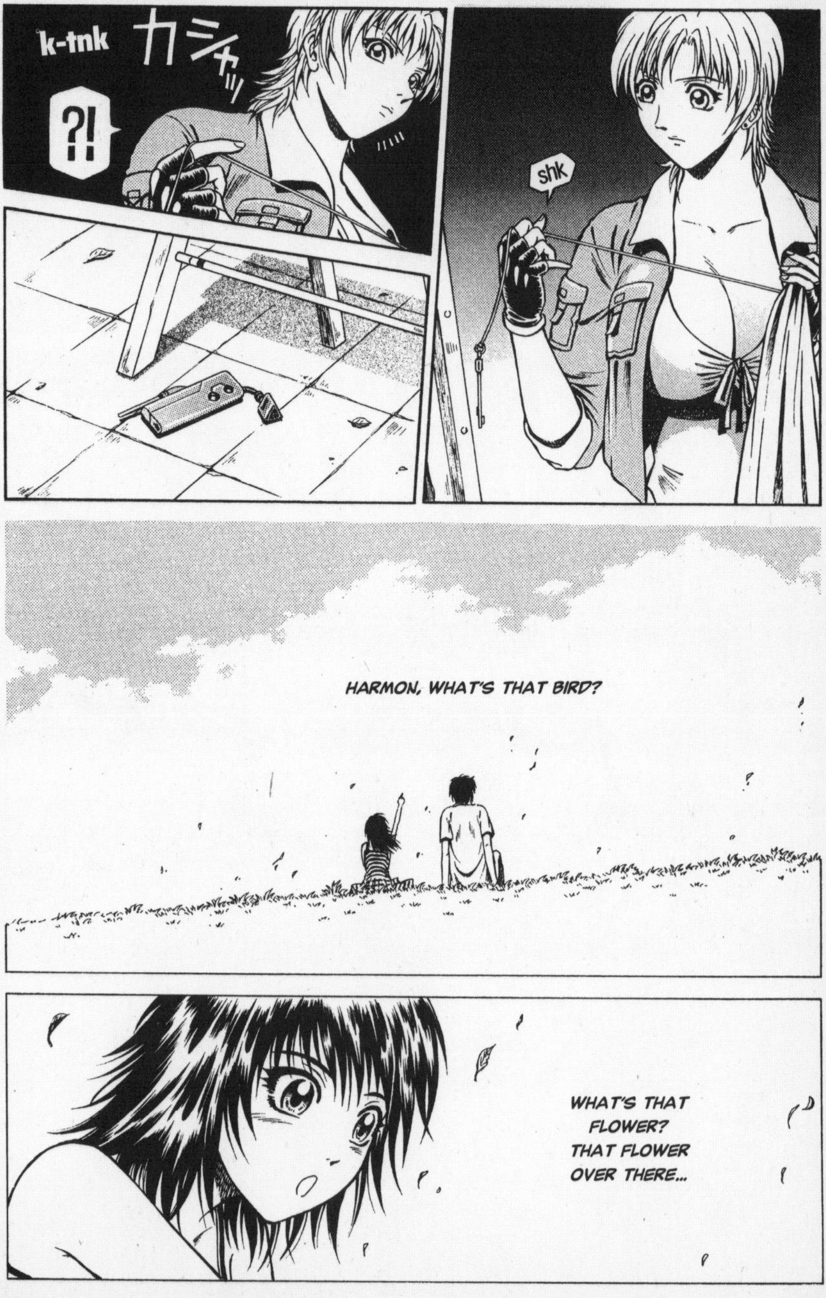
shk
k-tnk
カシャッ
?!
HARMON, WHAT'S THAT BIRD?
WHAT'S THAT FLOWER? THAT FLOWER OVER THERE...

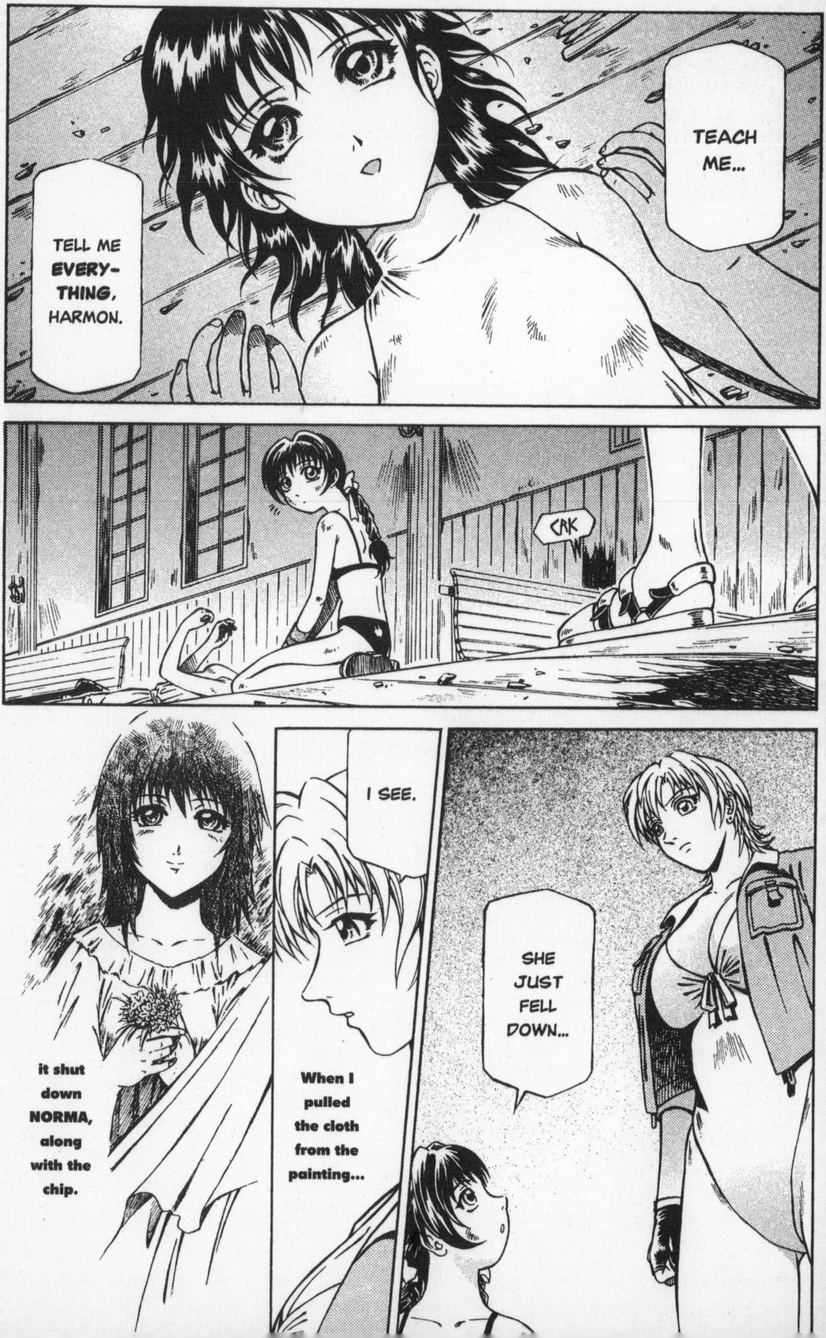
TEACH ME...
TELL ME EVERYTHING, HARMON.
CRAK
SHE JUST FELL DOWN...
I SEE.
When I pulled the cloth from the painting...
it shut down NORMA, along with the chip.

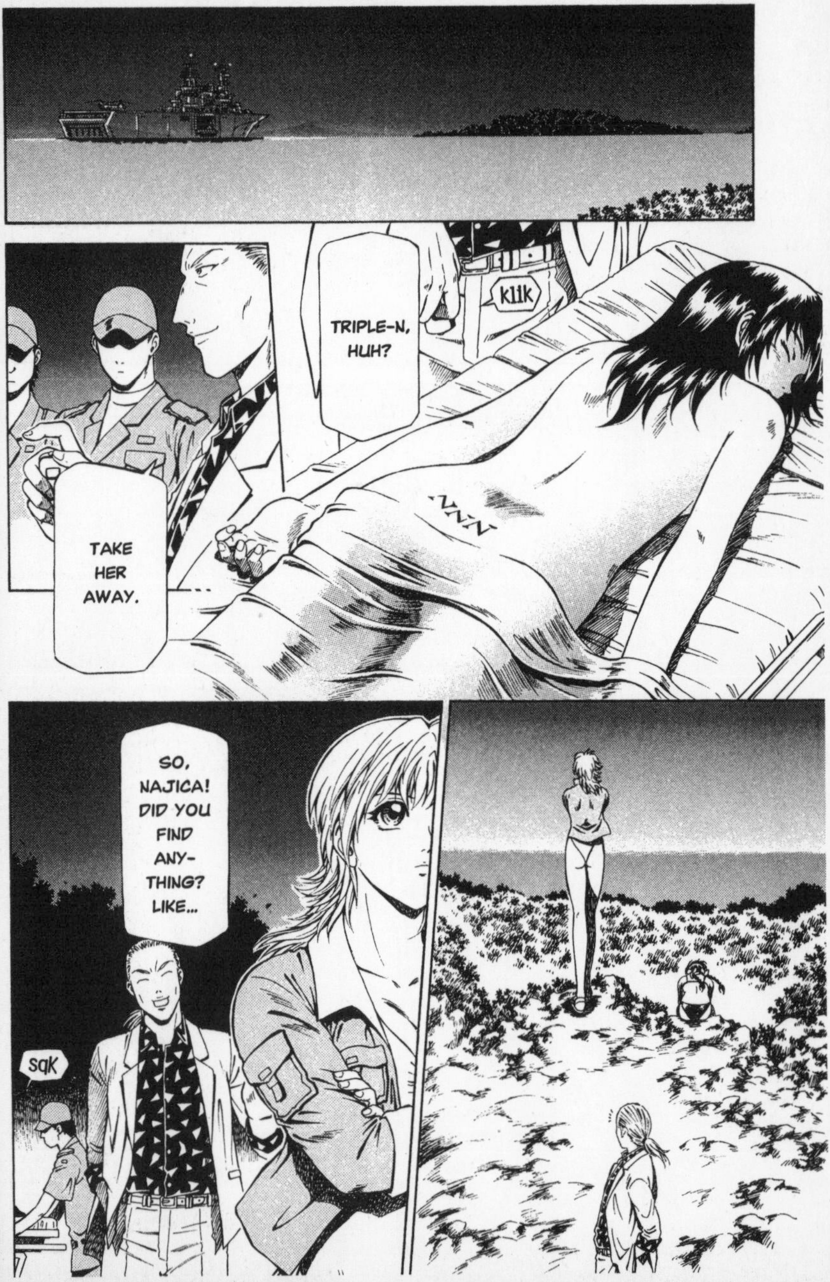
klik
TRIPLE-N, HUH?
TAKE HER AWAY.
SO, NAJICA! DID YOU FIND ANY-THING? LIKE...
sqk

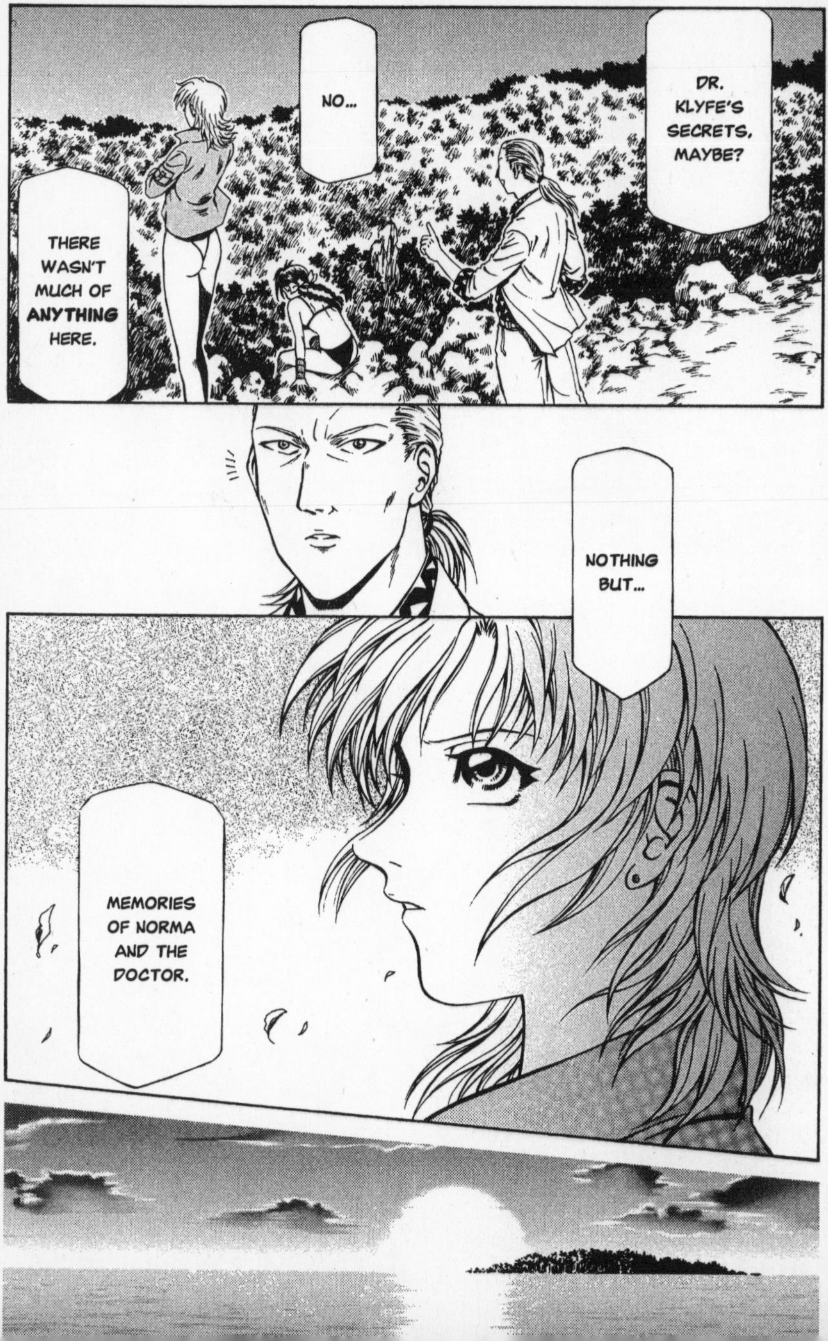
DR. KLYFE'S SECRETS, MAYBE?
NO...
THERE WASN'T MUCH OF **ANYTHING** HERE.
NOTHING BUT...
MEMORIES OF NORMA AND THE DOCTOR.

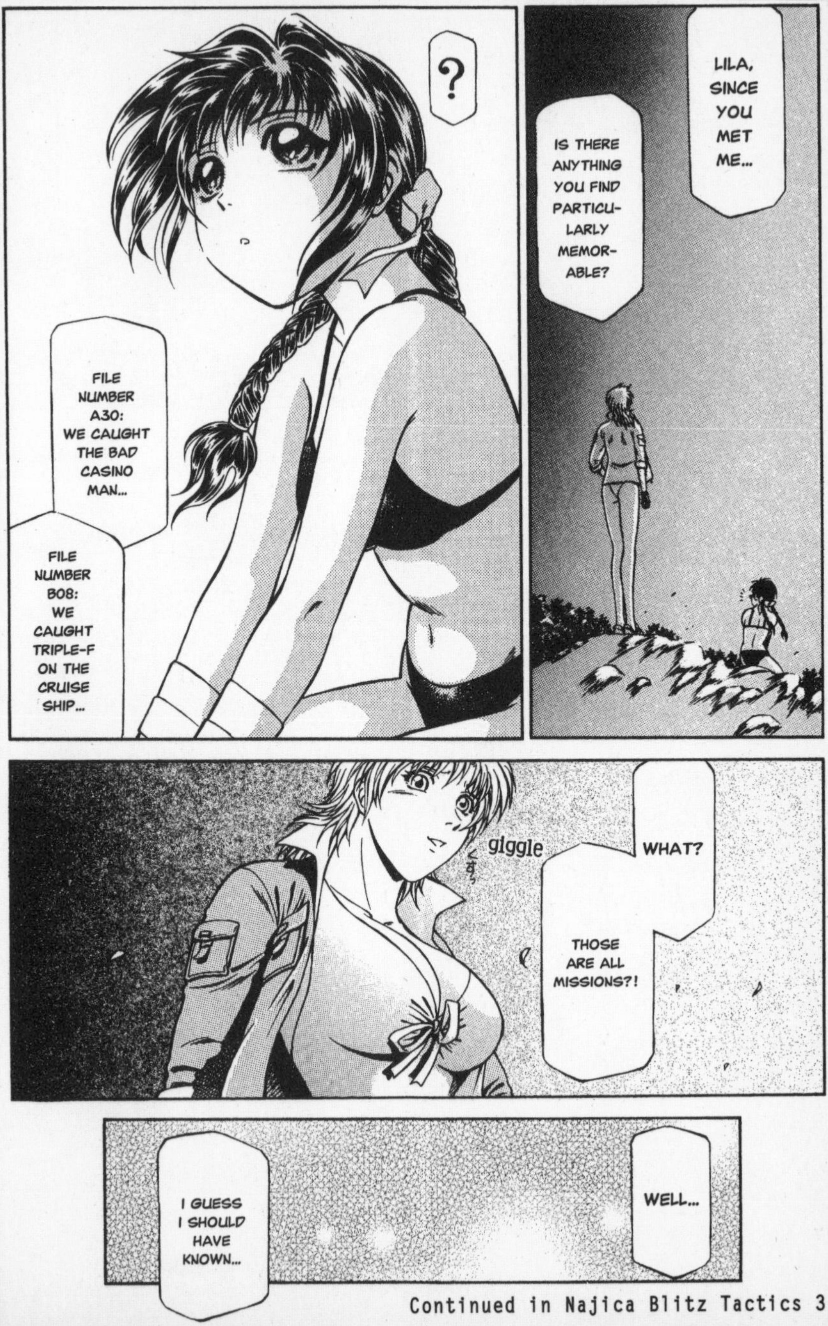
LILA, SINCE YOU MET ME...
IS THERE ANYTHING YOU FIND PARTICU-LARLY MEMOR-ABLE?
?
FILE NUMBER A30: WE CAUGHT THE BAD CASINO MAN...
FILE NUMBER B08: WE CAUGHT TRIPLE-F ON THE CRUISE SHIP...
WHAT?
giggle
THOSE ARE ALL MISSIONS?!
WELL...
I GUESS I SHOULD HAVE KNOWN...

Continued in Najica Blitz Tactics 3

Lila Blitz Tactics

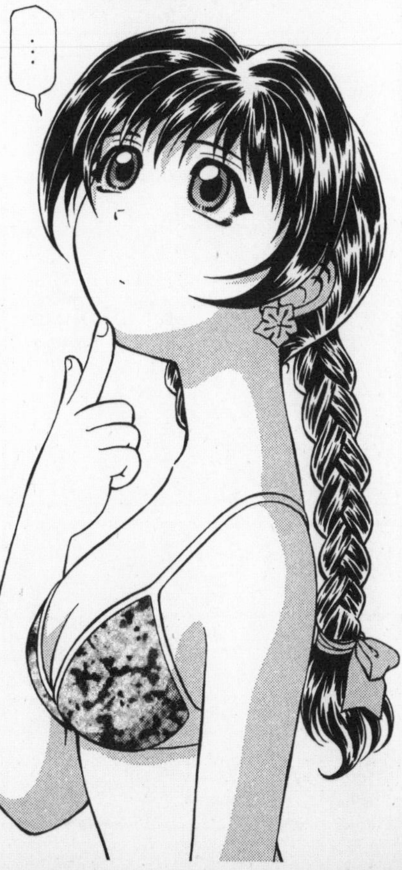
...

Najica's awesome!

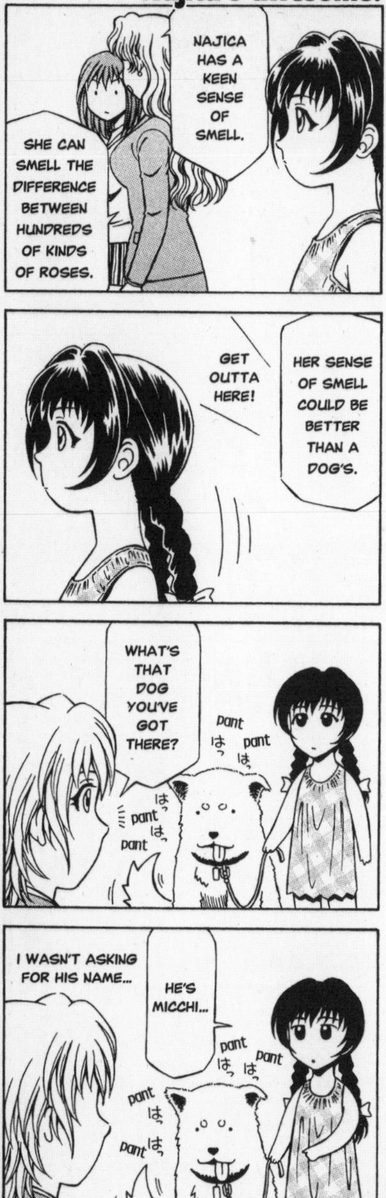
NAJICA HAS A KEEN SENSE OF SMELL.
SHE CAN SMELL THE DIFFERENCE BETWEEN HUNDREDS OF KINDS OF ROSES.
HER SENSE OF SMELL COULD BE BETTER THAN A DOG'S.
GET OUTTA HERE!
WHAT'S THAT DOG YOU'VE GOT THERE?
pant はっ pant はっ
はっ pant はっ pant
HE'S MICCHI...
I WASN'T ASKING FOR HIS NAME...
pant はっ pant はっ
pant はっ pant はっ

Being a Humaritt Pt. ①

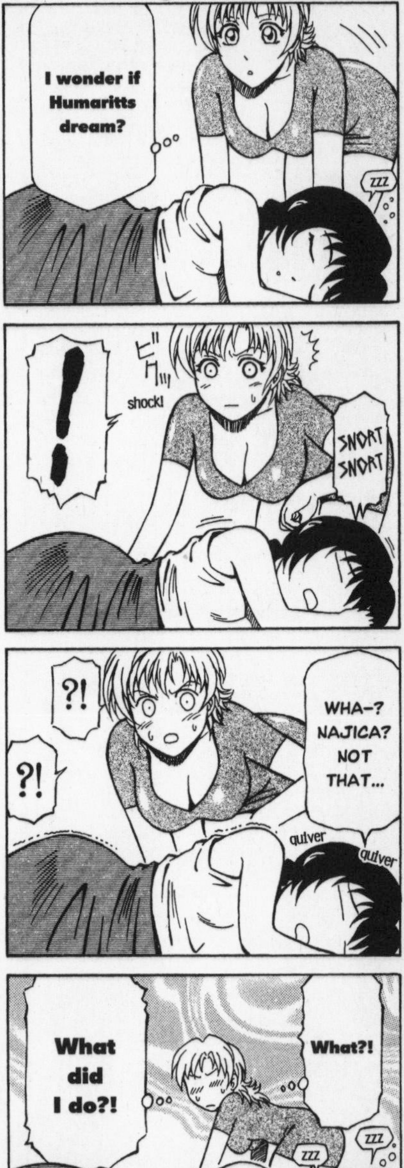

I wonder if Humaritts dream?
zzz
!
ビクッ
shock!
SNORT SNORT
WHA-? NAJICA? NOT THAT...
?!
?!
quiver
quiver
What?!
What did I do?!
zzz
zzz

Being a Humaritt Pt. ②

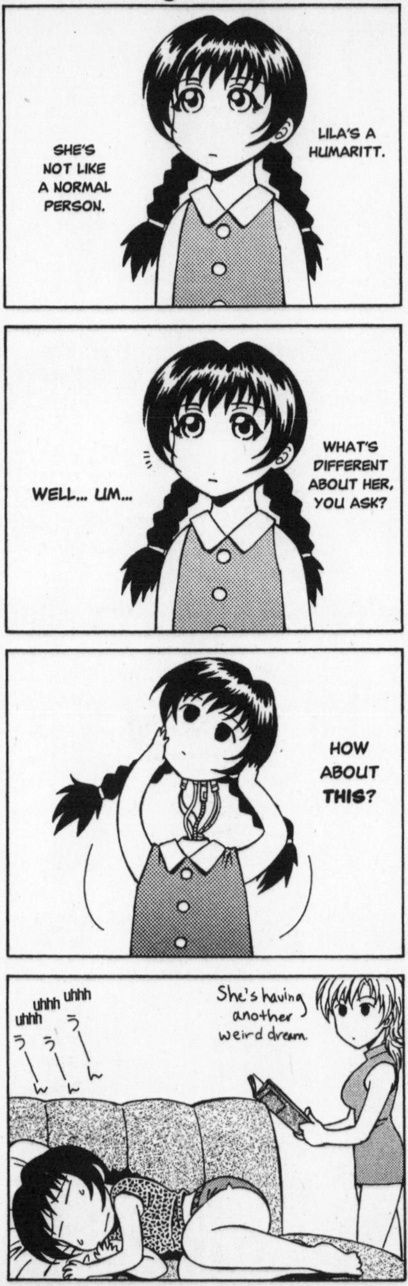

LILA'S A HUMARITT.
SHE'S NOT LIKE A NORMAL PERSON.
WHAT'S DIFFERENT ABOUT HER, YOU ASK?
WELL... UM...
HOW ABOUT THIS?
She's having another weird dream.
uhhh
uhhh
uhhh
う〜ん
う〜ん
う〜ん

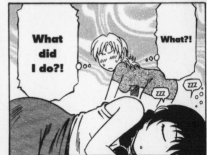

M-m Plump!!

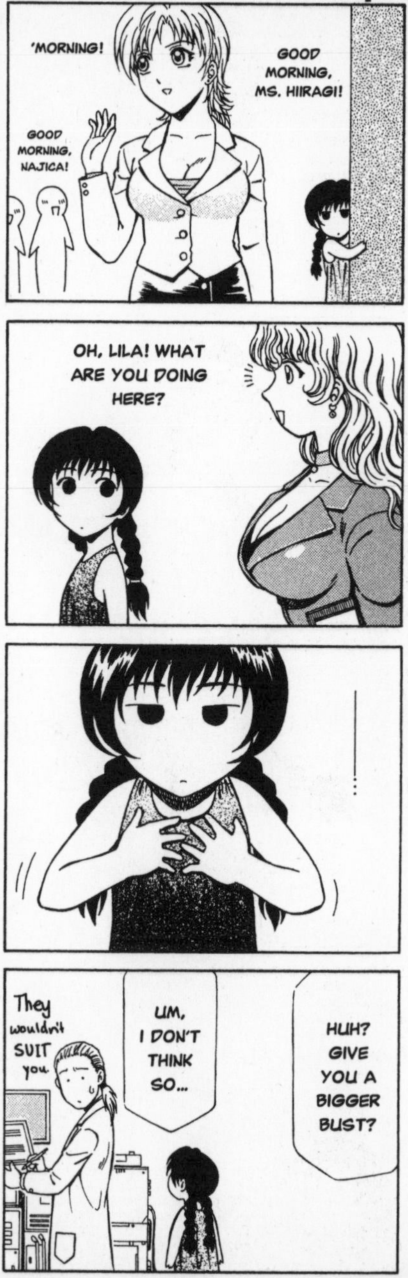
GOOD MORNING, MS. HIIRAGI!
'MORNING!
GOOD MORNING, NAJICA!
OH, LILA! WHAT ARE YOU DOING HERE?
……
HUH? GIVE YOU A BIGGER BUST?
UM, I DON'T THINK SO...
They wouldn't SUIT you.

I'll have what he's having!!

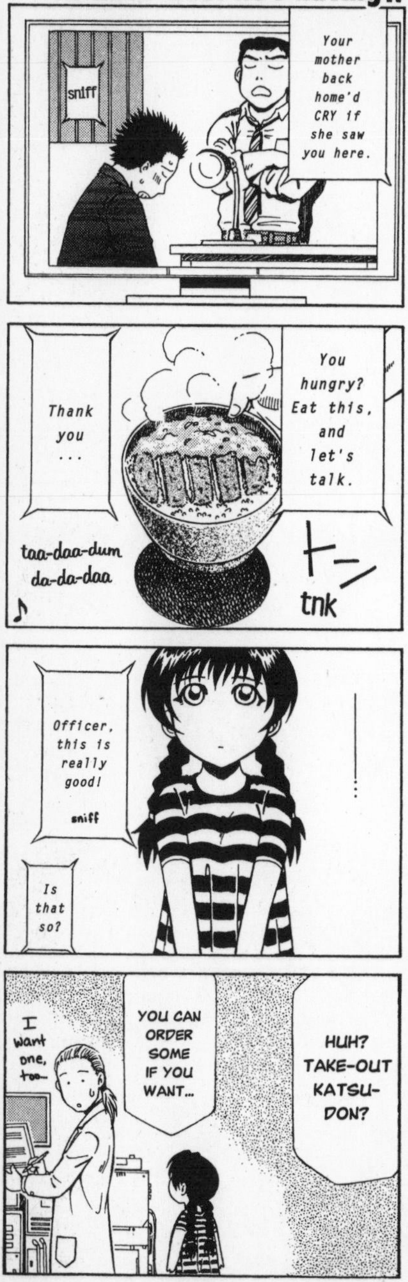
Your mother back home'd CRY if she saw you here.
sniff
You hungry? Eat this, and let's talk.
Thank you ...
tnk
taa-daa-dum da-da-daa ♪
……
Officer, this is really good!
sniff
Is that so?
HUH? TAKE-OUT KATSU-DON?
YOU CAN ORDER SOME IF YOU WANT...
I want one, too...

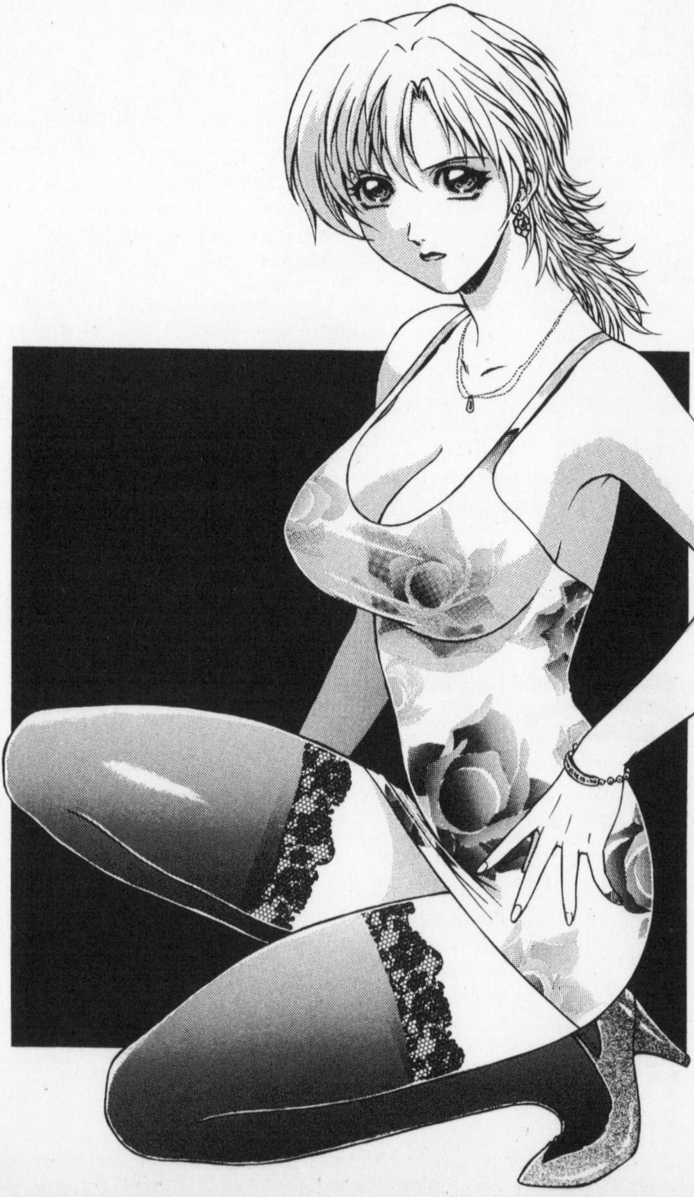

Najica Blitz Tactics
Volume 2

© 2002 by Takuya Tashiro/STUDIO FANTASIA • AFW/NAJICA Project/MEDIA FACTORY
First published in Japan in 2002 by MEDIA FACTORY, Inc.
English Translation rights reserved by A.D.Vision, Inc.
Under the license from MEDIA FACTORY, Inc., Tokyo.

Translator	**JOSH COLE**
Lead Translator/Translation Supervisor	**JAVIER LOPEZ**
ADV Manga Translation Staff	**KAY BERTRAND, AMY FORSYTH, BRENDAN FRAYN**
	HARUKA KANEKO-SMITH, EIKO McGREGOR AND
	MADOKA MOROE
Print Production/ Art Studio Manager	**LISA PUCKETT**
Pre-press Manager	**KLYS REEDYK**
Art Production Manager	**RYAN MASON**
Sr. Designer/Creative Manager	**JORGE ALVARADO**
Graphic Designer/Group Leader	**SHANNON RASBERRY**
Graphic Designer	**KERRI KALINEC**
Graphic Artists	**HEATHER GARY, SHANNA JENSCHKE,**
	AND GEORGE REYNOLDS
Graphic Intern	**MARK MEZA**
International Coordinator	**TORU IWAKAMI**
International Coordinator	**ATSUSHI KANBAYASHI**
Publishing Editor	**SUSAN ITIN**
Assistant Editor	**MARGARET SCHAROLD**
Editorial Assistant	**VARSHA BHUCHAR**
Proofreaders	**SHERIDAN JACOBS AND STEVEN REED**
Research/ Traffic Coordinator	**MARSHA ARNOLD**
Executive VP, CFO, COO	**KEVIN CORCORAN**
President, CEO & Publisher	**JOHN LEDFORD**

Email: editor@adv-manga.com
www.adv-manga.com
www.advfilms.com

For sales and distribution inquiries, please call 1.800.282.7202

ADV MANGA™ is a division of A.D. Vision, Inc.
10114 W. Sam Houston Parkway, Suite 200, Houston, Texas 77099

English text © 2004 published by A.D. Vision, Inc. under exclusive license.
ADV MANGA is a trademark of A.D. Vision, Inc.

ISBN: 1-4139-0042-9
First printing, October 2004
10 9 8 7 6 5 4 3 2 1
Printed in Canada

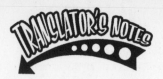

TRANSLATOR'S NOTES

Najica Vol. 02

PG. 05
Uniforms
Manga and anime fans are no doubt aware that *serafuku*, the sailor-inspired school uniform, is required wearing for girls in Japanese middle and high schools. Each school uses its own pattern and color scheme, so that a student from a different school is instantly recognizable. These variants also make some *serafuku* more "fashionable" than others—readers of *Full Metal Panic!* will recall how in volume 4, Tessa noted that the students at Fushimidai "must hate having to wear such old-fashioned uniforms."

For more on *serafuku*, see this entry at Japan-101 at:
www.japan-101.com/culture/japanese_school_uniform.htm

PG. 29
Rhodes
Located in the Aegean Sea, Rhodes is the largest of the Greek Dodecanese islands. The island (the name of which means "rose" in Greek) was once called "the Island of Sun" because of its patron deity, the sun god Helios. Not surprisingly, the island is famous for its year-round sunshine.

PG. 120
Iwo Jima
The southernmost island of the Ogasawara Archipelago. It was home to the most intense aerial bombing campaign of World War II, and gave rise to both a snapshot and a statue that became a national symbol—the six troopers raising a tilted flag atop a field of debris (actually the summit of Mt. Suribachi).

PG. 179
Katsu-don
Katsu-don is a common Japanese dish made of fried breaded pork cutlets served over a bowl of hot, sticky white rice.

LETTER FROM THE ADV MANGA TRANSLATION STAFF

Dear Reader,

On behalf of the ADV Manga translation team, thank you for purchasing an ADV book. We are enthusiastic and committed to our work, and strive to carry our enthusiasm over into the book you hold in your hands.

Our goal is to retain the spirit of the original Japanese book. While great care has been taken to render a true and accurate translation, some cultural or readability issues may require a line to be adapted for greater accessibility to our readers. At times, manga titles that include culturally-specific concepts will feature a "Translator's Notes" section, which explains noteworthy references to the original text.

We hope our commitment to a faithful translation is evident in every ADV book you purchase.

Sincerely,

Madoka Moroe

Haruka Kaneko-Smith

Javier Lopez
Lead Translator

Eiko McGregor

Kay Bertrand

ADV MANGA™

Brendan Frayne

Amy Forsyth

LETTTER FROM THE EDITOR

Dear Reader,

Thank you for purchasing an ADV Manga book. We hope you enjoyed the exciting espionage of the *Najica Blitz Tactics*.

It is our sincere commitment in reproducing Asian comics and graphic novels to retain as much of the character of the original book as possible. From the right-to-left format of the Japanese books to the meaning of the story in the original language, the ADV Manga team is working hard to publish a quality book for our fans and readers. Write to us with your questions or comments, and tell us how you liked this and other ADV books. Be sure to visit our website at www.adv-manga.com and view the list of upcoming titles, sign up for special announcements, and fill out our survey.

The ADV Manga team of translators, designers, graphic artists, production managers, traffic managers, and editors hope you will buy more ADV books–there's a lot more in store from ADV Manga!

ADV MANGA™

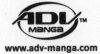

www.adv-manga.com

Publishing Editor Susan B. Itin	Assistant Editor Margaret Scharold	Editorial Assistant Varsha Bhuchar
Susan B. Itin	Margaret Scharold	VaBhu

From arresting assassins to rescuing Humaritts, Najica and Lila hardly have any time to work on their tans! After successfully securing their target from a bogus high school killer, Najica and Lila are living

Najica Blitz Tactics
Volume 3

the spy-life, heading to tropic ports and performing under CRI's watchful spotlight. These two bodacious babes battled their buns off against surprising enemies, and now more are coming their way. Surprising secrets about the Humaritts will be revealed when Najica and her trusty sidekick set off in search of a very important scientist—but will Shinba Industrial prove too mighty a menace for this gun-toting duo? Join Najica and Lila on their next exciting quest in *Najica Blitz Tactics* Volume 3!

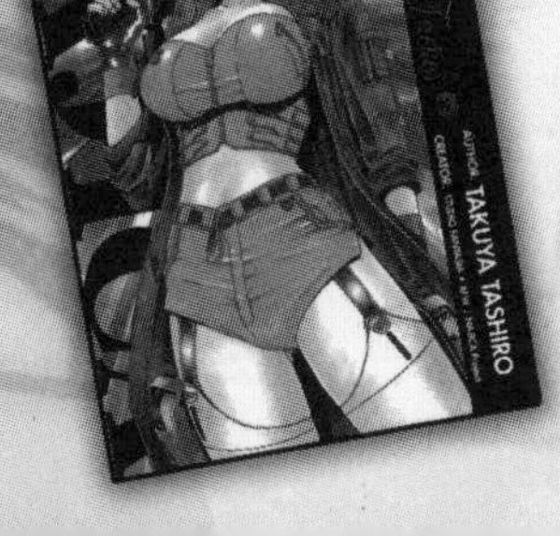
AUTHOR TAKUYA TASHIRO

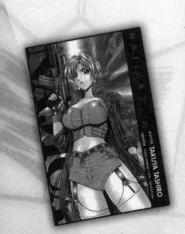

EDITOR'S

PICKS

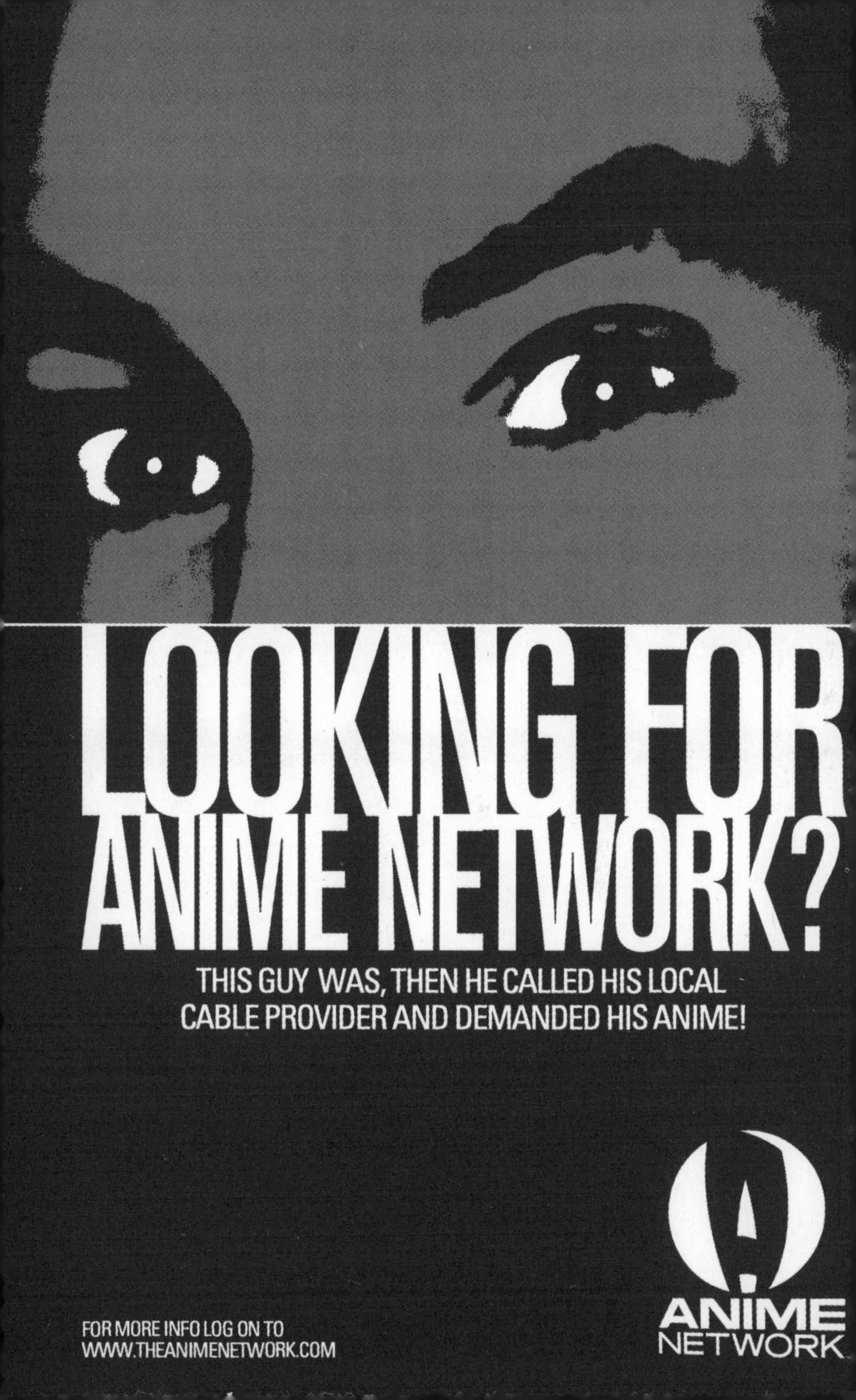
LOOKING FOR ANIME NETWORK?
THIS GUY WAS, THEN HE CALLED HIS LOCAL CABLE PROVIDER AND DEMANDED HIS ANIME!
FOR MORE INFO LOG ON TO WWW.THEANIMENETWORK.COM
ANIME NETWORK

MOVIES • ANIME • MANGA • VIDEO GAMES • TOYS

IF IT'S COOL, YOU'LL FIND IT EACH AND EVERY MONTH IN THE PAGES OF *NEWTYPE USA*, ALONG WITH FREE DVDS, POSTERS, POSTCARDS AND MUCH, MUCH MORE. *SUBSCRIBE TODAY!* GO TO WWW.NEWTYPE-USA.COM

IT BEGINS WHERE OTHER MAGAZINES END

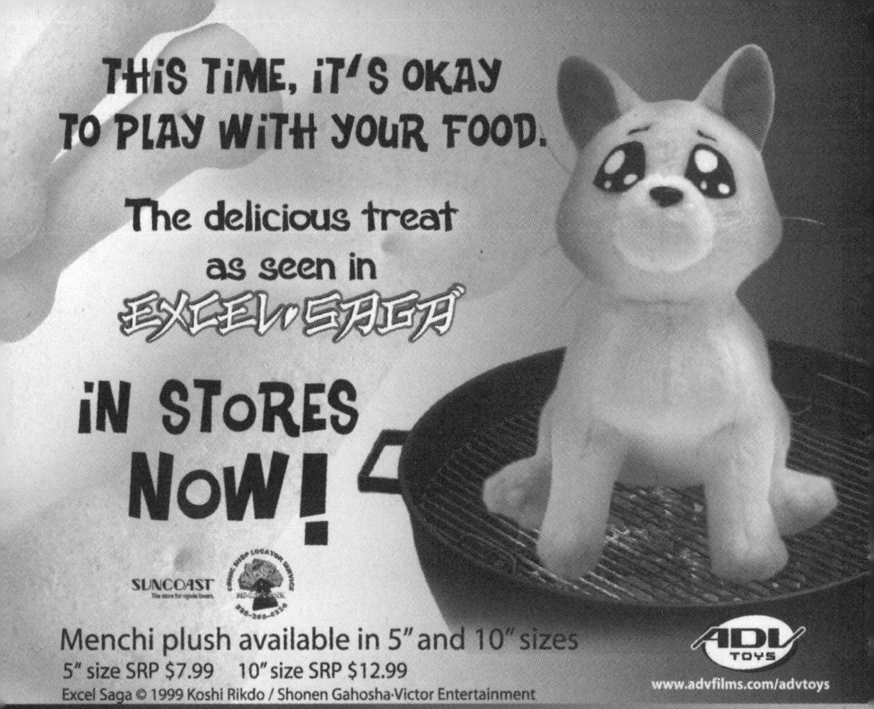
THIS TIME, IT'S OKAY
TO PLAY WITH YOUR FOOD.
The delicious treat
as seen in
EXCEL SAGA
IN STORES
NOW!
SUNCOAST
Menchi plush available in 5" and 10" sizes
5" size SRP $7.99   10" size SRP $12.99
Excel Saga © 1999 Koshi Rikdo / Shonen Gahosha·Victor Entertainment
ADV TOYS
www.advfilms.com/advtoys

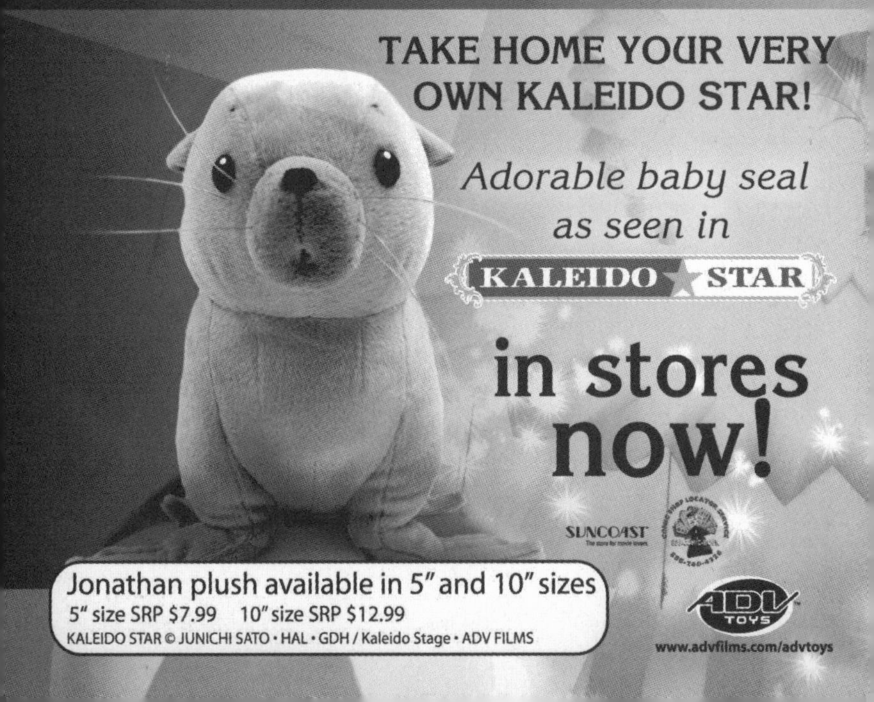
TAKE HOME YOUR VERY
OWN KALEIDO STAR!
Adorable baby seal
as seen in
KALEIDO STAR
in stores
now!
SUNCOAST
Jonathan plush available in 5" and 10" sizes
5" size SRP $7.99   10" size SRP $12.99
KALEIDO STAR © JUNICHI SATO · HAL · GDH / Kaleido Stage · ADV FILMS
ADV TOYS
www.advfilms.com/advtoys

[LOOKS CAN KILL]

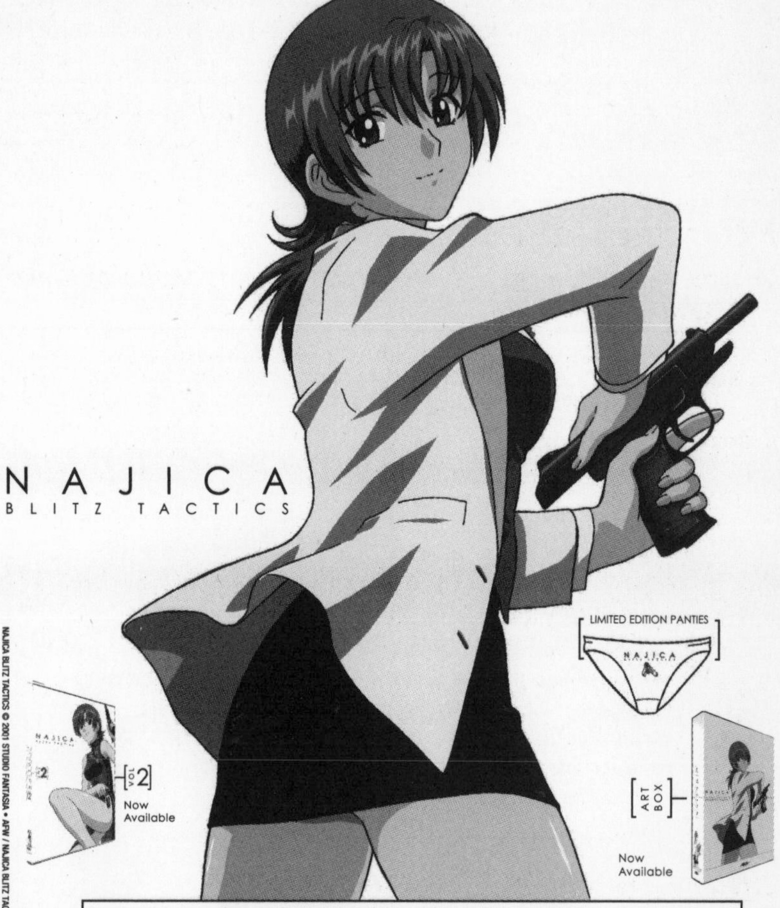
NAJICA
BLITZ TACTICS
LIMITED EDITION PANTIES
NAJICA
VOL 2
Now Available
ART BOX
Now Available

THE WORLD'S HOTTEST SECRET AGENT DOESN'T WEAR A TUXEDO. CHECK OUT HER FAVORITE EVENINGWEAR IN NAJICA BLITZ TACTICS VOLUME 2.

VOLUME 1 IS AVAILABLE AS A SINGLE DISC, OR IN A COLLECTOR'S EDITION PACKAGE WITH A CUSTOM SERIES ART BOX, FEATURING SPECIAL LIMITED EDITION PANTIES. VOLUME 3 GOES ON SALE NOVEMBER 11th.

ADV FILMS

WWW.ADVFILMS.COM

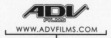

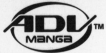

MANGA SURVEY

PLEASE MAIL THE COMPLETED FORM TO: EDITOR – ADV MANGA
c/o A.D. Vision, Inc. 10114 W. Sam Houston Pkwy., Suite 200 Houston, TX 77099

Name:________________________________
Address:______________________________
City, State, Zip:________________________
____
E-Mail:_______________________________
Male ☐ Female ☐ Age:________________

☐ ***CHECK HERE IF YOU WOULD LIKE TO RECEIVE OTHER INFORMATION OR FUTURE OFFERS FROM ADV.***

All information provided will be used for internal purposes only. We promise not to sell or otherwise divulge your information.

1. Annual Household Income (*Check only one*)

☐ Under $25,000
☐ $25,000 to $50,000
☐ $50,000 to $75,000
☐ Over $75,000

2. How do you hear about new Manga releases? (*Check all that apply*)

☐ Browsing in Store
☐ Internet Reviews
☐ Anime News Websites
☐ Direct Email Campaigns
☐ Online forums (message boards and chat rooms)
☐ Carrier pigeon
☐ Other:________________________
☐ Magazine Ad
☐ Online Advertising
☐ Conventions
☐ TV Advertising

3. Which magazines do you read? (*Check all that apply*)

☐ Wizard
☐ SPIN
☐ Animerica
☐ Rolling Stone
☐ Maxim
☐ DC Comics
☐ URB
☐ Polygon
☐ Original Play Station Magazine
☐ Entertainment Weekly
☐ YRB
☐ EGM
☐ Newtype USA
☐ SciFi
☐ Starlog
☐ Wired
☐ Vice
☐ BPM
☐ I hate reading
☐ Other:________________

4. Have you visited the ADV Manga website?
- ☐ Yes
- ☐ No

5. Have you made any manga purchases online from the ADV website?
- ☐ Yes
- ☐ No

6. If you have visited the ADV Manga website, how would you rate your online experience?
- ☐ Excellent
- ☐ Good
- ☐ Average
- ☐ Poor

7. What genre of manga do you prefer?
(*Check all that apply*)
- ☐ adventure
- ☐ romance
- ☐ detective
- ☐ action
- ☐ horror
- ☐ sci-fi/fantasy
- ☐ sports
- ☐ comedy

8. How many manga titles have you purchased in the last 6 months?
- ☐ none
- ☐ 1-4
- ☐ 5-10
- ☐ 11+

9. Where do you make your manga purchases? (*Check all that apply*)
- ☐ comic store
- ☐ bookstore
- ☐ newsstand
- ☐ online
- ☐ other:_____
- ☐ department store
- ☐ grocery store
- ☐ video store
- ☐ video game store

10. Which bookstores do you usually make your manga purchases at?
(*Check all that apply*)
- ☐ Barnes & Noble
- ☐ Walden Books
- ☐ Suncoast
- ☐ Best Buy
- ☐ Amazon.com
- ☐ Borders
- ☐ Books-A-Million
- ☐ Toys "Я" Us
- ☐ Other bookstore: _____

11. What's your favorite anime/manga website? (*Check all that apply*)
- ☐ adv-manga.com
- ☐ advfilms.com
- ☐ rightstuf.com
- ☐ animenewsservice.com
- ☐ animenewsnetwork.com
- ☐ Other:_____
- ☐ animeondvd.com
- ☐ anipike.com
- ☐ animeonline.net
- ☐ planetanime.com
- ☐ animenation.com